Generation 1.5 in College Composition

WITHDRAWAL

"...a well-organized volume with a strong emphasis on pedagogy."

Trudy Smoke, Hunter College, City University of New York

"Generation 1.5 is *the* most interesting topic of concern in ESL today, yet publications are few and far between.... The editors clearly know what they're doing.... They know the field, know the subject matter, and understand the problems.... This volume contributes to the thinking in the field."

Linda Lonon Blanton, University of New Orleans

Building on the work that has been done over the past decade, this volume provides theoretical frameworks for understanding debates about immigrant students, studies of students' schooling paths and language and literacy experiences, and pedagogical approaches for working with generation 1.5 students. Since the mid-1970s, U.S. colleges and universities have experienced a dramatic increase in the population of immigrant students who entered the educational system as children and developed complex bi- or multilingual repertoires throughout their adolescence. The term "generation 1.5" is used to describe these students because their immigrant and educational journeys position them somewhere between first generation adult immigrants and the U.S.-born second generation children of immigrant families.

Generation 1.5 in College Composition:
- is designed to help both scholars and practitioners reconceptualize the fields of College Composition and TESOL and create a space for research, theory, and pedagogy focusing on postsecondary immigrant ESL students
- provides *both* important new theoretical work (which lays the underpinnings for serious pedagogical innovation) *and* important new pedagogical approaches

Because of their varied and complex language and literacy profiles, generation 1.5 students are found in developmental English courses, college ESL courses, and mainstream college writing courses. This volume is directed to preservice and inservice teachers, teacher educators, and researchers involved with educating generation 1.5 students in these and other contexts.

Mark Roberge is Associate Professor of English in the Composition program at San Francisco State University.

Meryl Siegal is Ins ⁣akland, California.

Linda Harklau is ⁣ nguages program and the Linguistics program at the Un

Generation 1.5 in College Composition

Teaching Academic Writing to
U.S.-Educated Learners of ESL

Edited by
**Mark Roberge, Meryl Siegal, and
Linda Harklau**

Routledge
Taylor & Francis Group

NEW YORK AND LONDON

PE
1128
.A2
G434
2009

HARVARD UNIVERSITY
GRADUATE SCHOOL OF EDUCATION
MONROE C. GUTMAN LIBRARY

Gift

First published 2009
by Routledge
270 Madison Ave, New York, NY 10016

Simultaneously published in the UK
by Routledge
2 Park Square, Milton Park, Abingdon, Oxon OX14 4RN

Routledge is an imprint of the Taylor & Francis Group, an informa business

© 2009 Routledge, Taylor and Francis

Typeset in Minion by Wearset Ltd, Boldon, Tyne and Wear
Printed and bound in the United States of America on acid-free paper by IBT Global

All rights reserved. No part of this book may be reprinted or reproduced or utilized in any form or by any electronic, mechanical, or other means, now known or hereafter invented, including photocopying and recording, or in any information storage or retrieval system, without permission in writing from the publishers.

Trademark Notice: Product or corporate names may be trademarks or registered trademarks, and are used only for identification and explanation without intent to infringe.

Library of Congress Cataloging in Publication Data
Generation 1.5 in college composition : teaching academic writing to U.S.–educated learners of ESL / edited by Mark Roberge, Meryl Siegal, Linda Harklau.

p. cm.

Includes bibliographical references and index.

1. English language–Study and teaching–Foreign speakers. 2. English language–Rhetoric–Study and teaching–United States. 3. Report writing–Study and teaching (Higher)–United States. I. Roberge, Mark. II. Siegal, Meryl. III. Harklau, Linda. IV. Title: Generation one point five meets college composition.

PE1128.A2G434 2008

428.0071–dc22

2008025825

ISBN10: 0-8058-6442-3 (hbk)
ISBN10: 0-8058-6443-1 (pbk)
ISBN10: 0-203-88569-4 (ebk)

ISBN13: 978-0-8058-6442-7 (hbk)
ISBN13: 978-0-8058-6443-4 (pbk)
ISBN13: 978-0-203-88569-7 (ebk)

August 25, 2009

Contents

Preface

Harklau, Losey, and Siegal's *Generation 1.5 Meets College Composition: Issues in the Teaching of Writing to U.S.-Educated Learners of ESL* (1999) set out to explore and focus the topic of generation 1.5 immigrants—a term that typically refers to English language learners who arrive in the U.S. at an early age, obtain much or all of their education in U.S. K-12 settings, and arrive in college with various patterns of language and literacy that don't fit the traditional, "institutionally constructed" profiles of Developmental Writing, College ESL, or Freshman Composition. This volume, *Generation 1.5 in College Composition: Teaching Academic Writing to U.S.-Educated Learners of ESL*, extends rather than duplicates that scholarship; the individual chapters are written by researchers, theorists, and teachers who have actively engaged with generation 1.5 issues over the past decade. While the prior volume was intended to open a dialogue, the current volume is intended to extend that dialogue and serve as a text in teacher education courses in the field of TESOL, Composition, and Language Arts. It will help teachers-in-training (as well as current teachers who are interested in the topic) understand the breadth of scholarly approaches to the generation 1.5 topic, the current debates and controversies surrounding the topic, and most importantly, the variety of curricular and pedagogical approaches for working effectively with generation 1.5 students.

Overview of the Volume

Part I provides groundwork for understanding the discussions and debates surrounding the generation 1.5 topic, as well as the pedagogical and curricular approaches that are presented in this volume. These chapters will help readers understand the broader socio-political, economic, historical, and disciplinary forces that affect teaching and learning of multilingual students. They will also introduce readers to the interdisciplinary breadth of the topic: Roberge provides a teacher's perspective on generation 1.5 and argues that the notion of "generation 1.5" can serve as a valuable heuristic in teachers' discussions of educational access, educational equity, and student success. Harklau and Siegal discuss multilingual students from an educational policy perspective, highlighting questions about multilingual students in higher education. Louie provides an immigration studies perspective, using broad demographic data to argue that generational status is significant. Matsuda and Matsuda use archival methods to document the presence of immigrant students in higher education and they examine the treatment of immigrants in TESOL and Composition scholarship. Benesch uses critical discourse analysis to examine the terminology of generation 1.5 discussions.

Part II provides studies of generation 1.5 students and their schooling paths. These chapters include a variety of research approaches and they focus on a variety of institutional settings; they illustrate not just student characteristics and experiences, but also the variety of ways that we obtain and construct information about students. Allison uses ethnographic methods (observational data collection) to study reading and writing practices in high school classes in order to examine how generation 1.5 students are prepared for college reading and writing. Frodesen uses a longitudinal case-study method to examine a single student's academic literacy development over time. Crosby uses case-study interviews to study generation 1.5 students' reading and writing strategies. Mott-Smith combines critical discourse analysis of university documents with interviews of generation 1.5 students to examine discourses and perceptions of writing success and writing failure. Providing a perspective from a large cross-institutional study focusing on community college students, Patthey, Thomas-Spiegel, and Dillon examine student success, student progression, and student curricular choices.

Part III presents pedagogical and curricular approaches for working with generation 1.5 students. These chapters show how teachers, curriculum developers and program administrators have responded to the changing demographics of postsecondary writing classes. Murie and Fitzpatrick offer an academic enrichment model, one that runs counter to typical deficit-based models of student instruction. Holten discusses her experience designing a course specifically for generation 1.5 students, an alternative to a deficit-based curricular approach that sees students solely as "incomplete" language learners or solely as "deficient" native speakers. Reynolds, Bae, and Wilson discuss their experiences instituting a highly individualized pedagogy by which students work with writing associates. Johns offers what she has called a "socio-literate approach" that focuses on rhetorical flexibility. Schleppegrell takes a functional linguistics approach and presents ways of working with students on grammar that focus on discourse conditions rather than form. Finally Goen-Salter, Porter, and vanDommelen provide an overview of principles and practices that they have used with generation 1.5 students in the institutional contexts of a College ESL program, a Basic Writing program and a university tutoring center.

Feature of the Volume

In selecting chapters for this volume, we have drawn on established scholars, newer researchers, and seasoned teachers from a variety of institutional contexts. What they share is an interest in immigrant students' academic language and academic literacy development, student success, and educational equity.

We have encouraged authors to follow their own definitions of "generation 1.5" but we cautioned them to avoid deterministic descriptions of generation 1.5 students, i.e., "They are generation 1.5 students and therefore they are going to be X, Y, and Z." Instead we have encouraged authors to describe students and teachers in real educational situations, as well as the real pedagogical and curricular approaches that have led to student success.

We have included authors who embrace the notion of "generation 1.5" and find it useful in promoting educational success and educational equity. We have also included authors who are cautious about the term "generation 1.5," authors who do not use the term at all, and authors who are explicitly critical of the notion of "generation 1.5." The volume thus adds breadth and depth to the discussion of composition instruction and immigrant students.

Acknowledgments

We would like to thank the authors, who worked painstakingly and patiently through multiple rounds of manuscript review and revision. We would also like to thank Elizabeth Erchul, our graduate assistant, who put in countless hours preparing the manuscript for submission.

Part I
Frameworks

1 A Teacher's Perspective on Generation 1.5

Mark Roberge San Francisco State University

Over the past three decades, many U.S. colleges and universities have seen a dramatic increase in the number of students from immigrant families. This group of students is highly diverse: some students have been in the U.S. since birth while others arrived shortly before or even during their college years. Some enter college with complex bilingual or multilingual communicative repertoires while others enter college still strongly self-identifying as "ESL students." Some have had nurturing and enriching kindergarten through twelfth grade (K-12) schooling experiences that promoted and validated their language and literacy development in both English and their home language(s) while others have experienced numerous educational injustices in the U.S.: crowded, poorly equipped, underfunded schools; monolingual English "submersion" policies that offer students little linguistic or cultural validation and little academic support; deficit-oriented "ability tracking" policies that can keep students out of "mainstream" classes and deny students access to a rich, engaging, reading and writing curriculum; and both subtle and overt racial, ethnic, and linguistic discrimination.

As this group of students has become larger and more diverse, scholarship on immigrant students has also become more complex. Researchers and theorists have developed more nuanced views of immigrant populations and explored the great variety of language and literacy histories that students may bring to their schooling. Scholars have looked at "in-migrants" from U.S. territories such as Puerto Rico (see Urciuoli, 1991; Zentella, 2000); "parachute kids" who come to the U.S. on foreign-student visas to live with relatives or caregivers and attend K-12 schools (see Lee, 2006; Zhou, 1998); "transnationals" who experience multiple back-and-forth migrations between their home countries and the U.S. (see Sanchez, 2004); "second generation immigrants," i.e., U.S.-born children of immigrant parents (see Portes & Manning, 1986; Portes & Rumbaut, 2001); children growing up in linguistic enclave communities (see Portes & Schauffler, 1994); adolescent "unschooled" or "under-schooled" immigrants who arrive in the U.S. with minimal formal schooling experience yet enter the upper levels of the U.S. K-12 school system (see Meyer, 2000; Morse, 1997); and immigrants who are speakers of "other Englishes" (see Nero, 1997). In attempting to understand and describe the diversity of students from multilingual/multicultural immigrant families, scholars have introduced new terminology to highlight socio-cultural and linguistic issues previously obscured when students were theorized and studied using more generic categories such as "immigrant," "non-native," or "minority."

At the same time, scholars have become aware that existing educational and institutional labels, such as "ESL," "Basic Writing,"[1] and "Regular Composition," can serve to highlight or conceal, validate or invalidate, and define or convolute the histories, experiences, and educational needs[2] of individual students. I would argue that these institutional labels can perpetuate educational injustice: some students (typically the economically privileged as well as those who more closely fit traditional, institutionally defined profiles) receive a curriculum more tailor-made to their individual needs. Depending on the particular institution, this advantaged group *may* include:

- Foreign-visa students who are in intensive English programs (IEPs) or college ESL programs that are designed to build upon students' prior English as a Foreign Language (EFL) instruction in their home countries and provide a transition to U.S. university instruction.
- So-called "mainstream" students who place directly into Freshman Composition classes that are designed to dovetail with the college-preparatory classes that these students have taken in high school.
- Students who place into Basic Writing classes that are designed with a bias toward the needs of monolingual English-speaking students.

Unfortunately, other students (typically those who arrive with less economic or social capital and those whose histories, experiences, and individual needs don't match traditional institutional profiles) may be marginalized, their educational support being "outsourced" to tutoring centers, basic skills programs, or even other institutions, as is the case when universities send matriculated students "away" to community college for ESL or developmental writing courses.[3]

It is against this backdrop that I have seen the notion of "generation 1.5" take hold. The term originated in the field of immigration studies to describe the complex social position of Southeast Asian refugee children adapting to life in the U.S. during the 1970s and 1980s (see Rumbaut and Ima, 1988). The term adds complexity to the descriptions of immigrant populations. "First generation immigrants" are those who grow up in cultural and linguistic contexts outside the U.S. "Second generation immigrants" are the U.S.-born children of immigrant parents; these children grow up solely in a U.S.-cultural contexts, often in bilingual or multilingual communities. The "1.5 generation" therefore consists of those who immigrate as young children and have life experiences that span two or more countries, cultures, and languages. These terms have allowed immigration scholars to highlight things previously unseen, such as differences in educational and economic opportunity for students arriving at different ages.

In the early 1980s the term was taken up by the Korean-American community: *il cheom ose* (literally "generation 1.5") began to appear in both Korean and Korean-American media. For Koreans and Korean-Americans, the term signifies the complex cultural and linguistic position of immigrant children who are not *il se* (first generation adult immigrants) and not *i se* (U.S.-born Korean-Americans). The term also highlights the process of negotiating between two cultural and linguistic identities. In a study of Korean-American youth, Park (1999) describes the term as "a highly conscious category with complex cultural meaning," one that expresses a self-perception of in-between-ness, as reflected in the title quote: "I really do feel I'm 1.5." Anyone who has grown up in bicultural, bilingual, or binational families or has spent extended periods living in cross-cultural contexts is deeply familiar with the sense of in-between-ness and the process of identity negotiation reflected in such works.

The term "generation 1.5" entered the field of education in the late 1990s and has since become more widespread, appearing in the fields TESOL (Teaching English as a Second Language), Composition, and high school Language Arts. Like most terms in the field of education, it is used in varying ways by individual teachers and scholars, sometimes referring to all immigrant students, sometimes referring only to those in a narrower demographic range (e.g., pre-adolescent arrivals), and sometimes referring only to those who are encountering difficulties with academic language and academic literacy. Like most terms in education, it both highlights and obscures aspects of experience and identity. And like most terms within the field, it comes with its own "baggage" and its own set of controversies.

Why would various teachers and scholars of education adopt a term that is from the field of immigrant studies and that is used by an American immigrant community? Several explanations have been proposed, some of which are less than favorable: a propensity to marginalize students through the process of "othering," a tendency to homogenize or erase the experiences of multilingual students, a desire to valorize the notion of the "native speaker," or even an attempt to repackage old knowledge using new terminology. However, none of those explanations can adequately account for the spread of the term or the growing interest in students who might be considered part of the 1.5 generation. This interest is particularly evident at the "grassroots level" among educators who work with generation 1.5 students.[4] I would argue that progressive educators and scholars are using the term in a conscious and purposeful way, to accomplish something that is not accomplished by other pre-existing terms our field. So what is it that this term might accomplish?

The notion of generation 1.5 seems to have gained acceptance more readily among teachers and scholars who want to problematize the traditional institutional division between College ESL and Basic Writing. On an ideological level, both institutional categories are based on what I call a "nativist normativity," i.e., the assumption that growing up as a monolingual native speaker is the norm. The institutional assumption in many College ESL programs is that students are monolingual speakers of their "native" language and are in the process of acquiring a second language as an *overlay* on the "native" language. English is construed as something that is "second" and "foreign" for students. Students are seen as *learners of English* rather than *users of English*. Similarly, U.S. culture may be seen as something that is "second" or "foreign" to students, as in those stereotypical ESL writing prompts that ask students to compare something in their "home culture" to something in "U.S. culture." By contrast, the institutional assumption in many Basic Writing programs is that students are monolingual speakers of English who are somehow "deficient" and must be "fixed" or "remediated" so that they can go on to "regular" English classes; students are seen as "cognitively underdeveloped" native speakers of English (for a seminal critique of this cognitive reductionism see Rose's, 1988 article).

Neither institutional construct validates bilingualism or multilingualism. In fact, neither construct reflects the histories and identities of students who see themselves as neither "ESL" nor "native" (see Chiang & Schmida, 1999; Ortmeier-Hooper, 2008). As Valdés (2000) makes clear, a child growing up in a multilingual context is not simply a child who has two side-by-side, monolingual-like language proficiencies. Instead, the child has language practices and language proficiencies that are spread across a bilingual range in complex ways that change from one social context to another. The constructs of "native speaker" and "non-native speaker"—terms that often characterize the institutional divide of College ESL and Basic Writing—do little to describe the multiple discourse proficiencies, multiple literacies, and multiple identities that many students bring to classes (see Harklau, 2000; McKay & Wong, 1996). The notion of generation 1.5 challenges this nativist normativity and helps teachers, curriculum developers, and program administrators reconceptualize students as having complex and varied language repertoires that are rooted in the social, political, and historical contexts of students' lives.[5]

The notion of generation 1.5 may also gain acceptance more readily among teachers and scholars who want to problematize the distinction between "remedial" and "mainstream" students. As Rose (1985) pointed out, the notion of remediation is based on a "myth of transience" and its associated belief that the system can somehow solve the "remediation problem" and "fix" students so that they can be sent to "mainstream" classes. Even at my own university, a multicultural urban institution with an ethnically and linguistically diverse faculty and student body, this myth of transience is evident in institutional discourse. In a recent memo to the campus, a high-level administrator praised the university because a large percentage of students had been "successfully remediated within one year." Such rhetoric belies the complexity of generation 1.5 students' long-term language and literacy development processes. Students who exit a Basic Writing course at the end of one semester are the same students who enter Freshman Composition the next semester. Both courses are part of a long-term learning trajectory by which students develop and refine discourse proficiencies and academic literacies throughout their college careers and across the college curriculum. In short, multilingual students should not be seen as "remedial" and multilingualism is not something that can or should be "remediated."

The term generation 1.5 may also find resonance among teachers and scholars who wish to problematize the divisions between fields of K-12 Language Arts, TESOL, and College Composition. Scholarship that spans the K-12 and postsecondary levels has been sparse; scholars typically confine themselves to one context or the other and thus cannot adequately capture the *long-term* language and literacy development of generation 1.5 immigrant students. The field of TESOL and its ancillary field of College ESL have tended to focus on foreign-visa students and on recently arrived immigrants; discussion about long-term U.S. resident bilinguals has also been sparse. When such students have been the focus of research, theory, or pedagogy, these students are often subsumed within larger, more generic populations, such as "immigrants" or "residents." By contrast, the field of College Composition and its ancillary field of Basic Writing have tended to focus on monolingual students who are inexperienced writers, students who are speakers of various community dialects of English,[6] and students who are members of politically and economically oppressed racial and ethnic groups. In such scholarship, long-term U.S. resident bilinguals are very often subsumed within more generic categories such as "ethnic minority students." These categories highlight race and ethnicity as the defining characteristics of such students.

At my own institution I have seen the notion of generation 1.5 used to problematize and successfully challenge traditional policies, program structures, and pedagogies. Discussions about generation 1.5 have been a key factor in our:

- Developing writing courses that draw upon multilingual/multicultural students' funds of knowledge and experiences growing up in California. (Multilingual students have the option of selecting these courses rather than more traditional ESL courses or generic "mainstream" courses.)
- Instituting self-guided placement processes. (Because we cannot assume multilingual students will have particular self-perceptions or identities, we allow students to have a voice in their own program placements.)
- Eliminating punitive remediation policies and creating intellectually enriching, credit-bearing freshman-level writing courses for students who would formerly have been sent to non-credit classes.
- Reconceptualizing our College ESL program as a program open to *all* multilingual students and renaming the program "Composition for Multilingual Students" to eliminate the stigmatizing "ESL" label.
- Developing workshops on editing and revising that support multilingual students in their regular Composition classes rather than tracking students into more traditional ESL writing courses or grammar courses.
- Instituting more professional development opportunities for both graduate students and faculty who want to learn to work with a wide variety of multilingual students. (The notion of generation 1.5 functions as a useful heuristic as teachers develop a more complex picture of the linguistic and cultural diversity of our student body.)
- Broadening teacher training in both the TESOL and Composition graduate programs. (New teachers coming out of both programs may have generation 1.5 students in their classes.)

In my discussions with community college teachers and administrators, I have seen the notion of generation 1.5 functioning in similar ways, as part of a dialogue about educational change, by educators who want to promote access, equity, and student success.

What should we do, as teachers, curriculum directors, and program administrators, to participate more effectively such dialogues? First, we must broaden and deepen our understandings of the possible histories, experiences, and individual educational needs that students bring to their college writing classes. Similarly, we must develop a knowledge of the social, political, historical, and institutional factors that have shaped our students' lives. Only then can we broaden our pedagogical repertoires in *all* classroom contexts, and begin to break down the traditional institutional boundaries of College ESL, Basic Writing, and "mainstream" College Composition, categories that do little to mirror the realities of many of our generation 1.5 students.

The Social, Political, and Economic Context of Post-1965 Immigration

To broaden and deepen our understanding of students, we must first look at the social, political, economic, and historical context of immigration. In 1965, the U.S. government finally repealed the overtly racist National Origins Act of 1924, which for 40 years had severely restricted immigration from most non-European countries (see McKay & Wong, 2000). The new 1965 Immigration Act allowed a more equitable distribution of visas to applicants throughout the world, established family unification rather than nationality as a favored selection criterion, and increased the overall number of visas issued each year. The post-1965 influx of immigrants was joined by repeated waves of refugees. New immigrants and new refugees then began to bring additional family members to the U.S. through family-sponsored visas, which now account for almost two-thirds of all new immigration visas (Office of Immigration Statistics, 2006). Currently, about one million immigrants arrive in the U.S. each year, almost one-third of whom are children under the age of 18. This represents the largest inflow of immigrant children in U.S. history. These new demographics challenge us as educators to change our paradigms about who our students are and how we teach them.

The 1965 Immigration Act increased not only the number of immigrants but also the racial, ethnic, and linguistic diversity of the immigrant population. The relative flow of immigrants from Northern and Western Europe slowed considerably, replaced by an ever-growing influx of immigrants from Asia and Latin America, who now account for over three-quarters of the new immigrant population (Office of Immigration Statistics, 2006). Unlike previous generations of European immigrants, most post-1965 immigrants are "visible minorities;"[7] their "newcomer" status is more readily apparent and thus they are more vulnerable to racial and ethnic discrimination. This increasing diversity also has fueled negative "white-nativist sentiments" (McKay & Wong, 2000) that have lead to anti-immigrant policies such as California Proposition 187 (passed in 1994) that sought to limit health and education services to undocumented immigrants and their children, and California Proposition 227 (passed in 1998) which severely restricted bilingual education programs. Such anti-immigrant or anti-bilingual legislation can now be seen in many states throughout the U.S. The accompanying racial, ethnic, and linguistic discrimination may slow the integration process for newly arrived immigrants and place them at an economic and political disadvantage, as compared to earlier generations of European immigrants (see Portes & Rumbaut, 1996; Portes & Zhou, 1993).

In the post-1965 era, the immigrant population has also become more socioeconomically diverse. Some groups, such as migrant agricultural laborers, enter the U.S. with few resources or marketable skills while other groups, such as technology workers, enter with skills that are in high demand. Within-group and between-group differences have also become greater, making it difficult to generalize about the immigrant population as a whole or adopt educational policies that can better support immigrant children.

While the demographics of the immigrant population have changed considerably, so too have the economic conditions that immigrants face when they arrive in the U.S. During pre-1965 waves of immigration, a familiar (although by no means universal) process of economic integration was available to immigrant families: first generation non-English speaking immigrants typically had access to jobs in labor. Their second generation children who were fluent in English typically had access to more highly paid skilled industrial jobs, thus moving up into the economic middle class. Their third generation grandchildren who had access to more schooling opportunities might take literacy-intensive professional jobs, thus becoming firmly anchored in the economic middle or upper-middle class. However, over the past four decades, technological changes, globalization, and the movement of manufacturing to offshore locations have eliminated many well-paying skilled industrial jobs in the U.S., cutting off traditional routes of economic integration and upward mobility. The U.S. economy has become more hourglass-shaped, with ever-growing numbers of unskilled, low-paying service sector jobs at the bottom and highly skilled, high-paying, literacy-intensive information-oriented jobs at the top.

Immigrants now face the prospect of "segmented assimilation" (see Rumbaut, 1994). Some segments of the immigrant population—those who arrive with strong educational backgrounds or those who are able to obtain high levels of education in the U.S.—achieve rapid economic integration and upward mobility. In fact, college-educated immigrants often reach income parity with native-born U.S. citizens within their lifetimes. By contrast, other segments—those who arrive without education and who are unable to obtain further education in the U.S.—make little progress toward income parity (Portes & Zhou, 1992). Some segments of the immigrant population even experience "downward assimilation" (Portes & Rumbaut, 2001). In such cases, the children of immigrants end up with less social or economic capital than they would have acquired had they remained in their parents' home countries. It is clear that the changing economic conditions in the U.S. have placed additional pressure on immigrant children. In order to avoid downward economic assimilation and to secure a place in the shrinking middle class, they are under considerably more pressure to follow an academically oriented college-bound path.

Arrival, Adaptation, Acculturation, and Identity Formation

Immigrant families' arrival experiences are greatly affected by the circumstances surrounding their departure from their home countries. Immigrants who suffered oppression, who were displaced by political or economic crises, who had to leave on short notice, who spent time in refugee camps or third countries, or who were unable to bring along economic capital typically have greater difficulties establishing themselves in the U.S. Those who lack extended family in the U.S. or lack access to a cultural and linguistic enclave community (which can help maintain cultural ties and provide an extended support network) may also have more difficulties. However, regardless of families' circumstances of departure and arrival, and regardless of individual differences, immigrants who arrive as children, the "generation 1.5ers," share a number of common challenges.

Many Americans are under the mistaken impression that immigrant children adapt relatively easily to new cultural and linguistic surroundings. However, research suggests that immigrant children experience numerous psychological and social challenges that are often overlooked. (For an overview, see James, 1997.) Such challenges may be exacerbated by the fact that many immigrant families are reticent to make use of social services, due to cultural and linguistic barriers, practical obstacles such as a lack of availability in local neighborhoods, experiences with discrimination, and in the case of undocumented immigrants, legal issues.

School counselors note that immigrant children often experience anxiety and depression as they leave behind their familiar homeland and their established social relations (James, 1997). Various stage models of cross-cultural adjustment have been proposed; researchers have documented various stages of acceptance and rejection of the new cultural surroundings (e.g., Wait, Roessingh, & Bosetti, 1996). What such models and studies have in common is the recognition that cross-cultural adjustment and bicultural identity development are complex, long-term, open-ended processes. Educators cannot assume that these processes are somehow "complete" simply because a student has been in the U.S. for a long time.

Studies indicate that immigrant children often shoulder significantly more responsibilities than U.S.-born children (see Orellana, 2003). Many immigrant parents work long hours in multiple jobs in order to make enough money to support their families in the U.S. Therefore, many immigrant children fend for themselves to a greater extent than non-immigrant children. When parents are away from home, older siblings often must play a parenting role for younger siblings. Furthermore, immigrant youth are sometimes under pressure to begin work at an early age so that they can support their families. Many immigrant children also do a significant amount of language brokering and literacy mediation for their non-English speaking parents, thus taking on adult responsibilities at a very early age (Tse, 1996). Therefore, many immigrant students will have significantly more responsibilities than non-immigrant students—responsibilities that may take away from the time and energy they can devote to schooling.

Perhaps the most commonly recognized challenge for immigrant children is that of intergenerational values conflict. Although immigrant children tend to experience considerable cognitive and emotional stress in adapting to a new culture, they usually reposition themselves more readily than their parents. This repositioning may bring children into conflict with their parents' expectations, especially regarding traditional gender roles, traditional parent–child relationships, and schooling (see Kibria, 1993; Zhou & Bankston, 1998). Immigrant children thus often need to navigate between two very different social worlds on a daily basis, worlds with conflicting norms, values, and expectations.

The process of acculturation and identity formation is particularly complex for generation 1.5 children who arrive at a very young age. Acculturation has traditionally been seen as a "zero sum game" of assimilation in which immigrant children progressively give up their home culture and accept American culture. (For a review of assimilation theories and controversies, see Alba & Nee, 1997.) However, scholars now realize that immigrant children negotiate complex multicultural identities (see McKay & Wong, 1996). An immigrant who arrives at a young age faces a twofold task— continuing to develop a "home culture" identity, while simultaneously developing a U.S. cultural identity. When this process is successful, immigrants develop confident bicultural identities with strong attachments to both cultures (see Rotheram-Borus, 1993). When the process is unsuccessful, immigrants may become dually alienated. In his 1997 ethnographic study, *Personas Mexicanas: Chicano High Schoolers in a Changing Los Angeles*, Vigil (1997) notes that some students feel highly alienated from both European-American culture and Mexican culture.

Over the past several decades, the process of identity negotiation has become more complex as hyphenated identities (e.g., "Asian-American") have become more important in U.S. society. For example, a generation 1.5 child who arrives from Vietnam must negotiate at least a threefold identity: as a Vietnamese, as an American, and as an Asian-American. Similarly, a generation 1.5 child from Mexico negotiates aspects of Mexican, American, and Chicano (Mexican-American) identities. While immigrant children tend to identify primarily with their *national heritage identities*, U.S. society tends to impose *ethnic and racial identities* (see Kibria, 2000) upon individuals. Thus Dominicans are seen as simply "Latino," Cambodians are seen simply as "Asian," etc. New immigrants often resist these ethnic or racial labels, especially when they entail a self-perceived loss of status, identity, or heritage. The process of negotiating a multicultural identity may be especially difficult for immigrant children who come to the U.S. before they have had significant life experiences in their home countries. These children must negotiate their home-culture identity, in spite of the fact that they may have little memory of their home countries. This problem is highlighted when ESL teachers assign typical newcomer-oriented ESL tasks such as comparing America with one's "home country."

Recently, scholars have noted a new pattern of acculturation and identity formation among immigrant children: acculturation without assimilation. In other words, both generation 1.5 immigrants and U.S.-born second generation immigrants have increasingly maintained aspects of their home culture identities instead of rapidly "Americanizing." (For a review and critique of assimilation theories, see Alba & Nee, 1997.) This phenomenon has led immigration scholars such as Rumbaut (1996) to refer to today's U.S.-born children of immigrants as "the new second generation," a generation that no longer follows the traditional multigenerational path of linguistic, cultural, and economic assimilation. This new pattern is particularly visible among ethnolinguistic groups that see themselves as part of transnational diasporas; the pattern challenges the notion that assimilation is a prerequisite for success (Gibson, 1998; see also Hinkel, 2000; Sridhar & Sridhar, 2000). Educators must resist the defunct notion that assimilation and school success go hand in hand.

Complicating identity development issues is the fact that generation 1.5 children often experience linguistic, cultural, and racial discrimination in their schools, their communities, and society at large. In school, teachers may harbor conscious or unconscious prejudices and thus underestimate immigrant students' potential (see Valdés, 1998). Conversely, teachers may place undue expectations on students; this is often the case with Asian immigrants who feel pressured to live up to the "model minority" stereotype (Conchas & Peréz, 2003; Suzuki, 1994). Students may also experience fourfold discrimination from their classmates:

- U.S.-born white classmates may regard generation 1.5 students as "foreigners."
- U.S.-born same-ethnicity classmates may see generation 1.5 students as being too "backward." (For example, some students report being disparagingly called "F.O.B." or "fresh off the boat" by their U.S.-born, same-ethnicity classmates.)

- Recently arrived immigrants who still have strong linguistic and cultural ties to their homelands may regard generation 1.5 students as "too Americanized."
- Members of other U.S. minority groups may perceive generation 1.5 students as "competing" for access to an increasingly limited array of economic and social opportunities within U.S. schools and society.

All of the above factors result in a multispeed, multidimensional process of adaptation, acculturation, and identity development. The post-1965 immigrant children thus tend to follow more complex and varied paths of linguistic, cultural, social, and economic integration, with more varied options and outcomes, even children within the same family. In fact, identity itself has become an increasingly complex phenomenon as immigrants now face numerous "identity options" that they can, to a certain extent, freely negotiate (see Kibria, 2000). Educators must develop an awareness of the identity options that students face and the factors that shape their identity choices; at the same time educators must remain aware that each student will follow a unique path in negotiating these choices.

K-12 Schooling and the Pathway to College

Immigrant children typically confront more disruptions and discontinuities along their pathway from kindergarten to college than do U.S.-born children (see ESL Intersegmental Project Commission, 2000). Immigrants who arrive before first grade experience a disruption when they enter U.S. schools, encounter an English-dominant culture, and are forced to navigate mainly or solely in English. Immigrants who arrive during elementary school, middle school, or high school may experience a disruption when they face a new schooling system, a curriculum that may not align with the curriculum of their home countries, a new language of instruction, and a new school culture. The disruption can be even greater for immigrants who have received little or no schooling in their home countries when they enter the U.S. (Morse, 1997) and for refugee children who have missed years of schooling during their migratory process (Bosher & Rowecamp, 1998). In addition, new immigrants to the U.S. often relocate several times before finding a permanent place to live; their children thus experience additional interruptions as they switch between schools that have differing placement policies, programs, and instructional practices.

Most K-12 schools assess incoming immigrant students to determine whether they need specialized language support. However, the quality of the assessment varies considerably between states and between school systems within a given state. In California, schools use the "Home Language Survey," a series of questions about the child's use of languages other than English. A "yes" answer to any of the survey questions is supposed to trigger a more thorough assessment process. Unfortunately, there may be a significant delay between initial identification and the more thorough assessment; during this time period, a child may languish in an inappropriate classroom at an inappropriate level (ESL Intersegmental Project Commission, 2000). Even when assessments are carried out in a timely manner, the effectiveness of assessment tools is often questionable. Especially at the younger grade levels, assessment tools can mistake minimal oral fluency for English proficiency, thus denying students access to special instructional support.

Even when effective assessment mechanisms are used, placement options and services for immigrant students may be limited. One commonly favored option is the "newcomer school" or "newcomer program" where recently arrived immigrant children may be placed while adjusting to U.S. school life and learning English. The value of newcomer schools and programs has been debated. Critics argue that such schools and programs may enhance segregation, add yet another disruption to students' long-term schooling path, and delay students' entry into mainstream school life (see Feinberg, 2000). Advocates claim, on the other hand, that such schools and programs provide an entry point for newcomers, assist them with the adaptation and acculturation process, affirm the value of home cultures, and help newcomers build confidence and self-esteem (see Herzberg, 1998).

When newcomer programs are unavailable or inappropriate, ESL or bilingual classes often serve as the initial placement and the nexus of support for immigrant students. However, ESL and bilingual classes vary greatly in scope and function. Some classes take on a more general educational empowerment mission with teachers serving as advisors and intermediaries between the students and school personnel (see Harklau, 1994a). Other classes have a more limited scope, focusing merely on language instruction. As educators, we must be aware that students' prior experiences in newcomer, ESL, and bilingual programs will greatly shape their perceptions of classes targeted toward multilingual students.

As immigrant students advance along their educational pathways, they face a bewildering variety of programs, classroom placements, and instructional approaches (bilingual, ESL, immersion, two-way immersion, sheltered content, remedial/developmental, pull-out, and mainstream). This occurs because multilingual students are treated in different ways within each segment of the K-to-college pathway (ESL Intersegmental Project Commission, 2000). In California, most immigrant students start out designated as "English Learners" (ELs). Students are typically redesignated as "English Proficient" (EP) within a few years. However, generation 1.5 immigrants may be redesignated as English language learners as they move along their pathways. When students enter high school, community college, and 4-year colleges, they are particularly vulnerable to redesignation as "ESL students," a prospect that most students find highly demoralizing because they feel they have already "made it out of ESL." It is imperative that schools create curricular options for students that do not bear the stigmatizing "ESL" label.

In K-12 schools, immigrant students may face two equally problematic English placements—premature mainstreaming on the one hand and long-term ESL tracking on the other. In the era of No Child Left Behind and high stakes accountability, schools are under pressure to mainstream students long before the students are fully equipped to deal with the language and literacy demands of mainstream classes. In such classes, immigrant students may receive little or no instructional support. On the other hand, when immigrant students are tracked into ESL classes for years on end, they may have little contact with native English speakers and may receive an education consisting only of mechanical grammar drills, worksheet pedagogy, and seatwork. Harklau (1994b) documents how certain groups of ESL students manage to navigate their way out of the ESL track and find strategies for succeeding in the college-prep track. However, some groups of students remain "stranded" in the ESL track for much longer; such segregation may arise from latent racial and ethnic prejudices of school officials (see Valdés, 1998). When students enter an English class, their prior experiences with premature mainstreaming or long-term ESL tracking can greatly complicate the attitudes they will have toward their current placement.

Those immigrant students who successfully exit K-12 ESL classes face two additional problematic placement options: high track classes (sometimes called academic, honors, or college-bound) and lower track classes (sometimes called basic, regular, or remedial). In high track classes, students may receive richer linguistic input, more opportunities for oral interaction, and more stimulating instructional practices. However, students must "compete" with U.S.-born native English speakers for the floor, a prospect that can be quite daunting if the instructor fails to structure activities to accommodate students of varying oral proficiencies in English. In lower track classes, students may find the tasks and the oral interaction more manageable. However, linguistic input in low track classes is generally poorer, tasks are more mechanical, and classroom interaction tends to be minimal, as many teachers avoid interactive activities in order to control "behavior problems" (see Oakes, 1985). Multilingual students entering a college English class will thus have a broad range of educational histories; some will have followed educational pathways that have fostered success and prepared them well for college while other students have experienced trajectories full of discontinuities and problematic placements.

Student Success in K-12 Schools

A number of theories have been advanced to explain immigrant students' success (or lack of success) in K-12 schools. Ogbu's theoretical construct of *voluntary versus involuntary* minorities is perhaps the best known[8] (see Ogbu & Simon, 1998). Ogbu suggests that children from immigrant families tend to have a success orientation toward school because their families come to the U.S. voluntarily to seek out economic opportunities and better living conditions. Conversely, he suggests that children from non-immigrant minority groups (e.g., African-Americans and native peoples) tend to have an oppositional orientation toward school because these children are part of groups that have been colonized, oppressed, or brought to the U.S. involuntarily. While voluntary minorities tend to accept the power structures of school and society as legitimate, involuntary minorities tend to resist these structures because they are well aware of the oppressive nature of such structures. However, as Gibson (1998) points out, immigrant children who come at an early age do not fit into Ogbu's dichotomy. Generation 1.5 students may share traits of both voluntary and involuntary minorities. Their experiences with racial, ethnic, and linguistic discrimination may lead them to identify with other U.S.-born minority groups and thus they may develop a general attitude of resistance toward schooling and viewing school as an instrument of social oppression.

Home–school mismatch theories have also been proposed to explain the success and failure of immigrant children. Such theories are predicated on the notion that different socio-economic and socio-cultural groups belong to different discourse communities (see Gee, 1990). U.S. school structure and instructional practices generally fit closely with the values, norms, and behaviors of middle-class white families, thus giving their children a significant advantage when they enter school. Students who come from other linguistic, cultural, and economic backgrounds may have more difficulty negotiating the academic environment because school discourse practices do not affirm and build upon the discourse practices that students bring from their home communities (see Heath, 1983).

It has also been suggested that acculturation is a determinant of success in K-12 schools. Traditionally, both school personnel and scholars in the field of education have assumed that immigrant children's educational successes were correlated with their level of cultural and linguistic assimilation into U.S. society. However, over the past 20 years, a number of scholars have shown that strong home culture identity is positively correlated with motivation and academic performance. In fact, rapid cultural and linguistic assimilation has been linked to educational failure, rather than success, particularly among certain segments of the immigrant population (Bosher & Rowecamp, 1998). This may be due to the fact that students who rapidly give up their home language or home culture identity cut themselves off from valuable support and funds of knowledge in their home communities.

Overall, immigrant children experience the same segmented assimilation that is experienced by the general immigrant population. Some children use schooling as a path for upward mobility while others flounder in U.S. schools or drop out. Bankston and Zhou (1997) have referred to this pattern as the "bifurcation of immigrant youth." In their study of schooling in New Orleans, they discuss how Vietnamese youth faced two socially imposed identities, which the authors characterize as "valedictorians" and "delinquents." Some youth identified more with the success-orientation that is part of the Asian-American "model minority" myth, while others identified more with the youth gang identity.

Language Acquisition and Language Practices in Home, School, and Community

New immigrants to the U.S. tend to settle in specific regions. Over the past several decades the most important magnet regions have been in California, New York, Texas, Florida, New Jersey, and Illinois. Within magnet regions, immigrants often settle in ethnolinguistic enclave communities that are characterized by complex patterns of linguistic interaction. These communities contain monolingual home language speakers, monolingual English speakers, and multilinguals who range from home language dominant to English dominant (Valdés, 2000). Within these communities, the functions of English and the home language are particular to specific social contexts and they are spread over a variety of registers and domains. To be a full member of the community and participate in all social institutions, children must both maintain their home language and develop English proficiency (see Zentella, 1997). They must also adapt to the localized language practices of the community, practices that generally differ from language use in the home country. Within an enclave community, both the home language and English undergo modification and influence each other through such processes as semantic extension and linguistic borrowing (see Ardila, 2005). In addition, interlocutors often use complex patterns of code-switching that require speakers to be proficient in both languages. As members of bilingual/diglossic communities, generation 1.5 children thus develop complex linguistic repertoires that go far beyond the "academic English" that is valued in school settings.

Until the 1960s, many scholars thought that the acquisition of a second language at an early age carried negative cognitive consequences, "overloading" and "confusing" the child.[9] In fact, many educators advised immigrant parents to switch to English when addressing their children, even in cases where the parents had only a minimal command of English. Scholars now recognize that children navigate multilingual development without negative cognitive repercussions, and that the multilingualism can actually promote cognitive development.

As generation 1.5 children acquire English, they face all challenges characteristic of any second language acquisition process. Their English competence goes through a long interlanguage stage as it gradually approximates the English of their fellow interlocutors and their environment. This interlanguage is characterized by a high degree of diachronic and synchronic variability based on factors such as task difficulty, emotional state, or context. Learners may experience periods of apparent "backsliding," as their interlanguage develops and "reorganizes" itself. Learners' linguistic performance may be quite uneven, with some areas and domains highly developed and others underdeveloped. Both the rate of acquisition and the ultimate state of English proficiency vary greatly from individual to individual due to social and psycholinguistic factors that are still only partially understood. Some learners develop English proficiencies that are similar to those of U.S.-born monolingual students while others retain a distinct "non-native-like" feature, a process that has traditionally been referred to as "fossilization"[10] (see Fidler, 2006; Han & Odlin, 2006).

However, several factors may make generation 1.5 students' acquisition processes different from those of the adult immigrant language learners. Immigrant youth often learn much of their English through informal oral/aural interaction with friends, classmates, and co-workers, through interaction with English-dominant siblings and members of their extended families, and of course, through input from media. Children who begin English acquisition after the so-called "critical period"[11] and who acquire language predominantly through oral/aural interaction may not notice small syntactic, morphological, or lexical features of English, especially those features that are not stressed in speech. In such cases, the learner might not develop dexterity with these grammatical features. Like native monolingual English speakers who have limited experience with text, oral/aural English learners may not be aware of language features that are encoded primarily in formal written English. In their speech, they may also rely heavily on pragmatic discourse moves rather than lexical, syntactic, or morphological specificity. (Those who are bilingual are well aware that one can develop strong communication competence without attending to small grammar features.) Like monolingual English speakers, oral/aural language learners may become highly proficient oral communicators in school settings; however, they may face difficulty when confronted with school writing tasks that require attention to formal written conventions. In addition, like monolingual English speakers, oral/aural language learners generally lack the meta-linguistic terminology necessary for understanding teachers' explanation of written linguistic conventions.

While the classroom-based language acquisition experiences of immigrant students have been studied in some detail at the elementary school level, less is known about their experiences at the high school level (Harklau, 2000). Immigrant students who arrive during middle school and high school have often had some English instruction in their home countries. This instruction is often text based, focusing on reading and grammar. Therefore, even those who have had instruction usually arrive in the U.S. quite unprepared for the challenges of fast-paced classroom interaction. On the other hand, this prior training may give later-arrival students a meta-linguistic understanding of English, which can later facilitate their language acquisition, particularly in the area of formal academic writing. In fact, many later-arrival immigrant students report that they rely heavily on the instruction that they received in their home countries.

Socio-economic factors add complexity to the language acquisition processes and language repertoires of immigrant children. Many attend inner-city or rural schools where their interlocutors are speakers of various community dialects of English, such as African-American English Vernacular (AAEV) and Chicano English (CE). Many of their interlocutors are also language learners whose own speech is characterized by high variability. When confronted with academic writing tasks, immigrant students may produce prose that contains both learner-like features and features that mirror their peer-group interlocutors. They thus often face double censure from teachers—both for "ESL errors" and for "nonstandard errors." When a student's writing contains linguistic features that may be related to *either* language learning *or* dialect, it may be difficult for teachers to tailor their feedback and explanations to the individual student. When language features are related to a student's *home dialect*, teachers typically want to affirm that home dialect while teaching editing strategies that will help the student produce a more formal academic prose. When language features are related to a student's interlanguage development, teachers generally want to correct and explain what they perceive to be "errors."

After immigrant children arrive in the U.S., their home language proficiency may follow one of two main routes. Their proficiency may continue to grow through interactions with other home language speakers and interactions with text; this is often the case for children who acquired literacy skills before immigrating to the U.S. and for children who are able to attend bilingual classes or home-language literacy programs. Conversely, an immigrant child's home language proficiency may cease development and even backslide. In such cases, children do not develop a lexically and syntactically rich, age-appropriate command of their native language as they mature. The process of language shift and home language loss may occur quite rapidly. Of the group of immigrants who arrive between age 0 and age 14, approximately 20% will shift to English dominance within the first 5 years of U.S. residency, 40% will switch within the first 10 years, and 66% switch within the first 20 years. In fact, 10% of immigrants age 0 to 14 will eventually lose their home language completely. Those immigrants who arrive after age 15 appear to fare much better; few of these individuals lose their home language over the course of their lifetime. (See McKay & Wong, 2000 for a complete discussion of immigrant children's language loss and the associated statistics.) Again, educators must be aware of the range of language histories that students bring to our classes. Students' self-perceptions of their "most comfortable" language, their "preferred" language, their "best" language, their "first" language, or "second" language may not follow a pattern that educators traditionally expect.

College Experiences

Recent studies have shown that within a given ethnic group, immigrant children are more likely than non-immigrant children to attend college, even when confounding variables such as socio-economic status have been factored out (Vernez & Abrahamse, 1996). However, immigrant youth often face a number of challenges when they enter college. First, they may experience an identity change. As Harklau (2000) notes, in high school, immigrant students are often seen by teachers and administrators as the "good kids" (i.e., the most diligent) when compared to U.S.-born students. This is especially true in low-track high school classes where immigrants may be studying alongside U.S.-born students whom teachers see as "behavior problems." However, when immigrant students arrive at college, they may find that their identity in ESL and English classes changes. If they are placed in college-level ESL classes, they may find themselves studying alongside newly arrived foreign-visa students who have come to the U.S. with ample social, intellectual, and economic capital, as well as strong meta-linguistic training. Such immigrants, whom teachers and program administrators now compare to foreign students, may be seen as "the under-prepared," "the slackers," or the "behavior problems," for example, because they are already used to the informal character of U.S. schools.

Most students find that college as an institution is fundamentally different from high school. Society tends to treat K-12 education as a *right*; therefore, K-12 schools are characterized by an abundance of *support services* to help students take advantage of that right. By contrast, society tends to perceive postsecondary education more as a *meritocratic institution*; therefore postsecondary schools are characterized by an abundance of *gatekeeping mechanisms* that sort students by merit. Even with the advent of open admissions of the 1970s and the expanding "urban mission" of many public colleges, most college English departments find themselves caught between the conflicting goals of supporting linguistic minority students while at the same time maintaining what faculty and administrators perceive as traditional academic standards.

Immigrant college students also may face challenges typically associated with other so-called "non-traditional" students. Many are first in the family to go to college. Many are struggling economically, sometimes working full time to support their families when their non-English speaking parents have limited earning potential. Even when supportive of education, the families might have little understanding of what the college experience entails. Such families may pressure students to take unreasonable course loads in order to finish at an accelerated pace. In addition, recent anti-remediation mandates in many state college systems have put additional pressures on immigrant students to complete their ESL coursework "in record time" or face disenrollment or loss of financial aid.

Researchers in the field of education have noted that immigrant students are poorly served at the college level (Harklau, Losey, & Siegal, 1999; Rolph, Gray, & Melamid, 1996; Ruiz-de-Valasco & Fix, 2000). Academic services specifically targeted toward immigrants are sparse. Many institutions have an "office of international students" that supports and coordinates services to foreign-visa students. However, these services are typically unavailable to immigrant students, even recent arrivals (Reid, 1998). Within English programs, the curricular structures that track students into ESL, Basic

Writing, and "mainstream" classes offer no clear placement options for those immigrant students who are long-term U.S. residents, yet are still working on academic language development. After several years in U.S. schools, such students usually feel that they no longer "fit" in newcomer-oriented ESL classes but they may also feel unready for the language and literacy demands of English classes that are taught by teachers with little or no TESOL training. With time, English placement becomes even more problematic, especially when students shift to English dominance and yet still retain features in their speech and writing that are learner-like or ESL-like (Frodesen & Starna, 1999; see also Valdés, 1992).

The ways that postsecondary institutions currently label and categorize students tend to obscure the immigrant student population and conflate these students' experiences, characteristics, and needs with those of other populations (Harklau, Losey, & Siegal 1999), making it more difficult to design academic support programs to serve these students. *Ethnic labels* associated with diversity mandates are problematic because they conflate immigrants with U.S.-born minorities. For example, newly arrived Southeast Asian immigrants and fourth generation Chinese-Americans are both labeled "Asian-American." *Linguistic labels* such as "ESL" are problematic, especially at the college level, because they conflate immigrant students with foreign-visa students who often come to the U.S. with ample social and economic capital (Vandrick, 1995), strong meta-linguistic English training (Reid, 1997), and strong academic skills. *Academic labels* such as "remedial" or "basic writer" are problematic because they conflate immigrant students with monolingual U.S. students who may have very different language and literacy histories, experiences, and needs (Braine, 1996). Furthermore, all of these labels are problematic because they reduce immigrant students' needs to a single dimension and overlook other social, cognitive, and affective factors associated with the immigration experience, biculturalism, and bilingualism.

Conclusions

I have attempted to provide a perspective on generation 1.5 and present some of the things we know about the range of experiences generation 1.5 students may bring to our classes. However, as I noted in an earlier article on generation 1.5 (Roberge, 2002, 108)

> any attempt to describe a *group* of students is fraught with difficulty. Immigrant students' experiences are extremely diverse, even among members of the same family. These varied experiences are heavily affected by factors such as the geographic area of settlement, community demographics, the local political climate, school characteristics, and the presence or lack of extended family. Furthermore, student identity itself is fluid, multifaceted, and socially constructed (Harklau, 2000) and even the term "generation 1.5" may be problematic, for it implies that these students are somewhere "between" first and second generation immigrants when they may have experiences, characteristics, and educational needs which, in fact, differ markedly from both of these groups.

Despite these complexities, it is my hope that the notion of generation 1.5 will function as a useful heuristic in our ongoing discussions about ways to promote educational access, educational equity, and student success for linguistically and culturally diverse students.

Notes

1. I use the term *Basic Writing* because it is prevalent in the field of Composition, not because I consider students "basic."
2. The notion of "student needs" has come under criticism because it can be used to marginalize students. However, I consciously use the term here because I believe that in order to promote educational access and equity we must strive to meet the educational needs of *all* students.
3. One of our state universities in California has refused to provide developmental writing courses for students; if students score poorly on the entry-level writing exam, the students are required to take courses taught by the local community college.
4. My own notions of generation 1.5 have been shaped primarily by the hundreds of generation 1.5 students whom I've taught and whom I've advised over the past 6 years, as part of our self-directed placement policy. My views have also been shaped by my colleagues who are generation 1.5 immigrants themselves.
5. I recently attended a conference presentation that used a similar term, Complex Language Background (CLB) students. I prefer the term generation 1.5 because it highlights students' immigration experiences.
6. I use the term *community dialect* rather than the normative and pejorative term, *nonstandard*. The term community dialect focuses on the student's language use within his/her own local community.
7. This term is used in Canadian scholarship, but it captures well the issue of the racial and ethnic discrimination.
8. Ogbu's scholarship has generated much controversy and criticism. I include Obgu's typology here because his thinking has been highly influential.
9. Unfortunately, one still encounters many school personnel who believe that multilingual students should speak only English at home.
10. The notion of fossilization as a psycholinguistic phenomenon has come under critique.
11. Like fossilization, the notion of the critical period as a psycholinguistic phenomenon has also come under critique. However, those who have acquired multiple language at varying ages are well aware of the difficulties that arise when one begins a language at a later age.

References

Alba, R.D. & Nee, V. (1997). Rethinking assimilation theory for a new era of immigration. *International Migration Review, 31*(4), 826–874.

Ardila, A. (2005). Spanglish: An Anglicized Spanish dialect. *Hispanic Journal of Behavioral Sciences, 27*(1), 60.

Bankston, C.L. & Zhou, M. (1997). Valedictorians and delinquents: The bifurcation of Vietnamese American adolescents. *Deviant Behavior, 18*(4), 343–364.

Bosher, S. & Rowecamp, J. (1998). The refugee/immigrant in higher education: The role of educational background. *College ESL, 8*(1), 23–42.

Braine, G. (1996). ESL students in first-year writing courses: ESL versus mainstream classes. *Journal of Second Language Writing, 5*(2), 91–107.

Chiang, Y. & Schmida, M. (1999). *Language identity and language ownership: Linguistic conflicts of first-year university writing students.* In L. Harklau, K. Losey, & M. Siegal (Eds.), *Generation 1.5 meets college composition: Issues in the teaching of writing to U.S.-educated learners of ESL* (pp. 81–98). Mahwah, NJ: Lawrence Erlbaum Associates.

Chung, H.C. (2000). English language learners of Vietnamese background. In S.L. McKay & S.C.

Wong (Eds.), *New immigrants in the United States: Readings for second language educators* (pp. 216–231). Cambridge, UK: Cambridge University Press.

Conchas, G. & Pérez, C. (2003). Surfing the "model minority" wave of success: How the school context shapes distinct experiences among Vietnamese youth. *New Directions for Youth Development. Special Issue: Understanding the Social Worlds of Immigrant Youth* (Issue Edited by Carola Suárez-Orozco, Irina L.G. Todorova), *2003*(100), 41–56.

ESL Intersegmental Project Commission. (2000). *California pathways: The second language student in public high schools, colleges, and universities.* Sacramento: Intersegmental Council of Academic Senates in conjunction with the California Community Colleges Chancellor's Office.

Feinberg, R.C. (2000). Newcomer schools: Salvation or segregated oblivion for immigrant students? *Theory into Practice, 39*(4), 220–227.

Fidler, A. (2006). Reconceptualizing fossilization in second language acquisition: A review. *Second Language Research, 22*(3), 398–411.

Frodesen, J. & Starna, N. (1999). Distinguishing incipient and functional bilingual writers: Assessment and instructional insights gained through second-language writer profiles. In L. Harklau, K. Losey, & M. Siegal (Eds.), *Generation 1.5 meets college composition: Issues in the teaching of writing to US-educated learners of ESL* (pp. 61–80). Mahwah, NJ: Lawrence Erlbaum Associates.

Gee, J. (1990). *Social linguistics and literacies: Ideology in discourse.* London: Falmer Press.

Gibson, M. (1998). Promoting academic success among immigrant students: Is acculturation the issue? *Educational Policy, 12*(6), 615–633.

Han, Z. & Odlin, T. (Eds.) (2006). *Studies of fossilization in second language acquisition.* Clevedon, UK: Multilingual Matters.

Harklau, L. (1994a). ESL versus mainstream classes: Contrasting L2 learning environments. *TESOL Quarterly, 28*(2), 241–272.

Harklau, L. (1994b). Tracking and linguistic minority students: Consequences of ability grouping for second language learners. *Linguistics and Education, 6*(3), 221–248.

Harklau, L. (2000). From the "good kids" to the "worst": Representations of English language learners across educational settings. *TESOL Quarterly, 34*(1), 35–67.

Harklau, L., Losey, K., & Siegal, M. (Eds.) (1999). *Generation 1.5 meets college composition: Issues in the teaching of writing to US-educated learners of ESL.* Mahwah, NJ: Lawrence Erlbaum Associates.

Heath, S.B. (1983). *Ways with words: Language, life and work in communities and classrooms.* Cambridge, UK: Cambridge University Press.

Herzberg, M. (1998). Having arrived: Dimensions of educational success in a transitional newcomer school. *Anthropology and Education Quarterly, 29*(4), 391–418.

Hinkel, E. (2000). Soviet immigrants in the U.S.: Issues in adjustment. In S.L. McKay & S.C. Wong (Eds.), *New immigrants in the United States: Readings for second language educators* (pp. 352–368). Cambridge, UK: Cambridge University Press.

James, D.C.S. (1997). Coping with a new society: The psychosocial problems of immigrant youth. *Journal of School Health, 67*(3), 98–101.

Kibria, N. (1993). *Family tightrope: The changing lives of Vietnamese Americans.* Princeton, NJ: Princeton University Press.

Kibria, N. (2000). Race, ethnic options and ethnic binds. *Sociological Perspectives, 43*(1), 77–95.

Lee, A. (2006). Asian American studies: Identity formation in Korean American parachute kids. *CUREJ: College Undergraduate Research Electronic Journal,* University of Pennsylvania. Retrieved August, 2007, from http://repository.upenn.edu/curej/7.

McKay, S.L. & Wong, S.C. (1996). Multiple discourses, multiple identities: Investment and agency in second-language learning among Chinese adolescent immigrant students. *Harvard Educational Review, 66*(3), 577–608.

McKay, S.L. & Wong, S.C. (2000). *New immigrants in the United States: Readings for second language educators.* Cambridge, UK: Cambridge University Press.

Meyer, L. (2000). Barriers to meaningful instruction for English learners. *Theory Into Practice, 39*(4), 228–236.

Morse, S.C. (1997). *Unschooled migrant youth: Characteristics and strategies to serve them.* Charleston, WV: ERIC Clearinghouse on Rural Education and Small Schools (ED 405 158).

Nero, S. (1997). English is my native language … or so I believe. *TESOL Quarterly, 31*(3), 585–593.

Oakes, J. (1985). *Keeping track: How schools structure inequality.* New Haven, CT: Yale University Press.

Office of Immigration Statistics, Homeland Security. (March, 2006). *U.S. Legal Permanent Residents: 2006.* Washington, DC: Office of Immigration Statistics.

Ogbu, J.U. (1992). Adaptation to minority status and impact on school success. *Theory into Practice, 31*(4), 287–295.

Ogbu, J.U. & Simons, H.D. (1998). Voluntary and involuntary minorities: A cultural–ecological theory of school performance with some implications for education. *Anthropology and Education Quarterly, 29*(2), 155–188.

Orellana, M. (2003). Responsibilities of children in Latino immigrant homes. *New Directions for Youth Development. Special Issue: Understanding the Social Worlds of Immigrant Youth* (Issue Edited by Carola Suárez-Orozco, Irina L.G. Todorova), *2003*(100), 25–39.

Ortmeier-Hooper, C. (2008). English may be my second language, but I'm not "ESL." *College Composition and Communication, 59*(3), 2008.

Park, K. (1999). "I really do feel I'm 1.5": The construction of self and community by young Korean Americans. *Amerasia Journal, 25*(1), 139–163.

Pérez, B. (Ed.) (1998). *Sociocultural contexts of language and literacy.* Mawah, NJ: Lawrence Erlbaum Associates.

Portes, A. & Manning, R.D. (1986). The immigrant enclave: Theory and empirical examples. In S. Olzak & J. Nagel (Eds.), *Competitive ethnic relations* (pp. 47–68). Orlando, FL: Academic Press.

Portes, A. & Rumbaut, R. (1996). *Immigrant America: A portrait.* Berkeley: University of California Press.

Portes, A. & Rumbaut, G. (2001). *Legacies: The story of the immigrant second generation.* Berkeley: University of California Press.

Portes, A. & Schauffler, R. (1994). Language and the second generation: Bilingualism yesterday and today. *International Migration Review* (Special Issue: The new second generation), *28*(4), 640–661.

Portes, A. & Zhou, M. (1992). Gaining the upper hand: Economic mobility among immigrant and domestic minorities. *Ethnic and Racial Studies, 15*(4), 491–523.

Portes, A. & Zhou, M. (1993). The new second generation: Segmented assimilation and its variants. *Annals of the American Academy of Political and Social Sciences, 530*(1), 74–96.

Reid, J. (1997). Which non-native speaker: Differences between international students and US resident (language minority) students. *New Directions for Teaching and Learning, 70,* 17–27.

Reid, J. (1998). "Eye" learners and "ear" learners: Identifying the language needs of international students and US resident writers. In J.M. Reid & P. Byrd (Eds.), *Grammar in the composition classroom: Essays on teaching ESL for college-bound students* (pp. 3–17). Boston, MA: Heinle & Heinle.

Roberge, M. (2002). California's generation 1.5 immigrants: What experiences, characteristics, and needs do they bring to our English classes? *CATESOL Journal, 14*(1), 107–130.

Rolph, E., Gray, M.J., & Melamid, E. (1996). *Immigration and higher education: Institutional responses to changing demographics.* Santa Monica, CA: RAND Corporation.

Rose, M. (1985). The language of exclusion: Writing instruction at the university. *College English, 47*(4), 341–359.

Rose, M. (1988). Narrowing the mind and page: Remedial writers and cognitive reductionism. *College Composition and Communication, 39*(3), 267–302.

Rotheram-Borus, M. (1993). Biculturalism among adolescents. In M. Bernal & G. Knight (Eds.), *Ethnic identity: Formation and transmission among Hispanics and other minorities* (pp. 81–104). New York: SUNY Press.

Ruiz-de-Velasco, J. & Fix, M. (2000). *Overlooked and underserved: Immigrant students in U.S secondary schools.* Urban Institute. Retrieved August, 2006, from www.urban.org/immig/overlooked2001.html.

Rumbaut, R. (1994). The crucible within: Ethnic identity, self-esteem, and segmented assimilation among children of immigrants. *International Migration Review, 28*(4), 748–795.

Rumbaut, R.G. (1996). Ties that bind: Immigration and immigrant families in the United States. In A. Booth, A.C. Crouter, & N. Landale (Eds.), *Immigration and the family: Research and policy on US immigration.* Hillsdale, NJ: Lawrence Erlbaum Associates.

Rumbaut, R.G. & Ima, K. (1988). *The adaptation of Southeast Asian refugee youth: A comparative study.* Final Report to the U.S. Department of Health and Human Services, Office of Refugee Resettlement, Washington, DC: U.S. Department of Health and Human Services. San Diego, CA: San Diego State University (ERIC Document Reproduction Service ED 299 372).

Sanchez, P. (2004). At home in two places: Second-generation Mexicanas and their lives as engaged transnationals. Berkeley: University of California, Berkeley, Center for Latino Policy Research.

Sridhar, K. & Sridhar, S.N. (2000). At home with English: Assimilation and adaptation of Asian Indians in the United States. In S.L. McKay & S.C. Wong (Eds.), *New immigrants in the United States: Readings for second language educators* (pp. 369–390). Cambridge, UK: Cambridge University Press.

Suzuki, B. (1994). Higher education issues in the Asian American community. In M. Justiz, R. Wilson, & L. Björk (Eds.), *Minorities in higher education* (pp. 258–285). Phoenix, AZ: Oryx Press.

Tse, L. (1996). Language brokering in linguistic minority communities: The case of Chinese- and Vietnamese-American students. *Bilingual Research Journal, 20*(3–4), 485–498.

Urciuoli, B. (1991). The political topography of Spanish and English: The view from a New York Puerto Rican neighborhood. *American Ethnologist, 18*(2), 295–310.

Valdés, G. (1992). Bilingual minorities and language issues in writing: Toward professionwide responses to a new challenge. *Written Communication, 9*(1), 85–136.

Valdés, G. (1998). The world outside and inside schools: Language and immigrant children. *Educational Researcher, 27*(6), 4–18.

Valdés, G. (2000). Bilingualism and language use among Mexican Americans. In S.L. McKay & S.C. Wong (Eds.), *New immigrants in the United States: Readings for second language educators* (pp. 99–136). Cambridge, UK: Cambridge University Press.

Vandrick, S. (1995). Privileged ESL university students. *TESOL Quarterly, 29*(2), 375–381.

Vernez, G. & Abrahamse, A. (1996). *How immigrants fare in US education.* Santa Monica, CA: RAND Center for Research on Immigration Policy.

Vigil, J.D. (1997). *Personas Mexicanas: Chicano high schoolers in a changing Los Angeles.* Ft. Worth, TX: Harcourt Brace.

Wait, D.L.E., Roessingh, H., & Bosetti, L. (1996). Success and failure: Stories of ESL students' educational and cultural adjustment to high school. *Urban Education, 31*(2), 199–221.

Zentella, A.C. (1997). Latino youth at home, in their communities, and in school: The language link. *Education and Urban Society, 30*(1), 22–30.

Zentella, A. (2000). Puerto Ricans in the United States: Confronting the linguistic repercussions of colonialism. In S.L. McKay & S.C. Wong (Eds.), *New immigrants in the United States: Readings for second language educators* (pp. 137–164). Cambridge: Cambridge University Press.

Zhou, M. (1998). "Parachute kids" in Southern California: The educational experience of Chinese children in trans-national families. *Educational Policy, 12*(6): 682–704.

Zhou, M. & Bankston, C. (1998). *Growing up American: How Vietnamese children adapt to life in the United States.* New York: Russell Sage Foundation.

2 Immigrant Youth and Higher Education

An Overview

Linda Harklau   University of Georgia
Meryl Siegal   Laney College

Amid anxieties about an hourglass economy and the effects of globalization, there is a new sense of urgency in the U.S. regarding access to postsecondary education. The fact is that high school can no longer be the educational finish line for most students, including language minority students. In a postindustrial age, tertiary education (including associate and bachelor's degrees, technical training and certificate programs) is indeed becoming a necessity for many Americans. Unskilled jobs in goods-producing fields such as manufacturing and agriculture are experiencing long-term stagnation and decline (Bureau of Labor Statistics, 2004). Other unskilled jobs in industries such as food service rely on a continuing turnover of young workers and immigrants who are willing to tolerate poor wages and few opportunities for advancement (Education Trust, 2003). Yet a recent report published by the Educational Testing Service (Kirsch, Braun, Yamamoto, & Sun, 2007) observes that given current trends, overall levels of literacy and numeracy in the U.S. population

> will have decreased [by 2030] by about 5% while inequality will have increased about 7% percent. Put crudely, over the next 25 years or so, as better-educated individuals leave the workforce they will be replaced by those who, on average, have lower levels of education and skill.
>
> (p. 4)

Postsecondary education is vital for the individual well-being of youth since college educated people are likely to be wealthier and even healthier than those who do not go to college (Education Trust, 2003; Leonhardt, 2005). Economist Benjamin Friedman has argued that "economic growth is not merely the enabler of higher consumption; it is in many ways the wellspring from which democracy and civil society flow" (2005). Furthermore, on a societal level, the U.S. will need increasing numbers of workers with postsecondary training in order to meet demands in professional and related occupations in computers, healthcare, and education (Bureau of Labor Statistics, 2004; Gordon, 2005, p. 80). One in five children in the U.S. is now the child of immigrants (Capps et al., 2005), meaning that first and second generation immigrant youth will increasingly bear the burden of economic growth in the U.S. (Bureau of Labor Statistics, 2004; Hayes-Bautista, Schink, & Chapa, 1988). Given national and global economic and demographic trends, there is clearly an urgent need to get even first generation language minority students into higher education and keep them there.

In this review, we begin by assessing what we know about the number of language minority students, particularly immigrant youth, participating in higher education. We then contextualize the situation of immigrant students and their college composition experiences within the broader context of trends in U.S. postsecondary education. We suggest that changing demographics call for increased awareness of issues related to "generation 1.5" students at the college level. As this volume illustrates, language— or multilingualism—may be the one commonality that links the otherwise disparate group of college-going language minority students. It is also the issue most seized upon as a defining feature, and often a deficit, in language minority college students. Yet we argue here for a more expansive view of language minority students in higher education. We find that over the past 10 years, immigrant and other language minority student issues have increasingly become confounded with and subsumed by broader, politically charged issues of minority access to higher education. These include barriers to college access, shrinking financial aid, and the demise of affirmative action and arguments over the role of diversity in higher education.

In this chapter we use the term "language minority" (United Nations Office of the High Commissioner for Human Rights, 1998) to mean students whose home or first language is a language other than English and who are bilingual or multilingual. The term also serves as a reminder that those who speak a language other than English may face discrimination similar to other non-dominant racial, ethnic, or cultural groups in American society.

The Numbers

How many language minority students are enrolled in American colleges and universities? The short answer is, we do not know. Unlike K-12 public schools that are compelled to administer home language surveys for entering students, higher education is not mandated to keep track of students' home languages. While the College Board (2002) recommends that colleges collect such information as part of "best practices" in admissions and lists it as a possible mitigating factor in admission practices, in reality colleges vary considerably in whether they collect such information at all and if so, in the level of detail. The major federal college enrollment database, the Integrated Post-secondary Data System (IPEDS) (National Center for Education Statistics, n.d.-c) does not require that colleges collect data on students' home languages—they are only required to collect enrollment and graduation rates in the broad categories of Black non-Hispanic, White non-Hispanic, Hispanic, and Asian/Pacific Islander, and race unknown. Broadly based categories such as these confound African American students from Atlanta with Somali refugees, Spaniards with children of Mestizo migrant workers, and the children of Taiwanese entrepreneurs with Hmong refugees.

Moreover, students' self-reports of race and ethnicity on college applications and SAT questionnaires are becoming less and less useful. For reasons that are unclear, the number of people who decline to report race and ethnicity has doubled in the past 15 years (Gilroy, 2005), skewing attempts to assess diversity in college admissions and retention. Another—although also inexact—source of information consists of federally funded nationally representative longitudinal surveys such as the Educational Longitudinal Survey (National Center for Education Statistics, n.d.-b) and the Beginning Postsecondary Students Survey (National Center for Education Statistics, n.d.-a). Unfortunately such surveys may be based on sample sizes that are too small to disaggregate immigrant data (Bailey & Weininger, 2002). Regional or systemwide data on language minority college enrollment, especially from large systems such as the University of California (Regents of the University of California, n.d.) and the City University of New York (CUNY) (Bailey & Weininger, 2002) often include fuller samples and thus can be a profitable source of information. So too can cross-institutional data such as the southern California consortium of public 2- and 4-year colleges and universities tapped by Patthey-Chavez and colleagues (Patthey-Chavez, Thomas-Spiegel & Dillon, 1998; Patthey-Chavez, Thomas-Spiegel & Dillion, this volume).

In all, while we do not know exactly how many linguistic minorities are currently enrolled in higher education, when triangulating from such sources it is clear that language minority youth form an increasing percentage of the students in the secondary school "pipeline" to college. By 2014, the high school graduating class is expected to be almost 20% Hispanic and almost 7% Asian American (Western Interstate Commission for Higher Education, 2004). Many of these youth are immigrants or children of immigrants. At the K-12 level, immigrant youth are most concentrated in secondary schools, where about one-third of the children of immigrants are immigrants themselves (Capps et al., 2005). That means that language minority youth in secondary schools may have been educated abroad, may have experienced disruptions in schooling, and are likely to be learning language and a new academic system at the same time they are preparing for college. The number of children of immigrants in secondary schools has been increasing faster than that in elementary schools (72 versus 39%) (Capps et al., 2005), suggesting that the number of language minority youth coming to college may be accelerating.

About one-half of immigrant parents and immigrant youth were born in Latin America and the Caribbean, with over a third born in Mexico (Capps et al., 2005). Although the vast majority of "Limited English Proficient" newcomers in secondary school classrooms fall into the "Hispanic," and to a lesser extent, "Asian American" ethnic categories, no country besides Mexico contributes more than 4% of foreign-born youth, suggesting that the population of foreign-born children is very diverse (Capps et al., 2005).

Another source is broad demographics of college-going minority youth. College enrollment nationally is growing. Enrollment at public institutions jumped by 1.2 million students between 1995 and 2001 (Harvey & Anderson, 2003/2004, p. 9), and is expected to continue to grow more slowly through 2009 (College Board, 2005; Western Interstate Commission for Higher Education, 2004). These enrollment jumps will not be spread evenly across regions, however. Established immigrant settlement areas such as California, Florida, and New York will bear a significant proportion. In the Peralta Community College urban district of northern California, for example, 84% of students in fall 2006 reported that English was *not* the primary language they spoke at home. Likewise, cross-institutional data in southern California (Patthey-Chavez et al., 1998) show that 18% of enrollees in ESL writing and composition courses could be considered "generation 1.5" students. At the state level in 2005 about 40% of students admitted to the University of California systemwide reported that they spoke languages other than English at home (Regents of the University of

California, n.d.). However, recent changes in patterns of immigrant settlement in the U.S. have resulted in major influxes of language minority students in areas of the Midwest and Southeast that have not traditionally hosted immigrant populations (College Board, 2005; Western Interstate Commission for Higher Education, 2004). At the college level, the growth in Hispanic enrollment outpaced other demographic groups, growing by 75% in the decade from 1991–2001 (Harvey & Anderson, 2003/2004, p. x). In the same decade, Asian American enrollment in college expanded by 53% (Harvey & Anderson, 2003/2004, p. x).

Yet in spite of continuing demographic growth in overall numbers of language minority youth in secondary schools and colleges, the statistics on language minority student enrollment and retention in higher education are a mixed picture at best. Some analysts such as Vernez and Abrahamse (1996) have reported excellent outcomes for immigrants in higher education. They found that immigrants were overall *more* likely than American-born peer cohorts to attend college and, once there, to persist and receive a degree. Similar results are reported by Patthey-Chavez et al. (this volume) and Bailey and Weininger (2002). On the other hand, Gray, Rolph, and Melamid (1996) reported that first generation Latino students were *less* likely than those in the second or third generation to go to college. While Hispanic college enrollment has increased numerically, their enrollment as a proportion of the population showed little improvement from 1991 to 2001 (Harvey & Anderson, 2003/2004), and continues to lag substantially behind the proportion of White students attending college.

Barriers to College Access and Retention

While it is clear that language minority students are quickly becoming a substantial part of the college-going population in the U.S., there are nevertheless troubling indications of continuing barriers to college-going for many under-represented groups, and language minority students in particular, as well as problems with retention once they are there. For one thing, areas that attract new immigrants are frequently the same ones experiencing overall demographic growth. As a result, colleges may be overenrolled and have increased competition for limited college spaces (College Board, 2005). At institutions focusing on baccalaureate and graduate education, language minority students with less familiarity with English might also be penalized by an admissions process that privileges SAT scores. As Freedle (2003) observes, the SAT and other standardized tests used in college admissions and placement such as Advanced Placement exams have persistently shown bias against non-White and non-middle-class groups, and new versions of the SAT and ACT need to be evaluated for such bias. Since the 1980s scholars have noted at least two potential problems with such tests that might have a particularly adverse effect on newcomers who are less conversant with English (Durán, 1986; Pennock-Román, 1986). First, test items may be less intelligible to English learners, and second, timed test formats may make it difficult for some examinees who are reading more slowly in a non-native language to get through all the items. Furthermore, many would argue that such standardized tests contain cultural content and assumptions that put minority students, particularly newcomers, at a disadvantage (Pennock-Román, 1986). In a survey of college admissions practices, the

College Board (Rigol, 2003) found that a growing number of colleges give special consideration to applicants for whom English is not a first language. However, students placed in this admission pool are evaluated for a limited number of places against students with a variety of special admissions factors including first generation college-going, applicant's geographic location, socio-economic status, and academic and community service endeavors outside the classroom.

The "open admissions" policies of many community colleges may make them more attractive starting points for language minority students. For example, the majority of Hispanic students are enrolled in associate institutions (Fry, 2004). Many colleges allow students to complete lower division general education requirements for admission and then transfer to a baccalaureate institution. In fact, some public university systems may have an automatic transfer policy for students who have completed required coursework with a certain grade point average (e.g., University of California, Davis, 2008). Yet significant questions have been raised about whether first enrollment in associate colleges might lead to poorer retention and transfer in the long run (Fry, 2004). Overall, Hispanic students persist at half the rate of White students (Fry, 2004) and made no gains in persistence between 1989 and 1995 while Whites gained (Harvey & Anderson, 2003/2004). Moreover, the number of students who left associate colleges without a degree rose to almost 60% in the 1990s (Harvey & Anderson, 2003/2004). On the face of it, Asian American and Pacific Islander students overall had the highest rates of earning bachelor's degrees and lowest percentage of students dropping out (Harvey & Anderson, 2003/2004). However, scholars caution that this masks considerable ethnic and social class variability within the very broad pan-ethnic designation (Lee, 2006; Louie, 2001). In all, we are in need of more research on the college-going patterns and goals of language minority students and students from other underrepresented groups, particularly at associate colleges.

Shrinking Financial Aid

College affordability has been an escalating issue over the past two decades. Countries contributing the greatest numbers of contemporary immigrants to the U.S. are all substantially poorer than the United States (Capps et al., 2005), suggesting that immigrants are likely to come from low income backgrounds. Over the past 10 years college costs have been rising but median household income has not, suggesting that students are finding college less and less affordable (College Board, 2005). More financial aid is being provided at the state level (College Board, 2005) but both state and federal financial aid has been moving away from need-based awards (Atwell, Melendez, & Wilson, 2004; College Board, 2005).

In his study of Asian Americans, Kiang (1992) notes that immigrants were more likely than international students to be working class, and often spent considerable time working off campus. Likewise, Fry (2004) notes that Hispanic students are more likely than Anglo students to have financial responsibilities to the family that can impede college participation and retention. There is long-standing evidence that ethnicity and income level have distinct effects on family willingness to use student loans to finance education (see, e.g., Orfield, 1992). Perhaps for this reason, financial aid has been found to be a key issue in retention of Hispanic students in community colleges

(Padron, 1994). In all, then, the barriers regarding college affordability present an increasing challenge.

Student Body Diversity and Language Minority Students

There has been remarkably little policy discussion regarding language minority students in higher education. In 1996 Gray et al. (1996) surveyed faculty and administrators and found little awareness about immigrant educational issues. In fact, many respondents confused American language minority youth with international students. In the intervening years, even in light of dramatic demographic changes, little new attention has been given to these issues. Perhaps one reason for the lack of attention is that language minority student issues have been overshadowed by legal and legislative battles over universities' use of race or ethnicity as a factor in admissions (U.S. Department of Education, Office of Civil Rights, 2003). A great deal of recent research and policy analysis aims to show the benefits of ethnic and racial diversity on U.S. college campuses (see, e.g., Alger et al., 2000; Gurin, Dey, Hurtado, & Gurin, 2002).

With affirmative action under siege, colleges seem to be reluctant to recognize the inadequacies of the traditional demographic descriptors of Hispanic, Asian, and Pacific Islander, etc. In recent years, however, there has been increasing recognition that colleges have paid too little attention to *intra*group diversity within broad ethnic categories (Louie, 2001; Smith & Wolf-Wendell, 2005). Rong & Brown (2001) for example, note that immigrants and their children will constitute 12% of the Black population in the U.S. by 2010, yet little research has looked specifically at the educational attainments of African and Afro-Caribbean *immigrant* youth. As a result, while universities often talk about "diversity," the way they talk about it paradoxically masks the diversity to be found in the student population. Language minority students are for the most part overlooked. There is little explicit discussion of their college experience, and research and statistics are inadequate to tell us how they are dealt with when they arrive or their ultimate fate in college.

Alternatively, language minority students are defined by institutions of higher education purely in terms of their multilingual backgrounds, and even more specifically in terms of possible perceived deficits in English. Their multilingualism is often labeled as "remedial" or "developmental." It is presumed that once a language minority student has completed a series of coursework, the student will be able to perform just like native speakers. Such a view does not consider research that indicates that up to a decade is needed in order to develop language skills. Nor does this view consider the role that learner identity and societal representation of non-native speaking immigrant students play in language learning. In the absence of a discussion concerning language learning and immigrant students, universities seem to rely on local, ad hoc policies for language minority students that are inconsistent across institutions and systems (see, e.g., Bunch & Panayotova, 2006).

Conclusions and Recommendations

Considering the overwhelming demographic evidence that the population of first generation immigrant language minority students is rapidly increasing in postsecondary education, it is quite surprising how little research attention has been devoted to the subject. It seems that language minority student issues have been folded into much broader and highly charged policy debates about minority enrollment and retention in higher education.

One symptom and consequence of this is the increasing prevalence of research that is funded or suggested by sources outside of the academy. Much of the work on college pathways has shifted over the past 10 years out of traditional peer-reviewed scholarly sources and into reports issued by foundations and professional organizations. While such work often fills important gaps in existing knowledge, it also completely bypasses scholarly peer review and is thus vulnerable to political agendas that could influence both the research questions and interpretations of the data.

Language minority students are also an integral part of post-Michigan-decision era efforts to find new, innovative ways to diversify students, faculty, and campus environments (Williams, Berger, & McClendon, 2005). There is also growing recognition that there are significant ethnic and racial disparities in college retention and achievement (Bauman, Bustillos, Bensimon, Brown, & Bartee, 2005; Gándara, 1999). Scattered research reports suggest that language minority students may feel isolated or alienated on college campuses (Ngo, 2002; Osajima, 1993; Swaminathan & Alfred, 2001/2002). We need considerably more research on campus climate for these students and its effects on achievement and retention.

Another issue that has come to the fore in recent years is the debate on undocumented immigrant access to college. This issue garners attention that is disproportionate to its actual impact on college campuses. For example, according to the Urban Institute (Capps & Fix, 2005), undocumented students form less than 3% of America's secondary school students. If their college enrollment mirrors that of residents, fewer than 2% of immigrants seeking entry into college are undocumented. Yet at this writing, if one does an online search for "immigrants" and "higher education," over half the web-based sources in the top 20 are about undocumented immigrants. Likewise, the defeat of immigration legislation in 2007 and accompanying opposition to the Development Relief and Education for Alien Minorities (DREAM) Act suggest that this issue strikes a cultural nerve that is totally disproportionate to its material impact on college enrollments.

Another trend in U.S. higher education is the surge of interest in globalization and internationalization. In a recent Institute of International Education report, it was noted that "in just the last decade [1985–2005], study abroad increased 144 percent up from 84,403 in 1994/1995 [to 205,983]" (IIE, 2007). Concurrently, there seems to be an increasing focus on college campuses to get students to think about issues in international rather than regional or national terms as well. While one might think this would create increased interest in and support for multilingual students on campus, it oddly enough seems to be focused almost completely outward, toward exporting students to other places. We would hope that college campuses could exploit this interest and create connections with the already existing ethnic and linguistic diversity on college campuses.

Finally, we have an increasing amount of research and policy initiatives in recent years to enhance the K-12 college pipeline for students from under-represented groups (ESL Intersegmental Project, 2000; Kazis, Vargas, & Hoffman, 2004; Pathways to

College Network, 2001; Venezia, Kirst, & Antonio, 2003). Yet we often see an implicit tone of rebuke in this work suggesting that high schools and associate colleges are not doing an adequate job of preparing students. This focus leaves baccalaureate and graduate institutions "off the hook" for communicating across institutional boundaries or changing the way that *they* work with feeder institutions, or for making substantial changes in the way that they educate first- and second-year baccalaureate students from under-represented groups (Gritsch de Cordova & Herzon, 2007). However, models are currently emerging that involve a more fundamental level of communication and integration of high schools, community colleges, and four year institutions to close the gap in language minority student college retention and degree completion (see, e.g., Kazis et al., 2004) and more work is needed in this area.

References

Alger, J.R., Chapa, J., Gudeman, R.H., Marin, P., Maruyama, G., Milem, J.F., et al. (2000). *Does diversity make a difference? Three research studies on diversity in college classrooms.* Washington, DC: American Council on Education and American Association of University Professors.

Atwell, R.H., Melendez, S., & Wilson, R. (2004, July). *Reflections on 20 years of minorities in higher education and the ACE annual status report.* Washington, DC: American Council on Education.

Bailey, T. & Weininger, E.B. (2002). Performance, graduation, and transfer of immigrants and natives in City University of New York community colleges. *Educational Evaluation and Policy Analysis, 24*(4), 359–377.

Bauman, G.L., Bustillos, L.T., Bensimon, E.M., Brown, M.C., & Bartee, R.D. (2005). *Achieving equitable educational outcomes with all students: The institution's roles and responsibilities.* Washington, DC: American Association of Colleges and Universities.

Bunch, G.C. & Panayotova, D. (2006). From high school to community college: Language testing, placement policies, and access to higher education. Paper presented at the annual meeting of the University of California Linguistic Minority Research Institute, Irvine, CA.

Bureau of Labor Statistics. (2004). *Tomorrow's jobs. Occupational Outlook Handbook, 2004–5 Edition* (Bulletin No. 2540). Washington, DC: U.S. Department of Labor.

Capps, R. & Fix, M.E. (2005). *Undocumented immigrants: Myth and reality.* Washington, DC: The Urban Institute. Retrieved February 6, 2008, from www.urban.org/publications/900898.html.

Capps, R., Fix, M., Murray, J., Ost, J., Passel, J.S., & Herwantoro, S. (2005). *The new demography of America's schools: Immigration and the No Child Left Behind Act.* Washington, DC: The Urban Institute.

College Board. (2002). *Best practices in admission decisions: A report on the third College Board conference on admissions models.* New York: College Board.

College Board. (2005). *The impact of demographic changes on higher education. Summary of conference discussions.* Washington, DC: College Board.

Durán, R.P. (1986). Prediction of Hispanics' college achievement. In M.A. Olivas (Ed.), *Latino college students* (pp. 221–245). New York: Teachers College Press.

Education Trust. (2003, Winter). A new core curriculum for all: Aiming high for other people's children. *Thinking K-16, 7*(1), 1–29.

ESL Intersegmental Project. (2000). *California pathways: The second language student in public high schools, colleges, and universities. Updated with revised writing proficiency descriptors, writing samples, and user's guide.* Sacramento, CA: California Teachers of English to Speakers of Other Languages (CATESOL) and California Community Colleges Chancellor's Office.

Freedle, R.O. (2003). Correcting the SAT's ethnic and social-class bias: A method for reestimating SAT scores. *Harvard Educational Review, 73*(1), 1–44.

Friedman, B. (2005). Meltdown. A Case Study. *Atlantic Monthly.* July/August. Retrieved February 6, 2008, from www.theatlantic.com/doc/200507/friedman.

Fry, R. (2004). *Latino youth finishing college: The role of selective pathways.* Washington, DC: Pew Hispanic Center.

Gándara, P. with Maxwell-Jolly, J. (1999). *Priming the pump: Strategies for increasing the achievement of underrepresented minority undergraduates.* New York: College Board.

Gilroy, M. (2005). American Council on Education issues annual status report on minorities. *Hispanic Outlook in Higher Education, 15*(19), 9–11.

Gordon, E. (2005). *The 2010 meltdown. Solving the impending jobs crisis.* Westport, CT: Praeger.

Gray, M.J., Rolph, E., & Melamid, E. (1996). *Immigration and higher education: Institutional responses to changing demographics.* Santa Monica, CA: RAND.

Gritsch de Cordova, H. & Herzon, C. (2007). *From diversity to educational equity: A discussion of academic integration and issues facing underprepared UCSC students.* Research and Occasional Paper series: Center for Higher Education, University of California, Berkeley. Retrieved February 6, 2008, from http://cshe.berkeley.edu.

Gurin, P., Dey, E.L., Hurtado, S., & Gurin, G. (2002). Diversity and higher education: Theory and impact on educational outcome. *Harvard Educational Review, 72*(3), 330–336.

Harvey, W.B. & Anderson, E.L. (2003/2004). *Minorities in higher education: Twenty-first annual status report.* Washington, DC: American Council on Education.

Hayes-Bautista, D.E., Schink, W.O., & Chapa, J. (1988). *The burden of support: Young Latinos in an aging society.* Stanford, CA.: Stanford University Press.

Institute of International Education. (2007). *Current trends in U.S. study abroad and the impact of strategic diversity initiatives.* IIE Study Abroad White Paper series. Retrieved February 6, 2008, from www.iienetwork.org/file_depot/0–10000000/0–10000/1710/folder/62450/IIE+Study+Abroad+White+Paper+I.pdf.

Kazis, R., Vargas, J., & Hoffman, N. (2004). *Double the numbers: Increasing postsecondary credentials for underrepresented youth.* Cambridge, MA: Harvard Education Press.

Kiang, P.N. (1992). Issues of curriculum and community for first-generation Asian Americans in college. In H.B. London & L.S. Zwerling (Eds.), *First-generation students confronting the cultural issues* (pp. 97–112). New Directions for Community College, No. 80. San Francisco, CA: Jossey-Bass.

Kirsch, I., Braun, H., Yamamoto, K., & Sun, A. (2007). *Executive summary. America's perfect storm. Three forces changing our nation's future.* Princeton, NJ: Educational Testing Service. Retrieved February 6, 2008, from ets.org/stormreport.

Lee, S.J. (2006). Additional complexities: Social class, ethnicity, generation, and gender in Asian American student experiences. *Race Ethnicity and Education, 9*(1), 17–28.

Leonhardt, D. (2005, May 14). A closer look at income mobility. *New York Times.* Retrieved February 6, 2008, from www.nytimes.com/2005/05/14/national/class/15MOBILITY-WEB.html.

Louie, V. (2001). Parents' aspirations and investment: The role of social class in the educational experiences of 1.5 and second generation Chinese Americans. *Harvard Educational Review, 71*(3), 438–474.

National Center for Education Statistics. (n.d.-a). *Beginning postsecondary survey.* Retrieved December 11, 2007, from http://nces.ed.gov/surveys/bps/.

National Center for Education Statistics. (n.d.-b). *Educational Longitudinal survey.* Retrieved December 11, 2007, from http://nces.ed.gov/surveys/els2002/.

National Center for Education Statistics. (n.d.-c). *Integrated postsecondary education data system.* Retrieved April 14, 2006, from http://nces.ed.gov/ipeds/.

Ngo, B. (2002). Contesting "culture": The perspectives of Hmong American female students on early marriage. *Anthropology and Education Quarterly, 33*(2), 163–188.

Orfield, G. (1992). Money, equity, and college access. *Harvard Educational Review, 62*(3), 337–372.

Osajima, K. (1993). The hidden injuries of race. In L.A. Revilla, G.M. Nomura, S. Wong, & S. Hune (Eds.), *Bearing dreams, shaping visions: Asian Pacific American perspectives* (pp. 81–92). Pullman: Washington State University Press.

Padron, E.J. (1994). Hispanics and community colleges. In G.A. Baker (Ed.), *A handbook on the community college in America: Its history, mission, and management* (pp. 82–93). Westport, CT: Greenwood Press.

Pathways to College Network. (2001). *A shared agenda: A leadership challenge to improve college access and success.* Boston, MA: Pathways to College Network.

Patthey-Chavez, G.G., Thomas-Spiegel, J., & Dillon, P. (1998). Tracking outcomes for community college students with different writing instruction histories. Paper presented at the California Association for Institutional Research, San Diego, CA.

Pennock-Román, M. (1986). Fairness in the use of tests for selective admissions of Hispanics. In M.A. Olivas (Ed.), *Latino college students* (pp. 246–277). New York: Teachers College Press.

Regents of the University of California. (n.d.). *Statfinder.* Retrieved November 30, 2007, from http://statfinder.ucop.edu/statfinder/default.aspx.

Rigol, G.W. (2003). *Admissions decision-making models: How U.S. institutions of higher education select undergraduate students.* New York: College Board.

Rong, X.L. & Brown, F. (2001). The effects of immigrant generation and ethnicity on educational attainment among young African and Caribbean Blacks in the United States. *Harvard Educational Review, 71*(3), pp. 536–565.

Smith, D.G. & Wolf-Wendell, L.E. (2005). *The challenge of diversity: Involvement or alienation in the academy? ASHE Higher Education Report* (New edition—originally released in 1989 Vol. 31:1). Hoboken, NJ: Wiley.

Swaminathan, R. & Alfred, M.V. (2001/2002). Strangers in the mirror: Immigrant students in the higher education classroom. *Adult Learning, 12/13*(4/1), 29–32.

United Nations Office of the High Commissioner for Human Rights. (1998). *Fact Sheet No. 18 (Rev. 1), Minority Rights.* Retrieved February 6, 2008, from www.unhchr.ch/html/menu6/2/fs18.htm.

U.S. Department of Education, Office of Civil Rights. (2003, March). *Race-neutral alternatives in postsecondary education: Innovative approaches to diversity.* Washington, DC: U.S. Department of Education.

University of California, Davis. (2008). Undergraduate admissions. Retrieved February 6, 2008, from http://admissions. ucdavis.edu/.transfers.

Venezia, A., Kirst, M.W., & Antonio, A.L. (2003). *Betraying the college dream: How disconnected K-12 and postsecondary education systems undermine student aspirations.* Stanford, CA: Stanford Institute for Higher Education Research.

Vernez, G., Abrahamse, A., with Quigley, D. (1996). *How immigrants fare in U.S. education* (ERIC document reproduction service no. ED 399 320). Santa Monica, CA: RAND Center for Research on Immigration Policy.

Western Interstate Commission for Higher Education. (2004). *Knocking at the college door. 2003.* Boulder, CO: Western Interstate Commission for Higher Education.

Williams, D.A., Berger, J.B., & McClendon, S.A. (2005). *Toward a model of inclusive excellence and change in postsecondary institutions.* Washington, DC: Association of American Colleges and Universities.

3 The Education of the 1.5 Generation from an International Migration Framework
Demographics, Diversity, and Difference

Vivian Louie Harvard University

Since the Immigration Act of 1965 reopened large-scale immigration to the United States, immigrant children have become a substantial presence in the nation's schools. Today, the children of immigrants, both U.S.- and foreign-born, comprise a fifth of the nation's population under the age of 18, and a quarter of these children come from low income families. By the year 2015, the children of immigrants will likely comprise 30% of the nation's K-12 population (Fix & Passel, 2003). This new immigration intersects with key educational and labor market transformations in the United States. Many children of immigrants, both foreign- and U.S.-born, are attending urban public K-12 schools undergoing reforms aimed at reducing the achievement gap while struggling with a lack of resources. Along with their native peers, the children of immigrants[1] confront a postsecondary system of education that is more accessible than it ever has been and yet, increasingly stratified. The educational stakes will prove substantial, as the bachelor's degree has increasingly become the key to a middle-class lifestyle, not only in the United States but progressively on the global stage as well (Contreras, 2002; Furstenberg, Rumbaut, & Settersten, 2005; Long, 2007; Louie, 2005, 2007; Wilson, 1980, 1987).

In this chapter, I address the 1.5 generation from an interdisciplinary international migration framework, one that elaborates on the economic, and socio-cultural contexts around immigration broadly speaking, and those specifically pertaining to the 1.5 generation. In the first half of the chapter, I will outline the demographics of the immigrant population, following with a discussion of settlement patterns, the needs of immigrant children in our K-12 schools and the challenges therein, and their transition to college. In the second half, I will pay particular attention to the 1.5 generation along these lines, outlining the utility of this demographic label, and ways in which the experiences of 1.5 generation individuals intersect with and are distinct from their second generation counterparts or the U.S.-born children of immigrants.

There are high stakes surrounding the outcomes among the children of immigrants. The implications for social mobility affect not only individuals but ethnic groups as well. By virtue of their sheer numbers, the outcomes among the children of immigrants will determine the trajectories of the ethnic groups to which they belong (Portes & Rumbaut, 2001). Those outcomes can be higher education and upward social mobility, or they can be low levels of education and its implications (Gans, 1992). In the contemporary United States, low levels of education have become associated with a "spiral of cumulating disadvantage and downward mobility" (Rumbaut, 2005, p. 1083).

There are national implications as well. Without a highly skilled, technologically sophisticated, and educated workforce, the United States faces losing its competitive edge in the global arena at a time when knowledge has become a determining factor in the wealth of nations. In the last few decades, the immigration of the highly skilled and highly educated has helped the United States to maintain its competitive advantage (Grissmer, 2005). As the recently failed immigration bill demonstrated, the idea that educational credentials and skills should be criteria for entry continues to receive strong support from some economists and business leaders (Alba, 2007). Beyond the demise of the immigration bill, however, other trends signal that the pipeline of highly skilled labor from abroad has become blocked. On the receiving end, in the wake of the events of 9/11, the United States has paid greater scrutiny to the entry of international students. More international students are finding higher restrictions associated with entry, and if entrance is gained, the climate in the United States to be less hospitable (Stewart, 2005). On the sending end, an increasing number of international students are deciding to return to their countries of origin rather than permanently settling here. If such trends continue, the economic well-being of the United States will become more strongly tied to the development of its own domestic immigrant and non-immigrant talent than it has been in the recent past (Grissmer, 2005). As Alba (2007) points out, the stakes are high. For example, the United States' decision to invest in domestic talent by addressing inequities in its institutional infrastructures such as education could conceivably reduce the achievement gap. Seen from this perspective, the decision by the United States to increase the importation of highly skilled labor would represent a lost opportunity to make the kinds of systemic changes that would benefit both immigrants and non-immigrants and reduce racial and ethnic inequalities. It is within these high-stake contexts that immigration and education must be understood.

The New Immigration Post-1960s: Demographics, Settlement, and Schooling

Immigration has long been a part of the history of the United States. The previous waves of immigration that helped fuel the industrialization of the United States during 1840–1924 came disproportionately from South, Central, and Eastern Europe and as unskilled or semi-skilled labor (Pedraza, 1995). Fears that the immigrants, who settled in urban ethnic neighborhoods with their own forms of associational life, would refuse to shed their languages, religions (Catholicism and Judaism), and cultural mores gave rise to nativist sentiments (Alba & Nee, 2003; Lazerson, 1977; McGreevy, 1996; Waters, 1990). The rise of the common school movement, which led to the formation of public schools as we know them today, was partly grounded in the mission to Americanize the immigrant, and more importantly, the immigrant's children (Olsen, 1990; Ravitch, 2000; Weisz, 1976).

Nonetheless, the nativist movement continued to gain ground, culminating in the passage of restrictive laws called the Johnson Act (1921, 1924), also known as the Immigration Act of 1924.[2] Numerical limits were imposed on the total number of immigrants admitted each year, and quotas were established for each sending nation that favored Northwestern European sources of immigration. Overall, as Figure 3.1

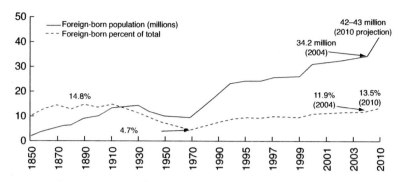

Figure 3.1 United States foreign-born population, 1850–2010 (source: Capps et al., 2005).

shows, there was a sudden and long-lasting decline in immigration. European migratory flows, which had reached a high of more than one million immigrants in 1907, had fallen to about 65,000 by 1937. Overall, immigration levels remained low until 1970 (Alba & Nee, 2003). It was during the decades between 1924 and 1970 that the descendants of these early immigrants eventually assimilated into the American mainstream (Alba & Nee, 2003).

The Immigration Act of 1965 represented a dramatic shift in immigration policy, and as Figure 3.1 shows, ushered in a new period of large-scale immigration that has transformed our nation's demographics. Under the new system, the Eastern hemisphere was assigned 120,000 visas per year, with up to 20,000 entries per country per year. No limits were set on the entry of spouses, children, and parents of U.S. citizens, and preference was given to family reunification and professional skills (Foner, 1987). By the year 2000, more than 60 million people, representing 22% of the total population in the United States, were either born in another country or the child of foreign-born parents.

Diversity in the Post-1960s Immigrant Population

The post-1960s immigration has differed from earlier waves on several important demographic indicators, and the new immigrants have been incorporated into economic and socio-cultural contexts much changed from those encountered by their predecessors (Alba & Nee, 2003; Pedraza, 1995). While there are diverse sending sources, more than three-quarters of the new immigrants are from Latin America, the Caribbean, and Asia; in fact, more than a quarter of the new immigrants are from Mexico (Rumbaut, 2004).[3]

The new immigration is bifurcated with some arriving as unskilled or semi-skilled labor with relatively little formal schooling, and other immigrants arriving with high levels of education, well above the American norm, and professional skillsets. The new immigrants meanwhile have entered a nation transformed by the fruits of the Civil Rights movement, with equality of opportunity now mandated by the state. This does not mean that nativism or negative attitudes have abated. There continue to be fears that immigration will alter our language (witness the English-only movement) and debates about whether immigrants serve as a benefit to or drain on the nation's economy (Contreras, 2002). In the following, I outline particular demographic indicators for new immigrants and the contexts they are encountering, in particular, settlement patterns, the K-12 schools attended by immigrant children, and the transition to college.

As distinct as they are from their predecessors, today's new immigrants are highly differentiated from one another, most immediately along the lines of national origins, but also vis-à-vis socio-economic status and documentation status; such differences are evident both within and between groups. While contemporary immigration is typically framed as a Latino-Asian phenomenon, the terms, *Latino* and *Asian*, refer to socially constructed categories that aggregate distinct groups, and in the process, obscure variation (Cooper, Coll, Thorne, & Orellana, 2005). As Rumbaut (2004) demonstrates, this becomes clear if we sort immigrants by socio-economic status (SES). As noted earlier, contemporary immigration is bifurcated socio-economically, bringing both unskilled and highly skilled labor. Rumbaut compares immigrants aged 25–34 to their U.S. counterparts on measures of educational and occupational attainment, and finds that immigrants can be found in all SES groups and that national origins tend to map onto socio-economic status. Thus immigrants from "low SES groups" tend to be from the sending nations of the Dominican Republic, El Salvador, Guatemala, Honduras, Haiti, Laos, and Cambodia. At the other end of the immigrant spectrum are "high SES groups" from many Asian, African, European, and South American nations along with Canada and Australia. In the mid-range were immigrants from a wide range of sending regions, including "Cuba, Costa Rica, Nicaragua, Panama, Colombia, Ecuador, Peru, Jamaica, Vietnam, Afghanistan and Iraq" (Rumbaut, 2004, p. 1188).

The undocumented immigrant population warrants attention. Although this represents a difficult population to measure, it is estimated that 11.1 million undocumented immigrants[4] comprised "30% of the foreign-born population in 2005," alongside legal permanent residents (28%) and naturalized U.S. citizens (31%) (Passel, 2006). Undocumented migrants have typically either arrived in the United States without the necessary documentation (via border crossings, for example), or continue to stay past the expiration of their visas. Mexico, El Salvador, and Guatemala are "the sending countries with the highest proportion of undocumented immigrants in the United States," a distinction that becomes further complicated by age of arrival, as I will discuss in the second half of this chapter (Rumbaut, 2004, p. 1181). Individuals from Mexico alone make up 56% of undocumented immigrants. Other regions of the world, however, are represented among the ranks of the undocumented, including Asians (13%), Europeans and Canadians (6%), and Africa and elsewhere (3%). In terms of labor force participation, undocumented immigrants are particularly clustered in the service industry, about 31%, with fewer numbers in professional occupations. It is a predominately recently arrived population, as two-thirds have been here less than 10 years. The complexity of this population is highlighted by the fact that individuals of multiple statuses can exist in one family, forming "mixed status" families; for example, it is estimated that 64% of the children in families without documentation are themselves U.S.-born and thus American citizens (Passel, 2006).

Finally, it is important to point out that patterns of contemporary immigration both depart from and map onto previous waves of immigration. For example, while the influx of Vietnamese and Laotians, post-1965, represents entirely new streams of immigration to the United States, Mexico has had a much longer, ongoing history of substantial labor migration; meanwhile, the new immigration has replenished the Chinese American population, which declined precipitously between 1882 and 1943, due to the Chinese Exclusion Act, and its restrictions on the entry of Chinese laborers.

Geographically speaking, new immigrants have tended to settle in what scholars describe as gateway cities (Miami, Los Angeles, New York) in destination states such as New York, California, Texas, Illinois, New Jersey, and Florida (Portes & Rumbaut, 2001). In these cases, newly arrived immigrants of low socio-economic status have often settled in urban, native minority neighborhoods already struggling with the departure of the middle class, industrial jobs, and investment on the part of the state; the results have been dauntingly high rates of poverty, unemployment, and crime as features of the neighborhood landscape (Portes, Fernandez-Kelly, & Haller, 2005; Wilson, 1987).

During the 1990s, a new trend emerged with immigrants moving to parts of the country that have had few contemporary experiences incorporating newcomers, such as the Rocky Mountains, and Midwestern and Southeastern states; the Limited English Proficient (LEP)[5] K-12 student population increased more than fourfold in North Carolina and Alabama in this time period, and more than doubled in Kentucky (Olsen, 2000; Rong & Preissle, 1997). More recently, researchers have turned their attention to how institutions and individuals that do not have a contemporary history of receiving immigrants on a significant scale have negotiated the process, and further, how the process might be improved (Gozdziak & Martin, 2005; Millard & Chapa, 2004; Zuniga & Hernandez-Leon, 2005). With a focus on Latinos, case studies in the states of Georgia, North Carolina, Maine, Colorado, Illinois, and Indiana provide insights into the challenges of formulating and implementing K-12 educational policies in such receiving contexts (Wortham, Murillo, & Hamann, 2002). One example is the binational partnership between two school districts in Georgia and a private university in Mexico, which worked to promote understandings of the educational system the Latino children were coming from and the skillsets and needs with which they were arriving as a way of better serving them (Zuniga, Hernandez-Leon, Shadduck-Hernandez, & Villarreal, 2002). Overall, the incorporation of newcomers into PK-12 schools in these regions remains a story to be written, given that many do not have the immediate infrastructure to serve immigrant children such as teachers well versed in the cultures the children are coming from, or the training to work with English language learners (Gibson, 2002). In the rest of this chapter, I will draw mainly on the schooling experiences of immigrant children in the central cities of destination states, given its focus in much of the existing literature.

Schooling Contexts Among the Children of Immigrants

A key feature of the urban neighborhoods that are home to many immigrant children is under-resourced and struggling public K-12 schools (Contreras, 2002; Portes et al., 2005; Rong & Brown, 2002). Immigrant children have been incorporated into public schools that were already grappling with budget shortfalls, and lagging academic standards prior to their arrival. At the same time, immigrant children from working-class backgrounds often do not have the sponsorship of their parents to navigate schooling processes. While having high expectations for their children's educational trajectories in the United States (Kao & Tienda, 1995), immigrant parents from working-class backgrounds typically do not have an adequate knowledge base about academic readiness and access (Lew, 2005; Louie, 2001, 2004). This can be traced to several reasons, including the parents' lack of fluency or facility in the English language, relatively low levels of formal schooling, lack of time due to labor intensive jobs, and differing cultural views about the role of schools and the role of parents; in short, what schools might perceive as a lack of interest on the part of immigrant parents might actually be a lack of knowledge and time, and also, a conception of schooling where the teacher knows best rather than the mainstream model of parental advocacy (Kao, 2004; C. Suárez-Orozco, 2001; Suárez-Orozco & Suárez-Orozco, 2001). One way to address this issue would be to facilitate greater school–family dialogues and partnerships, involving immigrant community-based organizations as an important lever in the relationship (Contreras, 2002; Goodwin, 2002).

Central to any discussion of serving the needs of immigrant students is the teaching force and teacher training; credential programs rarely require trainees to engage in any depth with the issues that immigrant students may face in adjusting to school life in America (Gibson, 2002; C. Suárez-Orozco, 2001). Beyond the relatively low proportion of teachers from racial minority backgrounds, teacher education programs have not foregrounded immigrant children, despite, as Goodwin (2002) notes, the decades-long and continuing trend of schools incorporating immigrant newcomer students. While the changing demographics occasioned by immigration is noted, schools do not necessarily identify immigrant children in their records, and immigrant children themselves tend to be subsumed in discussions of "children of color," "diverse children," "culturally and linguistically diverse students," and "minority children"; further, when immigrant students are specifically mentioned in teacher education materials, it is often in the context of English language learning (Goodwin, 2002, p. 160), rather than parental country of origin, or the child's own generational status.

Given the ethnic, socio-economic, and generational diversity among the children of immigrants, it is important to have more precise ways of identifying this population. Certainly, English language acquisition is crucial to the academic development of the children of immigrants (Suárez-Orozco & Suárez-Orozco, 2001). However, it is important to keep in mind that the children of immigrants have needs and experiences in addition to second language learning, and that these are crucial to understand as they may also bear upon their academic achievement. In working-class households, for example, the children of immigrants can be asked to serve as language and cultural brokers for their families, effectively asked to interpret the world of mainstream America, a task that can be time-consuming, challenging, and also positive, insofar as it brings about an increase in self-confidence (Buriel, Perez, DeMent, Chavez, & Moran, 1998; Orellana, 2001). Other children might have come as refugees or undergone family separations via migration, processes that produce psychological stresses that have little to do with English language learning per se, but might nonetheless affect their engagement and performance with school (Suárez-Orozco, Todorova, & Louie, 2002).

Overall, immigrant children, particularly those from low income backgrounds, have needs resulting from the migration process itself, including separation from loved ones, cultural dislocation, and stigmatizing characterizations of their national and/or ethnic origins (Goodwin, 2002; Suárez-Orozco & Suárez-Orozco, 2001; Suárez-Orozco et al., 2002). Such needs, however, intersect with the complexity of immigration, and can thus be experienced in different ways according to the particular language and parental country of origin. Thus, rather than practices grounded in the philosophy of one model fits all, there needs to be greater awareness of the diverse cultural backgrounds of students and "differentiated instruction" along these lines (Goodwin, 2002). In this way, schools can assist immigrant children in experiencing a sense of belonging, or attachment to schooling, that can shape positive academic pathways (Koyama, 2007).

At the same time, it is clear that immigrant children share needs and experiences in common with their native peers, such as the effects of economic disadvantage, and low expectations that cut across nativity status. On the face of it, for example, special education and bilingual education/ESL programs have little in common, given that they serve students with different academic needs, and from different racial and ethnic groups and nativity statuses. Thus, the Black male youth, who disproportionately comprise special education students, would seem to have very dissimilar educational experiences from the Latino, mainly foreign-born, youth, who make up bilingual/ESL students. Yet, a stigmatizing label of underachievement and relatedly, low expectations are conferred upon youth in both programs. In short, while the goals of such programs are to promote student achievement, the result can often be disengagement instead (Eckert, 1989; McDermott, 1987, 1997; Stein, 2004), and this process affects both immigrant and non-immigrant students.

College Pipeline: Ethnic Differences

How do such factors play out in the increasingly important high school to college transition? In drawing on the limited existing research on this question, I will also report on studies focusing not on immigrant status per se, but rather on racial/ethnic groups, e.g., Latinos, Whites, Blacks, and Asians. While not an adequate proxy for immigrant status, it is worth noting that certain groups largely comprise the foreign-born or the children of foreign-born parents, particularly among Mexicans, Cubans, Central and South Americans, and Asians (Rumbaut, 2004, p. 1169). Certainly, there are racial/ethnic differences. Fry's (2005) work with data collected by the U.S. Department of Education shows that Latinos tend to attend larger public high schools, with student enrollments of at least 1,838, higher student/teacher ratios, and a larger proportion of economically disadvantaged children (as measured by eligibility for free and reduced free lunch) than any other group. While the geographic concentration of Latinos can partly account for this trend—nearly four out of five Latino students attending public high schools are in the states of California, Texas, Florida, New York, Arizona, Illinois, and New Jersey—the disproportionate representation of Latinos in under-resourced public high schools exists even in those states. In other words, even in those states, Latinos and Whites are attending different public high schools. Exclusion can also occur among racial and ethnic minorities; when Latinos and Blacks live in the same cities, they are often attending different public high schools (Fry, 2005).

The Latino–Asian comparison is also relevant. Asians are nearly as likely as Latinos to be attending large public high schools (55% vs. 56.1%), also with high student/

teacher ratios. The key differences rest with the rate of poverty and racial/ethnic composition of the student body. Asians are nearly twice as likely to be attending public schools where less than a third of the students are eligible for free or reduced school lunch. Further, only 14.8% of Asians are attending public high schools that are more than 88% minority, as compared to a third of Latinos (Fry, 2005, pp. 25–26).

Additionally, there is evidence of differences in academic preparation for postsecondary education. Latinos who have completed high school are more likely to have taken less rigorous content courses. Drawing from the National Educational Longitudinal Study (NELS) and Follow-Ups, Swail, Cabrera, and Lee (2004, p. 5) find that "only 1 in 4 Latino students were qualified" for postsecondary education (both 2- and 4-year institutions). Part of this can be explained by mathematics learning, which remains a serious challenge for adequate postsecondary school preparation. Among Latinos, who have finished public high school, 58% finished their mathematics careers with standard geometry, as compared to 44% of all students. Given that 79% of the Limited English Proficiency (LEP) K-12 population is Spanish-speaking, it would seem that language ability and academic preparation are somehow intertwined, although more work needs to be done in this domain. In this vein, Harklau's ethnography (1994) has shown us that a different, though no less powerful, form of tracking occurs with language minority students at the secondary level. Faced with the task of assessing the abilities of foreign-born language minority students within the existing stratified system, educators employed much the same instructional materials and activities rather than develop new practices tailored to the newcomers' needs. Additionally, the norm was to place the language minority students in less rigorous, or "low track classes." As Harklau (1994) documents, students tracked in these classes could "jump tracks," or switch to a more rigorous mainstream curriculum, provided they first recognized the existence of tracks in the school, and then developed ways to leverage institutional agents on their behalf, not an easy task for immigrant children.

This issue of who makes it to postsecondary education is complex. As Portes et al. (2005) observe, the high educational aspirations expressed by today's immigrant children set them apart from many of their predecessors of the mid-nineteenth through the early twentieth centuries. Such ambitions, however, are in keeping with the aspirations of the new generation of young Americans (Schneider & Stevenson, 1999). Certainly, in the last few decades, there has been a dramatic rise both in numbers of institutions and enrollments, particularly among members of minority groups, women, low income students, and immigrants. At the same time, there has been increasing stratification among institutions of postsecondary education with divides along the lines of prestige between 4-year schools and 2-year community colleges, between public and private 4-year institutions, and among public and private 4-year institutions.[6] Meanwhile, the gains in opening up the college pipeline notwithstanding, Astin and Oseguera (2004) have found that parental education assumes a stronger role in the type of institution attended by students, with the children of highly educated parents more likely to attend the nation's most selective institutions. Finally, paths through postsecondary education have increasingly become more complex than the previously straightforward route of entering college directly from high school, and then finishing in 4 years (Rumbaut, 2005). Individuals are coming in and out of the system at different points in their lives and for different lengths of time. Transfers can occur in the transition from a 2-year to a 4-year institution, and between 4-year institutions (Goldrick-Rab, 2007).

Along these lines, a recent report of the Institute of Higher Education Policy discusses the different educational paths taken by immigrants, and variations therein according to race and ethnicity. Asian and White immigrants are more likely to attain bachelor's degrees, although there is variation by income in both groups. Meanwhile, Erisman and Looney (2007), the authors of the report, found that Black immigrants are more likely to be non-traditional undergraduates, meaning that they are older than 30 and tend to have dependants; of all the immigrant groups, Blacks were the most likely to get a certificate or associate's degree. Finally, Latino immigrants face a daunting set of blockages in the college pipeline, including substantial rates of dropping out of high school and college, and low rates of degree completion.

To sum up, the new immigrant population in the United States is a complex one, differentiated by national origins, time of arrival, socio-economic background, and documentation status, factors that can often intersect with one another. That said, a majority of the newcomers, particularly working-class immigrants, have settled in the central cities of destination states. There, they face challenging urban contexts, including under-resourced and under-performing schools. Educationally speaking, the newcomers have arrived at a point in American history when the college degree assumes substantial and increasing importance in social mobility. While access to postsecondary education is more open than it ever has been, there is also stratification and barriers in the college pipeline (Astin & Oseguera, 2004; Louie, 2005; Louie, 2007). As I will show next, the picture of immigration and education is further complicated by generational status.

Why Generational Status and the 1.5 Generation Matter

The existing research on immigration reveals a strong effect of generational status on the pace and mode of immigrant adaptation and educational attainment. Researchers have typically defined the first generation as foreign-born individuals, who migrate as adults (e.g., ages 18 and older), the second generation as the U.S.-born children of the aforementioned group of immigrants, and the third generation as the U.S.-born children of U.S.-born parents. The overall pattern is for increasing rates of high school and college graduation with successive generations, particularly for low SES groups (Rumbaut, 2004). However, the differences between arriving as an adult and as a child in the adaptation process have led researchers to subdivide the foreign-born population into the first and the 1.5 generations (Rumbaut, 2004). Generally speaking, the experiences of the 1.5 generation are similar to the first generation in that they are foreign-born, and yet can approximate those of the second generation as they have been educated and socialized here in the United States as well.

Within the 1.5 generation, age of arrival is a key line of difference, one with substantial human developmental and educational implications. Given the limitations of nationally representative data sets, which would ordinarily provide the most scope,[7] Rumbaut (2004) leverages different data to provide the following more refined categorizations grounded in stage of the life course at time of arrival, and implications for adaptation. The members of the 1.75 generation arrived in early childhood (0–5 years of age) and were not educated in their homeland; the members of the 1.5 generation arrived in middle childhood (6–12 years of age) and had some early schooling in their homeland but completed the bulk of their education here; and the members of the 1.25 generation arrived in adolescence (13–17 years of age) and may have had some secondary schooling in the United States.

Such distinctions, for example, matter in the crucial area of language assimilation, which Rumbaut defines as acquisition of English proficiency. Drawing on the 5-Percent Public Use Microdata Sample from the 2000 U.S. Census, with a focus on the years 1992, 1995, and 2002, Rumbaut (2004) found that generational status is linked to both English-language proficiency and proficiency in parents' language, with 85% of members of the second generation, for example, reporting that they spoke English very well in all three survey periods; members of the 1.5 generation were the least linguistically assimilated (it should be noted that the 1.25 generation was not included in this analysis). In another analysis, Rumbaut (2004) finds that members of the 1.25 generation, i.e., individuals who arrived between the ages of 13 and 17, are in fact the most "vulnerable" relative to other groups, except for the first generation, and thus might need further attention from researchers. Possible lines of inquiry include their incorporation into schooling: as teenagers, members of the 1.25 generation enter high schools, which are typically less equipped than elementary schools to deal with issues of content, language, and literacy relevant for immigrant newcomers (Fix & Passel, 2003). The later age of arrival might also have an effect on the development of second language skills (Jia, 2004). Finally, there might be developmental consequences to migrating at this particular stage of the life course. It is worth noting that Mexico, El Salvador, and Guatemala, which send high numbers of undocumented immigrants to the United States, also tend to send younger migrants. About half of the migrants from all three nations came as adolescents or young adults aged 18–24 (Rumbaut, 2004). Thus, the struggles of the 1.25 generation may be disproportionately experienced along with the effects of being undocumented among these groups.

The effects of being undocumented on the college pipeline are particularly felt among the 1.75, 1.5, and 1.25 generations, as these are individuals who have arrived at early enough ages to engage with the PK/K-12 system in the United States and along with their native classmates, see the transition to college as a possible option. It has been shown that undocumented children experience particular stresses associated with schools as an arm of the state that speak to the danger of being discovered (Suárez-Orozco & Suárez-Orozco, 2001). Moreover, due to their lack of valid documentation, such children do not typically qualify for in-state tuition or other kinds of financial aid, substantially raising the financial stakes associated with college.[8]

School-based ethnographic accounts, particularly at the secondary level, have highlighted the differences and similarities between the 1.5 and second generations. In Matute-Bianchi's (1986) fieldwork at a California high school, she delineates five groups of Mexican-descent students, and the different ways in which they are perceived by peers and teachers. It is clear that those students, who are more recently arrived from Mexico (who would be defined as the 1.5 generation, broadly speaking), stand out insofar as they are thought of as strongly ethnic and more hardworking than their co-ethnic peers. Lee (2001) finds similar characterizations of 1.5 and second generation Hmong at a Wisconsin public school. Teachers framed the 1.5 generation

Hmong as ethnic and serious about schooling, contrasting them with their more Americanized second generation counterparts, who were felt to be lagging academically and more prone to disruptive behavior. In Lee's fieldwork, however, the situation is revealed to be more complex. The second generation Hmong have both Hmong and American identities, and their negative attitudes towards schooling, though not uniform, could be traced to their perception of racial and ethnic discrimination in the United States.

At the same time, members of the 1.5 generation, particularly those who arrive in early and middle childhood, share a wide range of experiences in common with their second generation counterparts. Regardless of generational status, children of immigrants, particularly among the working class, help out at home in various ways, not only with household chores but also language brokering for their parents (Orellana, 2001). Similarly, children of immigrants witness the hardships, including the loss of language, culture, and status, often associated with their parents' migration journeys and lives in the United States (Lopez, 2001; Louie, 2004; Suárez-Orozco & Suárez-Orozco, 2001). The sense of being on their own in the schooling process, without adequate support from parents, teachers, or staff, combined with the sense of being different from the mainstream, is also experienced by both the 1.5 (broadly defined) and second generations (Lee, 2001; Louie, 2004), although there might be distinctions in how such issues play out, as discussed above.

Conclusion

After decades of low inflows of newcomers, post-1960s immigration has once again brought a substantial newcomer population to the United States. Given the stakes attached to higher education in the contemporary labor market, it is crucial to chart the processes and outcomes among immigrants, particularly those who engage with American institutions of schooling. This is an emergent interdisciplinary field of inquiry that intersects with several research domains, such as PK-16 schooling, language and learning, identities, and the transition to college. Still more needs to be learned about how immigrant students are faring in the United States educational system, their particular needs and those that intersect with native peers, and how to develop effective practices to serve them. Attention to generational status, particularly the 1.5 generation, will facilitate those inquiries and deepen our knowledge around immigration and education.

Notes

1. Please note that unless otherwise specified, my use of the terms, immigrant children and the children of immigrants, includes both the foreign- and U.S.-born.
2. Restrictions on immigration were first imposed on migrants from East Asia, who were much fewer in number than immigrants from Europe—it is estimated that only 100,000 Chinese were in the United States in 1880. Nonetheless, East Asian immigrants were the targets of even more pronounced hostility, which led to the Chinese Exclusion Act of 1882, the first federal exclusion law aimed at a specific nationality, and the Gentlemen's Agreement Act of 1907, which restricted immigration from Japan.
3. Alba and Nee (2003) have noted that the lawmakers behind the Immigration Act of 1965

initially expected immigration to come from Europe. Nonetheless, the United States continued and expanded immigration after it became clear that the new immigrants were coming from other regions of the world.

4. Passel (2006) employs the term, *unauthorized migrants,* which he defines as "a person who resides in the United States but who is not a U.S. citizen, has not been admitted for permanent residence, and is not in a set of specific authorized temporary statuses permitting longer-term residence and work" (p. i). In this chapter, I draw on this definition while using the term, undocumented immigrants.

5. Limited English Proficient (LEP) is the formal designation used by the federal government to determine a K-12 student's eligibility for state Second Language/Bilingual services, regardless of actual placement. An English language learner does not necessarily have to be an LEP student although the reverse is true.

6. Please see Gelber (2007) for further discussion.

7. According to Rumbaut (2004), nuanced analyses of the effect of generational status on outcomes require "data sources that contain information on the country of birth of the respondent; and if foreign-born, the age and date of arrival; and if, native-born the country of birth of the mother and father" (p. 1164). Please see Rumbaut (2004) for a more detailed discussion of the various data sets and relevant methodological strategies for overcoming their limitations, for example the decennial U.S. Census, the Public Use Microdata Samples of the decennial Census, and the Current Population Surveys.

8. First introduced to Congress in 2001, the DREAM Act, which has not been passed, outlines a college pipeline for foreign-born individuals arriving in the United States as children or young adolescents (the maximum cut-off for age of arrival is 15 years). In addition to the age requirement, a foreign-born individual must have spent more than 5 years in the United States, and be deemed of good moral character. Following high school graduation, individuals who meet the relevant criteria can apply for conditional legal residence of up to 6 years. At the end of this period, the student would have to have completed a degree from a 2-year college, finished at least 2 years of a 4-year college degree, or served in the U.S. military for at least 2 years. The end goal would be permanent residency (National Immigration Law Center, 2006).

References

Alba, R. (2007, June 19). Demographics and the golden door: The way we reform immigration could end our best hope for racial justice. *Los Angeles Times,* p. A17.

Alba, R. & Nee, V. (2003). *Remaking the American mainstream: Assimilation and contemporary immigration.* Cambridge, MA: Harvard University Press.

Astin, A.W. & Oseguera, L. (2004). The declining "equity" of American higher education. *Review of Higher Education, 27*(3), 321–341.

Buriel, R., Perez, W., DeMent, L., Chavez, D., & Moran, V. (1998). The relationship of language brokering to academic performance, biculturalism and self-efficacy among Latino adolescents. *Hispanic Journal of Behavioral Sciences, 20*(3), 283–297.

Capps, R., Fix, M.E., Murray, J., Ost, J., Passel, J.S., & Herwantoro Henandez, S. (2005). *The new demography of America's schools: Immigration and the No Child Left Behind Act, a report of the Urban Institute.* Washington, DC: Urban Institute. Retrieved July 1, 2007, from www.urban. org/url.cfm?ID=311230.

Contreras, A.R. (2002). The impact of immigration policy of education reform: Implications for the new millennium. *Education and Urban Society, 34*(2), 134–155.

Cooper, C., Garcia Coll, C.T., Thorne, B., & Faulstich Orellana, M. (2005). Beyond demographic categories: How immigration, ethnicity, and "race" matter for children's identities and pathways through school. In C.R. Cooper, C.T. García Coll, W.T. Bartko, H. Davis, & C. Chatman (Eds.), *Developmental pathways through middle childhood: Rethinking contexts and diversity as resources* (pp. 181–206). Mahwah, NJ: Lawrence Erlbaum Publishers.

Eckert, P. (1989). *Jocks and burnouts*. New York: Columbia University Press.

Erisman, W. & Looney, S. (2007, April). *Opening the door to the American dream: Increasing higher education access and success for immigrants*. Washington, DC: Institute for Higher Education Policy.

Fix, J. & Passel, M. (2003). *U.S. immigration: Trends and implications for schools*. Urban Institute. Retrieved July 17, 2007, from www.urban.org/url.cfm?ID=410654.

Foner, N. (1987). Introduction: New immigrants and changing patterns in New York City. In N. Foner (Ed.), *New immigrants in New York* (pp. 1–33). New York: Columbia University Press.

Fry, R. (2005). *The high schools Hispanics attend: Size and other key characteristics*. Washington, DC: Pew Hispanic Center.

Furstenberg, F., Jr., Rumbaut, R., & Settersten, R., Jr. (2005). On the frontier of adulthood: Emerging themes and new directions. In R. Settersten Jr., F. Furstenberg Jr., & R.G. Rumbaut (Eds.), *On the frontier of new adulthood: Theory, research, and public policy* (pp. 3–25). Chicago, IL: University of Chicago Press.

Gans, H. (1992). Second generation decline: Scenarios for the economic and ethnic futures of the post-1965 American immigrants. *Ethnic and Racial Studies, 15*(2), 173–193.

Gelber, S. (2007). Pathways in the past: Historical perspectives on access to higher education. [Electronic version.] *Teachers College Record, 109*(10). Retrieved June 29, 2007, from www.tcrecord.org.

Gibson, M.A. (2002). The new Latino diaspora and educational policy. In S. Wortham, E.G. Murillo, & E.T. Hamann (Eds.), *Education in the new Latin diaspora: Policy and the politics of identity* (pp. 241–252). Westport, CT: Ablex Publishing.

Goldrick-Rab, S. (2007). What higher education has to say about the transition to college. [Electronic version.] *Teachers College Record, 109*(10). Retrieved June 29, 2007, from www.tcrecord.org.

Goodwin, A.L. (2002). Teacher preparation and the education of immigrant children. *Education and Urban Society, 34*(2), 156–172.

Gozdziak, E.M. & Martin, S.F. (2005). *Beyond the gateway: Immigrants in a changing America*. Lanham, MD: Lexington Books.

Grissmer, D. (2005, May). Closing the nation's racial achievement gaps. Panel presented at Harvard University, Graduate School of Education.

Harklau, L. (1994). Jumping tracks: How language-minority students negotiate evaluations of ability. *Anthropology and Education Quarterly, 25*(3), 347–363.

Kao, G. (2004). Social capital and its relevance to minority and immigrant populations. *Sociology of Education, 77*(2), 172–175.

Kao, G. & Tienda, M. (1995). Optimism and achievement: The educational performance of immigrant youth. *Social Science Quarterly, 76*(1), 1–19.

Koyama, J. (2007). Approaching and attending college: Anthropological and ethnographic accounts. [Electronic version.] *Teachers College Record, 109*(10). Retrieved June 29, 2007, from www.tcrecord.org.

Jia, G. (2004). The acquisition of English and maintenance of first language by immigrant children and adolescents in North America. In U. Gielen & X. Jaipaul (Eds.), *Childhood and adolescence: Cross-cultural perspectives and applications*. Westport, CT: Greenwood Publishing Group.

Lazerson, M. (1977). Understanding American Catholic educational history. *History of Education Quarterly, 17*(3), 297–317.

Lee, S.J. (2001). More than model minorities or delinquents: A look at Hmong American high school students. *Harvard Educational Review, 71*(3), 509–528.

Lew, J. (2005). *Asian Americans in class: Charting the achievement gap among Korean-American youth*. New York: Teachers College Press.

Long, B.T. (2007). The contributions from economics to the study of college access and success. [Electronic version.] *Teachers College Record, 109*(10). Retrieved June 29, 2007, from www.tcrecord.org.

Lopez, G. (2001). The value of hard work: Lessons on parent involvement from an (im)migrant household. *Harvard Educational Review, 71*(3), 416–437.

Louie, V. (2001). Parents' aspirations and investment: The role of social class in the educational experiences of 1.5 and second generation Chinese Americans. *Harvard Educational Review, 71*(3), 438–474.

Louie, V. (2004). *Compelled to excel: Immigration, education, opportunity among Chinese Americans.* Stanford, CA: Stanford University Press.

Louie, V. (2005). Immigrant student populations and the pipeline to college: Current considerations and future lines of inquiry. *Review of Research in Education, 29*, 69–106.

Louie, V. (2007). Who makes the transition to college? Why we should care, what we know, and what we need to do. [Electronic version.] *Teachers College Record, 109*(10). Retrieved June 29, 2007, from www.tcrecord.org.

McDermott, R. (1987). The explanation of minority failure, again. *Anthropology and Education Quarterly, 18*(4), 361–364.

McDermott, R. (1997). Achieving school failure, 1972–1997. In G.D. Spindler (Ed.), *Education and cultural process: Anthropological processes* (pp. 110–131). Prospect Heights, IL: Waveland Press.

McGreevy, J.T. (1996). *Parish boundaries: The Catholic encounter with race in the twentieth century urban North.* Chicago, IL: University of Chicago Press.

Matute-Bianchi, M.E. (1986). Ethnic identities and patterns of school success and failure among Mexican-descent and Japanese-American students in a California high school: An ethnographic analysis. *American Journal of Education, 95*(1), 233–255.

Millard, A.V. & Chapa, J. (2004). *Apple pie and enchiladas: Latino newcomers in the rural Midwest.* Austin: University of Texas Press.

National Immigration Law Center. (2006 April). *DREAM ACT: Basic Information.* Retrieved June 29, 2007, from www.nilc.org.

Olsen, L. (1990). Then and now: A comparative perspective on immigration and school reform during two periods in American history. *California Perspective, 1.* Oakland, CA: California Tomorrow.

Olsen, L. (2000). Children of change overview. *Education Week, 20*(4), 31.

Orellana, M.F. (2001). The work kids do: Mexican and Central American immigrant children's contributions to households and schools in California. *Harvard Educational Review, 71*(3), 366–389.

Passel, J.S. (2006) The size and characteristics of the unauthorized migrant population in the U.S.: Estimates based on the March 2005 Current Population Survey. Washington, DC: Pew Hispanic Center.

Pedraza, S. (1995). Origins and destinies: Immigration, race, and ethnicity in America. In S. Pedraza & R.G. Rumbaut (Eds.), *Origins and destinies: Immigration, race, and ethnicity in America* (pp. 1–20). Belmont, CA: Wadsworth.

Portes, A. & Rumbaut, R. (2001). *Legacies.* Berkeley: University of California Press.

Portes, A., Fernandez-Kelly, P., & Haller, W. (2005). Segmented assimilation on the ground: The new second generation in early adulthood. *Ethnic and Racial Studies, 28*(6), 1000–1040.

Ravitch, D. (2000). *The great school wars: A history of the New York City public schools.* Baltimore, MD: Johns Hopkins University Press.

Rong, X.L. & Brown, F. (2002). Immigration and urban education in the new millennium: The diversity and the challenges [editorial]. *Education and Urban Society, 34*(2), 123–133.

Rong, X.L. & Preissle, J. (1997). *Educating immigrant students: What we need to know to meet the challenge.* Thousand Oaks, CA: Corwin Press.

Rumbaut, R. (2004). Ages, life stages, and generational cohorts: Decomposing the immigrant first and second generations in the United States. *International Migration Review, 38*(3), 1160–1205.

Rumbaut, R. (2005). Turning points in the transition to adulthood: Determinants of educational attainment, incarceration, and early childbearing among children of immigrants. *Ethnic and Racial Studies, 28*(6), 1041–1086.

Schneider, B. & Stevenson, D. (1999). *The ambitious generation: America's teenagers, motivated but directionless.* New Haven, CT: Yale University Press.

Stein, S. (2004). *The culture of education policy.* New York: Teachers College Press.

Stewart, D.W. (2005, May 8). The brain drain: U.S. colleges losing foreign students. *Boston Globe*, p. K12.

Suárez-Orozco, C. (2001). Afterword: Understanding and serving the children of immigrants. *Harvard Educational Review, 71*(3), 579–589.

Suárez-Orozco, C. & Suárez-Orozco, M. (2001). *Children of immigration.* Cambridge, MA: Harvard University Press.

Suárez-Orozco, C., Todorova, I., & Louie, J. (2002). Making up for lost time: The experience of separation and reunification among immigrant families. *Family Process, 41*(4), 625–643.

Swail, W.S., Cabrera, A.F., & Lee, C. (2004). *Latino youth and the pathway to college.* Washington, DC: Pew Hispanic Center.

Waters, M. (1990). *Ethnic options.* Berkeley: University of California Press.

Weisz, H.R. (1976). *Irish-American and Italian-American educational views and activities, 1870–1900.* New York: Arno Press.

Wilson, W.J. (1980). *The declining significance of race: Blacks and changing American institutions.* Chicago, IL: University of Chicago Press.

Wilson, W.J. (1987). *The truly disadvantaged: The inner city, the underclass, and public policy.* Chicago: University of Chicago Press.

Wortham, S., Murillo, E.G., & Hamann, E.T. (2002). *Education in the new Latin diaspora: Policy and the politics of identity.* Westport, CT: Greenwood Publishing Group.

Zuniga, V. & Hernandez-Leon, R. (2005). *New destinations: Mexican immigration in the United States.* New York: Russell Sage Foundation.

Zuniga, V., Hernandez-Leon, R., Shadduck-Hernandez, J.L., & Villarreal, M.O. (2002). The new paths of Mexican immigrants in the United States: Challenges for education and the role of Mexican universities. In S. Wortham, E.G. Murillo, & E.T. Hamann (Eds.), *Education in the new Latin diaspora: Policy and the politics of identity* (pp. 99–116). Westport, CT: Greenwood Publishing Group.

4   The Erasure of Resident ESL Writers

Paul Kei Matsuda and Aya Matsuda   Arizona State University

Every way of seeing is also a way of not seeing.

(Burke, 1935, p. 70)

In recent years, a growing number of teachers and researchers of college TESOL in North America have begun to pay attention to various issues surrounding a particular population of students that has come to be known as *generation 1.5* students.[1] The term first entered the consciousness of many TESOL and composition specialists in the late 1990s through a ground-breaking volume, *Generation 1.5 Meets College Composition: Issues in the Teaching of Writing to U.S.-Educated Learners of ESL*, edited by Linda Harklau, Kay M. Losey, and Meryl Siegal (1999). Within a few years, it became one of the most popular keywords among college TESOL specialists working in the United States, calling attention to the presence and needs of an increasing number of ESL students whose linguistic and educational backgrounds differed from those of international ESL students, who had long been the central focus—if not the sole focus—of college TESOL research and instruction.

Although publications that focus on generation 1.5 students frequently mention the rapid growth of this population as a rationale for their studies, demographics alone does not fully explain the surge of interest in this topic. As we will explain, the presence of resident ESL students had already been recognized by some prominent second language specialists by the mid-1950s (Slager, 1956) and the population continued to grow throughout the 1970s and the 1980's. By 1990, the foreign-born student population in U.S. higher education had exceeded the two million mark, 65 percent of whom were U.S. citizens (Otuya, 1994). Our task in this historical chapter, then, is to examine why college ESL specialists in the TESOL tradition long remained silent on the issue of resident ESL students—until the introduction of the term generation 1.5 in the last few years of the century. In so doing, we hope to illuminate the significance—as well as the side effects—of this powerful key term.

International Students and the Rise of College TESOL

To understand why resident ESL students have long been absent from the historical consciousness of college TESOL specialists, we must look back to the late nineteenth century, when resident students actually did not have a significant presence in U.S.

higher education. U.S. colleges in antebellum society were, at least on the surface, linguistically homogeneous for the most part (Russell, 2002). Those institutions focused on providing liberal arts education to a small number of students from privileged social backgrounds, leaving little room for the offspring of recent immigrants who did not speak a privileged variety of English. Although international ESL students had already been part of the system since the late eighteenth century and the number of government-sponsored international students was increasing in the late nineteenth century, they were exceptions rather than the rule. When the number of those students increased, institutions began to expect the students to have acquired a high level of proficiency in English before attending college, and the students or their sponsoring governments were responsible for bearing the cost of language preparation.[2]

U.S. higher education at the turn of the century went through a period of rapid growth, and several important changes took place that affected the make-up of the college student population.[3] One of the major changes was the shift from British-style liberal arts colleges to German-style research universities. During the nineteenth century, German higher education distinguished itself for its advancement in science and for the granting of Ph.D. degrees, attracting international students from various parts of the world. Many U.S. students went to Germany to obtain advanced degrees, and upon their return to the States, they began to create Ph.D.-granting research universities, beginning with the creation of Johns Hopkins University in 1876 (Connors, 1997). Another important development during this period was the passage of the Morrill Acts—first passed in 1862 and then extended in 1890—which led to the creation of public land-grant universities throughout the country. An important part of the land-grant mission was to prepare a highly skilled workforce in an increasingly industrialized society. To that end, land-grant institutions placed a strong emphasis on practical fields of agriculture and mechanics, and accepted a growing number of young men and women from a wider variety of socio-economic groups (Connors, 1997).

The shift of emphasis from the reproduction of the values of the privileged class to mass education in practical fields did not result in an increase of resident ESL students because of yet another important change that took place during this period: the creation in 1874 of the entrance exam at Harvard University, a practice that was adopted widely by many other institutions across the nation. As Connors (1997) points out, this development was motivated in part by the pervasive language attitude of the time that conflated language differences with class differences. The entrance exam at Harvard, for example, was designed to assess students' pronunciation as well as the use of grammar and convention of written English associated with the privileged social class (see also Brereton, 1995). The linguistic filtering through the entrance exam continued at least until the turn of the century, when standardized tests, such as the Achievement Test developed by the College Entrance Examination Board (College Entrance Examination Board, 1999), began to take over this function.

In the early twentieth century, U.S. universities made significant advancements in science and technology, and began to grow in popularity as destinations for international students, most of whom spoke English as a second language. During the first decade of the twentieth century, however, the number of international students was still relatively small; in 1911, there were 3,645 international students mostly at highly selective, internationally known research institutions (Kandel, 1945). Although language preparation was still considered to be the responsibility of individual students or their sponsoring governments, the need for providing additional language support became recognized gradually. In 1911, the English Department in the Engineering College at the University of Michigan created what is probably the first language support course for international students. Other research institutions—such as Columbia, Cornell, George Washington, Harvard, and Yale—also began to develop special English classes for non-native speakers. Many of these courses were ad hoc in nature, and focused on the needs of a growing population of international ESL students (see Matsuda, 2006).

The most significant impetus for the development of college TESOL came about as a result of the political shift after the conclusion of World War I in 1918, which also brought about a change in the prevailing language attitude. Because of an increasing political tension associated with the rise of totalitarianism, the U.S. government became interested in forming an alliance with Latin American countries, and the teaching of English to Spanish-speaking students from Central and South America became a matter of national security (Morley, Robinett, Selinker, & Woods, 1984). According to Harold B. Allen (1973), the U.S. Department of State and the Rockefeller Foundation sponsored, in the fall of 1939, an invitational conference at the University of Michigan to determine the best method for English language teaching for Latin American students, and Charles C. Fries' oral approach, which directly applied insights from descriptive linguistics, was chosen over other proposals (including one by C.K. Ogden and I.A. Richards). With grants from the State Department and the Rockefeller Foundation, the English Language Institute (ELI) opened its door in 1941 as the first intensive English program of its kind (Allen, 1973). Although the Institute later expanded its scope to include students from other countries, its pedagogy, which included a program to facilitate cultural adjustments, continued to focus on the needs of international students.

With the conclusion of World War II, the United States affirmed its status as the world's new superpower, and U.S. higher education saw an unprecedented influx of international students, replacing Germany as the most popular destination for international studies. In 1945, there already were over 10,000 international students. The number continued to rise rapidly from 82,709 in 1965 to 144,708 in 1970 (Zikopoulos, 1993). As a result, the international ESL student population reached a critical mass at many institutions, and the need to develop language support programs became undeniably clear. Michigan's pedagogical approach—along with its exclusive focus on international ESL students—were replicated in other parts of the country, as many institutions hired Michigan-trained instructors, and adopted the program structures and pedagogical materials developed at the Michigan ELI (Allen, 1973).

Although the intensive English program was effective in developing spoken language proficiency, it was inadequate in preparing students for the required first-year composition courses that had become a commonplace in U.S. higher education. For this reason, many institutions began to develop special sections of writing courses for international ESL students—often labeled "English for foreign students"—during the 1950s and 1960s. The growing need for college ESL instruction, coupled with ESL teachers' desire to professionalize, prompted the creation of the TESOL organization in 1966 (Matsuda, 1999). As we will discuss next, the development of college TESOL instruction in response to the presence and needs of international students had a lasting impact on the status of resident ESL students in U.S. higher education.

"Generation 1.5" Meets College TESOL

Although the ESL population in U.S. higher education had long been dominated by international students, the situation began to change in the mid-twentieth century. Resident ESL students began to enter U.S. higher education in large numbers by the 1950s and the 1960s, when developments such as the G.I. Bill and the Civil Rights Movement prompted many colleges and universities to open their doors to tradition-ally excluded groups of students (Kiester, 1994). One of the first to document the significant presence of resident ESL students in U.S. higher education was William Slager of the University of Utah. In 1956, *Language Learning* published Slager's article entitled "The Foreign Student and the Immigrant—Their Different Problems as Stu-dents of English," in which he noted the presence of "an equally large number of immigrants who have serious difficulties with English" (pp. 24–25).

Slager's description of "immigrant" students bears striking resemblance to the pro-totypical "generation 1.5" students:

> Many of these students have lived in the community for years; they may even have graduated from local high schools and have served in the armed forces. Yet their scores in the English language tests are often as weak as, or weaker than, those of the newly arrived foreign students.
>
> (p. 25)

He continued:

> Here are a few typical sentences from the compositions of Dutch immigrants. Because their language is so similar to English structure, they can often translate directly and get English patterns that are clear enough to pass uncorrected except in an academic environment. One frequent mistake is the position of "here" in "She will be at ten o'clock here." (*Zij zal om tien uur hier zijn.*) There will occa-sionally be a mistake in tense: "I am here since four years." (*Ik ben hier sinds vier jaar.*) Since the question pattern with *do* is new to the Dutch, you will find, "How much costed the house when it new was?" (*Hoe veel koste het huis toen het niew was?*) Here word order and the irregular verb also must be considered. Even so, the meaning in English is quite clear. Because he is not corrected, the immigrant makes habits of these non-English patterns. Therefore, he must not only learn a new pattern: he must unlearn an old one.
>
> (Slager, 1956, p. 28)

Slager's analysis is based on the then-dominant view of language learning as habit formation promulgated by the Michigan ELI, where Slager received his professional preparation. What is important to note here is that Slager is referring to the kind of issues that are commonly associated with "generation 1.5" students. It is significant that Slager, writing in as early as the mid-1950s, recognized that resident ESL students had characteristics and needs that differed either from speakers of dominant varieties of English or from international ESL students. He also recognized that ESL courses that were developed primarily for international ESL students were not appropriate for resident ESL students who were already fluent in spoken English and were already familiar with various U.S. cultural practices. For this reason, he called for the development of separate courses as well as teaching materials for an increasing number of resident ESL students in U.S. higher education.

A generous reading of Slager's work might suggest that it was an attempt to call attention to the problem of the exclusive focus on international students among college TESOL specialists at the time (Matsuda, 2003). However, the lack of organized responses from the college TESOL community seems to favor a different interpretation. That is, Slager's identification of the differing needs of resident ESL students did not function as a call for action; instead, it was taken as a justification for excluding resident ESL students from the purview of college TESOL specialists in the context of the then-emerging field of TESOL. As a result, when TESOL was established in 1966, college TESOL began to develop with an exclusive focus on international ESL students in intensive English programs or separate sections of first-year writing courses for international students. The effect of the split between resident and international ESL students continues to be felt; even today, some college TESOL specialists continue to resist having resident students in ESL courses—even when no other appropriate placement options are available (Matsuda, 2008).

While college-level TESOL specialists decided to focus on international students, the number of resident ESL students continued to increase as U.S. colleges and universities grew in number and became more inclusive than in the past. One of the events that prompted the growth of the resident ESL student population was the advent of the open admissions policy at many urban institutions, which began to accept any high school graduates who wished to obtain college education. The open admissions policy brought to colleges various kinds of differences that had previously been excluded from higher education—ethnic, cultural, economic, and, of course, linguistic. Among the new groups of students were foreign-born immigrants from Asia and Eastern Europe, who began to arrive in the United States in large numbers after the Immigration and Naturalization Services Act of 1965, which removed the restrictions placed by previous legislation, allowing previously excluded ethnic and national groups to immigrate into the country.

A prime example is the City University of New York (CUNY), an urban, multi-campus institution that opened its door to any New York City residents who had completed high school education. Many of the "open admissions students," as they were then called, did not have the kind of academic preparation that traditional students had, and attempts were made to address the needs of those students—by developing various academic support programs, including basic writing programs and ESL programs. At CUNY, where the ESL population was predominantly resident students, the salient distinction was not between international and resident ESL students but between native-born and foreign-born populations. This distinction often (but not always) coincided with that between native and non-native English speakers. By 1980, the foreign-born student population constituted 21.4% of newly entering students and 18.5% of transfer students (City University of New York, 1995). Recognizing the complexity of identifying linguistic and writing needs of students, however, CUNY also developed an elaborate, multi-tiered placement procedure to identify the differing needs of ESL students and so-called Speakers of English as a Second Dialect (SESD) students (Matsuda, 2003).

The influx of resident ESL students into U.S. higher education, however, was not met by a surge of interest in issues surrounding their presence and needs among mainstream college TESOL specialists. While the term *immigrant* appeared on the pages of *TESOL Quarterly* in as early as 1967 (Allen, 1967) it was used in connection with adult immigrants or children in schools. What is probably the first explicit mention of immigrant ESL students at the college level happened in the 1980s in reference to the student population at Seneca University in Ontario, Canada. They were "primarily immigrants" who are "extremely diverse in terms of objectives and background" (Carpenter & Hunter, 1981, p. 431). Throughout the 1980s, however, references to resident ESL students in U.S. higher education remained few and far between. Many books on second language writing that appeared in the early 1990s also focused almost exclusively on international ESL students (e.g., Kroll, 1990; Leki, 1992; Reid, 1993).

Resident ESL Students in the Professional Literature

As we have discussed, there was a dearth of explicit references in the TESOL literature to resident ESL students at the college level before the end of the 1980s, and the distinction between international and resident ESL students did not begin to enter the consciousness of many college TESOL specialists until around 1990. To many college TESOL specialists today whose disciplinary background is primarily in TESOL, then, it may seem that the presence of resident ESL students suddenly became an issue in the 1990s. Yet, this view is largely a discursively constructed fiction. As we have already mentioned, the presence of resident ESL students in U.S. education can be traced back to the mid-twentieth century. Furthermore, the discussion of resident ESL students began to appear in the 1970s. This development, however, escaped the attention of mainstream college TESOL specialists because it did not take place within the disciplinary context of TESOL. Instead, articles responding to the presence and needs of resident ESL students were being published in journals in composition studies.

When the *Journal of Basic Writing* (*JBW*) was created in the mid-1970s in response to the writing needs of open-admissions students, it included issues surrounding resident ESL writers within its scope—albeit marginally.[4] The inaugural issue of the *JBW* in 1975 included two articles (Lay, 1975; Rizzo & Villafane, 1975), followed by an article on the application of sentence combining to ESL writers a few years later (Davidson, 1977). Although the journal, which organized each issue around a specific theme for the first 10 years, was quiet on ESL issues during the first half of the 1980s, it began to publish a growing number of ESL-related articles in 1986, when Lynn Quitman Troyka became the editor and included the term "English as a second language" in the call for papers. Between 1986 and 1992, *JBW* published 15 articles focusing substantially on ESL writing (Benson, Deming, Denzer, & Valeri-Gold, 1992; Costello, 1990; Herendeen, 1986; Jie & Lederman, 1988; Johns, 1986; Kroll, 1990; Lay, 1992; Liebman, 1988; Patthey-Chavez & Gergen, 1992; Perkins & Brutten, 1990; Purves, 1986; Sanborn, 1987; Sternglass, 1989; Yorio, 1989; Zamel, 1990). While not all of them clearly defined the term *ESL*, many of them were concerned primarily with resident ESL writers.

The *JBW* was not the only composition journal that published articles related to ESL issues. In fact, some of the most substantial discussions of issues related to resident ESL writers in the early 1990s appeared in *Written Communication*, an international and interdisciplinary journal growing out of composition studies. In "Interpreting an English Competency Examination: The Frustrations of an ESL Science Student," Ann Johns (1991) presented a qualitative case study of Luc, a Vietnamese resident ESL student who came to the United States with his family when he was a high school student. She documented how the state-wide competency examination kept Luc in the "remedial" English classes "designed to prepare students for freshman-level writing competency" (p. 384) even though he had been successfully completing writing tasks in courses in his major. In the following year, *Written Communication* published "Bilingual Minorities and Language Issues in Writing" by Guadalupe Valdés (1992), which articulated how the "compartmentalization of the English-teaching profession" (p. 87) had led to the marginalization of bilingual minority students who were long-time residents of the United States. Reviewing the ESL writing research literature in the disciplinary context of TESOL, she pointed out that

> research on composing process of nonnative English language has focused primarily on students who can still be classified as incipient bilinguals. Moreover, many of the studies cited above have investigated the writing of elective and noncircumstancial bilinguals—foreign students who have been educated in their own countries and who have elected to enroll in American universities—rather than American bilingual minority students.
>
> (p. 113)

While issues related to resident ESL students were discussed within the disciplinary context of composition studies, college TESOL specialists continued to focus largely on international ESL students. The international-student bias among college TESOL specialists became most conspicuous in "Ideology in Composition: L1 and ESL" by Terry Santos (1992), which was published in the inaugural issue of the *Journal of Second Language Writing*. In arguing that Composition is more ideological and TESOL more pragmatic—a distinction that has been problematized from a number of perspectives (Benesch, 1993, 2001; Severino, 1993)—Santos (1992) contrasted Composition and TESOL in terms of their national and international foci, respectively. Despite Santos' proclamation that equated second language writing with international students, the *Journal of Second Language Writing* also included a number of articles that explicitly mentioned resident ESL writers (e.g., Braine, 1996; Severino, 1993; Williams, 1995). Yet, the discussion of resident ESL students in most of these articles was rather brief (with the exception of Severino, 1993), and the implications of the distinction were not always clearly indicated.

This is not to say that resident students were not included in the mainstream college TESOL discussion at all; they were simply not identified as such. Some researchers publishing in *TESOL Quarterly*, such as Ann Raimes, had been working with resident ESL students all along. Yet, the authors often did not make explicit reference to the student population. It may have been that the distinction between international and resident ESL students had not yet become salient in the minds of college TESOL specialists. Another possibility is that, because college TESOL specialists did not see resident ESL students as their concern, articles that mentioned resident ESL students explicitly were not well received—or accepted for publication. In retrospect, the lack of explicit distinction probably contributed to misunderstandings and unnecessary disagreements among ESL writing specialists throughout the 1980s. Realizing the seriousness of the problem, Raimes (1991) pointed out the importance of clarifying the student population in her historical overview of ESL writing pedagogy. She wrote:

> Our field is too diverse for us to recommend ways of teaching ESL in general. There is no such thing as a generalized ESL student. Before making pedagogical recommendations, we need to determine the following: the type of institution (high school, two-year college, four-year college, research university?) and the ESL student (undergraduate or graduate? freshman or junior? international student [returning to country of origin] or immigrant/refugee? with writing expertise in L1 or not? with what level of language proficiency?).
>
> (p. 420)

With this recognition, the situation began to change in the 1990s. In 1991, the City University of New York created a new journal, aptly called *College ESL*, which sought to create a forum for the discussion of issues related to resident ESL students. The focus on resident ESL students is apparent in the statement by its editor, Gay Brooks. She wrote:

> Our experience is defined in part by our ESL students—college-age and adult, living in urban centers, by and large permanent residents of the United States who have come as immigrants and refugees.... They differ in many ways from foreign students who come for education only and plan to return to their countries, and who are traditionally educated and middle-class. Most significantly, the ESL population is vastly heterogeneous. They have in common that English is not their first language, but that may be all.... We wanted a journal to talk about these students in the classroom, the university, the workplace, society, and the family and community, about how we teach them and meet their educational needs and about a host of issues related to them and their language development.
>
> (Brooks, 1991, p. i)

The creation of a separate journal with an explicit focus on resident ESL students seems to mark an emergence of a new community of inquiry—apart from the mainstream college TESOL. A decade later, however, the publication of *College ESL* was discontinued in the midst of a political shift in New York City that resulted in the elimination of academic support programs at CUNY's 4-year colleges. Since then, the journal's focus on resident ESL students—along with some of its editorial members—has been reintegrated into the *Journal of Basic Writing* (see Matsuda, 2006).

Beyond "Generation 1.5"

One explanation for the historical invisibility of resident ESL students, as Harklau has suggested, is that "a traditional bipartite division of labor between ESL and mainstream composition resulted in these students' institutional invisibility, often confounding them with international students" (Matsuda, Canagarajah, Harklau, Hyland, & Warschauer, 2003, p. 153). While we generally concur that the disciplinary division of labor between composition studies and second language studies (Matsuda, 1998, 1999) was a factor, the situation is complicated by yet another disciplinary division that emerged in the formative years of college TESOL: the division between international and resident students. As we have tried to show, college TESOL in the United States arose as a viable educational enterprise in response to a growing number of international ESL students in the early half of the twentieth century. Although the presence and needs of resident ESL students had already been recognized by the time TESOL became a field, the college TESOL community did not include resident ESL students within the scope of its work, and articles that explicitly and centrally addressed those students remained conspicuously absent from mainstream college TESOL publications. Instead, issues surrounding resident ESL students found a disciplinary home—or at least a shelter—in composition studies, which, ironically, is sometimes referred to as *L1* composition (Atkinson & Ramanathan, 1995; Santos, 1992). In other words, resident ESL students were not confounded with international students but were treated as a separate category outside of college TESOL. The invisibility of resident ESL students in college TESOL, then, was a result of the two dividing lines that were not aligned with one another. The condition was described in the early 1990s by Valdés (1992), but it did not seem to hold sway over college TESOL specialists—perhaps because the article appeared in a composition studies journal rather than a college TESOL journal.

By the early 1990s, college education had become a minimum requirement for a greater variety of jobs in the United States, and an increasing number of resident ESL students began to seek higher education as a precondition for upward mobility (Harklau, 1998). The issues surrounding resident ESL students were quickly approaching a "tipping point" (Preto-Bay & Hansen, 2006), although it did not quite tip. What finally tipped the balance was the publication of *Generation 1.5 Meets College Composition* (Harklau, Losey, & Siegal, 1999a), a book that has been frequently cited in publications dealing with resident ESL students. There are many possible reasons for the success of the book in calling college TESOL specialists' attention to resident ESL students—such as the timeliness of the publication, the quality of research and writing, and the publisher's ability to market the book widely. One of the most important reasons, we contend, is the expansive use of the term *generation 1.5*. Coined by sociologists Rubén G. Rumbaut and Kenji Ima (1988), the term originally referred to Southeast Asian refugees in Southern California who were "completing their education in the U.S. during the key formative periods of adolescence and early adulthood" (p. 22). Harklau, Siegal, and Losey (1999b), in their introduction to the landmark volume, extended the definition to include a broader population of students based on their linguistic and educational profile—i.e., graduates of U.S. high schools who are actively learning English. The term continued to expand in its scope; researchers are now beginning to include students who are currently in high schools or even in elementary schools (Schwartz, 2004; Yi, 2007). While the number of students who fall under this category was actually growing quickly, it seems that the term generation 1.5 has played a major role in creating a critical mass discursively by embracing various categories of students who had traditionally been represented by different terms, such as bilingual minority, immigrant ESL, resident ESL, or just plain ESL—or a subset of that population (Matsuda, 2008; Schwartz, 2004). To put it crudely, the term achieved its popularity because everyone who has a student who does not fit the traditional category can relate to it.

The expansive definition also has its drawbacks. Harklau, for example, has cautioned against expanding the definition too much, recognizing "the tendency to reify the term" in ways that essentialized students as "perpetual foreigners" who are "in need of remediation" (Matsuda et al., 2003, pp. 155–156). Schwartz (2004) has also pointed out that the term may have been "overused and its meaning has been diluted so that it no longer serves to be very useful in identifying, describing, and placing such students" (p. 43). In the process of expanding its definition, the term began to replace other terms that had been used in referring to diverse yet overlapping categories of students. Harklau et al. (1999b) were clearly aware of the existence of various and sometimes conflicting terms, as they wrote:

> The fact that authors [of chapters in the volume] differ on something so fundamental as a name for U.S.-educated English language learners shows just how difficult it is to fit these students into current ways of categorizing linguistically diverse college writers—ESL, developmental, regular (and by implication, how problematic those categories are).
>
> (p. 4)

Yet, by putting those contending terms into a single umbrella category, generation 1.5 *replaced*—rather than *consolidated*—them, imposing a newly constructed reality over existing, disparate realities. In effect, the term may have disconnected the current discussion from preceding conversations, making it seem as though the issues surrounding resident ESL students had not been addressed previously—or worse yet, that these students did not have a significant presence in higher education until the last decade of the twentieth century.

From the historical perspective, one of the major problems of the term is that it served as what Kenneth Burke (1966) has called a *terministic screen*. As he explained:

> *many of the "observations" are but implications of the particular terminology in terms of which the observations are made.* In brief, much that we take as observation about "reality" may be but the spinning out of possibilities implicit in our particular choice of terms.
>
> (p. 46; italics in the original)

That is, it is sometimes supposed that generation 1.5 students did not have a significant presence before the late 1990s because the strong illumination generated by the term has also blinded many college TESOL specialists from seeing what came before it. Practically speaking, new researchers would now search the database (or the web) with the keyword "generation 1.5" but they may leave out many of the categories that the term had replaced. It is true that *generation 1.5 students* did not exist in the literature; instead, they were variously referred to as *immigrant students* (Slager, 1956; Williams, 1995), *bilingual minority students* (Valdés, 1992), and more recently, *ear learners* (Reid, 1998). Or they were simply referred to as ESL students without a clear distinction from international ESL students. The irony is that the very term that has called attention to resident ESL students may have contributed to the collective amnesia among college TESOL specialists about the historical presence of those students as well as the professional discussion about this population.

A closely related problem is the imprecise nature of the term, which is a metaphorical borrowing from the immigration narrative. The notion of "1.5 generation" is based on the immigrant narrative of the mid-twentieth century, when the stigmatization of non-English languages—especially Asian languages—created a linguistic generation gap. In this narrative, which is itself an imprecise generalization, the first generation immigrants (*Issei*, to use the term used by the Japanese American community) are citizens of other countries who immigrated into the United States as adults. Because most of them did not begin to learn English until later in their lives, the narrative goes, they were often not proficient in English. The second generation immigrants (*Nisei*), children of the first generation immigrants, are those who were born in the United States, although in popular usage, the term sometimes refers to children who came to the United States early in their lives with their *Issei* parents. They were often functional bilinguals because they grew up speaking their parents' language as well as English. The third generation immigrants (*Sansei*) are U.S.-born grandchildren of the first generation immigrants who grew up speaking mostly English.

The term "1.5 generation" is meant to capture, albeit crudely, the linguistic characteristics of recent immigrant children whose linguistic profile falls somewhere between those of the first and second generation immigrants. The use of the term "generation 1.5", then, is best understood as metaphorical—it is not to be taken too literally. It is a functional category that does not refer to a precisely defined group of students. The awareness of the imprecise nature of the metaphor seems to be reflected in derivative terms such as generation 1.25 and 1.75. In fact, the whole notion of "generation" in referring to immigrants and their linguistic profile is inaccurate, since there are many first generation immigrants who are highly proficient in English. The "first generation" immigrants may also have brought with them their parents—who would then have to be called *generation 0* or *0.5*.

The imprecise nature of the term has also created much confusion about the very population it was designed to describe—it has allowed college TESOL specialists to talk to one another as if they are talking about the same issue while they may actually be thinking of completely different types of students. The problem becomes apparent when the term is used in contrast to other related terms. For example, here are some of the contrasts that can be found in published and unpublished articles, conference themes, and presentation titles, and even job ads for faculty positions:

"ESL and Generation 1.5"
"Generation 1.5 and immigrant"
"ESL, Generation 1.5, and international students"
"Generation 1.5 and international students."

Many of these categories are false distinctions; they are not mutually exclusive. The contrast between ESL and generation 1.5 is clearly problematic—generation 1.5 students are by definition non-native English speakers, but they are excluded from the category of ESL. This distinction has long been used as a justification for excluding resident ESL students from ESL programs that have traditionally been designed for international ESL students. "Generation 1.5 and immigrant" is also highly problematic for obvious reasons; generation 1.5 students, at least in Harklau et al.'s original usage, are primarily—though not exclusively—immigrant students. The confusion is especially evident in the third example, "ESL, Generation 1.5 and international students," which comes from a recent job ad for a tenure-track faculty position.

The problem of the binary between generation 1.5 and international students in the last example may be less obvious, but the differing criteria implicit in these terms create a problem of definition. Although the category of international student is based on the students' visa status and can be defined unambiguously, generation 1.5, taken as a functional category based on the characteristics of students, is not mutually exclusive with international students. For example, there are some international visa students in U.S. higher education who went through several years of high school education in the United States. Some may have come to the United States with their parents who were sent by their employers to branch offices located in the U.S. Others may have come to the United States as high school exchange students and, after a few years of high school education, went on to pursue higher education in the States—as was the case with one of the co-authors of this chapter. While the number of students in this category might be relatively small, that does not mean their presence and needs can be ignored.

We do not mean to argue that no ambiguity should be tolerated—we realize that ambiguity and redundancy are *sine qua non* of natural languages. Such ambiguity, however, is not appropriate for a technical term used in professional communication. What is especially problematic with the term generation 1.5 is that the imprecise definition of the term has, on the one hand, masked the historical presence of these students and efforts to address their needs while, on the other hand, creating confusion about the population of students that it is trying to describe. Schwartz (2004) has sought to overcome this problem in her study by using the term "cross-over" students in referring to the specific subset of resident ESL students in mainstream composition courses. The distinction based on immigration status can be delineated more precisely by the terms *resident* and *international*, although other aspects of student characteristics also need to be discussed (see Matsuda, 2008, for parallel continua of learner characteristics).

The ESL or multilingual student population—and we include both resident and international students in this category—is far more complex and diverse than a single, imprecise term can capture. As Raimes (1991) cautioned about the term ESL students, the term generation 1.5, if it were to be used at all, also needs to be used in ways that do not mask the diversity of students that it represents. In order to understand fully the student population under consideration, the characteristics of the students need to be described explicitly and multi-dimensionally each and every time.

Acknowledgments

We are grateful to the Graduate School of International Development, Nagoya University, whose generous support in the form of a visiting researcher position enabled us to complete the revision of this chapter.

Notes

1. In this chapter, we use the term *college TESOL* (not to be confused with the journal *College ESL*) in referring to a segment of the TESOL profession—to distinguish it from the discussion of ESL students taking place in other disciplinary contexts, such as the K-12 TESOL, bilingual education, and composition studies.
2. See Matsuda, 2006, for a detailed account of the historical presence of international students in U.S. higher education.
3. For detailed descriptions of changes in U.S. higher education in the nineteenth century, see: Connors (1997); Brereton (1995); Kitzhaber (1953/1990).
4. For a detailed discussion of the status of ESL issues in the *Journal of Basic Writing*, see Matsuda (2003).

References

Allen, H.B. (1967). Challenge to the profession. *TESOL Quarterly, 1*(2), 3–9.
Allen, H.B. (1973). English as a second language. In T.A. Sebeok (Ed.), *Current trends in linguistics: Linguistics in north America, Vol. 10* (pp. 295–320). The Hague, the Netherlands: Mouton.
Atkinson, D. & Ramanathan, V. (1995). Cultures of writing: An ethnographic comparison of L1 and L2 university writing/language programs. *TESOL Quarterly, 29*(3), 539–568.
Benesch, S. (1993). ESL, ideology, and the politics of pragmatism. *TESOL Quarterly, 27*(4), 705–717.
Benesch, S. (2001). Critical pragmatism: A politics of L2 composition. In T. Silva & P.K. Matsuda (Eds.), *On second language writing* (pp. 161–172). Mahwah, NJ: Lawrence Erlbaum Associates.
Benson, B., Deming, M.P., Denzer, D., & Valeri-Gold, M. (1992). A combined basic writing/English as a second language class: Melting pot or mishmash? *Journal of Basic Writing, 11*(1), 58–74.
Braine, G. (1996). ESL students in first-year writing courses: ESL vs. mainstream classes. *Journal of Second Language Writing, 5*(2), 91–107.
Brereton, J.C. (1995). *The origin of composition studies in the American college, 1875–1925: A documentary history*. Pittsburgh, PA: University of Pittsburgh Press.
Brooks, G. (1991). Introduction. *College ESL, 1*(1), i–ii.
Burke, K. (1935). *Permanence and change*. New York: New Republic.
Burke, K. (1966). *Language as symbolic action*. Berkeley: University of California Press.
Carpenter, C. & Hunter, J. (1981). Functional exercises: Improving overall coherence in ESL writing. *TESOL Quarterly, 15*(4), 425–434.
City University of New York. (1995). *Immigration/migration and the CUNY student of the future*. New York: City University of New York.
College Entrance Examination Board. (1999, September). *Measuring the SAT: The SAT does something different from achievement tests*. Retrieved February 1, 2000, from www.collegeboard.org/index_this/sat/html/counselors/measure/measuree.html.
Connors, R.J. (1997). *Composition-rhetoric: Backgrounds, theory, and pedagogy*. Pittsburgh, PA: University of Pittsburgh Press.

Costello, J. (1990). Promoting literacy through literature: Reading and writing in ESL composition. *Journal of Basic Writing, 9*(1), 20–30.

Davidson, D.M. (1977). Sentence combining in an ESL writing program. *Journal of Basic Writing, 1*(3), 49–62.

Harklau, L. (1998). Newcomers in U.S. higher education. *Educational Policy, 12*(6), 634–658.

Harklau, L., Losey, K.M., & Siegal, M. (Eds.) (1999a). *Generation 1.5 meets college composition: Issues in the teaching of writing to U.S.-educated learners of ESL.* Mahwah, NJ: Lawrence Erlbaum Associates.

Harklau, L., Siegal, M., & Losey, K.M. (1999b). Linguistically diverse students and college writing: What is equitable and appropriate? In L. Harklau, K.M. Losey, & M. Siegal (Eds.), *Generation 1.5 meets college composition: Issues in the teaching of writing to U.S.-educated learners of ESL* (pp. 1–14). Mahwah, NJ: Lawrence Erlbaum Associates.

Herendeen, W. (1986). Of tricksters and dilemmas in ESL writing classes: An epistolary account. *Journal of Basic Writing, 5*(2), 49–58.

Jie, G. & Lederman, M.J. (1988). Instruction and assessment of writing in China: The national unified entrance examination for institutions of higher education. *Journal of Basic Writing, 7*(1), 47–60.

Johns, A.M. (1986). The ESL student and the revision process: Some insights from schema theory. *Journal of Basic Writing, 5*(2), 70–80.

Johns, A.M. (1991). Interpreting an English competency examination: The frustrations of an ESL science student. *Written Communication, 8*(1), 379–401.

Kandel, I.L. (1945). *United States activities in international cultural relations.* Washington, DC: American Council on Education.

Kiester, E. (1994). Uncle Sam wants you … to go to college. *Smithsonian, 25*(8), 128–139.

Kitzhaber, A.R. (1990). *Rhetoric in American colleges, 1850–1900.* Dallas, TX: Southern Methodist University Press. (Original unpublished dissertation 1953.)

Kroll, B. (1990). The rhetoric/syntax split: designing a curriculum for ESL students. *Journal of Basic Writing, 9*(1), 40–55.

Lay, N.D.S. (1975). Chinese language interference in written English. *Journal of Basic Writing, 1*(1), 50–61.

Lay, N. (1992). Learning from natural language labs. *Journal of Basic Writing, 11*(2), 74–81.

Leki, I. (1992). *Understanding ESL writers.* Portsmouth, NH: Boynton.

Liebman, J. (1988). Contrastive rhetoric: Students as ethnographers. *Journal of Basic Writing, 7*(2), 6–27.

Matsuda, P.K. (1998). Situating ESL writing in a cross-disciplinary context. *Written Communication, 15*(1), 99–121.

Matsuda, P.K. (1999). Composition studies and ESL writing: A disciplinary division of labor. *College Composition and Communication, 50*(4), 699–721.

Matsuda, P.K. (2003). Basic writing and second language writers: Toward an inclusive definition. *Journal of Basic Writing, 22*(2), 67–89.

Matsuda, P.K. (2006). The myth of linguistic homogeneity in U.S. college composition. *College English, 68*(6), 637–651.

Matsuda, P.K. (2008). Myth: International and U.S. resident ESL writers cannot be taught in the same class. In J.M. Reid (Ed.), *Writing myths: Applying second language research to classroom technique* (pp. 159–176). Ann Arbor: University of Michigan Press.

Matsuda, P.K., Canagarajah, A.S., Harklau, L., Hyland, K., & Warschauer, M. (2003). Changing currents in second language writing research: A colloquium. *Journal of Second Language Writing, 12*(2), 151–179.

Morley, J., Robinett, B.W., Selinker, L., & Woods, D. (1984). ESL theory and the Fries legacy. *JALT Journal, 6*(2), 171–207.

Otuya, E. (1994). The foreign-born population of the 1990s: A summary profile. *Research Briefs, 5*(6), 1–10.

Patthey-Chavez, G.G. & Gergen, C. (1992). Culture as an instructional resource in the multiethnic composition classroom. *Journal of Basic Writing, 11*(1), 75–96.

Perkins, K. & Brutten, S. (1990). Writing: A holistic or atomistic entity. *Journal of Basic Writing, 9*(1), 75–84.

Preto-Bay, A.M. & Hansen, K. (2006). Preparing for the tipping point: Designing writing programs to meet the needs of the changing population. *WPA: Writing Program Administration, 30*(1/2), 37–57.

Purves, A.C. (1986). Rhetorical communities, the international student, and basic writing. *Journal of Basic Writing, 5*(1), 38–51.

Raimes, A. (1991). Out of the woods: Emerging traditions in the teaching of writing. *TESOL Quarterly, 25*(3), 407–430.

Reid, J. (1998). "Eye" learners and "ear" learners: Identifying the language needs of international student and U.S. resident writers. In P. Byrd & J.M. Reid, *Grammar in the composition classroom: Essays on teaching ESL for college-bound students* (pp. 3–17). New York: Heinle & Heinle.

Reid, J.M. (1993). *Teaching ESL Writing.* Englewood Cliffs, NJ: Regents/Prentice Hall.

Rizzo, B. & Villafane, S. (1975). Spanish language influences on written English. *Journal of Basic Writing, 1*(1), 62–71.

Rumbaut, R.G. & Ima, K. (1988). *The adaptation of Southeast Asian refugee youth: A comparative study.* (Final report to the Office of Resettlement.) San Diego, CA: San Diego State University. (ERIC Document Reproduction Service No. ED299372.)

Russell, D. (2002). *Writing in the academic disciplines: A curricular history* (2nd ed.). Carbondale: South Illinois University Press.

Sanborn, J. (1987). Obstacles and opportunities: Sentence combining in advanced ESL. *Journal of Basic Writing, 6*(2), 60–71.

Santos, T. (1992). Ideology in composition: L1 and ESL. *Journal of Second Language Writing, 1*(1), 1–15.

Schwartz, G.G. (2004). Coming to terms: Generation 1.5 students in mainstream composition. *Reading Matrix, 4*(3), 40–57.

Severino, C. (1993). The sociopolitical implications of response to second language and second dialect writing. *Journal of Second Language Writing, 2*(3), 181–201.

Slager, W. (1956). The foreign student and the immigrant: Their different problems as students of English. *Language Learning, 6*(3–4), 24–29.

Sternglass, M.S. (1989). The need for conceptualizing at all levels of writing instruction. *Journal of Basic Writing, 8*(2), 87–98.

Valdés, G. (1992). Bilingual minorities and language issues in writing: Toward professionwide response to a new challenge. *Written Communication, 9*(1), 85–136.

Williams, J. (1995). ESL composition program administration in the United States. *Journal of Second Language Writing, 4*(2), 157–179.

Yi, Y. (2007). Engaging literacy: A biliterate student's composing practices beyond school. *Journal of Second Language Writing, 16*(1), 23–39.

Yorio, C. (1989). The other side of the looking glass. *Journal of Basic Writing, 8*(1), 32–45.

Zamel, V. (1990). Through students' eyes: The experiences of three ESL writers. *Journal of Basic Writing, 9*(2), 83–98.

Zikopoulos, M. (Ed.) (1993). *Open doors 1992/93: Report on international educational exchange.* New York: Institute of International Education.

5 Interrogating In-Between-Ness

A Postmodern Perspective on Immigrant Students

Sarah Benesch   *College of Staten Island, City University of New York*

A critical perspective toward language policy emphasizes the importance of understanding how public debates about policies often have the effect of precluding alternatives, making state policies seem to be the natural condition of social systems … Moreover, a critical perspective aggressively investigates how language policies affect the lives of individuals and groups who often have little influence over the policymaking process.

(Tollefson, 2002, p. 4)

It may seem counterintuitive to begin a chapter in a collection devoted to generation 1.5 with a quote about language policy. The connection between the 1.5 metaphor and language policy, critical or otherwise, is not immediately obvious. Yet, I hope to show in this chapter that the generation 1.5 category, due to its modernist assumptions about languages and identities, may have the unintended effect of supporting exclusionary language and testing policies. That is, I will claim that language-assessment procedures adopted by universities in immigrant-receiving countries are often based on modernist beliefs, ones that ignore the linguistic complexity of the global diaspora. In doing so they may exclude immigrant students by constructing them as linguistically unprepared for university study, an assumption bolstered by the generation 1.5 metaphor. To counter this exclusionary tendency, I will propose a critical perspective, one informed by postmodern assumptions.

Briefly, modernist theories view languages as autonomous systems composed of constituent features that can be examined objectively, apart from context and users. Postmodern theories, on the other hand, reject the notion of languages as self-contained cognitive systems, assuming instead that language and identity are linked in fluid and unstable social relationships.

In this chapter, I will contrast modern and postmodern assumptions by interrogating the generation 1.5 trope of in-between-ness. In addition, I will propose alternative conceptualizations of immigrant students' identities and uses of language, hoping to encourage inclusionary policies. Before contrasting modern and postmodern theories, I next discuss the importance for English language teachers of theorizing language and identity.

English Language Teachers and Theory

English language teachers (ELTs) in postsecondary settings are often called upon to fulfill contradictory roles (Harklau, 2007). On the one hand, they may act as advocates for English language learners (ELLs), who are not always welcomed as full-fledged members of college communities, particularly if they are immigrants. Advocacy can include defending credit for ESL courses, securing proficiency retesting, and promoting tutoring, among other activities that support student retention.

On the other hand, ELTs are often positioned as gatekeepers who oversee reading and writing tests and courses. The tests serve not just as proficiency indicators but often as barriers to mainstream classes as well. The ESL courses, while intended to prepare students for the mainstream, may be perceived by students as impediments to earning credits toward degrees. Therefore, ELTs find themselves managing tests and courses that, while potentially helpful, also serve as gates.

How can the contradictions between advocacy and gatekeeping be reconciled, especially at a time when ELLs are precariously positioned as unprepared on many college campuses? How can ELTs make sense of their own varying positionings vis-à-vis educational institutions and students? One way is by carefully theorizing language and identity. Staking out clear theoretical positions allows ELTs to respond thoughtfully to policies that may be unfavorable to immigrant students. Conversely, leaving theoretical assumptions unexplored may lead to unintentional support for exclusionary policies, ones whose consequences may not have been intended. That is, according to Ricento and Hornberger (1996), "the discourse of schools, communities, and states help reinforce unstated beliefs so that teachers come to believe not only that what they are doing reflects explicit policies but that the policies are generally in the best interest of students" (p. 417).

To avoid the reinforcement of unfavorable policies, I propose more explicit theorizing of language and identity, first by critiquing modernist theories of language and then by presenting postmodern alternatives.

Modernist Theories of Language

The most popular introductory linguistics textbook, Fromkin and Rodman's *Introduction to Language*, now in its eighth edition, describes language as a set of discrete components, each building on the next:

> Speakers use a finite set of rules to produce and understand an infinite set of possible sentences. These rules comprise the grammar of the language and includes the sound system (the phonology), the structure of words (the morphology), how words may be combined into phrases and sentences (the syntax), the ways in which sounds and meanings are related (the semantics), and the words or lexicon.
>
> (Fromkin and Rodman, 1998, p. 27)

This and other linguistic textbooks treat phonetics, phonology, morphology, and so on, as constituents that together comprise language. Influenced by Chomsky, they treat syntax as the *sine qua non* of linguistics, the grammatical rules allowing native speakers to create novel sentences. Fromkin and Rodman (1998) also support the Chomskyan notion of a "universal grammar that is part of the human biologically endowed language facility" (p. 19). And with the assumption that universal grammar is a "scientific" concept, they believe that the "linguist's goal is to discover the 'laws of human language' as the physicist's goal is to discover the 'laws of the physical universe'" (p. 19).

Newmeyer (1986) applies the label "autonomous linguistics" to the study of language "apart from either the beliefs and values of the individual speakers of a language or the nature of the society in which the language is spoken" (pp. 5–6). He traces the origins of "autonomous linguistics" to comparative linguists of the nineteenth century who sought "a protolanguage for each language family." Comparative linguists attempted to "formulate the sound changes by which it descended into its various daughter tongues" (p. 19) through a study of "systematic correspondences in sound and meaning among the languages under investigation" (p. 18). In the twentieth century, according to Newmeyer, language-as-autonomous object became a more deeply entrenched construct with the acceptance of Saussure's distinction between *langue*, "the abstract system of structural relationships inherent in language, relationships that are held in common by all members of a speech community" (p. 32) and *parole*, "the individual act of speaking, which is never performed exactly the same way twice" (p. 32). *Langue* was embraced as the target of linguistic study while *parole* was set aside.

Language-as-autonomous object became an even-more deeply entrenched assumption with Chomsky's distinction between *competence* and *performance*, his version of *langue* and *parole*, as well as his *universal grammar* hypothesis. These concepts solidified linguists' study of language apart from its use and users:

> It should be clear that Chomsky did not challenge the idea that the grammar of a language can be characterized as an autonomous structural system. Far from it. By proposing a structural treatment of relations that hold between sentences (such as between *John threw the ball* and *the ball was thrown by John*), where most had believed that such treatment was not possible, his approach expanded the scope of autonomous linguistics.
>
> (Newmeyer, 1986, p. 71)

By claiming that theirs was the only scientific approach to language, Chomsky and other generative linguists were able to secure funding for their research and acceptance in academic departments. However, alongside this trend, in the 1960s and 1970s, sociologists and anthropologists with an interest in language-in-use began to study *performance*. Their goal was not to oppose or replace Chomsky's syntactic theory, but rather to complement it. To this end, they sought to discover the rules governing linguistic variation at the *surface level*, just as generative linguists sought syntactic rules at the *deep level*. Gumperz (1967), for example, described the work of "sociolinguists," as they began to call themselves, as the search for the rules of *linguistic interaction*:

> Linguistic interaction … is a process in which speakers take in clues from the outside environment and, by a culturally determined process of perception similar

to that which converts sounds into phonemes and meanings into words, arrive at appropriate behavioral strategies. These are, in turn, translated into verbal symbols.... Although this work is in its beginning stages, there are indications that persons behave in accordance with rules of social interaction which, like the rules of grammar, function below the level of consciousness. If this is the case, then linguistic and social categories are phenomena of the same order; and moving from statements of social constraints to grammatical rules thus represents a transformation from one level of abstraction to another within a single communicative system.

(p. 231)

Kress (2001) characterizes the work of Gumperz, Labov, and Hymes as *correlational sociolinguistics*, defined as an attempt to demonstrate that "certain forms of linguistic behavior can be shown to correlate quite clearly with certain aspects of social organization" (p. 33). For example, Hymes' and Gumperz's proposal for *communicative competence*, while going "well beyond the grammatical/syntactic competence proposed by Chomsky" (pp. 33–34), by hypothesizing a "close connection between language and the social," nonetheless "does so by leaving each as quite separate entities" (p. 34). It simply "invert[ed] the relation between the linguistic and the social ... mak[ing] the social prior" (p. 35).

Kress' critique of correlational sociolinguists' research is that though it assumed that "the social caused selections of different codes ... it did not reach into the organization of code: language remained a discrete autonomous system" (p. 35). Left out of this equation is the language users themselves; they are accorded no agency, no role in shaping language. Instead, language is viewed as a set of pre-existing codes acquired by speakers, who do not affect them. According to Kress, this view of the relationship between the social and linguistic is an "implausible theory" because it places form at the center while meaning is "marginal" (p. 37).

By contrast, in critical linguistics, which Kress claims is a "plausibly social view of language" (p. 37), speakers have agency, shaping "the cultural/linguistic resources available to them in their social environment and always within fields of power" (p. 37). That is, power is central to critical, or postmodern theories of language and "no part of linguistic action escapes its effects" (p. 35). The relationship between language and power is taken up next, in the discussion of postmodern theories of language.

Postmodernist Theories of Language

Postmodern discourse has retheorized the nature of language as a system of signs structured in the infinite play of difference, and in so doing has undermined the dominant positivist notion of language as either a permanent genetic code or simply a transparent medium for transmitting ideas and meaning.

(Aronowitz & Giroux, 1991, p. 75)

Postmodern theorists of language are concerned with shoring up the division between *langue* and *parole*, between *competence* and *performance*. Claiming that Saussure "massively narrowed the scope of linguistics" by disregarding everything but structure, including "history, politics, society, economics, culture" (Pennycook, 2004, p. 4), post-modernists aim to restore the social to linguistics, not as an add-on constituent, but as integral to its conceptualization. Opposing the proposition that *langue* "exists and subsists independently of its users" (Bourdieu, 1991, p. 44) and asserting that "[g]rammar defines meaning only very partially," Bourdieu calls for a recognition that "social heterogeneity is inherent in language" (p. 34). This recognition of social heterogeneity on the part of postmodernists requires a shift in attention from "uniformity" across languages to "variation" (Harris, 1990, p. 144) and ways that varieties, or discourses, are embraced or repressed in social contexts.

Postmodern theorists acknowledge variation and heterogeneity in a range of ways. However, all replace the notion of language-as-autonomous system with language as discourses shaped by social context. For example, Bourdieu (1991) theorizes language as discourses circulating in the "market" where they compete for social recognition. Opposing the modernist construction of *langue* as "a strictly linguistic competence, abstractly defined, ignoring everything that it owes to the social conditions of its production" (p. 38), he claims that:

> [t]he competence adequate to produce sentences that are likely to be understood may be quite inadequate to produce sentences that are likely to be *listened to*, likely to be recognized as *acceptable* in all the situations in which there is occasion to speak.
>
> (p. 55)

That is, according to Bourdieu, taking into account the "linguistic market" permits understanding how "[s]peakers lacking the legitimate competence are de facto excluded from the social domains in which this competence is required, or are condemned to silence" (p. 55).

Similarly, Rampton (1997) faults sociolinguistics for overlooking "diversity and variation" in the interest of "root[ing] out what it supposes to be orderliness and uniformity" (p. 330). Instead, he proposes examining relationships among competing discourses in a globalized world, focusing on "boundaries of inclusion and exclusion" (p. 330). More specifically, Rampton is concerned with ways that students negotiate relationships between standard varieties and diaspora vernaculars, claiming that "how well they do at school is itself very much dependent on how they manage the tension between school on the one hand, and a whole vernacular aesthetic on the other" (p. 332).

For his part, Pennycook (2004) proposes performativity, based on Austin's speech act theory and Butler's theory of performativity in gender studies, as a way to theorize relationships between language and identity. According to this theory, "language use is an act of identity that calls language into being" (p. 17). The focus of linguistic research from this perspective is "how we do things with words (and how words do things to us)" (p. 10), that is, both creativity and interpellation. According to Pennycook, the notion of performativity allows for "an anti-foundational view of language as an emergent property of social interaction and not a prior system tied to ethnicity, territory, birth, or nation" (p. 7).

Viewed together, the theories of Bourdieu, Rampton, and Pennycook point to the need to address the postmodern condition of "fragmentation, contingency, marginality, transition, indeterminacy, ambivalence, and hybridity" (Rampton, 1997, p. 330) through a study of language and power. Questions guiding postmodern investigations of language might include: How do students navigate the discourses of home, school, and peers? How do students perform their identities through a variety of discourses? When do they feel entitled to speak and when are they silenced? How do classroom discourses and assessment procedures encourage students to speak or discourage them from speaking?

These questions require a re-imagining of language users, not as those who must acquire a fixed system, one tied to a particular place and time, but, rather as speakers who are simultaneously interpellated by dominant discourses and creative inventors of newly formed discourses born of the postmodern diaspora.

In-Between-Ness as a Modernist Construct

The trope of "in-between-ness" in the generation 1.5 literature is illustrated in the following quote:

> Rising immigration rates across the United States have introduced a new term to the educational lexicon, Generation 1.5. This generation of students is sandwiched between their parents, who immigrated as adults, and their younger siblings, who were born here. Caught between two cultures and two languages, these students face unique academic challenges.
>
> (www.collegeboard.com/about/association/regional/middle/forum2007/
> pop61.html)

At first reading, the 1.5 construct seems to take the social into account. It links demographic and linguistic characteristics causally, pointing to possible effects of migration on the language use of those who left their countries of origin prior to adulthood. However, by mapping a modernist understanding of language onto the contemporary global diaspora, the 1.5 metaphor creates a mismatch. Adopting the modernist expectation that language users should develop proficiency in discrete languages tied to particular places, proponents of the 1.5 position express concern when these criteria are not met, claiming that 1.5 students "face unique challenges." Solutions to these "challenges" are offered, ranging from additional testing to special courses to tutoring, solutions that can serve to exclude students from mainstream courses (Benesch, 2008).

Rather than assuming that students have failed to acquire the sanctioned variety of L2, it may be more productive to look at social institutions and see what steps they could take to acknowledge changing demographics. That is, instead of claiming that students have neither L1 nor L2, that they are in-between languages and cultures, ELTs might instead explore ways to address the complexities of the global diaspora. Rejecting the language-as-autonomous system construct, one that ties a mythical standard language to place, they might examine the discourses of immigrant students, as Reyes (2007) has done. Her study of Southeast Asian teenagers in Philadelphia revealed that they spoke "a hybrid variety that frequently incorporated features of AAVE as well as features of Vietnamese, Khmer (Cambodian), Lao, or other home languages" (p. 64). Rather than viewing their discourses as non-standard or unacceptable, she analyzed ways that "Asian American teens constructed and used African American slang as an interactional resource to position themselves and each other relative to stereotypes of African Americans" (p. 65). Taking agency into account, she observed that they were performing emergent identities through a variety of linguistic resources. She discovered "how teens specified relationships between language, race, age, region, and class" (p. 65) through various discourses.

Harris, Leung, and Rampton (2002) warn that "if policy on standard English continues to embrace a primarily negative response to vernacular Englishes, treating them as phenomena to be eradicated and avoided ... it looks destined for continued resistance and failure" (pp. 44–45). That is, if English language teachers subscribe to modernist understandings of language as "grandiose abstract systems which the participants ought to be using in some ideal world" (Harris, 1990, p. 148), they participate in excluding diasporic students. Instead, they might attend to the claim "that marginality is actually a crucial experience" (Rampton, 1997, p. 330) for these students, and is therefore worth exploring rather than bemoaning.

Conclusion

Returning to the twin issues of language policy and the conflicting roles of English language teachers, what policies are engendered when the 1.5 metaphor is evoked? In this chapter, I have argued that the 1.5 concept, with its modernist assumptions about languages as autonomous systems supports, albeit unwittingly, assessment policies that demand standard English proficiency at a time of massive migration and linguistic flux. In place of that demand, I second Harris, Leung, and Rampton's (2002) warning about the consequences of treating vernacular Englishes "as phenomena to be eradicated and avoided." Maintaining this stance will indeed lead to "continued resistance and failure" (pp. 44–45) on the part of diasporic students who are silenced and excluded by this position.

I conclude this chapter by offering some implications for research of the 1.5 positioning of students, implications that take up Bhabha's (1994) challenge to address the "right of difference in equality" (p. xvii):

> If as Bucholtz and Hall claim, "identity is the social positioning of self and other" (p. 586), ELTs might consider the effects on their own positionings of the labels they apply to students. In other words, if they call students 1.5, what are they calling themselves? In terms of power, which groups are privileged by this label and how does that privileging manifest itself both in and out of the classroom?
>
> What are the vernacular Englishes spoken by diasporic students enrolled in high schools and colleges in immigrant-receiving countries? How can ELTs find support to study these vernaculars more extensively?
>
> In what ways are current language assessment policies driven by modernist assumptions? What might be alternative assessment procedures that could take students' varying discourses into account?

Future research on immigrant students' discourses might lead to postmodern understandings replacing modernist ones in the field of English language teaching.

This might, in turn, lead to language policies and assessment practices honoring their linguistic resources.

References

Arononowitz, S. & Giroux, H.A. (1991). *Postmodern education: Politics, culture & social criticism.* Minneapolis: University of Minnesota Press.

Benesch, S. (2008). "Generation 1.5" and its discourses of partiality: A critical analysis. *Journal of Language, Identity, and Education, 7*(3–4), 294–311.

Bhabha, H.K. (1994). *The location of culture.* London: Routledge.

Bourdieu, P. (1991). *Language and symbolic power.* Cambridge, UK: Polity Press.

Bucholtz, M. & Hall, K. (2005). Identity and interaction: A sociocultural linguistic approach. *Discourse Studies 7*(4–5), 585–612.

Fromkin, V. & Rodman, R. (1998). *An Introduction to language* (6th ed.). Fort Worth, TX: Harcourt Brace.

Gumperz, J.J. (1967). Supplement: Language and communication. *Annals of the American Academy of Political and Social Sciences, 373*, 219–231.

Harklau, L. (2007). Dilemmas in teaching college composition to "generation 1.5" students. Keynote presented at "Teaching, Languages, and the CUNY Student," John Jay College, March 2, 2007.

Harris, R. (1990). Communication and language. In N. Love (Ed.), *The foundations of linguistic theory: Selected writings of Roy Harris* (pp. 136–150). London: Routledge.

Harris, R., Leung, C., & Rampton, B. (2002). Globalization, diaspora, and language education in England. In D. Block & D. Cameron (Eds.), *Globalization and language teaching* (pp. 29–46). London: Routledge.

Kress, G. (2001). From Saussure to critical sociolinguistics: The turn towards a social view of language. In M. Whetherall, S. Taylor, & S.J. Yates (Eds.), *Discourse theory and practice: A reader* (pp. 29–38). London: Sage.

Newmeyer, F.J. (1986). *The politics of linguistics.* Chicago, IL: University of Chicago Press.

Pennycook, A. (2004). Performativity and language studies. *Critical Inquiry in Language Studies, 1*(2), 1–19.

Rampton, B. (1997) Second language research in late modernity: A response to Firth and Wagner. *The Modern Language Journal, 81*(iii), 329–333.

Reyes, A. (2007). *Language, identity, and stereotype among Southeast Asian American youth: The other Asian.* Mahwah, NJ: Lawrence Erlbaum Associates.

Ricento, T. & Hornberger, N. (1996). Unpeeling the onion: Language planning and policy and the ELT professional. *TESOL Quarterly 30*(3), 401–427.

Tollefson, J.W. (2002). Introduction: Critical issues in educational language policy. In J.W. Tollefson (Ed.), *Language policies in education: Critical issues* (pp. 3–15). Mahwah, NJ: Lawrence Erlbaum Associates.

Part II
Student Characteristics and Schooling Paths

6 High School Academic Literacy Instruction and the Transition to College Writing

Harriett Allison University of Georgia

In 1998, more than 90% of the ESL students at the southeastern U.S. community college where I taught had completed high school outside the U.S.; within 3 years, the college's ESL enrollment had grown from 16 to 160 students, almost 90% of whom were U.S.-educated English learners (ELs). Like many other college ESL instructors, my graduate TESL (Teaching English as a Second Language) program had focused on pedagogy for adult ELs educated outside the U.S., but by 2001 my classes had many more EL students who had graduated from area high schools and whose learner characteristics differed in significant ways from those I was accustomed to teaching. Although many of the newer students "sounded American" and were comparatively better acquainted with U.S. culture than their international classmates, their literacy skills were markedly different and in many ways less well-developed and sophisticated. Simultaneously, their writing and reading practices, while superficially resembling those of their English-only peers, revealed second language issues related to academic vocabulary and writing/reading fluency. These observations raised pedagogical questions about how and why these ELs were unique, which led to my wondering what their high school literacy experiences and preparation had been. However, searching for such information in academic sources was not productive, for little research exists on the acquisition of academic writing and reading skills of the group frequently referred to as generation 1.5 ELs, and even less examines their experiences as they negotiate the transition from secondary school to college (Harklau, 2004). Additionally, much of the available research has been done in settings where ELs have constituted a significant presence for longer periods of time (2004), and may not address situations in which generation 1.5 ELs are newcomers in school systems accustomed to teaching English-only students. To learn more about generation 1.5 ELs' pre-college literacy preparation, I designed a study that examines the following questions:

- What is the experience of selected generation 1.5 ELs in their transition from high school to college literacy tasks?
- How do these selected EL students describe and interpret their secondary and tertiary writing and reading tasks?

Background

Before the mid-1990s, most southeastern U.S. public school and university systems had little reason to concern themselves with the distinctive learning characteristics of generation 1.5 English language learners. Unlike states such as Florida, New York, and California, with a longer history of working with significant numbers of immigrant ELs, southeastern U.S. schools and colleges have only recently begun to see a rise in the immigrant student population. As immigrant enrollment grew, K-12 schools and community colleges have begun to develop pedagogy and support for EL learners. On the college level each institution has designed its own ESL program as needed with new EL enrollments; on the K-12 level, general program requirements are decided at the state level with implementation affected by variability at the school and district level. As a result, generation 1.5 EL students in the Southeast have experienced variable learning environments before they arrive in college classrooms. How do the pre-college literacy backgrounds and practices of these students match with the kind of literacy work they will do in college? The generation 1.5 students discussed here are U.S.-educated English learners, graduates of U.S. high schools who are matriculating in U.S. colleges, often at 2-year schools. While they may or may not have taken ESOL classes in high school, they are still learning academic English and the discourse practices of higher education when they matriculate.

College Literacy Demands

Before considering how generation 1.5 ELs are situated in regard to college writing, it is helpful to ask what literacy research tells us about writing and reading demands of postsecondary education. Approached in this order—first, analysis of college literacy demands followed by descriptions of representative high school literacy practices—readers can observe the accord, or lack thereof, between expectations in/across the two settings.

Writing and reading are intertwined in college literacy tasks (Carson, Chase, Gibson, & Hargrove, 1992b; Chase & Gibson, 1994) and when used together, they facilitate integration and learning of course concepts (Stahl, 2006). Moreover, they are critical means for learning and performing in postsecondary education—as sources of information, ways of processing information for coherent learning, and modes for presenting confirmation of academic progress. Of equal importance, as students undertake college coursework, writing and reading used integrally enable and enhance higher levels of learning and thinking (e.g., Wittrock & Alesandrini, 1990). The extent to which students can manipulate and exploit academic literacy determines in large part how successful their academic efforts will be, no matter whether they are enrolled in postsecondary institutions that emphasize research or community colleges (Hirvela, 2004). Research shows that writing and reading are not restricted to the composition classroom but occur in a purposeful relationship across the curriculum. In most college courses, literacy tasks range from note-taking a single day's lecture to visually reviewing a semester's collection of lecture and text notes to writing responses on final exams and writing papers based on using researchable sources. Largely at the postsecondary level, the expectation is that students will assemble and maintain content from lectures and printed sources, most commonly through written notes, and then re-construct and re-present this information through written course assessments.

Although writing and reading are frequently taught as separate skills—often without explicit acknowledgment or examination of their interrelationship (Carson & Leki, 1993; Hirvela, 2004)—in the real world of college, they are interwoven through-out course tasks and learning (Carson, 2001; Carson, Chase, & Gibson, 1992a; Carson et al., 1992b; Chase & Gibson, 1994). Research analyzing literacy demands of typical undergraduate curricula highlight the following factors:

- coursework in the introductory core curriculum, with the exceptions of composi-tion and literature classes, require students to read far more than they need to write (Carson et al., 1992a);
- as writing and reading requirements are not the same across disciplines, students make choices about what they need to write and read based on their interpreta-tions of instructor-generated course assessments (1992a);
- literacy tasks include reading from multiple texts and other sources, listening to and generating notes based on class lectures, integrating lecture notes with read-ings done before and after class, reading quiz and exam text, and writing to demonstrate knowledge and comprehension (Carson, 2001; Carson et al., 1992b).

Thus, students' interpretations of the types of responses and levels of thinking embed-ded in course assessments determine what and how they write, read, and study in spe-cific classes (cf., Alexander, 2005; Pugh, Pawan, & Antommarchi, 2000; Stahl, 2006). To be successful in college literacy tasks, the student must develop the ability to deter-mine how and when to read, and what and how to write about course content from print sources and lectures.

Perhaps the clearest and most influential development affecting college literacy tasks since Carson et al. (1992a) has been the burgeoning omnipresence of digital technology in education. Before students begin registering, many colleges routinely provide them with e-mail accounts through which important notices and other information is delivered, thus demonstrating the college's assumption that matriculated students will have online access and be able to function in a virtual environment.

Although writing and reading requirements of undergraduate curricula have not changed appreciably from what they were before the introduction of computers to higher education, the increasing role of digital technology, especially online resources, has intro-duced additional literacy dimensions and issues, especially for ELs (Pugh et al., 2000; Stahl, 2006). One source of digital technology's impact is the volume of content available through online resources, such that attending to and organizing the available information becomes a mammoth task in itself (Hirvela, 2004); now, the Internet's seemingly never-ending flow of information must be integrated with more traditional text sources (Grabe & Stoller, 2002; Hirvela, 2004; Hynd-Shanahan, Holschuh, & Hubbard, 2004). Con-sequently, as students now have ready access to a plethora of information, arbitrarily offered, they have an even greater need of organization, evaluation, and selection skills to determine the reliability of what they read (Lanham, 1994); furthermore, they must be able to integrate that content in academically appropriate ways as they compose reports, essays, quizzes and exam responses, and term papers (Hirvela, 2004).

Generation 1.5 ELs may be even more challenged in managing content from online sources than their English-only classmates in part because of unfamiliar vocabulary and culturally dependent references (2004). In addition, they need adequate language and discourse skills to comprehend and register the author's intent (Harklau, 2004); otherwise, the resources become impediments, not enhancements, to learning.

Another example of digital technology's impact in education is the advent of course enhancement DVDs developed and distributed by textbook publishers. These DVDs provide PowerPoint lectures for middle and high school teachers and college instructors to use with course texts. Along with teacher- and professor-generated notes made available online for downloading and printing, these publisher-produced lessons can influence not only how and what students read and write but also how they study.

Additional developments affecting student literacy activities and learning—in this instance non-digital—are changes in textbook formats that present content in a pre-annotated manner, thereby making it less likely that students will analyze text as they read and make notation of their conclusions. Items such as key terms and definitions appear in the margins, along with important dates and events. As the need for students to analyze the text they read declines, so do activities that can help them process and build their understanding (J.P. Holschuh, personal communication, February 7, 2006). Although little, if any, research investigating possible effects of these text modifications is available, it seems reasonable that having discrete information called out from the body of a text implicitly influences students to emphasize memorization tasks over concept development.

High School Literacy Experiences of Selected Generation 1.5 ELs

With this account of college literacy tasks, what have been generation 1.5 ELs' high school literacy practices and how well do they correspond with the writing and reading demands of college? I have collected data from an ongoing multiple-case study that describes the literacy experiences of selected ELs as they move from high school to college (Allison, 2007). Although the study focuses on reading practices and developed understandings of generation 1.5 ELs as they transition from secondary to tertiary settings, it also includes description and discussion of related writing tasks.

Study Design

Study Sites

The high school and college sites selected for this study are in a county in a southern state that had, until the 1990s, a relatively local, homogeneous student population with few if any minority language, English language learners. In the target public school systems, the minority language population has increased dramatically over the last 10 years, with some elementary schools made up of 95%+ enrollees whose home language is not English and one high school in which one-third of the students speak English as a second or third language. Both high school and college sites include students who have studied both English and regular course curricula in systems that were in the process of developing pedagogy and practices for ELs.

Participants

The data presented here come from responses of second semester senior students at the target high schools who are still in the process of acquiring academic English language skills and who intended to matriculate to a postsecondary institution in the fall. The participants were located by querying ESOL teachers at area high school sites with minority language students to identify eight to ten students who meet the criteria just described. Of the final eight participants of the high school phase, four matriculated in the fall, one at an urban university and three at a local community college. However, responses from all eight secondary school participants are included in the following discussion. Seven of the participants speak Spanish at home, while the eighth participant's home language is Chinese. Course levels, or tracks, of the participants varied according to individual schools, with five students who attended three different high schools enrolled primarily in mainstream classes (90%), and three students at another high school enrolled in a combination of Advance Placement, honors, mainstream, and ESOL-sheltered language arts coursework.

Findings

In-class Reading

In a number of social studies and science courses, assigned readings were PowerPoint slides, overheads, worksheets, quizzes, tests, text glossaries, and sometimes course textbooks. In place of students reading and synthesizing course text material, all study participants described a number of classes in which their teachers used ancillary DVDs to deliver PowerPoint lectures that are condensations of book content. In addition, these readings were predominately brief, decontextualized phrases, with some full sentences, emphasizing knowledge identification; in contrast, college assignments are primarily extended, connected passages from multiple sources emphasizing application, analysis, or evaluation. Typically, students were instructed to copy text from the PowerPoint slides verbatim as the teacher read what was on the screen. After the PowerPoint lectures, students read and completed worksheets, using the information they had copied from the slides. When study participants were asked if they *ever* read from the course text, all replied that if they couldn't find the answers in their notes, they sometimes "looked in the book." Three participants attending different schools made comments almost identical to the following:

> The teacher gives us the PowerPoints so we won't have to read all that in the book. All we need to know for the test is in the PowerPoint. We copy down the Power-Points from the screen and fill out the worksheets. The tests are like the questions on the worksheet.

One student, Jia, evaluated these PowerPoint-based lectures with these remarks: "His [a social studies teacher] PowerPoints are dumb, and he can't even read them. I think he get [*sic*] them from the teacher book. I hate them!" Although a course focus on textbook material is consistent with previous research on high school literacy practices (Carson et al., 1992a), such infrequent reading of the text itself is a recent development.

Quizzes and tests were directly related in content and form to the worksheets. These exercises usually consisted of matching, sentence completion, true–false, and multiple choice questions emphasizing knowledge and comprehension, with few items requiring application of course concepts. Furthermore, it appeared that teachers typically did not require students to respond to questions in the section labeled "Critical Thinking." On most of the worksheets reviewed, those activities were crossed out. Jia remarked that "You don't have to study or read the book if you do the worksheets because that's what's on the test." Other participants made similar observations about the direct relationship between worksheet content and tests. Elio said, "He makes his [worksheet] questions just like the test. You know what it's going to be."

Study participants also described the use of PowerPoint lectures in many of their science classes, along with remarks revealing a similar attitude in this subject area toward the unimportance of actually reading from books. Generally speaking, in both social studies and biology, course texts were used as reference sources for glossary—or as the students called them—"vocabulary tests" and for exercises such as answering questions at the ends of chapters. As Felicia commented, "She don't [sic] want us to have to read so much."

Classroom observations and teacher comments support these descriptions. The teachers interviewed said they provided outlines and summaries of text material that most closely matched the content of the mandatory state graduation and end-of-course standardized tests. According to one teacher participant,

> I give them the notes in a form they can copy down while I go over it verbally. If they don't understand, they can ask questions on the spot. The worksheets reinforce the lecture material, so they really don't have to study very much at all. There is a test every Friday, so they go over it again.

Clearly, these statements describe an increasing concern with standardized testing that plays out in teacher focus, pedagogical choices, and ultimately in the nature of literacy tasks in the classroom, all of which can adversely affect students' readiness for college literacy tasks.

In many language arts/literature classes, only the teachers read novels, short stories, poems, and essays aloud to the students, providing comments and attention prompts as they read. In the mainstream English courses observed during this study, readings were done in class under close direction from the teacher, but with an added variation. In an American Literature class, the day's lesson was *The Great Gatsby*. What was most interesting—and surprising—about the class was not the lesson on *Gatsby*; rather, it was that *the teacher* read, not the students. Copies of *Gatsby* were handed out and she began to read the assigned chapter to them, pausing from time to time to ask questions such as "What is happening here?" or "Do you recall who Nick is and why he is important?" Many—but not all—students were silently reading along with the teacher. After the class, when asked if this was a representative activity, the teacher's explanation was echoed by most of the teacher participants, "Only about 5–10% of the class will read the assignment if it's homework, so if I want them to understand the lesson and participate and be ready for the test, it has to be read in class." It should be noted that teachers in all disciplines observed did not read to their students. However, the practice of in-class reading of the content for the day's lesson appeared in other courses, with teachers typically directing students to read a sentence, paragraph, or section followed by a discussion or class activity.

Reading Outside Class

Students in language arts/literature, social studies, and science courses reported spending approximately 20–30 minutes per week on reading outside class. Sources cited first were worksheets and Internet sites, with textbooks mentioned infrequently. Unlike typical academic reading practices of college courses, as previously described, participants most frequently completed mainstream high school reading assignments at school in class under the teacher's close direction. Moreover, in each week the quantity of time participants read independently for high school assignments was 90% less than the time they will be expected to spend reading for college courses. Academic writing activities demonstrate a similar relationship in that secondary school teachers provided class time for participants to complete individual and group projects, essays, book reports, and other writing assignments; additionally, teachers were available for clarification of and consultation on tasks. Although college class activities include group work, for the most part matriculated students will complete writing assignments independently outside scheduled class time without immediate access to instructor responses.

Mechanical Writing and Reading Tasks

Writing tasks in many mainstream classes required students to follow assignment-specific rubrics and formats, and tended toward brief, short-answer responses; worksheets and rubrics directed students to locate and employ specific content in their written responses. Generally speaking, teachers gave detailed, specific instructions about what and how students should complete literacy tasks, leaving little need for them to exercise personal choice and creativity. In many of the observed social studies and science classes, writing activities consisted of copying PowerPoint slide content, filling in short-answer worksheets, answering discrete item quiz questions using content from worksheets, constructing project posters and reports, and completing glossary activities. Students were required to use teacher-generated rubrics for reports and poster activities. Mainstream language arts/literature writing included warm-up "sponge" activities and two- to three-page essays and projects/posters composed according to teacher-generated rubrics. In contrast, the literacy tasks college instructors assign provide far more general directions; thus, each person must make decisions about locating and selecting appropriate content, and then organizing it for submission.

Student Reading Strategies

Reading activities appeared to encourage students to use a single strategy: skimming for pre-selected content. For the most part, students skimmed assigned text from printed and online sources to locate specific information. There was no prompting of readers to "question" the text to develop an understanding of content and concepts, and text structure and its relation to meaning received little or no attention. Although from time to time teachers had students read a paragraph or page in class, participants reported that their most frequent reading task in social studies was looking through their notes (copied from PowerPoint lectures), and occasionally textbooks, to find specific, pre-identified information. They described this activity as "skimming to get the answers." When queried, none of them stated that they read their social studies texts to identify and connect concepts, or to locate and organize supporting information.

In addition to the typical skim-reading task, one participant described an activity called "Guided Reading" in which the class responded to worksheet prompts instructing them to refer to certain pages and locate main ideas and other text features, hence "guided reading." These activities could be interpreted as scaffolding; however, the scaffolding appeared to be a permanent fixture as the exercises did not lead to independent student text analysis. Moreover, students were not asked to complete the task without explicit directions to specific pages and paragraphs. Most of the writing activities in literature classes, and in other disciplines involving projects and reports using text, were similarly scaffolded in that students were instructed to complete teacher-provided rubrics. As one student commented, "I just fill out what the rubric says: 'Background,' 'Major Accomplishments,' you know, just find it online and put it in."

Uses of Internet Source Material

Generally speaking, participants made favorable comments about using online instruction and resources. One participant who had not passed a required language arts class was enrolled in an online, individually paced course called "Credit Recovery," so named because it allows students to retake failed courses for graduation credit. She commented that

> I like the Credit Recovery course because it is on the computer and I can repeat something as much as I want to. I read better when I can do it my way, so I try to do it like that when I can.

This student's perspective points to a positive effect of printed text for ELs' learning. Harklau (1999) notes that this emphasis on visual as opposed to spoken content presentation encourages learning and participation for EL students because they can access information at a rate and in a manner more conducive to individual comprehension than oral/aural content interaction. Other study participants queried made similar comments about the relative ease of print assignments compared to listening and speaking activities.

Students reported that they evaluated and selected online materials according to site design and content, and they infrequently cited sources, used reliability criteria, or concerned themselves with plagiarism issues. No participants questioned the reliability of the websites they found; if the "facts" were there and the site was easy to navigate, i.e., if it provided headings directing them to the information they needed, the reference was considered a good one. Only three students—all at one school, Hilltop—mentioned the issue of plagiarism and volunteered that their teachers were very strict about this. Students at other schools whose coursework included web material said they copy-pasted relevant information into their papers without attribution.

When using Internet sources, many participants reported scanning web pages for headings that directed them to rubric-required content or answers, and then skimming the section to locate teacher-prescribed information. Maria said,

> It's easy [to use the Internet as a reference] because I use Ask.com, and the web page on Marbury vs. Madison has headings like "Background" that gives the information we have to put in our reports. I just find the kinds of things we are supposed to have and I copy that into my slides. The teacher gives us a rubric and I fill it out.

Discussion

In sum, for these EL participants writing and reading exercises directly connected to their textbooks have become less important activities than they were for the students described in studies carried out 10 and 15 years ago (e.g., Carson et al., 1999a), and if anything, literacy tasks are more closely determined by what will be assessed on high stakes standardized tests. In addition, the text material these participants read was less connected and cohesive than previously described. Generally speaking, teachers spelled out specifically how students were to structure their writing assignments, exactly what content they should focus on, and how they were to engage in meaning-making. When they did read extended passages, the reading strategy used most often was skimming for specific information, with written responses taken directly from the text. Finally, although digital technology is an increasing presence in these high school classrooms, little if any awareness of appropriate Internet use was included in most mainstream literacy activities.

Hilltop High School, the Exception

Thus far, I have described themes in ELs' perceptions of their writing and reading tasks common to all four high schools. However, ELs at one of the four study sites, Hilltop High, clearly had opportunities and support not found at the other schools. As a result of test scores and other assessments, the institution had been designated as a school "In Need of Improvement." In addition, it has the highest drop-out rate and lowest socioeconomic status of the six high schools in the county. Despite what seemed to be disadvantages, the school actively encouraged students to read more than the other three. Although all the system's high schools are supposed to set aside time for individual, in-class reading each day, this was the only school where I observed it actually being done. The three participants from Hilltop talked about a school-wide requirement to begin every class with 10 minutes of silent reading. Students self-selected whatever they want to read, and the classroom teacher recorded their selection in the students' agendas. Manny read course-related material, while Tran read religious tracts from his church. Although this practice can be seen as a small, perhaps superficial, effort, it represented a striking difference from the attitude toward reading observed at the other schools.

I also found that Hilltop's writing activities were challenging for these ELs; for example, when I reviewed the assignments Manny had composed for his British Literature class, I discovered that the teacher encouraged students to grapple with difficult text (readings included *Beowulf* and Jane Austen) and then use that content in thoughtful essays. The instructor also had students revise their essays, working through a series of drafts, and most remarkably, he emphasized the importance of careful source attribution. In light of the somewhat cavalier attitude toward plagiarism I had observed in classes at other sites, this teacher's attitude, coupled with the rigor he demanded throughout the course, was noteworthy. It should be noted that one study participant in particular, Manny, responded to the challenge and wrote very thoughtful, concise essays of which he was rightfully proud.

This high school differs from the other three schools in additional, and for three study participants, important ways. Although two EL participants at other schools had taken honors classes (one had completed two courses; another had completed one), one of the students at Hilltop, Ramon, had finished two honors classes in the fall semester and was enrolled in two more in the spring: Chemistry and Human Anatomy and Physiology. What is even more remarkable is that he was simultaneously in ESOL Language Arts. Tran was enrolled in an AP writing course, and Manny had taken one AP and five honors classes, also while enrolled in ESOL Language Arts.

Finally, according to Ramon's descriptions of his American Government teacher, students at Hilltop are challenged more than at the other schools, and are not spoon-fed as much. "Mr. Carson is very tricky. You have to really pay attention and understand what you read in his class. It's not easy. You have to think." Classroom observations supported Ramon's assertion. During an American Government class devoted to test review, most of Mr. Carson's questions—addressed in a random order to individual students—called for application or analysis responses. This practice was not observed in any mainstream class at the other schools.

EL Academic Language Issues

When asked whether they encountered any problems reading in English, seven of the eight focus students said the primary challenge was vocabulary. After further discussion, it became clear they meant course-specific terminology, which was explicitly taught through worksheet exercises and use of text glossaries. When queried about new or unfamiliar words that weren't in the glossary, all replied that they did occasionally note them and look them up but only one student could recall an example, "allocate." Two students said, "When I see a word I don't know, I just ask the teacher and he/she tells me what it means." None of their teachers followed up with further work on vocabulary items that weren't course-specific; that task was left to individual student initiative. One participant, whose first language is Chinese, kept a list of new words, their definitions, and examples of use; others did not. The other seven, all of whom spoke Spanish at home, volunteered that when possible they used Spanish to determine meanings of unfamiliar words. However, in light of the limited use of independent literacy activities in the courses I observed, I am not surprised that participants did not find a significant amount of unfamiliar vocabulary.

In the opinion of many participants who had ESL support in high school, the courses they said presented significant literacy challenges were their ESOL classes. Their designating ESOL as more difficult than mainstream coursework came as a surprise. When Elio was asked about his transition from ESOL to core classes, he replied that "It was so easy after ESOL. I guess ESOL was harder because we were learning the English, but writing and reading in the next courses was a lot easier." A number of participants also cited Language Arts writing and reading tasks as demanding, making statements like, "There was so much it was hard to keep up!" and "I didn't understand a lot of it because it was old [Shakespeare and Chaucer]." However, most of them found the novels and short stories to be interesting and engaging. Although they did not recall titles, they spoke excitedly about the stories they had read.

Participants' Choices of Reading Strategies

Most participants appeared surprised and puzzled when asked if they read differently according to specific assignments; generally speaking, they replied, "[we] do what the teacher tells us" or "I read the instructions on the worksheet or at the end of the chapter and do what it says." Understandably perhaps, they hadn't yet developed the notion of selecting reading strategies according to task or domain. However, when asked to compare the ways they read in literature classes with the ways they read in social studies, they were aware of using different approaches. For example, one student commented, "In Language Arts I just read for what's happening and I see it in my mind. In Government, I am looking for something that will be on the test."

Meta-Cognitive Awareness

Half the participants described some meta-cognitive awareness about their literacy tasks. Notably, however, this was not the result of the instructors prompting, nor did it appear that teachers reinforced the practices students employed; rather, these ELs said they developed individual approaches when they were first learning English and have continued to apply them in their coursework. For example, Sonia observed,

> When I read, I make a picture and then I remember the story. I do the same thing in Biology and I can understand and remember the way things work better. I have to put it in my own words to learn it.

Likewise, Veronica said, "I like to outline what I read. I like to be organized, and outlines help. Sometimes I do this on paper and other times I just think it out in my head." Ramon concurred, "The reading is easy; it's what comes after the reading that's harder, you know the understanding what it means. So I think when I'm reading about what it says." Again, Rosa commented, "I read better when I can do it my way, so I try to do it like that when I can." Jia moaned, "I read SO SLOW! I just figure out what is important and read that. I leave out the other stuff. If I didn't, I would never finish." And Diego explained,

Oh, the courses in high school history and government were so easy because we learn all that in middle school history and civics. I just think about what I already know and then I put the new things where they belong.

From the remarks of these six participants, it appears that these ELs engage actively, not passively, with their literacy tasks and assignments. Unlike their monolingual classmates, they did not limit their writing and reading activities to teacher-required tasks. All five described engaging in the kind of writing and reading that leads to generative processing of course content; in completing tasks, they analyze, organize, and assemble the material into a form that makes sense to them. One EL remarked, "I can't just copy it; I have to put it in my own words so I will understand." When high school teacher participants were queried about the likelihood of all their students voluntarily making notes on or restating readings or class discussions and lectures, most responded that their native English-speaking students in mainstream (and some Advanced Placement and Honors classes) almost never took any notes unless they were required to do so. A high school teacher acknowledged, "They won't write down anything unless I make them. In fact, I have them keep the notes I give them in a notebook that I grade at the end of the semester. That's the only way they'll take notes." When asked if the same were true for their EL students, they replied that it was not, "I see Jia writing down words she doesn't know and other things we've talked about in class. She even comes in as soon as the building is open in the morning to make sure she understands the material." Significantly, it appeared that they were more active readers precisely because of their background as ELs. In this sense, then, ELs may actually have an advantage when, in college, they will need to be active, not passive, readers and writers as they engage in more integrative literacy tasks.

Although these students' dynamic approaches to academic tasks equip them with learning strategies critical for college literacy tasks, in most of the current studies ELs did not appear to have clear notions of how college learning might differ from what they had experienced in high school. When participants were asked to describe how college literacy tasks would be different from high school, all said they thought "It will be harder." As a follow-up they were asked how they thought it would be more difficult; half said they didn't really know but according to Veronica, "my teachers say it will just be harder than high school so I should study now." Those who did respond with ideas about this greater difficulty characterized it as a need to memorize more. Ramon explained, "They say it will be harder. You have to have courage and work hard, so I will just memorize more." When queried, he said he did not make deliberate efforts to retain or to rehearse information because he "just automatically remembers it."

Summary

In some ways, data from this study describe secondary school literacy experiences consistent with those outlined by Carson et al. (1992a). In their study, high school literacy experiences were characterized as teacher-directed, with writing and reading expectations explicitly defined, and in and out of class activities and assignments "very much based on, and tied to, the course text" (1992a, p. 3). In determining what and how to present course information, teachers paid close attention to end-of-course standardized testing that controlled whether a student received credit for a course; these course assessments were also regarded as important to teachers' reputations as effective instructors (Carson et al., 1992a).

Yet the data also show significant changes in the secondary school environment over the past 15 years. For one thing, the use of high-stakes tests has increased since the Carson et al. work and continues to affect significantly the nature of literacy practices ELs encounter in high school. At the study's school sites, teachers described situations in which students could have at least three and as many as four "finals" or tests in a single course: a teacher-prepared course final, a state-mandated end-of-course test, a state-required graduation test covering a discipline area, and, in Advanced Placement courses, an AP final exam.

Unlike the high school classrooms examined in Carson et al. (1992a), digital technology is now a significant presence and pedagogical tool in educational settings. Previous analyses of college literacy tasks demonstrate the importance of students' capacity to tell the difference between important and less important subject matter in textbooks, and to analyze, synthesize, and organize reading and lecture information (Carson et al., 1992a). When online resources are added to the mix, application of analysis, synthesis, and evaluation skills becomes even more critical (Hirvela, 2004). In contrast, high school literacy work as described by study participants leaned heavily toward use of a single source for knowledge, recognition, and recall activities closely supervised by classroom teachers, a condition unlikely to provide a smooth segue from secondary school to college studies.

Pedagogical Implications and Recommendations: Make it Real

As I reflect on my conversations with student participants and consider the challenges awaiting them in higher education, my foremost concern is not about their English proficiency, but about the paucity of opportunities they have had to rehearse college literacy activities. I was also struck by the extraordinary range and unpredictable diversity in their high school learning experiences and opportunities, and in the wide variation of preparation for college learning (see also Bailin, 2006; Harklau, 1999). These realities confound efforts to match individual students' high school literacy experiences with appropriate pedagogical intervention and support they may need for college. However, acknowledging that college ESL coursework cannot "fix" generation 1.5 ELs is a starting point; from this position we can begin to devise appropriate curricula and support programs.

One approach that does not avoid but allows for the diversity of EL academic characteristics is one that teaches writing and reading strategies EL students can apply as needed according to discipline and task. For example, academic vocabulary knowledge influences reading comprehension, word choices in writing, perception and reproduction of appropriate registers, and the ability to use written source materials. Thus, writing and reading courses should include strategies for building ELs' academic lexicons and their ability to recognize suitable discourse practices according to discipline and setting.

Much of the literature on English learners catalogs their academic disadvantages: underdeveloped writing skills, limited academic vocabulary, struggles with reading tasks, unfamiliarity with academic discourse, and less than sufficient strategies for reading and composition (Burt, Peyton, & Van Duzer, 2005). Yet, little has been written about rethinking ways that the reading/writing connection can be exploited. This tack may provide opportunities not only for addressing the very problems cited above but also for enhancing student learning in general.

As success in higher education requires students to do more than memorize and reproduce what they hear or read, positive educational outcomes for generation 1.5 students depend on more than improving their competency in semantic processing and production and then committing material to memory, or knowing which verb form is appropriate in a given sentence. They must be able to "think critically," selectively managing the ever-increasing flood of information available in a digitally enhanced learning environment—discerning which information is valuable, which information needs to be checked, and finally synthesizing information so they can comment on it and use it at a later date. Students also need to determine how best to re-present their learning through writing. Hence, developing policies, programs, and pedagogy that go beyond second language issues and help these ELs creatively and effectively use the writing/reading relationship is especially important.

Learning support courses have traditionally been designed for monolingual, English-speaking students who need additional instruction in order to achieve institutional or system minimum scores on standardized reading, math, and/or English usage tests. Although generation 1.5 students have shared similar school experiences with these students, the two groups are different in significant ways. Typical learning support students grow up in an English-speaking environment and develop a natural sense of English syntax and morphology. The same cannot be said of generation 1.5 students whose home language most often is not English. Consequently, writing courses that address their particular and individual issues are critical for their progress in coursework across the curriculum.

Generation 1.5 ELs also differ from typical learning support students in the amount of English vocabulary they can use in writing and reading. While English-first students usually enter college with vocabularies of 10,000 to 100,000 words, ELs beginning academic work tend to have access to 2,000 to 7,000 words for writing (Burt et al., 2005). Although there have been no definitive studies assessing academic vocabulary knowledge of generation 1.5 students, anecdotal estimates place the number at fewer than 10,000. So, teaching realistic and effective methods for tackling this concern can advance ELs' learning potential in all their coursework.

Granted, trying to address the unique learning characteristics and issues of 15 to 25 different ELs at the same time in the same class is no easy matter. However, adopting an approach that teaches discipline-specific strategies for literacy tasks and simultaneously responds to each student's particular set of concerns can open a college ESL classroom to new possibilities. As scholars note:

> Teachers can productively shift to thinking strategically so that they can co-construct strategic interventions on the fly, or at the point of need (Nelson, 1991). Like other types of scaffolded instruction, this "strategic habit of mind" (Collins, p. 210) balances student independence, strategy acquisition, and task completion with teacher-as-mediator or scaffold.
>
> (King & O'Brien, 2002, p. 49)

Teaching in this manner is far more demanding of instructors than working within lesson plans that begin a class with activities already laid out for every moment. Such an approach will likely be at odds with existing curriculum and syllabi, yet ESL pedagogy needs to allow for students' unique learning characteristics and experiences. This approach also means we need to develop texts and other materials that are practical and flexible enough to be used in "teaching on the fly" (King & O'Brien, 2002, p. 49). Most of all, we need to respect the strengths that our students bring to the classroom and use them to build ESL pedagogy that responds to their real literacy learning needs.

References

Alexander, P.A. (2005). The path to competence: A lifespan developmental perspective on reading. *Journal of Literacy Research, 37*(4), 413–436.

Allison, H.A. (2007, April). College bound generation 1.5 readers in high school. Paper presented at the meeting of the American Association of Applied Linguistics, Costa Mesa, CA.

Bailin, S. (2006). Failure in a college ESL course: Perspectives of instructors and students. *Community College Journal of Research and Practice, 30*(5), 417–431.

Burt, M., Peyton, J.K., & Van Duzer, C. (2005). *How should adult ESL reading instruction differ from ABE reading instruction?* Center for Adult English Language Acquisition website. Retrieved June 1, 2007 from TUwww.cal.org/caela/esl%5Fresources/briefs/readingdif.htmlUT.

Carson, J.G. (2001). A task analysis of reading and writing in academic contexts. In D. Belcher & A. Hirvela (Eds.), *Linking literacies: Perspectives on L2 reading–writing connections* (pp. xii, 351). Ann Arbor: University of Michigan Press.

Carson, J.G., Chase, N.D., & Gibson, S.U. (1992a). *Literacy analyses of high school and university courses: Summary descriptions of selected courses*. Atlanta, GA: Center for the Study of Adult Literacy, Georgia State University. (ERIC Documents ED 366 259.)

Carson, J.G., Chase, N.D., Gibson, S.U., & Hargrove, M.F. (1992b). Literacy demands of the undergraduate curriculum. *Reading Research and Instruction, 31*(4), 25–50.

Carson, J.G. & Leki, I. (1993). Introduction. In J.G. Carson & I. Leki (Eds.), *Reading in the composition classroom: Second language perspectives*. Boston, MA: Heinle & Heinle.

Chase, N.D. & Gibson, S.U. (1994). An examination of reading demands across four college courses. *Journal of Developmental Education, 18*(1), 10.

Collins, J. (1998). *Strategies for struggling writers*. New York: Guilford Press.

Grabe, W. & Stoller, F. (Eds.) (2002). *Teaching and researching reading*. London: Longman.

Harklau, L. (1999). The ESL learning environment in secondary school. In C.J. Faltis & P. Wolfe (Eds.), *So much to say: Adolescents, bilingualism, and ESL in the secondary school* (pp. 42–60). New York: Teachers College Press.

Harklau, L. (2004, October). From high school to college: English language learners and shifting literacy demands. Paper presented at the 10th Biennial Composition Studies Conference, Durham, NH.

Hirvela, A. (2004). *Connecting reading and writing in second language writing instruction*. Ann Arbor: University of   Press.

Hynd-Shanahan, C., H   ., & Hubbard, B.P. (2004). Thinking like a historian: College students' reading of r   torical documents. *Journal of Literacy Research, 36*(2), 141–176.

King, J. & O'Brien, D.(Adolescents' multiliteracies and their teachers' need to know: Toward a digital déte   . Alvermann (Ed.), *Adolescents and literacies in a digital world* (pp. 40–50). New Yor   ng.

Lanham, R. (1994, Ma   onomics of attention. Paper presented at the 124th annual meeting of the Associ   search Libraries, Austin, TX.

Nelson, M. (1991). *At the point of need: Teaching basic and ESL writers.* Portsmouth, NH: Boynton/Cook.

Pugh, S.L., Pawan, F., & Antommarchi, C. (2000). Academic literacy and the new college learner. In R. Flippo & D. Caverly (Eds.), *Handbook of college reading and study strategy research* (pp. 25–42). Mahwah, NJ: Lawrence Erlbaum.

Stahl, N.A. (2006). Strategic reading and learning, theory to practice: An interview with Michele Simpson and Sherrie Nist. *Journal of Developmental Education, 29*(3), 20–27.

Wittrock, M.C. & Alesandrini, K. (1990). Generation of summaries and analogies and analytic and holistic abilities. *American Educational Research Journal, 27*(3), 489–502.

7 The Academic Writing Development of a Generation 1.5 "Latecomer"

Jan Frodesen   University of California, Santa Barbara

As an ESL composition teacher for more than two decades and as an ESL program director since the early 1990s, I have witnessed the immense changes in the immigrant student populations entering California colleges and universities. Increasingly, those of us who develop composition courses, as well as conduct initial writing placements, must consider the special situations of bilingual students who have spent enough time in U.S. schools (at least 4–5 years) to reject the "ESL" designation as a stigmatizing label but who, on the other hand, still experience serious difficulties in college level writing. Many of these learners, as junior high or high school newcomers to the U.S., are eager to learn English in order to interact with and be accepted by their American peers as well as (and sometimes secondarily) to achieve academically. Unfortunately, as Laurie Olsen (1997) has so poignantly described in *Made in America,* her 2-year ethnographic study of immigrant newcomers at a California school she calls "Madison High," these learners more often than not find themselves both figuratively and literally on the margins of their schools. Linguistic and social prejudices prevent them from developing meaningful social relationships with native English-speaking peers, some of whom ridicule their accented English; as a result, the newcomers may form "ESL ghettos," or exclusive L1 social groups along the perimeter of their school courtyards. In addition, these English language learners often lack access to a curriculum that gives them the language skills they need for advanced level work. As Olsen puts it, "The reality is that few immigrants get the preparation they need academically or the language development required for academic success" (p. 11). Upon entering a college or university, these underprepared students may find themselves overwhelmed by language demands; at the same time, they find ways to lessen these demands, choosing majors that emphasize mathematical abilities and courses that do not require papers and that assess only with multiple choice exams. These L2 learners may call upon peers—including native English speakers if they find willing ones—to "check" drafts for courses with writing requirements (read: correct errors, rewrite unidiomatic language). As researchers have noted (e.g., Johns, 1991; Leki, 1995), students who develop academic coping strategies to get around language deficiencies often, in terms of overall grade point averages, look very successful.

This chapter presents a case study of the academic language development of Jinny,[1] a permanent resident from Taiwan. In contrast to immigrant learners who enter the U.S. at a very young age, Jinny belongs to the group of somewhat "later-arrived" U.S.-educated immigrants. Moving to the U.S. at the age of 15 with only the barest foundation in

English, she found herself, like so many of the students whose voices were heard in Olsen's Madison High study, struggling to establish new social, cultural, and linguistic identities as an American and as an English speaker in a southern California high school. Despite the immense challenges of attaining a high school education while simultaneously adjusting to a new culture and developing second language proficiency, upon graduation Jinny realized her goal of entering a selective research university.

My interest in Jinny and her academic language development during her university years arose from two concerns: one related to my role as a composition teacher and the other as a program administrator. First of all, Jinny was my student for three 10-week quarters; the first of these quarters she was enrolled in an ESL composition class and two subsequent quarters in weekly individual writing tutorials. In the composition course, I had been concerned with the considerable difficulties Jinny experienced developing syntactic and lexico-grammatical accuracy in her papers. Thus, I had encouraged her to enroll in my tutorial course in the hopes that she would make more progress with individualized instruction.

A second concern motivating this examination of Jinny's English language learning history and writing development derived from the continuing discussions among faculty in our campus ESL and writing programs about how and where to place bilingual students in composition courses. Along with several colleagues from my campus writing program, I was interested in exploring through studies of individual learners the results of campus placement decisions for bilingual students entering our university from U.S. high schools. Each spring our ESL program places all entering freshmen who have been designated as "ESL" on the basis of their performance on the University of California Analytical Writing Placement Exam, formerly known as the Subject A Examination. In this diagnostic exam, high school students who have been admitted to University of California (UC) campuses have 2 hours to read a 700 to 1,000 word passage and write an essay, most of which are later holistically scored by trained writing and ESL instructors in a single session at the Berkeley campus. Descriptors for these holistic scores include both rhetorical and linguistic features; for non-passing essays, descriptors refer to levels of error in grammar and word choice. A non-passing score requires that the student be placed into a preparatory composition course. Non-passing essays with significant errors characteristic of second language writers are designated ESL; this distinction is confirmed by at least one ESL specialist. On those UC campuses such as mine that have ESL composition programs, faculty making placement decisions must decide whether these students are best served by placement into an ESL or a mainstream writing course.

In our case study research, my colleagues and I focused on the writing development of several students who had received ESL designations on their diagnostic writing exams but different placements, some in ESL and some in mainstream composition.[2] In the case of Jinny, I wanted to document the kinds of writing progress she made during her coursework in both ESL and mainstream composition and to identify educational, social, and cultural factors that might have helped or hindered her academic language development, beginning with her arrival in the U.S. and continuing through three of her four years at the university. I also hoped this study would help to inform our campus writing placement procedures.

During the time I was working with Jinny in tutorials, my writing program colleagues and I were intrigued by Guadalupe Valdés' (1992) discussion of different types of bilingual learners and their special instructional needs. One group of learners, whom Valdés termed "incipient bilinguals," was characterized as still acquiring fluency in English and producing writing with frequent and varied grammatical errors. The other group, termed "functional bilinguals," had advanced English proficiency but produced systematic errors persisting after years of English instruction. Valdés maintained that "incipient bilinguals" need ESL instruction, whereas "functional bilinguals" should receive specialized instruction within mainstream composition. She pointed out that educational institutions need to establish criteria to distinguish these two kinds of learners and that institutional placement mechanisms for entering students often do not take into consideration important information about learners' educational needs.

These issues were among those my colleagues and I wanted to explore through our case studies. We hoped that by investigating individual students' educational backgrounds, academic language learning histories, and university-level writing development, we would gain insights into the wisdom of our placement procedures and the value of specialized ESL instruction for bilingual students. We also wished to gain a better understanding of how to determine when generation 1.5 learners should be considered "functional bilinguals." As will be seen in Jinny's case, the distinctions between the two kinds of bilingual learners Valdés described are not easily made, even with considerable information about a learner's background. This study poses a challenge to the idea that placement criteria that can be established that would distinguish the two groups based on samples of writing. In addition, this study attests to the complex variables that may influence the academic literacy development of advanced learners of English.

The data used for Jinny's case study were her diagnostic Subject A Examination, drafts and final papers from two ESL courses and two Writing Program courses, audiotaped tutorials, and one audiotaped and transcribed interview; Jinny gave permission for all of these data to be used for this study.

The Beginnings of Jinny's U.S. Education

Like many other Taiwanese immigrants in southern California, Jinny's family established residence in the United States solely to provide their children better educational opportunities than those available in Taiwan. The family made the transition in stages, with Jinny's college-age sister and father moving in 1989 to a city about 20 miles south of downtown Los Angeles, while Jinny, the second of three daughters, remained in Taiwan with her mother and younger sister. A year later, the rest of the family followed, and Jinny, at the age of 15, began her American education at the ninth grade level, in a high school with a large Asian student population.

Jinny's English proficiency prior to her arrival in the United States was minimal. For 2 years she had studied English 3 hours a week in her junior high school, where she, in her words, "learned the basics like A, B, C, D and the basic sentence like, you know, 'Today I play.'" Spending most of their class time working on grammar and writing exercises, the students rarely spoke English in class; based on her description of these classes, it is no wonder that Jinny arrived in the United States having studied English but unable to speak more than a few words. When asked how she had at first coped in an American school with such limited English skills, Jinny focused on the social alienation, on the difficulty of making friends with anyone other than Chinese speakers: "you don't, you make fre—it hard to, it's hard to make friend. Like, so, mmm ... I—just my friends all Chinese and someones like Americans they come by making fun of you and ... is bad." She also focused on the ostracism she encountered in some of her classes: "when I was freshman I really don't like my P.E. because you need to play like with a group and it is hard to find people to play with you. So you were kind of by yourself."

With such limited opportunities for social interaction in English, Jinny found it difficult to use outside the classroom the English she was learning; perhaps partly as a result of this, she remained in ESL classes throughout her high school education rather than making the transition into mainstream English. Judging from her descriptions, Jinny's ESL courses did little to help her develop either spoken or written discourse competence. In fact, they resembled the English curriculum in her Taiwanese junior high school: lots of grammar and writing, not much speaking. Unfortunately, she had the same ESL teacher all 3 years of high school, one who, in Jinny's opinion, didn't really know how to teach English to non-native speakers; as Jinny put it, she just knew how to give assignments. When the classes did have discussion activities, they were typically unstructured small group discussions, which, as Jinny recalls, often ended up as an opportunity for students to converse in their native languages. As she tells it, her experience contrasts sharply with the rich language environment of the ESL class described in Harklau's (1994) ethnographic study of ESL versus mainstream classes in a secondary school. Classes taught by a veteran ESL teacher in Harklau's research featured small groups led by the teacher and her aides, discussions in which every student was called on several times, open-ended questions for students to answer with sample responses modeled by the teacher, and extended composition projects. In addition to oral and written comprehensible input enhanced by visual aids and comprehension checks, there was, overall, emphasis on structured participation and self-expression. In Jinny's ESL classes, although the classes provided little structured interaction, Jinny did at least have an opportunity to make friends and to speak English with students from Korea and Japan as well as with some Chinese students whose dialect was different from hers.

During the summer after her first year of high school, Jinny asked her parents to fund an expensive Scholastic Assessment Test (SAT.) preparation course since she wanted to apply to colleges. In her university placement essay written during her senior year, she describes this experience, explaining that her parents were "amazed" by her desire to take the course. Thus, Jinny's goals to further her education appeared to be intrinsically motivated rather than stemming from any kind of parental pressure to attend college. According to Jinny, while she was taking the preparation course, whenever her parents found her doing anything besides studying English, they would, she wrote in her essay, "scold on me for waste my time." Jinny's efforts to achieve an acceptable (albeit marginally so) SAT score appear to have paid off. Despite her struggles with English, she scored 330 on the verbal section, much lower certainly than her math score, which was close to 700, but with a total high enough to gain her admission to a UC campus. Thus, upon graduating high school, Jinny followed in her older sister's footsteps, becoming the second child in her family to gain admission to a 4-year research university.

Assessment of Jinny's Writing as an Entering UC Undergraduate

The two on-campus ESL specialists who reread Jinny's Subject A Exam, which had received both a non-passing score and an ESL designation, disagreed on the placement, with one rater placing her into the lowest of three ESL courses offered for undergraduates and the other into the middle level. A third rater agreed with the middle level placement. The differing rater judgments were due, perhaps, to the unevenness of Jinny's essay in both development and grammatical control.

Jinny's Subject A task was to summarize and evaluate an excerpt from Gloria Watkins' (bell hooks) book *Talking Back*. In the passage, Watkins describes her family's resistance to her leaving her small Kentucky hometown to attend Stanford University; they feared, as Watkins saw it, that they would lose her forever. Watkins then discusses how honest communication helped her to maintain family bonds and to value skills and talents various family members had, regardless of their educational level. Jinny's response to the prompt, which asked writers to identify both the conflicts and the sources of connections Watkins describes and then react to her analysis, was to some extent rhetorically appropriate: she responded directly to the first part of the topic, noting conflicts and connections, and then related her own experience, discussed above, of her parents' not wanting to fund an SAT preparation course because they didn't believe she was a serious scholar. Her language use, however, obscured meaning in a number of places, creating considerable distraction for readers with the frequency of errors throughout. Jinny's linguistic difficulties no doubt contributed significantly to the assignment of the holistic scores to her essay at the system-wide scoring session: two scores of '2' on a six-point scale, indicating serious difficulties in reading and writing.

Jinny's Subject A essay did demonstrate some skill, on both rhetorical and mechanical levels, in using source materials in her writing. She had attempted to interweave Watkins' points in her own discussion, noting similarities between her experience and Watkins' and using the passage to support her conclusion. She had also taken care to underline the title of Watkins' book and had used quotation marks for some phrases taken from the passage. The development of her essay did not entirely succeed, however, most noticeably due to comparisons that seemed inappropriate, at least from an American cultural perspective. For example, in likening her own experience to Watkins' uncertainty about the value of education, an uncertainty stemming from her parents' ambivalence toward book learning, Jinny stated: "As same as her feeling, it really drive me insane, sometimes." This comparison, which followed the discussion of her parents' scolding her for wasting time when she was not preparing for the SAT, seemed inappropriate since, based on the content of her essay, Jinny's parents, unlike Watkins, did not disapprove of her studying. Another faulty comparison in her concluding paragraph related the appreciation Watkins developed for her family with Jinny's feeling that parents should support their children and make them feel like a "better" or "superior" person.

These problems, stemming perhaps from a misunderstanding of the passage, would not warrant the low holistic scores Jinny received. Nor would the weaknesses in content development account for her subsequent placement by the campus ESL instructors into an ESL course two levels below the Writing Program preparatory composition course. The language errors in Jinny's essay largely accounted for her non-passing score and placement. Her essay most certainly fit Valdés' (1992) incipient bilingual description of "having many errors." More significant, however, were the types of errors; they indicated a writer who would most likely need more than one-quarter of ESL instruction to write effectively in mainstream classes across the curriculum.

A relatively short essay for this exam at 439 words, Jinny's response did not have a single error-free sentence. While this measure of errors does not distinguish serious errors from less serious ones, it does tell us something about writing proficiency. Along with the many word level problems (verb tense, verb forms, word forms, noun number, article usage, agreement errors), Jinny's essay had a number of sentence structure problems that prevented a clear understanding of her ideas. Consider, for example, the following paragraph from her essay, one that summarizes part of the Watkins' passage:

> From her view, "keeping far to home" was the biggest problem they have. Her parents adamantly opposed her to attend Stanford University because they fear that they would lose her forever and they thought college education might do to her minds even they felt unenthusiastically acknowledge its importance. Watkins says, "resolution and reconciliation" has been important to her and both of it affects her development as a writer. But from her parents, they didn't understand why she could not attend a college nearby. To her parents, they thought any college would graduate, and make her become a teacher. Such as these make Watkins felt so utterly painful and led to intense conflict.

Similar to many other inexperienced academic writers (often referred to as "basic writers" in the composition literature), Jinny had borrowed phrases from the source text, paraphrasing only slightly if at all, and had used them in ways that do not fit syntactically or semantically into her sentences. Watkins' phrases "their fear that they would lose me forever," "they feared what college education might do to her mind," "they unenthusiastically acknowledged its importance," "they did not understand why I could not attend a college nearby," and "I would graduate, become a school teacher" are all taken from the text, minimally changed to indirect forms of reported speech (e.g., "I" to "she") and used as the core information for her summary. Campbell (1990) notes that this use of background information, which she terms "Near Copies," may result from an awareness of the need to paraphrase but at the same time an inability to do so appropriately under time constraints. In making changes to the borrowed sentences, Jinny had produced structures that reflect a lack of linguistic knowledge regarding syntactic collocation constraints (e.g., the error resulting from replacing the verb "fear" with "thought"; the complementation error created by inserting "unenthusiastically acknowledge its importance" after "felt"). One phrase was misquoted: the unidiomatic "keeping far to home" was actually "going so far from home" in the passage. The inability to edit misquotes appears to be a common problem among developing L2 writers; what stands out as obviously misquoted to a native speaker or fluent bilingual due to faulty syntax or missing words will often go unnoticed by a developing bilingual writer even when she reads the sentence aloud.

Jinny's essay did attempt a variety of sentence structures; in fact, the variety of sentences, as structurally problematic as they were, argued for a higher ESL placement level than that for writers who produce strings of simple sentences or compound ones joined by coordinating conjunctions such as "and." It was difficult to evaluate Jinny's entering essay in terms of vocabulary usage, which may be considered a subcategory of grammatical competence, since much of the essay has appropriated phrasing from the text, both with and without citation. The amount of borrowing from the source text, combined with inappropriate collocations, such as "a rich class" to describe the expensive SAT preparation course, suggested that Jinny had not yet acquired the lexical resources in English needed to accomplish successfully academic writing tasks at the university level.

On the level of discourse competence, Jinny's Subject A essay also demonstrated a need for further language development. Although Jinny did use discourse markers for cohesion and topic shifts, they were usually in some way problematic. She often introduced topics with noun phrases that reflect Chinese topic/comment structure (as well as informal speech), producing what composition handbooks sometimes term "double subjects": "Gloria Watkins, her passage from the book *Talking Back*, describes the conflicts as separating her." Sometimes a transition was insufficiently elaborated (as in the use of "truly" to indicate agreement with ideas stated in a previous paragraph) or unidiomatic ("as same as my feeling").

In summary, the overall impression we get from the analysis of Jinny's entering Subject A Exam is of a writer who had not yet acquired a level of grammatical and discourse competence needed for college level writing. On the other hand, her attempts to use complex sentence structures, to create text coherence through transitional phrases and reference, to use citation conventions, and to interweave source material and her own ideas indicated skill in the basics of essay writing. Consequently, Jinny's on-campus placement into the middle level of ESL seemed, to paraphrase Huot (1996), a recognition of both her limitations and her promise as a writer.

University Writing Development and Ongoing Assessment

As it turned out, Jinny ended up spending four quarters in ESL before being promoted to a mainstream composition course in the Writing Program. Three of these quarters involved classroom courses, including a required repeat of the highest level, ESL 3, with me as her instructor. Jinny then spent an additional quarter working in tutorial twice a week with me. She did not make the transition to the Writing Program composition course until the spring of her sophomore year. At that time she continued with the ESL tutorial course in conjunction with the preparatory writing course. Thus, I was directly involved with Jinny's writing development for an entire year.

During the time she was enrolled in my ESL 3 course (fall quarter of Jinny's sophomore year), Jinny's behavior and writing proficiency were similar to those of many of the other female Asian students in the class. In discussions, she was reticent. She sometimes seemed embarrassed to speak out in class when called on and rarely volunteered answers, but would occasionally venture a response if I looked directly at her while raising a question. Like the female Hispanic students in Losey's (1995) study of student output in a mixed monolingual and bilingual classroom, Jinny may have, during whole class discussions, felt intimidated by some of the more orally proficient male and female students. These students were from European, middle Eastern, and Hispanic backgrounds, all of them older than the other undergraduate students in the class. While Jinny's class participation in whole class activity was not high, she did participate actively in the frequent small group tasks and was in every other way a "good student," turning in all assignments and meeting with me frequently to work on draft revisions.

By the end of the quarter in which Jinny had enrolled in ESL 3 for the second time, she had completed three quarters of university level ESL; she had written a number of papers based on assigned readings, with required drafts for peer response and instructor conferences, and had completed many other assignments intended to help students improve editing skills, increase academic vocabulary, and develop syntactic complexity. However, her writing portfolio, consisting of in-class and out-of-class writing, indicated that she was still struggling with language at the sentence level, producing a variety of structural errors such as incorrect complements and relative clauses. In Jinny's portfolio introduction essay, addressed to the ESL instructors who would be reading it, she enthusiastically summarized the improvements she had made over the quarter and cited the work on editing and revision that had helped to advance her writing skills. She emphasized how she had learned to recognize her own errors and correct them. While these activities may indeed have helped Jinny in the long run, her writing for the quarter did not demonstrate the kind of proficiency that would seem necessary for successful completion of a mainstream composition course.

On the other hand, a comparison of Jinny's ESL 3 essays with the Subject A Exam she wrote in her senior year of high school indicated development in discourse competence as well as somewhat more sophisticated expression. Her essays had more overall fluency and in general used transitions and other cohesive devices more appropriately. The following example from the first unrevised draft of her final out-of-class essay, an argument for continued government funding of research to explore possibilities of extraterrestrial life, illustrates both the rhetorical strengths and grammatical difficulties typical of Jinny's writing at that time:

> Nowadays, many scientists are interesting on study if there are other civilizations besides human beings on Earth. However, some people think it is a waste of time and money in studying and researching intergalactic civilizations. On the contrary, they deem it the government should use these moneys in other appropriate uses such as to provide some welfare programs which can precisely benefit people. In my opinion, I think it is a wise use of money to examine and study civilizations in outer space. By doing this is not only a new discovery in the scientific field, but also to the advantage of us in some ways.

This excerpt from Jinny's essay, with its frequent, and, in some cases, serious structural errors, reflects the English proficiency of a learner still actively acquiring English; while the ideas are comprehensible, there remain numerous problems with complementation, such as the gerund rather than infinitive structure "in studying and researching," with word forms (the present participle "interesting" instead of the past participle; the base form "study" rather than the gerund "studying"), and with mixed constructions, such as in the last sentence that employs "doing this" as both the object of an introductory prepositional phrase and the subject of the sentence and that lacks parallelism in the structures linked by the correlative conjunctions "not only ... but also." The ESL designated essays of entering freshmen whom we place into mainstream composition courses have neither the frequency nor, in general, the seriousness of error that was still evident in Jinny's writing.

Because of Jinny's continued difficulties with sentence and word level structures, during the ESL portfolio reading sessions, the ESL Program decided to place her into a one-to-one tutorial course I taught. During the 20 sessions of the tutorial, Jinny's participation, like that of the Mexican women in Losey's (1995) study, was markedly different from her classroom behavior: in contrast to her timidity in class, Jinny frequently controlled interactions in the tutorials, asking questions, explaining her motivations for structures she had produced in her writing, and even frequently interrupting the instructor to clarify a point or raise a question about something she did not understand. Such behavior suggests that she was quite motivated to improve her writing skills. With Jinny's ESL 3 portfolio writing serving as the "text" for grammatical instruction and editing practice, she seemed to gain an understanding of some of the structural constraints in English that she had frequently not observed, such as the uses of various types of *that* in clause formation (complements, relative clauses, comparative clauses). She also learned correct forms of idiomatic expressions that she had previously misused in her papers. Whether this intensive work in fact helped Jinny develop more control of sentence level structures and use more appropriate vocabulary in the long run is not clear, even with her successful completion of two mainstream composition courses, Writing 1 and 2, in which she received B-grades. From looking at her in-class writing and drafts versus final papers in the Writing 2 course, it was obvious that much of Jinny's success had resulted from her diligence in getting instructor and tutorial assistance with revision. She seemed to have steadily developed her rhetorical competence; as a result, her final papers were quite acceptable. And her fluency appeared to have improved by the end of the first mainstream course, subsequently noted by her Writing 2 instructor, who commented on how much she had written in 20 minutes on her first day writing sample. In-class writing and drafts of out-of-class papers, however, while syntactically more mature, retained a high frequency of word and sentence level errors as evidenced by the following excerpt from an in-class writing:

When I came to United States, I had problem on speaking and writing English. My writing skill was very low even sometime people had hard time reading my paper.... Now I still continue learning English and learning how to write better and trying to improve my English at the same time. For me, I think this is a discovery, because learning English is a long process, and through the process I am not only learning English but also discover the mistakes I have been made and then improve these.

From the writing sample alone, Jinny would still seem to be at a stage in which additional ESL instruction is needed since her errors are so frequent and varied. In the excerpt above there are frequent missing articles, a feature more characteristic of bilinguals still actively acquiring English than is incorrect article usage such as using *the* when no article should be used. The lack of an appropriate comparative structure in the second sentence (using *very low* instead of *so low that*) is also one that more proficient writers would have edited. The omission of the *be* auxiliary for progressive *am learning* in the second sentence and the misused passive verb in the last sentence (perhaps confused with a restrictive relative clause structure such as *that have been made*) are further examples of language errors typical of learners who are still acquiring English grammar and syntax.

A Final Assessment: Jinny as a Functional Bilingual

At the end of her third year at the university, Jinny had been in the US for 7 years. After four quarters of university ESL instruction in addition to two quarters of mainstream composition, Jinny's writing still fit Valdés' description of that produced by learners still acquiring English. Recent research suggests that the number of years it takes second language learners to achieve near native-like academic English proficiency is greater than was previously thought (Collier, 1989). Yorio's (1989) study (cited in Valdés, 1992) found that non-native speakers with 5 to 6 years of residency had difficulty producing native-like writing after exiting ESL classes. Although almost all our ESL students making the transition to mainstream classes retain, like the students in Yorio's study, some non-native forms, those like Jinny who continue to have considerable problems with sentence and clause structure as well as idiomatic phrasing cause a great deal of concern for mainstream composition teachers. Yet, many such students maintain above average academic records during their college careers, raising questions as to what constitutes reasonable expectations for linguistic accuracy in academic work.

Although Jinny was overall a successful student in her majors of Mathematics and Business Economics, her educational and social paths at the university and the strategies she used to cope with her language difficulties may, in some ways, have contributed to her lack of progress in developing greater proficiency in English. At the end of her junior year, she had avoided taking the third required writing course in the Writing Program. Like one of the international students in Leki's (1995) study of coping strategies used by ESL students to meet university writing demands, Jinny had adopted the strategy Leki calls "taking advantage of the first language and culture." She had met other university writing requirements through courses in the Chinese department where, she says, "[it] is easy to get good grade." To meet her other course requirements for graduation, she chose courses that were primarily mathematically based, feeling more comfortable, she said, in these classes than in ones that required a lot of reading.

Though Jinny's oral English was somewhat fluent, it was quite ungrammatical. By nature rather shy, she rarely, if ever, spoke voluntarily in her classes, using English only when she was involved in a group project. Away from the university, she spoke Chinese almost exclusively in her social interactions; when asked what percentage of her time she spent speaking Chinese and what percentage English outside of classes, she responded: "I would say all Chinese.... We think is weird if you know how to speak Chinese but you speak English." All in all, Jinny's use of English as both a high school student and college student was largely restricted to classroom contexts and even there her productive use of spoken English was quite limited.

As Valdés (1992) has discussed, deciding how long an individual can remain a "language learner" is a complex question. In considering the transition of learners from an acquisitional to a functional stage, she states: "[N]o matter how many features remain that are non-native-like, there is a point at which an individual must be classified as a functional bilingual rather than as an incipient bilingual" (pp. 101–102). When that point occurs and how to recognize it are among the complex questions that arise for those who make writing placements. Even if it had been possible to classify Jinny as a "functional bilingual" upon entry to the university, it seems likely that the additional specialized instruction she received in the ESL composition courses and tutorials helped her develop her academic reading and writing proficiency.

In fact, Jinny's life post-college appears in one sense to validate her status as a functional bilingual. In a follow-up telephone conversation years after she had graduated, it turned out that she was employed by an international firm and had a position in which she had to spend a great deal of time speaking English on the telephone. As a result, her oral fluency had improved considerably, a feat she had not been able to accomplish in school, perhaps partly because of her limited associations with English speakers outside the classroom. On the other hand, given these reported gains in oral proficiency, Jinny could also be considered to be still acquiring English. This is not to deny her functional bilingual status but to suggest that language learning occurs in many different discourse domains and thus is an ongoing and even lifelong process.

Implications

In reflections over time on the interviews, conversations, and writing samples used to tell Jinny's story, I have considered the implications of her experience from different perspectives. From one perspective, her situation points to the difficulty ESL programs may have in knowing when to promote students into mainstream composition courses with confidence they will be successful learners in these contexts. Many of us who teach 10- or 12-week courses find it difficult to determine whether or not our instructional efforts have made a difference. Because I worked intensively with Jinny one-on-one over several quarters, I was able to see both the progress she made toward understanding English syntax and the limits of what we could accomplish together. McKay and Wong (1996) raise the question of why some learners are able to progress in the target language in some contexts and others don't. In their study of junior high school students, they examined the multiple discourses of learners in and out of classrooms and stressed that L2 learners who lack proficiency in English and must negotiate complex social identities in communicative situations seek ways to gain communicative power that may be counterproductive to developing L2 proficiency. This could include resistance to certain forms of instruction in teaching contexts or dependence on L1. Citing Peirce's (1995) work on social identity, McKay and Wong agree that the simplified notion of learner motivation might be better replaced by the concept of investment, in which individuals value language development in relation to their communicative needs in establishing identities in social interactions. It is no surprise then, that L2 learners such as Jinny, who are shut out of meaningful communication in the target language, both in their classroom settings and in their social life outside the classroom, enter universities after years of U.S. schooling without having developed academic language proficiency. Like many bilingual immigrants who began their life in the U.S. in California secondary schools, Jinny held painful memories of being made fun of and ostracized by native English speakers, finding acceptance only with her native Chinese-speaking friends and other L2 students in her ESL classes, and recalled few opportunities for meaningful negotiated language interactions in her classrooms.

Obviously, as educators we cannot force L2 immigrant and native English-speaking students to interact socially outside our classrooms. However, educational institutions can develop curricula, programs, and extracurricular activities that encourage meaningful, negotiated oral interaction in the classroom for all students, L2 and native English-speaking learners alike. Academic literacy is not limited to reading and writing; learners must also develop academic oral proficiency (Scarcella, 2003). In observations of mainstream secondary classes, Harklau (1994) found the lack of interaction between mainstream teachers and L2 learners "quite striking": students were often "withdrawn and noninteractive" in these classes, with little opportunity for producing extended discourse. She noted that the L2 learners often just "tuned out" mainstream instructional interactions, especially when teachers got off topic or used language the students could not understand, such as puns, irony, or sarcasm. In addition to structuring meaningful opportunities for interaction within classrooms, schools can help native English-speaking students better understand and appreciate the difficulties of learning a second (in contrast to a foreign) language. As one example, at a Los Angeles high school, students were allowed to speak only in Spanish (whether or not they knew the language) for a day so that non-native Spanish speakers could get a better sense of how it felt not to be able to communicate in their native language. More generally, high school curricula could offer linguistic or sociolinguistic courses exploring issues in second language acquisition and language diversity in American culture. This suggestion is included in *Academic Literacy: A Statement of Competencies Expected of Students Entering California's Public Colleges and Universities* (Intersegmental Committee of the Academic Senates, 2002) in its section discussing ways that teachers and administrators can work together to ensure the special needs of English language learners. Through such courses, native speakers of English could gain greater sensitivity to the challenges their L2 peers experience in developing English proficiency.

Current research in K-12 contexts has increasingly focused on the broader social contexts of learning and the influence of social interactions on academic language development in K-12. From Jinny's experience and that of many other L2 learners who come to the U.S. as adolescents, it is often the case that even the most intensive intervention at the college level cannot make up for the lack of enriching and meaningful language learning environments during the junior high or high school years. Thus, educators must increase collaborative efforts to provide rich language experiences and appropriate feedback on language output for L2 learners in ESL and mainstream contexts.

In terms of placement and instruction for advanced bilingual writers at the university level, this study suggests that it may be difficult, if not impossible, to define criteria that distinguish different types of bilinguals solely on the basis of writing samples and years of U.S. education. The analysis of Jinny's writing development supports the findings of other studies that the writing of bilingual students may retain many non-native-like features despite years of specialized instruction. Yet, these writers can still benefit from form-focused attention to their writing needs. Consequently, writing instructors in mainstream as well as ESL programs will need to consider what are realistic expectations for advanced bilingual learners and how best to help them make continued progress in their academic language development.

Acknowledgments

I am grateful to Christine Holten, Mike Rose, and the editors of this volume for their helpful comments and suggestions on drafts of this chapter.

Notes

1. Jinny is a pseudonym.
2. The histories of two of these students have been described in Frodesen and Starna (1992).

References

Campbell, C. (1990). Writing with others' words: Using background reading text in academic compositions. In B. Kroll (Ed.), *Second language writing: Research insights for the classroom* (pp. 211–230). Cambridge, UK: Cambridge University Press.

Collier, V. (1989). How long? A synthesis of research on academic achievement in a second language. *TESOL Quarterly, 23*(3), 509–531.

Frodesen, J. & Starna, N. (1999). Distinguishing incipient and functional bilingual writers: Assessment and instructional insights gained through second-language writer profiles. In L. Harklau, K. Losey, & M. Siegal (Eds.), *Generation 1.5 meets college composition: Issues in the teaching of writing to U.S.-educated learners of ESL* (pp. 61–80). Mahwah, NJ: Lawrence Erlbaum Associates.

Harklau, L. (1994). ESL versus mainstream classes: Contrasting L2 learning environments. *TESOL Quarterly, 28*(2), 241–272.

Huot, B. (1996). Toward a new theory of writing assessment. *College Composition and Communication, 47*(4), 549–566.

Intersegmental Committee of the Academic Senates. (2002). *Academic literacy: A statement of competencies expected of students entering California's public colleges and universities.* Sacramento, CA: Intersegmental Committee of the Academic Senates.

Johns, A. (1991). Interpreting an English competency examination: The frustrations of an ESL science student. *Written Communication, 8*(3), 379–401.

Leki, I. (1995). Coping strategies of ESL students in writing tasks across the curriculum. *TESOL Quarterly, 29*(2), 235–260.

Losey, K. (1995). Gender and ethnicity as factors in the development of verbal skills in bilingual Mexican American women. *TESOL Quarterly, 29*(4), 635–659.

McKay, S.L. & Wong, C.S. (1996). Multiple discourses, multiple identities: Investment and agency in second-language learning among Chinese adolescent immigrant students. *Harvard Educational Review, 66*(3), 577–608.

Olsen, L. (1997). *Made in America: Immigrant students in our public schools.* New York: The New Press.

Peirce, B.N. (1995). Social identity, investment and language learning. *TESOL Quarterly, 29*(1), 9–31.

Scarcella, R. (2003). Academic English: A conceptual framework. University of California Linguistic Minority Research Institute Technical Report 2003–1, Santa Barbara, CA.

Valdés, G. (1992). Bilingual minorities and language issues in writing: Toward professionwide responses to a new challenge. *Written Communication, 9*(1), 85–136.

Yorio, C. (1989). Idiomaticity as an indicator of second language proficiency. In K. Hyltenstam & L.K. Obler (Eds.), *Bilingualism across a lifespan: Aspects of acquisition, maturity and loss* (pp. 55–72). Cambridge, UK: Cambridge University Press.

8   Academic Reading and Writing Difficulties and Strategic Knowledge of Generation 1.5 Learners

Cathryn Crosby   West Chester University

Generation 1.5 students vary greatly in the level of academic reading and writing preparation that they receive in U.S. K-12 schools. Because of this and because of the prolonged time that it takes to acquire academic English, students may enter college unprepared for the complex and language intensive reading and writing tasks that are demanded of college freshmen.

As a means of completing academic reading and writing tasks and overcoming difficulties, studies have shown that ESL students, including generation 1.5 learners, use a variety of strategies when engaging in reading and writing tasks. For example, Block (1986) found the academic reading strategies in her study of ESL readers could be categorized as general strategies, which include anticipating reading content, recognizing text structure, integrating information, questioning information in the text, interpreting the text, using general knowledge and associations to understand the text, monitoring comprehension of the text, self-correcting reading behavior, and reacting to the text, and specific strategies, which include paraphrasing, rereading, and questioning the meaning of a word, clause or sentence. Carson, Chase, Gibson, and Hargrove (1992), in their analysis of the academic reading strategies utilized by L2 students in an undergraduate history course, found vocabulary was very important, and that it was imperative for students to have vocabulary acquisition strategies, including dictionary usage skills and the ability to recognize and use context clues.

In Raimes' (1987) study of ESL college student writers, she found L2 writers utilized several different strategies, such as planning, rehearsing, rescanning, rereading, and revising and editing, to respond to informal and formal writing course tasks. A study on students' academic writing strategies across the curriculum conducted by Leki and Carson (1994) showed strategies like task management, such as managing text, managing sources, and managing research in academic writing were quite prevalent. Other strategies they found were rhetorical strategies for organization and coherence, language strategies for grammar and vocabulary, and cognitive strategies for developing and expanding ideas in writing, arguing logically in writing, and analyzing texts. Another study by Leki (1995) focused on the academic writing strategies of ESL students in various courses across the curriculum at the start of and throughout their college experience, and examined the academic writing strategies that participants in her study brought with them, and how these were altered and developed during the course of the study. In her study, she found a myriad of strategies, which included relying on past writing experiences to help with current writing tasks, using current experience or feedback as a means of evaluating the effectiveness of the strategies being used and to adjust them when necessary, and using previous ESL writing training as a resource for writing in other courses.

Studies of the strategies utilized by generation 1.5 learners to complete and overcome academic reading and writing tasks show that the strategies they utilize vary from one learner to another. For example, Johns' (1992) case study of the academic reading and writing strategies of a Laotian student in her first year of college found this student to be exceptional in regards to the strategic repertoire she utilized to help her accomplish the variety of academic reading and writing tasks and difficulties she encountered in college. Some of the difficulties with academic reading and writing that freshmen typically encounter in college include challenges in studying for exams that cover vast amounts of reading for the course and problems with understanding writing assignments that differ from one class to another and even from one assignment to another (Johns, 1992). The strategies Johns' case study participant utilized when completing course tasks and encountering difficulties included connecting and applying the assigned reading and writing tasks to meet her own needs and interests, making analogies, and predictions, planning, looking for underlying structures and concepts in course material, utilizing different ways of strategic thinking, and the integration of academic lexicon into these structures and concepts.

In another study on generation 1.5 learners, four in their first year of college encountered academic reading and writing tasks that were similar to those they had encountered in high school (Harklau, 2001). These included the use of multiple choice tests and textbooks. Because of this similarity, the participants were able to utilize the strategies they had already developed while in high school. However, because some tasks they encountered in their first year of college were different from what they experienced in high school, other academic reading and writing strategies that the participants utilized in their first year of college were different from what they experienced. These included strategies such as reading and understanding course syllabi, taking notes, and writing academically.

Understanding the strategic knowledge generation 1.5 learners use to overcome the difficulties they can face with academic reading and writing tasks is important because it can help college writing instructors have a better understanding of our students as academic readers and writers, and what their particular academic literacy needs are. By learning what these strategies are, we can develop the repertoire of strategies we use to teach academic reading and writing. This in turn can facilitate our students' progress (Bialystok, 1981) and raise students' awareness regarding the strategies they use and the effectiveness of them (O'Malley & Chamot, 1993). Consequently, it is imperative to examine the specific difficulties that generation 1.5 learners have with academic reading and writing tasks, and the strategic knowledge they use to complete and overcome these tasks. This chapter describes a case study that investigated the academic reading and writing difficulties two generation 1.5 learners encountered with the assignments in their first year college composition course as well as the strategies they utilized to complete the assignments and overcome the difficulties.

Study Design

In 2006, I conducted a study examining the academic reading and writing of two generation 1.5 learners. My purpose was to provide a better understanding of the challenges these students faced in completing tasks and the strategic knowledge they utilized in overcoming these challenges in their first year composition course. The following questions were asked: What academic literacy difficulties did these generation 1.5 English learners face in completing the tasks they encountered? What academic literacy strategies did learners utilize to overcome these difficulties?

Two generation 1.5 English learners enrolled in their first year at a tertiary institution in a midsized urban city in the Midwest were purposefully selected for the study. Andrew (a pseudonym), one of the participants, is from Vietnam and bi-literate in Vietnamese and English. He grew up in a somewhat literate home environment where he observed only his mother practicing written literacy. Andrew came to the U.S. at the start of his junior year in high school. The schooling he had in Vietnam was consistent and included about 5 years of English instruction, which mostly focused on grammar translation. At the American high school he attended, Andrew did not take ESL courses in high school because they were not offered; instead, he was mainstreamed directly into English Language Arts courses. I came to know Andrew and his academic literacy ability when he was a student in my advanced ESL composition course in his first year of college. From observations of his writing performance, Andrew particularly struggled with finding and using outside sources in his writing, a key component of the course curriculum.

Tiffany (a pseudonym), the other case study participant, is from Taiwan. Unlike Andrew, Tiffany is multi-literate (Taiwanese, Mandarin, English, and Japanese) and grew up in a home in which she was exposed to different types of literacy, including the reading of fiction, non-fiction, and academic texts. Like Andrew, Tiffany came to the U.S. at the start of her junior year. Her experiences in American secondary schools included reading a range of academic texts and opportunities to write academic texts (e.g., "the research paper") that required she use sources to support her ideas. However, the amount of academic reading and writing she did was relatively minimal.

The case study participants were recruited based on the following criteria: identification as a generation 1.5 learner (a non-native speaker of English having been educated in the U.S. K-12 school system prior to entering a tertiary institution) and enrollment in a composition course.

The study design included a case study methodology and employed a process of triangulation to establish reliability and validity of the data (Denzin & Lincoln, 2000). Data collection occurred over two academic quarters, approximately 6 months in length, in the belief that a prolonged engagement with the case study participants would increase the reliability and validity of the data collected (Stake, 2000). Data sources included participant interviews and academic literacy logs. The interviews were carried out by specifically inquiring about, discussing, and questioning the participants' academic literacy difficulties and strategies.

All interviews were audio taped with the participants' consent. Transcriptions of the interviews were made immediately following each interview and were numbered, coded, and analyzed for common themes and/or patterns, for multiple instances in the data to find meaning, for single instances in the data to find meaning, and across cases for similarities and/or differences (Creswell, 2003). The transcriptions were also used to do member checks, which were used in this study as a means for establishing credibility (Denzin & Lincoln, 2000). Perspicuous interview segments were chosen for analysis and inclusion to illustrate these themes and patterns.

Academic literacy logs were used as a means of keeping track of participants' literacy tasks and to raise their awareness of their own academic literacy strategies. By discussing what they recorded in their literacy logs, participants were able to focus their attention on what they understood and what they needed to know about their academic literacy strategies. Awareness of their academic literacy strategies allowed them the opportunity to learn more about them, evaluate their effectiveness, and make adjustments where and when necessary.

Findings and Discussion

Academic Reading Difficulties and Strategies

Andrew reported difficulty with understanding lexical items in academic reading tasks in his college composition course. In general, Andrew's perception of academic reading was relatively positive, although he claimed that he was "not a big fan" of it in his first language or in English. In one of our interviews, Andrew reported that he did not have difficulties with (academic) reading in his L1:

c: How well do you read in your native language?
a: Read real well. I don't have trouble with reading.

Likewise, he also claimed to not have difficulties with academic reading in English. However, despite these claims, Andrew did not identify himself as an academic reader, stating, "I'm not a reader. I'm not a reading person."

In spite of Andrew's positive perspective on academic reading, he faced difficulties with not understanding what he was reading because of his limited lexicon. In fact, this was the only issue he raised in interviews regarding difficulties with academic reading. Because of this difficulty, Andrew recognized that it took him a great deal of time to read and that he was unable to effectively use the course readings to complete assigned writing tasks. Students in Andrew's college composition course were regularly asked to complete assigned readings and then produce a short essay based on his understanding of the readings. The purpose of the task according to the course syllabus was to help students prepare for class discussions, use analytical concepts and techniques, think critically about writing and reading habits, record thinking done during the class about the reading and writing, and provide a source material for use in other course assignments (English 110 course syllabus, Winter 2006). The expectation was that students would produce academic writing in this short essay that would include a strong thesis or primary argument, good use of evidence and citation, effective organization strategies, and thorough editing. One of the essays Andrew completed was on Marianne Hirsch's "Reframing the Human Family Romance." The expectations for this essay were to write about the overall form and organization of Hirsch's essay and the relationship between its parts. Even though students were encouraged to use multiple quotations from the essay, Andrew was able to incorporate only a single direct quote in his essay. When asked why he had not used more quotations, Andrew expressed frustration with the "academic" nature of the vocabulary in the text and amount of time that it took to read the assignment. He did not mention any difficulties with the topic, the overall writing task, or the mechanics of integrating quotes into a writing passage; he simply attributed his problems to the vocabulary in the text, as can be seen in the following interview segment:

A: Mostly I can read it [assigned course reading], but I don't get what trying to say … Probably too academic for me.
C: What do you mean by too academic?
A: Like the word, the word of choice they use, just some big word and the way they write the sentence. It take like times to understand it. Their, they way they use example and connect their ideas are different from a normal essay, so…

Because Andrew perceived his reading difficulties to be mainly lexical in nature, he most frequently relied on the lexical reading strategy of using the dictionary to help him understand the outside sources he chose to incorporate in his research paper for his college composition course:

C: Were there other difficulties [with reading the outside sources], like with language?
A: Yeah, 'cause they used a lot of big words in there [outside sources].
C: So the vocabulary…?
A: Yeah, I gotta keep my dictionary handy.

Tiffany's perception of academic reading was very different from that of Andrew's in that she claimed to "hate reading in English." This is a seeming contradiction to her multilingual, multi-literate background. One might expect that someone who already knows many languages would like to learn and use them. However, this is not Tiffany's case, as can be seen in one interview segment.

T: … like, I hate English reading. So far what I read that was most interesting was "Mother Tongue." Other things are hard to understand and boring.
C: What was so hard to understand?
T: I have no idea. I understand every single word. It just doesn't make any sense.

Like Andrew, Tiffany also faced the difficulty of understanding the assigned readings for her college composition course. However, her difficulty was somewhat different from Andrew's. Tiffany's main challenge as a reader was contextualizing the reading she was doing for her courses. In the interview segment below, Tiffany discusses the difficulties she had with comprehending the article "Ethnicity: Identity and Difference" by Stuart Hall that students were asked to read and analyze rhetorically in a composition. The assignment, according to the syllabus, asked that students comprehend the text in order to summarize and analyze it as well as integrate direct quotations to support the analysis (English 110 course syllabus for Spring Quarter, 2006). Tiffany, however, found that she neither had the background knowledge about the topic necessary to help her understand the content of the article nor did she identify with the content of the text from a sociologist's perspective. As a consequence, Tiffany reported that it took her about 10 hours to complete the rhetorical analysis. Her discussion of the struggles she had with understanding the article can be seen here:

C: You keep saying that it was difficult to understand. Why was that?
T: Why was that? The author who wrote the article was a sociologist. At first when I didn't understand the article, I went to my friend and she asked if this was a sociology class. I'm like no, it's an English class, so I think the article tend more to the sociology part and what the author thinks identity is based on the sociology view, so I thought it was really hard to understand. The tone and the terms he was using. Like he talked about Karl Marx and how his opinion relates to identity. I'm like okay, he's the person who came up with Communism. That's all I know. Like I understood every single word, but I don't understand what he was talking about. Like I read it and I read it and I'm like Oh my god, I'm dying. But every single word I could understand what he is trying to say.

In this segment, Tiffany recognized and pointed out what she did and did not understand about the article. For example, she understood that Karl Marx originated Communism, and understood the meaning of every individual word in the text. However, she was frustrated by the fact that despite her understanding of the words and sentences, it was not enough to help her understand it in its totality because she lacked the necessary background knowledge. And as evidenced in the interview transcript, this caused her great frustration. Like Andrew, Tiffany's difficulty in comprehending the article interfered with her ability to complete the academic writing task. These students' experiences thus highlight the importance of the reading–writing connection (Hirvela, 2004) and illustrate that academic writing difficulties of generation 1.5 learners may be more reading-related than writing-related.

However, unlike Andrew, Tiffany, in attempting to overcome this difficulty with academic reading, utilized a strategy that she previously used because it effectively helped her learn unknown words.

C: What was so difficult about [vocabulary] quiz 5 and 6?
T: Vocabulary that was hard to remember.
C: Why?
T: ... when I first started to learn English, people always a-p-p-l-e, apple, apple, apple, like that. But for me, it was more the pronunciation than just memorizing the alphabet. So I was trying to sound it [the word] out. So that's easier to understand, and it takes less time too.

As can be seen here, when Tiffany had difficulty remembering vocabulary, she invoked a strategy she had used previously to help her remember lexicon. From Tiffany's previous experience with learning vocabulary, she discovered that emphasizing pronunciation, or what Ong (1982) refers to as "oral memorization," was an effective strategy for learning. However, Tiffany found this strategy did not work as well with academic literacy tasks in her composition course as it had with previous tasks in other courses because of the difficulty she had with pronunciation. In the same interview she stated, "It was hard [learning the lexicon] because some of the words were really hard to pronounce". What she found from trial and error across academic contexts was that this strategy did not work. However, even if the strategy was not successful, it is nonetheless significant that Tiffany employed strategies for her academic reading.

In all, then, while both Andrew and Tiffany faced difficulties with academic reading in their composition course, the sources of these difficulties were quite different. Andrew's major difficulty was in working with a limited lexicon that in turn limited his comprehension of the text. Tiffany, on the other hand, had no trouble decoding the text, but faced a difficulty that was probably not unlike many of her native English-speaking peers; namely, a lack of the background knowledge and schemata necessary to contextualize and interpret the meaning of texts. With regard to strategies of academic reading, Andrew and Tiffany discussed utilizing what they had available to help them overcome difficulties with academic reading or to complete academic reading tasks: various lexical strategies. What the comparison of the difficulties and strategies of these two generation 1.5 learners shows us is the level of understanding and notions they have of academic reading. We can also see how with Andrew there was more of a match between the difficulty faced and strategy used; both were more at the semantic level. On the other hand, with Tiffany, the difficulty she faced was at the conceptual level, whereas the strategy she used was more at the semantic level.

Academic Writing Difficulties and Strategies

Both Andrew and Tiffany faced difficulties with academic writing as well, but again the sources of their difficulties were quite different. For Andrew they were primarily mechanical while for Tiffany they were more holistic.

Andrew believed that the key to becoming a successful academic writer was to acquire more grammatical and lexical knowledge. In the following interview segment, Andrew discusses studying for the Test of English as a Foreign Language (TOEFL) during his senior year of high school. Part of the preparation included learning to write an academic essay.

A: I pretty much … just read books on TOEFL and essay, but I didn't really do the essay. I just learned the grammars and listening.

C: Why didn't you do the essay?

A: 'Cause like I don't really like writing that much 'cause it takes time. And the other stuff doesn't matter. But if you know a lot of grammar, you can expand your writing.

Andrew's comment suggests that he believes that one does not need to actually write in order to improve one's writing; one only needs to improve vocabulary and grammar. In a subsequent interview, he elaborated on this notion:

A: 'Cause I can write what I want to express, but in order to know what you want to write, you need word to describe it, and there are so many different words. You can use words to describe one thing that are different from formal writing, it's just normal. So what I mean is if you know a lot of words, you can change your style and make your essay more interesting.

This suggests that Andrew almost equated increased writing proficiency with an increased lexicon. This is consistent with the frequent lexical difficulties he encountered with the academic reading tasks during the study. Andrew was far from unique in this regard (see previous research by Hartman & Tarone, 1999; Lowry, 1999; Reid, 1997; Santos, 2004). In short, Andrew's understanding of how he could improve his academic writing focused primarily on the mechanical level, on English grammar and lexicon.

Andrew considered "grammar" to be his greatest academic writing challenge in most of the academic writing tasks he did for the course. In discussing the feedback he received from his instructor on essays, he stated:

A: I didn't read all the comments here, but I think she wants me to work on the grammars…

Likewise, a little later in the same interview, when we returned to discussing the mini essays for the course, he once again focused on grammar:

C: I forgot to ask you about the difficulties that you had in regards to [writing the mini essays].
A: Difficulty? … Grammar.

In response to difficulties with academic writing in his college composition courses, Andrew reported that he used more academic writing strategies than reading strategies. His most frequently mentioned strategy was to focus on stages of the composing process in order to help him complete writing tasks. For example, in the following transcript segment, Andrew discusses the different stages in the writing process he used to help him overcome the difficulty of organizing his thoughts in an essay for his college composition course:

C: How do you go about trying to overcome the difficulty of putting together your thoughts for the essay?
A: Well, the idea probably came from when we meeting and those idea came from that. And then I was trying to read over my old draft, and trying to revise it and fit the ideas. When I do that, I check for grammar and trying to use different words too, just like use all the techniques I learned in writing essays, academic.

Here we can see that going through the stages of the writing process including writing tutorials, multiple drafting, editing, and particularly Andrew's approach to revising his writing, in themselves constituted good writing in Andrew's view.

As previously discussed, Andrew's notion of academic writing emphasized fully knowing the grammar and lexicon of a language. Likewise, grammar was highly prominent in his notion of the writing process. While he had a notion of what the writing process includes, looking at grammar during revision seems to be the most salient step in the process for him.

Tiffany's notion of success in academic writing is quite different from Andrew's. While Andrew believed that improvement in writing came from knowing more about structure and vocabulary, Tiffany believed that improvement in writing comes from understanding the source(s) one is writing about. So while Andrew took a more mechanical view of writing improvement, Tiffany's beliefs about writing improvement were grounded more at the level of academic discourse, where writing is viewed as being source-based rather than experience-based. Tiffany realized that one cannot write without a source, and one must understand it in order to write about it. Likewise, Tiffany believed that the key to understanding academic texts is to become familiar with the language indicative of a particular academic discourse community. She therefore did not interpret her difficulties as primarily a problem of limitations associated with being a second language learner. On the other hand, Andrew believed that the key to understanding academic texts was to focus on learning more grammar and lexicon. Tiffany's beliefs about academic writing point toward an ideological view; she sees academic writing as being understood and situated within a specific context. On the other hand, Andrew's beliefs point toward an autonomous view of academic writing, where it consists merely as skills for completing academic literacy tasks detached from a context.

Unlike Andrew, Tiffany's greatest difficulty as a writer was "developing" her essays. By "developing" she meant writing analytically and including the right kind of supporting evidence. One of the academic writing tasks for Tiffany's college composition course was to write an analytical summary. In the following interview segment, Tiffany discusses the specific difficulty she had with writing this assignment:

T: The summary, when I was in English 107, we did the descriptive summary, so I had trouble trying to understand the difference between descriptive and analytical summary. Basically you wrote a descriptive summary and then you analyze it … It took me 2 hours. It was so hard. I thought it was hard. Like the summary part wasn't hard. The analyzing part was hard 'cause you need to get the author's point and what he was talking about.

From her discussion, we can see that Tiffany's difficulty with writing an analytical summary seemed to stem from two problems. One was her lack of prior experience with and understanding of diverse writing genres. The other was her struggles with understanding the source text used for the analysis.

Because of her lack of understanding of source texts, she found it difficult to develop support. In the following interview segment, Tiffany discussed this difficulty in the context of an analytical summary assignment for her college composition course, where students were asked to choose an article from four that they had read for the class and summarize and analyze it. Tiffany chose the article "Mother Tongue" by Amy Tan.

c: So you were to summarize and analyze the text and you've written the first draft. What difficulties did you have?

t: Analyzing

c: Can you say more about that?

t: I got the author's major point, the main point, and then I just need to say how the author approached the main point. From the article it would be the experiences that she gave to approach her point. Why the language was so important to speak perfect English. But then it was not long enough. I need to find another major point that she was talking about. But it was hard for me to find a second major point 'cause I was so focused on the first major point. So it took me a while to find the second major point.

While Tiffany seemed to understand one of the author's main points of the article she chose for this task, she still struggled in finding another main point to include in her discussion of the task, which may have been that she had not given enough thought to her analysis of the text.

In regards to academic writing strategies, like Andrew, Tiffany discussed the use of stages in the writing process as strategies for completing and overcoming difficulties with academic writing tasks; however, her notion of writing process is different from that of Andrew's. The interview segments below highlight the stages of the writing process that Tiffany used to complete an in-class essay for her college composition course:

t: First I had to think about it [the topic].

t: I spent a lot of time thinking before I started to write.

First, Tiffany thought about the topic on which she was writing. Then, after she thought about the topic, she wrote and reserved time at the end to edit for grammar errors:

t: I went back through for grammar and stuff. And I think the grammar was okay. The only thing I'm not sure about is if it was interesting to the instructor.

Tiffany's notion of writing process contrasts with Andrew's in that she spent considerable time thinking before writing. Even at the end of the process, her main concern was whether her writing was interesting, not whether the grammar was correct. On the other hand, Andrew's notion of the writing process focused almost exclusively on grammar and lexical choice.

Following instructors' feedback for academic writing tasks was another academic writing strategy frequently discussed by Tiffany. The variety of academic writing genres assigned, especially in the college composition course, and her relative unfamiliarity with these genres because of the prevalence of multiple choice or short answer exercises in other academic contexts may have been the reason she focused on following instructors' feedback for academic writing tasks. Tiffany's frequent use of academic reading and writing strategies may be in part because, as reported in the literature, female ESL learners discuss using language learning strategies more frequently than males (Green & Oxford, 1995). Tiffany discussed using both written and oral feedback from her instructors including instructor notes in the margins of her papers and writing tutorials where she and the instructor discussed a piece of her writing face to face.

An example of how Tiffany followed an instructor's written feedback can be seen in the interview transcript below. After spending about 10 hours trying to decipher what the text meant, Tiffany e-mailed her instructor to ask for help. The instructor responded to Tiffany's e-mail with an interpretation of what the text meant and suggestions as to how to utilize the understanding of the text when writing the assignment.

T: ... I read the e-mail first and kinda put it in my own. Then I printed it out and went back to the book and this topic relates to what the author said in the first article. It had four different sections as well, so I kinda thought the section three related to that section.

From Tiffany's solicitation of her instructor's help on this assignment, we can see that Tiffany viewed the instructor as a holder of knowledge, that is, the instructor understood the text and could provide Tiffany with this understanding. Tiffany also saw value in the instructor's understanding of the text, so much so that she utilized the instructor's feedback in order to write her paper. Tiffany reported that after reading through and thinking about the instructor's response, it took her just a couple hours more to complete the assignment. However, because of the importance of completing the assignment rather than developing her own understanding of the text, Tiffany utilized her instructor's understanding of the text as a substitute for her own.

Tiffany frequently discussed strategies for developing writing and completing academic writing tasks for her college composition course. In the following interview segment, Tiffany discusses her difficulty with development for a summary analysis essay for her college composition course. In this assignment, students needed to find points of analysis of a text they chose to analyze and summarize. Tiffany chose Amy Tan's essay, "Mother Tongue." In the process of completing the assignment, Tiffany had difficulties analyzing the text because of what she reported as her lack of experience with analysis. When she was finally able to find a point from the text she could analyze, she reached a place where she could not find another. In the interview transcript below, we see a discussion of the strategy she used to help her come up with another point of analysis:

C: Did you find one [another point of analysis]?
T: Yeah, well, I don't know if it's a major point, but I just made it up. The second strategy was to see the routine that she used over and over again. That was a strategy in our book that you count the words. How many times she use, and a lot of the time it means it's important. I didn't count the words, but I count what she was approaching, and I thought that would be a good second major point.

At the beginning of Tiffany's response, we can see that she was a bit uncertain about the second point of analysis she chose because she did not know if it was an important point to analyze from the text. From the interview segment we can see that she used a strategy of writing development that came from the course textbook and modified it to fit her own purposes in writing. Rather than counting repetitive words in the text, Tiffany chose to count the repetitive approaches Tan included in the text.

In all then, the participants had varying difficulties with regard to academic writing, including grammar (Andrew) and development (Tiffany). These results also seem to echo some discussions in the literature about the academic writing difficulties observed in other generation 1.5 learners (Reid, 1997; Thonus, 2003). Strategies that both these students used in their academic writing included frequent discussion of the stages in the writing process. However, previous research has not shown how students may follow instructors' writing feedback and strategies for writing development (Ferris, 1999). The comparison of these two students emphasizes that participants' notions of academic writing are based on previous experience with academic writing in their L1 and L2 or foreign language(s). It also highlights learner differences when it comes to examining difficulties and strategic knowledge. Finally, it shows that writing proficiencies can vary even within roughly the same level. For example, Andrew's writing difficulties and the strategies he utilized to overcome them focused more on academic writing at the semantic level, whereas for Tiffany, they focused more on academic writing at a rhetorical level.

Conclusions and Recommendations

In this chapter, I related case studies of two generation 1.5 learners in order to understand their differing academic literacy difficulties and the academic literacy strategies they utilized to overcome these difficulties to successfully complete academic tasks.

Findings from these case studies have several implications for teaching and curriculum development. For one thing, they suggest that instructors must keep in mind that they may have generation 1.5 learners in their courses and critically examine their pedagogy to see that it is as inclusive as possible. For example, while academic lexicon was one of the most frequently reported difficulties that these generation 1.5 learners faced in academic reading, it was not part of the teaching and curricula in all but one college composition course that Tiffany took. Clearly lexicon is an area that needs to be represented in college composition curricula when classes include generation 1.5 learners. Furthermore, even when generation 1.5 learners may possess strategies for deciphering academic lexicon, they may not always be effective. For example, Parry (1991) found that English learners who used the strategy of guessing lexical meaning from context were unable to use it effectively. Likewise, a number of studies show that the context in which an unknown word appears is not always clear and guessing requires a vast vocabulary (Folse, 2004; Pino-Silva, 1993; Schatz & Baldwin, 1996). Consequently, it is important for instructors to examine their teaching and curricula to ensure they are meeting generation 1.5 learners' academic literacy needs and helping them to establish and/or adjust the academic literacy strategies they may already possess.

The findings of this study also highlight the differences between these two students' approaches to academic reading and writing. While both Andrew and Tiffany reported difficulties with lexicon in their academic reading, grammar was more an issue for Andrew than Tiffany. Learners like Andrew could benefit from grammar instruction in college composition courses. This might include providing students with editing exercises that target their errors (see, e.g., Valdés, 1992). At the same time, it is important to keep in mind that most generation 1.5 learners do not possess the meta-language about English grammar that many international students do. When students have learned grammar through oral input and unsystematic exposure to grammar rules (Reid, 1997), they may not possess a meta-language for grammar. It is therefore important to make sure the grammar work we provide them in our courses is accessible to them, with minimal grammar jargon, and that it teaches them how to use grammar rather than learning about grammar.

In contrast to Andrew, Tiffany found developing content in writing was a difficulty. These results echo the case studies done by Frodesen and Starna (1999) showing that generation 1.5 learners can struggle with the rhetorical issue of writing development. They suggest that generation 1.5 learners and other students with similar academic writing needs in courses like college composition need to be explicitly taught strategies for writing and text development. These findings also show the importance of providing learners with readings that are understandable to learners (or can be made so through instruction). Both Andrew and Tiffany had difficulties in understanding the readings they were assigned to write on for their college composition courses and these problems made it difficult for them to complete the assigned writing tasks. Therefore, it is important for instructors to carefully choose readings to include as part of writing tasks and to not assume that readers all possess the same level of background or cultural knowledge.

Another means of helping generation 1.5 learners develop content in their writing is by providing them with exercises and activities that introduce them to strategies to develop support. For example, Bloch and Crosby (2006) used blogging in a beginning college ESL composition course with generation 1.5 learners. Because these learners came to the course with strong oral proficiency but weaker skills in academic literacy, blogging assignments served as a bridge to develop their writing proficiency without concern for issues of rhetoric or composition. Gradually, these generation 1.5 learners were introduced to the conventions of academic writing by, for example, using student blogs as an outside source to be incorporated into academic writing such as a synthesis essay. In addition, highlighting development in writing samples may help generation 1.5 learners see its structure and organization, which may in turn help them better conceptualize this aspect of academic writing. Helping learners to identify parts of their writing that need development also provides them with tools they need to move toward becoming autonomous writers.

The differences in writing difficulties between the two participants in this study suggest that it is important for instructors to discover the academic literacy strategies generation 1.5 learners possess. This can be done with the administration of a simple needs assessment. It is also important not only to be aware of the academic literacy strategies demanded by the tasks in our courses but also, if necessary, incorporate formal and informal instruction in our curricula to help these learners gain the academic literacy strategies they need to complete the tasks. As we saw in this study, some of the academic literacy tasks the generation 1.5 learners completed assumed background knowledge and strategies that they neither possessed nor were taught. For example, Tiffany struggled to understand an article on sociology that she did not have the background knowledge to understand. This points to the need on the part of instructors for an increased awareness of the background knowledge generation 1.5 learners possess and structure instruction and curricula accordingly.

Although the findings present only a small part of a much bigger picture of the academic literacy experiences of these learners, the participants in this study hopefully help us to see more clearly from their perspective what it means for them to utilize strategies to overcome difficulties with academic literacy tasks in the college composition classroom.

Acknowledgments

I am indebted to Alan Hirvela and George Newell for their help with initial drafts of this manuscript. I am also indebted to the editors of this volume for their help in transforming part of my dissertation into a publishable manuscript.

References

Bialystok, E. (1981). The role of conscious strategies in second language proficiency. *Modern Language Journal, 65*(1), 24–35.

Bloch, J. & Crosby, C. (2006). Creating a space for virtual democracy. *Essential Teacher, 3*(3), 38–41.

Block, E. (1986). The comprehension strategies of second language readers. *TESOL Quarterly, 20*(3), 463–494.

Carson, J., Chase, N., Gibson, S., & Hargrove, M. (1992). Literacy demands of the undergraduate curriculum. *Reading Research and Instruction, 31*(4), 25–50.

Creswell, J.W. (2003). *Research design: Qualitative, quantitative, and mixed methods approaches.* Thousand Oaks, CA: Sage.

Denzin, N. & Lincoln, Y. (Eds.) (2000). *Handbook of qualitative research* (2nd ed.). Thousand Oaks, CA: Sage.

Ferris, D. (1999). One size does not fit all: Response and revision issues for immigrant student writers. In L. Harklau, K. Losey, & M. Siegal (Eds.), *Generation 1.5 meets college composition: Issues in the teaching of writing to U.S.-educated learners of ESL* (pp. 143–157). Mahwah, NJ: Lawrence Erlbaum Associates.

Folse, K. (2004). *Vocabulary myths: Applying second language research to classroom teaching.* Ann Arbor: University of Michigan Press.

Frodesen, J. & Starna, N. (1999). Distinguishing incipient and functional bilingual writer profiles. In L. Harklau, K. Losey, & M. Siegal (Eds.), *Generation 1.5 meets college composition: Issues in the teaching of writing to U.S.-educated learners of ESL* (pp. 61–79). Mahwah, NJ: Lawrence Erlbaum Associates.

Green, J. & Oxford, R. (1995). A closer look at learning strategies, L2 proficiency, and gender. *TESOL Quarterly, 29*(2), 261–297.

Harklau, L. (2001). From high school to college: Student perspectives on literacy practices. *Journal of Literacy Research, 33*(1), 33–70.

Hartman, B. & Tarone, E. (1999). Preparation for college writing: Teachers talk about writing instruction for Southeast Asian American students. In L. Harklau, K. Losey, & M. Siegal (Eds.), *Generation 1.5 meets college composition: Issues in the teaching of writing to U.S.-educated learners of ESL* (pp. 99–118). Mahwah, NJ: Lawrence Erlbaum Associates.

Hirvela, A. (2004). *Connecting reading and writing in second language writing instruction.* Ann Arbor: University of Michigan Press.

Johns, A. (1992). Toward developing a cultural repertoire: A case study of a Lao college freshman. In D.E. Murray (Ed.), *Diversity as resource: Redefining cultural literacy* (pp. 183–201). Alexandria, VA: TESOL.

Leki, I. (1995). Coping strategies of ESL students in writing tasks across the curriculum. *TESOL Quarterly, 29*(2), 235–260.

Leki, I. & Carson, J. (1994). Students' perceptions of EAP writing instruction and writing needs across the disciplines. *TESOL Quarterly, 28*(1), 81–101.

Lowry, M. (1999). Lexical issues in the university ESL writing class. *CATESOL Journal, 11*(1), 7–27.

O'Malley, J. & Chamot, A. (1993). *Learning strategies in second language acquisition.* Cambridge, UK: Cambridge University Press.

Ong, W. (1982). *Orality and literacy: The technologizing of the word.* London: Methuen.

Parry, K. (1991). Building a vocabulary through academic reading. *TESOL Quarterly, 25*(4), 629–653.

Pino-Silva, J. (1993). Untutored vocabulary acquisition and L2 reading ability. *Reading in a Foreign Language, 9*(2), 845–857.

Raimes, A. (1987). Language proficiency, writing ability, and composing strategies: A study of ESL college student writers. *Language Learning, 37*(3), 439–467.

Reid, J. (1997). Which non-native speaker? Differences between international students and U.S. resident (language minority) students. *New Directions for Teaching and Learning, 70,* 17–27.

Santos, M. (2004, February). Some findings on the academic vocabulary skills of language-minority community college students. *Focus on the Basics, 6*(3), 7–9.

Schatz, E. & Baldwin, R. (1986). Context clues are unreliable predictors of word meanings. *Reading Research Quarterly, 21*(4), 439–453.

Stake, R. (2000). Case studies. In N. Denzin & Y. Lincoln (Eds.), *Handbook of qualitative research* (pp. 435–454). Thousand Oaks, CA: Sage.

Thonus, T. (2003). Serving generation 1.5 learners in the university writing center. *TESOL Journal, 12*(1), 17–24.

Valdés, G. (1992). Bilingual minorities and language issues in writing. *Written Communication, 9*(1), 85–136.

9 Responding to High-Stakes Writing Assessment

A Case Study of Five Generation 1.5 Students

Jennifer A. Mott-Smith Towson University

This chapter examines the experiences of five generation 1.5 students with a writing proficiency exam (WPE) at a large public urban university.[1] It focuses on the impact that passing or failing had on the students' accommodation or resistance to the norms and values about language and literacy that were embedded in the discourses of *standard language ideology* and *standards* of the high-stakes testing process. As we examine the students' invocation of these discourses, we see how the students regarded the notion of standard language. We also see how they saw themselves, in terms of such things as writing ability and attitudes toward ESL status. Additionally, we find forms of resistance to the WPE, such as the suspicion of racism, the belief that the university did not adequately prepare students for the exam, and the discourse of joy in writing.

While WPEs may be roadblocks to the academic achievement of many students, they may present a particular problem for some generation 1.5 students. Research has indicated that non-native English-speaking students tend to pass WPEs at a lower rate than native English speakers (Ching & Moore, 1993; California State University Graduation Writing Assessment Requirement [CSU GWAR] Review Committee, 2003; Janopoulos, 1995; Murphy, 2001; Ruetten, 1994). One reason for this discrepancy may be that the home language of generation 1.5 students is not the standard English required on WPEs. As many have argued (Gee, 1986; Weedon, 1987), different social groups are associated with different language forms that in turn are constitutive of people's identities. Rather than growing up with a standard English vernacular that approximates the language of school and the academy, many generation 1.5 students grow up in multilingual communities where they speak hybrid forms involving the mixing of languages (see Zentella, 1997). These hybrid forms provide important identity markers. However, when generation 1.5 students encounter WPEs, they find that to be successful they must leave aside their familiar forms and adopt a standard academic English form. In this study, the WPE required that students adopt a single-voiced rhetorical position that did not encourage them to explore hybrid perspectives in their writing (cf., Mountford, 1999).

The Discourses of the WPE

At the site of my study, I collected and examined numerous university documents that discussed the WPE.[2] Several important discourses emerged from these documents and I explore here the discourses of *standard language ideology* and of *standards*. Discourse reflecting *standard language ideology* defined a standard English form, most obviously through the exam scoring criteria. Proficiency in this form was positioned as necessary for demonstrating that one was a university-educated person and that one was ready for the workplace. Two university documents explained, for instance, that the exam measures "capabilities generally accepted as the mark of a university-educated person" (Harwood, 1999, p. 1; Office of the Provost et al., 1998, p. 1). Thus, the standard English form required to pass the exam was positioned as *the* mark of education, and the possibility that a person who used a different form was educated was made remote.

The discourse of *standards* set up opposing notions of standards on the one hand to access and retention on the other. One report stated, for instance: "the campus is as strongly committed to academic excellence as to equal access" (Offices of the Provost & the Dean of Undergraduate Education, 1995, p. 3). And again: "The university is constantly exploring strategies for improving the level of retention of our students without sacrificing the quality of the degree we offer" (Offices of the Provost & the Dean of Undergraduate Education, 1995, p. 20). Within this equation, linguistic and racially subordinated minority students were labeled "high risk" (Offices of the Provost & the Dean of Undergraduate Education, 1995, p. 20) and "non-traditional" (Offices of the Provost & the Dean of Undergraduate Education, 1995, p. 18; Harwood, 1999, p. 4). It was said that these students were "the products of deficient prior education" (Offices of the Provost & the Dean of Undergraduate Education, 1995, p. 17).

Occasionally, references specifically to linguistic minority students were made. A report entitled *The Performance of Two Cohorts of Students on the Writing Proficiency Requirement* claimed that, "The idea that less prepared students or students whose first language is not English require more effort and time to learn to read analytically and write in expository style should come as no surprise" (Harwood, 1999, p. 4). This statement was made to explain why non-native English-speaking students may have to attempt the WPE repeatedly before they pass. However, neither this statement nor other university documents recognized the research-supported positions that literacy skills are transferable, or that students who write analytically in their native language also tend to write this way in English (Cummins, 1979).[3]

These students were seen as threatening university standards. The discourse held them responsible for their own exam failure rather than analyzing the ways in which the university contributed to that failure. The student handbook *Nine Elements of Proficiency in Writing*, for instance, stated: "Most students who prepare conscientiously pass the exam on the first try" (2003, p. 2), implying that students who do not pass on the first try are not conscientious.

Study Design

The data presented here come from interviews with five generation 1.5 students conducted between March 2004 and February 2005. I recruited the participants by posting flyers, setting up a table in a busy corridor, e-mailing student organizations, and soliciting references from students and faculty at the university where I worked as an ESL instructor. Three participants approached me having seen the publicity, one was referred by a student, and one was referred by a faculty member. This last participant, Cat, was referred specifically because she had left the university due to experiences with the WPE.

I conducted three fifteen-minute interviews with each participant. The interviews followed Seidman's (1991) structure for interviewing: the first interview established the life story context; the second explored the specifics of the students' WPE attempts; and the third provided an opportunity for the participants to make meaning of their exam experience. All interviews were transcribed and coded using both open and theory-based codes. Analyses of accommodation emerged from a power relations analysis based on Carspecken (1996). Analyses of resistance emerged primarily from the open coding process.

The students were Cat (23), John (28), Marina (20), Sherry (24), and Vivian (29).[4] Cat was a U.S.-born ethnic Chinese who mixed Cantonese and English at home. John immigrated to the U.S. from Argentina at the age of 13; he was an ethnic Korean and spoke Korean at home. Marina immigrated to the U.S. from the Middle East at the age of 9; she spoke Arabic at home. Sherry immigrated from the PRC at the age of 14; she spoke Mandarin at home. Vivian immigrated to the U.S. from Vietnam at the age of 12; she spoke Vietnamese at home.

Of this group, Cat stood out in that she was U.S.-born, while the other four were immigrants. Cat was also the only first generation college student, and the only person who spoke of being discriminated against in the U.S. as a racially subordinated minority. Marina also stood out as different in that she was the only student to have entered the university as a first-year student; the other four were transfer students.[5]

The Students' Discourses

The Discourse of Standard Language Ideology

The students showed that they valued the standard language rules as defined by the exam scoring criteria. Vivian, for example, said: "And that's one of the things I believe in: the organization and structure requirement, the eight-fold requirement on the WPR [Writing Proficiency Requirement]."[6,7] Moreover, when asked what they thought good writing was, the students mentioned rules similar to those defined by the exam. In all, the students cited 14 components of good writing, namely, answering the question, citations, clarity, conciseness, effect on reader, flow, grammar, introduction–body–conclusion structure, main point, meaning, organization, spelling, supporting with quotes and paraphrase, and vocabulary. Of these, 12 were included in the scoring criteria or in the text of the student handbook; only "effect on the reader" and "conciseness" were not mentioned.

However, there was a slight difference in emphasis between students who passed the exam on the first attempt (John, Sherry, Vivian) and those who failed (Cat, Marina). Those who passed made statements consistent with the scoring criteria. In fact, two of them emphasized grammar to an even greater extent than the student handbook, which states, "It is unlikely that an exam will fail merely because it contains a few spelling or punctuation errors" (*Nine Elements of Proficiency in Writing*, 2003, p. 3). Vivian, for example, believed that the exam was looking for perfect grammar:

> Yeah, the correct grammar like verbs, yeah, I mean nouns, verbs, adjectives, all of that. It have to be correct grammar. *Why?* I mean [laughter in voice], you took the

test, you have to get grammar. I mean you already passed English 102, so your grammar have to be perfect. And if you still have problems with grammar and this is really a serious grammar structure, and then you have to take the grammar English again.

Having passed the WPE, these students seemed to feel that they were now in a position to endorse the imposition of the standard language.

Students who failed, by contrast, invoked the WPE scoring criteria themselves in order to define good writing. For example, when I asked Cat what good writing was, she responded:

> It's the same thing what I thought that the WPR [Writing Proficiency Requirement] want. It's just having the quotes and everything to back up your argument, stating your introduction, of course your argument, and then you write. Just answer the question; that's what the instruction is. And on the rest of the time, the body, you just back it up with quotes or paraphrase, whatever you want. And at the end, make sure you argued your argument. And then at the end, just do your conclusion and just wrap it all up, basically restate your argument.

In invoking the scoring criteria, Cat demonstrated that she understood the WPE requirements while at the same time expressing her outrage and incomprehension about having failed the exam three times.[8] When Marina invoked the scoring criteria, she was acknowledging that she did not fully understand why she had failed, and representing herself as an obedient student prepared to learn in the exam prep course.

Despite their support of the standard language as defined by the scoring criteria, two students (John, Marina) made a distinction between learning how to write well and learning what they needed to pass the WPE. For example, John said: "I don't really know what they're looking for. I just know how to pass it. That's all I researched [laughs] before the exam." Thus, these students were not simply obedient to the exam norms, but were actively negotiating their way through the requirement.

The Standards Discourse

As we have seen, three students passed the exam on the first attempt, while two failed it. For those who passed, the process was short, taking a few weeks at most to prepare the reading set and write the required essay. For those who failed, the process was long, taking months to attend counseling sessions, take required prep courses, file appeals, and wait for the next exam sitting. Both of these students failed the exam more than once, and facing the delay in attaining their goal of a college diploma and the threat of never earning one were stressful experiences. Cat suffered a loss of confidence in her writing ability, suspension, and eventual departure from the university. Marina also suffered a loss of confidence in her writing ability, causing her to change her major from law to business.

Not surprisingly, passing and failing affected the students' regard for the norms and values of the WPE differently. Students who passed ended up supporting the exam, although Vivian and Sherry thought that some changes should be made to it. Both

Vivian and John invoked the discourse of standards to justify the requirement. The students who failed, on the other hand, thought that the WPE should be abolished. They also invoked the standards discourse, not to justify the exam, but to attempt to understand their failure, wrestling with the negative labels put on linguistic minority students.

Vivian and John were the students who invoked the discourse of standards to justify the exam. Vivian's understanding was based on her knowledge of the California State University system, where she had completed a B.A.:

> Well, I came from California and the thing I experienced in California that most of the students grad from four year college they cannot write the essay when they get into the real world. And that's brought to the attention to the governor in California and they said they have graduate students, but when they do some kind of research for the company, they cannot do the writing. So when I see they have the writing proficiency over here, I think it's better. So they have at least they be able to write it.

John understood that standards were related to the university's accreditation. He also recognized that the university's reputation was maintained by the exam:

> I understood why the college would think it would be a requirement, because to make sure the graduates are able to perform. I mean, it would be embarrassing if they can't [laughter in voice]. So I think college would be embarrassed if its graduate cannot perform English in a certain level. And so I think I understand where they're coming from and stuff. So it is a bother, but I feel like it's not a big deal at all.

John's remarks targeted non-native English-speaking students. Thus, he distinguished linguistic minority students as threatening university standards just as the university documents did:

> if I was in charge of the university, I would wanna make sure that no non-English speaking graduates will be able to be sended out there [laughter in voice] with a diploma and they are just can't perform. And I think it will be embarrassing; it will give a bad reputation towards the education level of the university and all that, so.[9]

John seemed to support the exam because he believed that it helped counter the reputation of the university as not rigorous. In preparing to apply to dental school, he had an instrumental approach to college and saw the university as "just a stepping stone for me." I believe that John wanted to maintain the value of his degree because he thought it would help him get into graduate school. Thus, he was content to seek success on the university's terms. Consistent with this analysis, John was one of two students who explicitly rejected the notion of resistance to the exam. When I asked him how he would describe the exam to an incoming student, he revealed that, to him, the notion of resistance was distasteful:

Well, when people ask me about it, I just say that, "Oh, it's like a requirement that the college gives," and that's it [laughs]. I don't feel like I need to explain it or something. I just feel like it's just something that you need to do. That's it, you know? I don't really question why. I guess I'm more pleasant. I'm not gonna question the authority of it [laughter in voice]. I'm not disruptive that way maybe. But I didn't think it was such a big deal once I found out what it entailed. Like, it wasn't as hard or as long as I thought in the beginning, so.

Both Vivian and John were confident in their writing ability. Vivian said that she found writing in general to be easy. While John did not like to write, he felt that he was a good writer:

If I compare my writing to other people, I feel like I'm more precise, or like just more clear on my statements and flow of thought than other people. Yeah. Which is why I feel like my writing is better usually than most people.

Both students felt confident going into the exam, and for both, passing seemed to reinforce their understanding of themselves as good writers. This experience seemed to lessen their sensitivity for students who did not pass. Both students made statements blaming other students for their own failure. Vivian, for example, asserted that students failed because "they do not put enough effort in there." However, as we spoke during the interviews, Vivian backed off her position of upholding strict standards by means of the WPE. She even suggested that an oral version of the WPE could be used to demonstrate students' critical thinking abilities, since it was not fair to prevent hardworking students from graduating.

The "High-Risk" Label

Cat and Marina, students who had failed the WPE more than once, also invoked the standards discourse, not to justify the exam, but to attempt to understand their failure, wrestling with the negative labels put on linguistic minority students. Cat wondered out loud whether her public urban education had prepared her adequately to write in college. Referring to herself and a friend who also had not passed the WPE, she said:

And me and her, we've been going through a lot. We're like, "What the hell is wrong with us, you know?" And then we started thinking, "Is it the Boston Public's fault?" Because [laughs] we went to the Boston Public Schools that— We're like, "What the heck? What went wrong?"

Cat theorized that the level of English required by her high school classes may have been more basic than that demanded at the university. She explained that her high school had been a minority school with virtually no White students, and that those graduates who went to college tended to go to this public university. Cat reported that her high school teachers had not held high expectations for her academic achievement:

What they call us is an exam school, but we're graded the third one out of three. We're the third one. And people see it as, they're wannabees of the BLA, the Boston Latin Academy, and everything. We're not all that great and everything. So we want to prove to them because they already had the prediction, like, "Fifty percent of you guys aren't going to go to college," and everything. They made that, you know, "A lot of you guys are going to get pregnant, get married young or something's gonna happen. You guys won't finish college." And it's just our determination we're going to get into college and finish it. And that's how it is.

In addition to race, Cat recognized that class was involved:

The Boston Public, they always made fun of it, how it's not as good as the private schools, you know? Supposedly the private schools, I guess, they're more deter-mined to get the good straight A students from these classes, and for us—because we either went through Boston Public and some teachers are the greatest, some are the worst. And we see it as, I know that people in Boston Public, they don't have as much dedication I guess as the private schools. Because like in my classes, we had been making theories about private schools teachers versus the public school teachers. Because the private school teachers get paid more and the public schools don't. And maybe, we were thinking, maybe they don't have as much ded-ication as the private schools because they're not getting paid as much. And, I dunno, maybe they don't care as much. Because we had teachers that [chuckles], basically, like they will test you; they don't teach you anything. If you don't learn on your own, you're basically gonna get an F on your test.

From her high school experience, Cat had learned how to study on her own. She convened study groups to analyze the WPE reading sets and solicited faculty guidance. As an ethnic Chinese, she saw herself as particularly hardworking. Thus, when she failed the exam not once but three times, she not only lost confidence in herself, but she also started to resist the exam, believing that there was something wrong with it:

Well, things about it I don't understand is, it just makes you feel like—doing this test makes you feel like you can't write papers. You can't write any kind of papers. Because then I think about, well, all the papers I been writing supposedly for all these courses I've been taking for the WPR [WPE], I been passing them. Doesn't that show you that maybe I'm competent to write a paper? Maybe there's some-thing wrong with this test, or the people that's grading it actually. So it just made me confused, like I don't understand what's going on [chuckles lightly]. I was just lost.

Cat was particularly confused by the exam failure after taking the WPE prep course:

Because [in the course] they try to use the same exact format [as the exam] basi-cally ... They prepared you very well ... It became very easy. It's like, "Okay, okay, I get it." And then I'm like, "How could I fail again?" [chuckles lightly] It just didn't make sense at all. Like if I failed the test, why didn't I fail all the other courses then, you know? Why wouldn't the teacher just say, "Okay, you have major, major problem" [chuckles lightly] … I don't understand like how, if this test supposedly determine if I could graduate or not, like how all this time I've been passing these courses, because they all have writing in them. And it just didn't make sense to me at all.

Cat struggled with a precarious balance between thinking there was something wrong with her, and thinking there was something wrong with the exam scoring. She began to suspect that the scorers were racist, a possibility that her mother reinforced:

And then talking to my mom, she's like, "You always have to remember that [that your name is Chinese]." And I'm like, "Oh gosh" [chuckles]. And I'm hoping it's not, but then I just started thinking like, "What else can it be? What else can it be?" It's just like, it didn't make sense. I was doing well in my other classes and everything. It just didn't make sense.

In the end, Cat failed the exam three times, was suspended, and left the university. Cat did not drop out, but rather, felt "forced out."

Marina invoked the standards discourse in a different form. Consistent with the university documents' expectation that students whose first language is not English would naturally have difficulty passing the WPE, she explained that she was behind because she was an ESL student. She saw ESL status as a weakness reaching all the way back to fourth grade, when she had first started school in the U.S. She explained:

… in elementary school, and even in sixth grade, they always had an ESL teacher for me. Or instead of learning the regular English, I would go to the ESL teacher in a different room and just learn the basic English. So I've always been behind with English.

Marina also saw ESL status as the cause for the exam failure, concluding, "I'm pretty sure the whole ESL thing had something to do with it."

Like Cat, Marina was confused by the fact that she had passed her writing courses but not the WPE:

But, I mean, how did I get so far ahead without failing my courses? It's because I know enough how to write, and enough for the teachers who grade me, who are older, who've been teaching for years and years, to say, "This is a good paper, good job." You know? "You could have worked on this a little bit more, but overall it's a good paper." You know? If teachers give me the good grade, then it's fine.

And like Cat, Marina started resisting the exam. Marina resented that students alone should suffer the high-stakes consequences of failure when the university had failed to prepare them adequately. She gave this critique:

If the school sees that the classes aren't teaching us well, then they should go and attack teachers to teach better, not attack students to take that test. Because I heard the only reason it started was, in the 1970s, they felt that [the university] was giving an inflation, like grades, to the students, and so they had that test to make sure everyone is on top of things. And that kind of gets me mad. If there's a problem within how they teach, why do they have to make the students do something extra, you know, just to prove that the teachers are doing the right thing? ... They should look at the problem from the beginning, make it harder to get into [the university], you know? Because it's not that hard to get into here [laughter in voice], you know? Make it harder to get in here, be stricter about your teachers, have department heads look over the course syllabuses more, talk to the professors more, you know? If that's the problem, then go a different way at it.

Despite this critique, Marina rejected organized resistance to the WPE. She scoffed at the idea of joining a campus group that opposed the exam:

I wouldn't even join them because I wouldn't—[laughs] well, I wouldn't laugh at them, but in my head I would just look at them and laugh like, "What are you doing?" [laughter in voice] *Why?* Because the rules are rules. Like, "You're not special, anymore. You're not that special that they're gonna cancel the WPR for you."

And despite the fact that she saw ESL as her difficulty, Marina did not want to ask for help for this reason:

But I'm not gonna go up to the writing proficiency and be like, "Hey, English is my second language; give me a break." Because it doesn't work that way. It's like calling out for pity help. That won't get you anywhere.

Rather, Marina sought help through the official channels available to her, through the WPE office and prep course. In the face of the *high-risk* label, she represented herself as an earnest student who was willing to be taught. Marina failed the exam twice and was just beginning the prep course when I interviewed her. After the study, she hired a private tutor to help her pass, and she finally did.

The Discourse of Joy in Writing

Sherry, who passed the WPE on the first attempt, was unlike the other students who passed in that she did not invoke the standards discourse to justify the exam, she did not feel entirely confident about her writing ability, and she did not blame other students for their failure. Rather, Sherry spoke a discourse of joy in writing. She loved language, and read and wrote for fun. For her, the WPE was an extension of this. Unlike all the other students, Sherry saw the exam as a learning process, an opportunity to improve her writing skills, and believed it gave her an opportunity to express her own views.

However, Sherry's discourse of joy also led to her resisting some aspects of the exam process:

It's kind of a tough situation because at first, I wasn't ready to do it, because I feel like I have to. Because for students over seventy-five credits, and then if you're more than a junior, you have to take that. Otherwise, they tell you, right, "Oh, you'll be on probations." And then you can't take certain classes.... So a lot of students feel like they're forced to do it. So in that way it's not a good way of approaching students. Like if you forced, then you don't really have the joy of writing and then learning.

Like Marina, Sherry recognized that her English writing was "weak," and on the advice of her parents, had chosen to major in computer science. However, she remained committed to improving her writing:

But I mean, each semester I will always take one writing class anyways. *Why?* One, is to have diversity in the classes. Because usually I will take two CS [computer science] class and then two non-CS class. So one of them is usually writing, not necessarily in English class, but somehow has to involve with my writing English. *So why is that diversity important to you?* 'Cause I want to constantly improve myself, especially constantly like to improve my writing in English.

Sherry had begun to regret her choice of major, believing that if she had majored in English, it would have made her competitive with native-born Americans in the workplace. She also saw that most computer science majors were immigrants from China or India, and felt that she wanted to be in a more ethnically diverse major. Unlike Marina, Sherry did not seem to see her ESL status as holding her back.

University Responsibility for Exam Outcomes and the Bifurcation of the Student Body

The findings of this study show that the discourse of *standards* present in university documents bifurcated the student body into good and bad students. From the outset, linguistic minority students were positioned on the "bad" side. In this study, both students who passed and those who failed reacted to this positioning. The students who failed experienced an inner struggle in the attempt to represent themselves as good students. Two of the three students who passed seemed to join the "good" side by expressing support for the exam and blaming students who had failed for their own failure.

However, the data do not show that the passing students were more conscientious students than the failing ones. For example, the failing students described hours of diligent preparation for the exam, while John, who passed, mentioned that he had not even read the entire reading packet prior to entering the testing room. In addition, all five students embraced the standard language ideology endorsed by the university. Cat and Marina were not "bad" students. Both demonstrated their academic abilities through successful coursework. Cat, for instance, was involved in a study with an Asian American Studies Professor that demonstrated her ability to do academic research. She also worked in a community center with recently arrived immigrant children, demonstrating her ability to connect academic learning to community needs.

The data do show, however, that John joined Cat and Marina in the belief that the university did not prepare them for the exam. There are several arguments that can be made to support this belief. First, some students felt that the courses intended to prepare them for the WPE (English 101 and 102, the first-year seminar, and the intermediate seminar) did not do so. John, speaking of the intermediate seminar, was clear on this point: "It didn't prepare me at all. I don't think it helped me at all." He explained:

> I think people who already knew how to write did well in the class; people who did not, didn't do too well. I don't think they actually learned anything. Pretty much he [the professor] just assumed that just making somebody continue writing, get into the habit of writing, will increase their chances or help them for the WPR. But the only time he actually gave us feedback on it [our writing] was doing the two major papers that we wrote, out of three, because those we did a first draft and turned it in and he gave it back to us with feedback. But the comments didn't help me, and the others, and I don't think it helped them as much either.

In addition, Marina, who was the only student in the study to have taken both English 101 and 102 at the university prior to attempting the WPE, earning the grades of B and A respectively, nevertheless failed the exam.

The second argument is that many students do not take the courses intended to prepare them for the WPE because they are transfer students. John, Vivian, Sherry, and Cat had all taken their first-year English courses at other institutions, and had had the first-year seminar waived. Taking these arguments together, it seems likely that, rather than being prepared for the WPE by the university, the students were prepared by prior writing experiences. John was explicit in fact in crediting his first-year composition teacher in community college for his ability to write. Contrasting the prior writing experiences of the students who passed with those who failed also supports the argument that students were prepared for the exam by prior experiences. All three students who passed had studied at the university level in the U.S. prior to beginning the current degree. Vivian had both an associate's and bachelor's degree, and had completed a year of law school; John had an associate's degree; and Sherry had taken math and science courses at an Ivy League institution. In addition, Vivian had also worked for 8 years as a paralegal. The students who failed the WPE, on the other hand, had not had prior university experience but were typical high school graduates.

An additional point is that the process designed to help students who have failed by bringing them to the point of passing did not help Cat or Marina. Both students were frustrated that the WPE office had not informed them of the exam prep courses before sanctions came into play. Neither found the office staff's feedback on their exam writing to be helpful. And both students failed the exam again after having taken the prep course. Cat wondered aloud whether this process was a form of punishment, and Marina used the metaphor of an attack in war to describe it. I believe that the process that the university makes students such as Cat and Marina go through is stigmatizing and may be humiliating enough to make them leave school. To the extent that the curriculum does not adequately prepare students for the exam, and to the extent that it compels them to proceed through this process after failing, the university is responsible for some students' failure and the negative impacts of that failure. It is tragic that high-stakes WPEs have such devastating consequences on the otherwise successful academic careers of generation 1.5 students.

Where Do We Go From Here?

North (1996) has argued that it was the acceptance of minority students into college after World War II that led to the belief that the bachelor's degree had lost its value. This devaluation of the degree led, in turn, to the demand for more accountability (North, 1996). It was this demand for accountability that brought about an increased dependence on standardized testing (Giroux, 1988). And, perhaps ironically, it is standardized testing that may have such dire consequences for some minority students.

What are the possible reasons for academically successful non-native English-speaking students to fail a WPE (cf., Byrd & Nelson, 1995; Johns, 1991)?[10] Interestingly, the two students in this study who failed were two of the students who had begun their schooling in English the earliest (Cat in kindergarten, Marina in fourth grade). By contrast, John, who passed, had been studying in English since seventh grade, and Sherry had studied in English only in ninth and tenth grade, leaving school thereafter to attain a GED. This might seem ironic, considering the claims made in reports like the one quoted above: "students whose first language is not English require more effort and time to learn to read analytically and write in expository style" (Harwood, 1999, p. 4). The situation is more complex than reports like this one suggest; passing a WPE depends on more than length of English study.

Passing a WPE in English may be related to one's first language literacy skills. Cat and Marina reported having less-developed home language literacy than the students who passed. Marina also implied that she may have been ill-prepared by her prior ESL classes. While it is possible that these classes did not challenge her adequately to master academic writing skills, it is also possible that her lack of literacy skills in her home language held Marina back in these classes. A direction for further research, then, is to investigate how particular kinds of first language literacy experiences relate to standardized testing outcomes (cf., Ching and Moore, 1993).

Passing a WPE may also be related to issues of socio-economic class. Social class in the United States cannot be ascertained solely through income levels, but involves a set of indicators, including income, and also consumption patterns, career and job choices, and education. In this study, first generation college student status is one indicator of social class. Cat was the only first generation college student, and she reported that her family lived in low-income housing ("the projects,"). By contrast, all the students who passed (as well as Marina, who failed) had at least one parent who had graduated from college. Sherry's father was a chemical engineer doing research at an Ivy League institution. Vivian's parents, although they had no experience with U.S. universities, had both majored in English in college in Vietnam and had worked for the U.S. government until the fall of Saigon. Cat may have been at a disadvantage in terms of the class-related issues of familiarity with college and knowing how to navigate one's way through the system.

A second, more subtle influence of social class in WPE outcomes may involve differences in language forms and functions. The findings of sociolinguists such as Heath (1983), and the work of sociologists/anthropologists such as Pierre Bourdieu, who has explored issues of language and power through his work on "cultural capital" (Bourdieu & Passeron, 1977), suggest that social class has an influence on discourse patterns. Although Vivian's parents were no longer working in the field for which they had been trained, they may have been able to instill in Vivian the language functions and forms that are needed for academic achievement, which may in turn have been cemented by her long experience writing as a paralegal. I suspect that one important form that they exposed her to was standard Vietnamese. While Cat, Marina, and Vivian all reported that they mixed languages, Vivian explained that her father was strict with her, insisting that she produce prescriptively correct Vietnamese. Cat, by contrast, spoke "Chinglish" to her father and he used this mixed language or a simplified Chinese with her. By broaching the issue of social class and language use, I am suggesting that educational researchers and practitioners need to interrogate further the assumptions related to class that are integral to our understandings of literacy and writing proficiency.

In addition to investigating influences on testing outcomes, we also need to urge university administrators to consider seriously the overwhelmingly negative impacts of high-stakes testing on immigrant students. Assessment may be firmly established in the structures of our universities, but high-stakes outcomes measures are not the only way to assess our programs and demonstrate high standards. Contextualized forms of assessment such as portfolios or classroom assessment are better ways to assess students.

Finally, this analysis of the discourse of *standards* shows us the negative effects that labels such as "high risk" may have on students. While I do not believe that we can easily change the discourses that are currently in use, I think that we should be mindful of their effects as we pursue research and policy changes that affect generation 1.5 students.

Notes

1. The findings presented here are part of a larger study, *Multilingual student perspectives on a writing proficiency exam* (Doctoral dissertation, Harvard Graduate School of Education, 2006).
2. Documents included Undergraduate Catalogues 1997–1999, 1999–2000, 2000–2001, 2002–2003; *Schedule of Courses*, published every semester, 2001–2004; *Nine Elements of Proficiency in Writing: A Student Manual, revised Fall 2003*; "Readers' Report for Students Who Must Repeat the WPE"; "Writing Proficiency Evaluation Reader's Report"; "Handout for IS Instructors"; Printout of WPR website (retrieved August 19, 2004 from www.umb.edu/academics/wpr); *The Status of the Writing Proficiency Examination: A Report to the Office of Civil Rights, U.S. Department of Education, Region 1*, Offices of the Provost and the Dean of Undergraduate Education, University of Massachusetts Boston, December 1995; *The Status of the Writing Proficiency Examination: A Follow-Up Study*, Offices of the Provost, the Dean of Undergraduate Education, and the Director of the Core Curriculum in the College of Arts and Sciences, University of Massachusetts Boston, January 1998; *The Performance of Two Cohorts of Students on the Writing Proficiency Requirement: A Summary of Studies Prepared for the Office of Civil Rights*, Alan Harwood, Associate Dean for Undergraduate Education, University of Massachusetts Boston, May 1999; *An Analysis of Outcomes for the Writing Proficiency Requirement: Chart Book of Preliminary Results, Placement Committee Presentation*, Kevin B. Murphy, Office of Institutional Research and Policy Studies, May 10, 2001; *The Writing Proficiency Requirement at the University of Massachusetts Boston: Interim Report*, Kevin B. Murphy, Office of Institutional Research and Policy Studies, January 24, 2002.

3. The report also inadvertently recognized that the general education courses designed to prepare students for the exam were not doing so. Rather, many students had to acquire writing proficiency through the WPE process, specifically, in the prep course that students could take only after failing the exam.
4. Participants chose whether to use their own names or an alias, and chose their own aliases.
5. To put this in perspective, 72% of the new students in the 2002–2003 school year were transfers (*University of Massachusetts Boston Statistical Portrait Fall 2002*).
6. The "nine elements" were replaced by the "eight elements" in fall 2004. When Vivian said "the eight-fold requirement," she was referring to these eight scoring criteria.
7. Quotes are edited to make them easier to read. I omitted some false starts, repetitions, and filler words. I used ellipses to indicate that the response in the interview was longer than the quote given, editor's brackets to indicate the manner in which something was said, and italics to indicate interviewer's utterances.
8. In fact, because Cat could talk so fluently and convincingly about what was required to demonstrate proficiency on the WPE, I found it hard to understand why she had failed three times.
9. I interpret John's reference to "non-English speaking graduates" to mean non-native English-speaking graduates, as there are no non-English speaking students at the university.
10. In this study, I did not look at the students' actual exam writing in order to analyze why they might have passed or failed. Of course, doing so would shed light not only on student ability but also on the reliability of the exam scoring.

References

Bourdieu, P. & Passeron, J.-C. (1977). *Reproduction in education, society, and culture.* Beverly Hills, CA: Sage Publications Inc.

Byrd, P. & Nelson, G. (1995). NNS performance on writing proficiency exams: Focus on students who failed. *Journal of Second Language Writing, 4*(3), 273–285.

California State University Graduation Writing Assessment Requirement Review Committee. (2003). *A review of the CSU graduation writing assessment requirement (GWAR) in 2002.* Retrieved August 3, 2005, from www.calstate.edu/AcadAff/GWAR_review_2002.shtml.

Carspecken, P.F. (1996). *Critical ethnography in educational research.* New York: Routledge.

Ching, R.J. & Moore, C.A. (1993). ESL assessment: What we learn when we open Pandora's box. *Metropolitan Universities, 3*(4), 35–46.

Cummins, J. (1979). Cognitive/academic language proficiency, linguistic interdependence, the optimal age question and some other matters. *Working Papers on Bilingualism, 19*, 197–205.

Gee, J.P. (1986). Orality and literacy: From the savage mind to ways with words. *TESOL Quarterly, 20*(4), 719–746.

Giroux, H.A. (1988). Literacy and the pedagogy of voice and political empowerment. *Educational Theory, 38*(1), 61–75.

Heath, S.B. (1983). *Ways with words: Language, life and work in communities and classrooms.* Cambridge, MA: Cambridge University Press.

Janopoulos, M. (1995). Writing across the curriculum, writing proficiency exams, and the NNS college student. *Journal of Second Language Writing, 4*(1), 43–50.

Johns, A.M. (1991). Interpreting an English competence exam: The frustration of an ESL science student. *Written Communication, 8*(3), 379–401.

Mountford, R. (1999). Let them experiment: Accommodating diverse discourse practices in large-scale writing assessment. In C.R. Cooper & L. Odell (Eds.), *Evaluating writing: The role of teachers' knowledge about text, learning, and culture* (pp. 366–396). Urbana, IL: National Council of Teachers of English.

Murphy, K.B. (2001). *An analysis of outcomes for the writing proficiency requirement: Chart book of preliminary results.* Boston: University of Massachusetts, Office of Institutional Research and Policy Studies.

North, S.M. (1996). Upper-division assessment and the postsecondary development of writing abilities. In E.M. White, W.D. Lutz, & S. Kamusikiri (Eds.), *Assessment of writing: Politics, policies, practices* (pp. 148–157). New York: Modern Language Association of America.

Ruetten, M.K. (1994). Evaluating ESL students' performance on proficiency exams. *Journal of Second Language Writing, 3*(2), 85–96.

Seidman, I. (1991). *Interviewing as qualitative research: A guide for researchers in education and the social sciences.* New York: Teachers College Press.

Weedon, C. (1987). *Feminist practice and poststructuralist theory.* New York: Blackwell Publishing.

Zentella, A.C. (1997). *Growing up bilingual: Puerto Rican children in New York.* Malden, MA: Blackwell Publishing.

10 Educational Pathways of Generation 1.5 Students in Community College Writing Courses

Genevieve Patthey Los Angeles City College
Joan Thomas-Spiegel Los Angeles Harbor College
Paul Dillon Los Angeles City College

In 1960, the state of California created a "master plan" for kindergarten through college education in the state. In that plan,

> The California Community Colleges have as their primary mission providing academic and vocational instruction for older and younger students through the first two years of undergraduate education (lower division). In addition to this primary mission, the Community Colleges are authorized to provide remedial instruction, English as a Second Language courses, adult noncredit instruction, community service courses, and workforce training services.... The transfer function is an essential component of the commitment to access. The University of California (UC) and California State University (CSU) are to establish a lower division to upper division ratio of 40:60 to provide transfer opportunities to the upper division for community college students, and eligible California Community College transfer students are to be given priority in the admissions process.
>
> (www.ucop.edu/acadinit/mastplan/mpregents091503.pdf, pages 4–8)

Outside of California, community colleges have similar goals. The nation's community colleges are a point of access into higher education for those students who most often do not fit the traditional college student profile (Council for Adult and Experiential Learning, 1999; Justice & Dornan, 2001). Students at community colleges often describe themselves through their other responsibilities first and as a student last. Most have familial and work obligations that take precedence, leaving them with limited time to devote to study and classes. Most are part-time students (California Community Colleges Chancellor's Office, 2003) who may not have qualified for less accessible higher education institutions.

Yet, meeting the academic needs of students without a college-preparatory education remains an important goal of all community college instruction, and this turns community colleges into "a site where contradictions meet" (Lewiecki-Wilson & Sommers, 1999). Community colleges enroll the majority of U.S. students seeking a higher education, particularly for traditionally underrepresented minorities and immigrants (Bailey & Weininger, 2002), the most likely groups of origin for generation 1.5

students. This unparalleled access is assuming increasing importance as state university systems are raising the academic bar and phasing out remediation programs (Bailey & Weininger, 2002; Roueche & Roueche, 1999; Sternglass, 1999). In addition, high schools are increasingly phasing in writing exams that students must pass to graduate and earn their diplomas (California Department of Education, 2006). Students who experience academic difficulties turn to the one educational institution maintaining open access—the community college. Community college faculty members more often than not face groups of students with a huge range of academic preparation, and have to negotiate the contradiction of finding ways to address the divergent needs of their students while still maintaining college standards.

In open admissions institutions, pre-collegiate composition teachers walk a razor's edge as they work to turn the promise of access into a reality by preparing students for college classes, but find that many students have far greater language learning needs than can reasonably be met by available classes. As Sullivan observes, "English teachers perform much of the 'cooling out' function at community colleges" by "most often [delivering] bad news to students about their ability to do college-level work" (2003, p. 379). Yet while we know of many developmental students who "struggle or fail" (p. 379), we also know of many students who persevere and succeed, perhaps after stopping out a semester or two, or after attending a different institution for one semester (Adelman, 1999; Dillon, 2001; Sternglass, 1997).

How well do community colleges fulfill this particular, unique mission for generation 1.5 students? To date, studies on the effects of raised standards of academic achievement invariably conclude that English learners lag significantly behind their peers. Second language acquisition research has for years shown that academic language development lags behind conversational fluency (August & Hakuta, 1998; Cummins, 1999). Rumberger & Gandara (2004) conclude that "the achievement gap is sizeable at all grade levels and puts English learners further and further behind their English-only counterparts" in the California public education system (p. 2). In a review aimed at identifying strategies leading to "Academic Success for English Learners," Olsen (2006) observes:

> Since passage of the federal No Child Left Behind Act, English learners have become an increasing focus of concern as educators struggle to implement instructional approaches and programs to ensure achievement for these students.... Despite major policy efforts to impact EL achievement, the gap between English learners and English-fluent students has remained virtually constant in the past decade.
>
> (p. 1)

Early studies of exit exam outcomes also identify English learners as a group less likely to succeed (Goossen, 2005) and thus more likely to be denied their high school diplomas. For those inclined to continue their education despite such initial disappointments, community colleges are the logical choice. Given current open admissions and diagnostic assessment practices at these institutions, most of these students will begin their higher education in developmental language classes, or classes that are more than one level below college English as defined by the state legislature.

Ironically, by developing and delivering developmental coursework to meet the needs of the diverse students entering college with open admission policies, community college writing programs figure prominently in institutional gatekeeping. These programs often are deeply involved in the shaping and implementation of assessment programs meant to uphold "college standards" as well as place students into developmentally appropriate coursework, much of it pre-collegiate. While most courses have no English prerequisite outside of the English series, more educationally successful students (those who graduate and/or go on to attend a 4-year university) are more likely to have been assessed into higher levels of English or math, generally at college level or one level below. Stop-outs (those students who take classes and then cease sometimes for many semesters or years) and inter-institutional movements between community colleges as well as between other higher education institutions, make it difficult to evaluate the progress of developmental students or the success of developmental programs. Moreover, since the objective of developmental instruction is to prepare students for college-level work, its success cannot truly be evaluated without access to that college-level work upon completion of the developmental program. Precisely because of open admissions and students' desire to transfer to a 4-year college, we wanted to see how successful developmental education was in this regard and we began to study the academic paths of all students beginning their college careers with developmental writing instruction (Patthey-Chavez, Dillon, & Thomas-Spiegel, 2005). In the current study, we examine the paths taken by likely generation 1.5 students and compare their achievements using the measures we developed to gauge developmental progress for the whole population. The question addressed is how well do community colleges meet the academic needs of generation 1.5 students? We answer this question through analysis of data that tracks the students through their composition courses. Furthermore, we compare our results with the larger student cohort group.

Data and Methods

Founded in 1999, the Intersegmental Project to Assure Student Success (IPASS) is a regional data-sharing consortium that includes 14 community colleges in four districts and two state universities in California. One of the consortium's goals is to track the progress of developmental students and to compare their demographic profiles and academic outcomes with the profiles and outcomes of more traditional students. To that end, the consortium has assembled all the enrollment records and available student demographic information from participating institutions into a comprehensive database. We draw on the results of a large study of IPASS enrollment records from nine community colleges and two universities tracking the progress of all composition students from 1990 to 2000 (Patthey-Chavez et al., 2005). In the comprehensive study, students starting their composition instruction with English as a Second Language (ESL) or pre-collegiate composition classes at any time from Spring 1990 to Spring 1998 were selected, "tagged" according to their starting point, and tracked through Fall 2000. Longitudinal tracking was adjusted to give all students a minimum of five semesters (from Fall 1998 to Fall 2000 for students starting in Spring 1998) to progress through the composition sequence, resulting in an adjusted n of 238,032 students. For the current study, likely generation 1.5 students were identified using three primary variables: age (under 22 years), primary language other than English, and completion of a U.S. high school. Using these variables, 43,964 students, or 18.4% of the total population, were identified as likely generation 1.5 students. Among the students working their way through different forms of academic remediation, we find many generation 1.5 students. Overall results confirm a troubling relationship between lack of preparation and lack of progress, with less well-prepared students less likely to progress to college-level work than better-prepared students. However, students fitting the generation 1.5 profile appear more likely to make progress both with their academic writing and with their college studies. Results thus shed light on the complexities of developmental instruction as it intersects issues of language and immigration status.

Our intersegmental partnership made it possible to track students with different entering academic profiles in one large, urban region of California as they progressed through the region's developmental and college course sequences, thus taking advantage of an alternate route to academic resources. The partnership made it possible to track the progress of a variety of developmental students through composition, English language learning, and mathematics programs designed to get them "college-ready." There are various kinds of data that inform this study.

We collected data on educational goals and generation 1.5 status. Having a clear goal at the onset of matriculation at a community college is associated with academic success. Each semester at registration in a community college, students may declare educational goals. The 13 specific goals can be grouped into five basic categories: (1) vocational training and certification, (2) transfer, (3) terminal associate's degree, (4) basic skills development, and (5) undecided or unknown. Table 10.1 displays the declared educational goals for three groups of students: those who began college in a developmental English course, those who began in college-level English, and those identified as generation 1.5 students. Not all students enter community college intent on higher education degree goals. Many students simply desire improved English and math basic skills. At the time of the study, those who desired vocational certificates rarely required completion of college-level English. It is important to remember that many students (40–60%) never intend to complete the English progression examined in our study in full. Of the study population, 91% (215,765) filed a goal at the beginning of their first semester. Of these, 35% of students starting with developmental coursework selected vocational goals, 20% indicated a transfer goal, 15% indicated a desire to improve their basic skills, 5% indicated they wanted to complete a terminal

Table 10.1 Percentage of Education Goals upon Entrance to College by Beginning Level of English and Generation 1.5 Cohorts

Educational goal	Began in developmental English (%)	Began in college-level English (%)	Generation 1.5 (%)
Vocational	35	24	23
Transfer	20	44	30
Basic skills	15	5	18
Associate's degree	5	4	7
Undecided	24	24	23

degree, and a further 24% described themselves as undecided. Not surprisingly, proportionally more students starting with college English (44%) selected transfer; proportionally fewer indicated a vocational goal (24%) or a desire to improve their basic skills (5%), and a similar number indicated they wanted to complete a terminal AA-degree (4%) or that they were undecided (22%).

As indicated in Table 10.1, goal selection for likely generation 1.5 students was the following: 30% chose transfer, 23% chose vocational improvement or certification, 18% selected basic skills improvement, 7% wanted to complete a terminal associate's degree, and 23% started out undecided. This distribution puts likely generation 1.5 students somewhere between the developmental and the college-prepared groups in our previous more comprehensive study (Patthey-Chavez et al. 2005) with regard to transfer goals. Some entering generation 1.5 students set lower educational goals with more emphasis on basic skills and an associate's degree than other groups. Yet, importantly, their emphasis on transfer to higher degrees remains the most frequently chosen goal, as it is for students who began in college-level English classes.

Regarding the sequence of English composition courses we focused on in this study, as is to be expected, the English composition sequences of 14 institutions do vary, but they have enough in common for the purposes of this analysis. We identified and operationalized three pre-collegiate starting points: (1) beginning ESL writing (ranging from one to four semesters in participating community colleges); (2) advanced or academic ESL writing (ranging from one to three semesters; in some colleges, students can use these courses for transfer credit, but they are not able to substitute for "College English I"); and (3) pre-collegiate writing instruction (ranging from one to two semesters, with courses alternatively called "English Fundamentals" or "Beginning English Reading and Writing"). The aim for both advanced ESL classes and "English Fundamentals" classes is to prepare students for "Intermediate Reading and Composition," and that course in turn prepares students who so desire to progress to "College English I." Students aiming to transfer are also required to complete a second semester of college composition, "College English II." Typically, there is no ESL-oriented College English I or II. "Intermediate Reading and Composition" satisfies the composition competency requirement for an associate's degree at most community colleges in the region and cannot be classified as developmental according to the State Chancellor's Office and funding legislation, particularly for students with vocational goals. A model of progression through the English composition sequence is shown in Figure 10.1.

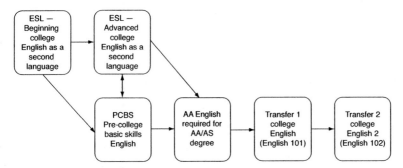

Figure 10.1 English and ESL composition course progression.

Table 10.2 provides an overview of the starting points for each of the 238,032 students in the comprehensive study, as well as a comparison of the starting points for the 43,964 students with generation 1.5 characteristics.

According to Roberge (2002) and Goen, Porter, Swanson, and VanDommelen (2002), generation 1.5 students who have ESL features in their writing are often placed into either advanced ESL or pre-collegiate composition courses upon matriculation into college. The starting points of our sample students diverge from the overall population in that direction, with almost twice as many generation 1.5 students starting with pre-collegiate basic skills instruction than the overall population, and a lower number starting with either intermediate (AA-applicable) or college-level English composition. Initial enrollments in ESL are not much higher than for the general population, perhaps because of the same resistance to the "ESL stigma" noted by earlier studies. By state law, students self-select either the ESL or ENL (English as a Native Language) assessment, and are thus placed within the series based on that initial choice. Group progress was assessed using the following outcome measures:

- highest English composition course completed;
- group GPAs (grade point averages) in both AA-level English and College English (Transfer 1) according to starting point;
- completion of community college units; and
- transfer to partner universities.

The outcomes for the larger study population provided a basis of comparison for the outcomes of likely generation 1.5 students, a comparison to which we now turn.

Success in English Composition Courses

We monitored student progress through the college composition sequence for both the comprehensive study population and the generation 1.5 subset. For the comprehensive study, an important goal was to assess the chances of progress through college composition (the course we call Transfer 1) for students with four different starting points: (1) Beginning ESL, (2) Advanced ESL, (3) Pre-collegiate or basic composition, and (4) associate's degree-applicable composition (AA-English). We monitored the pass rates for all groups in their first composition course, and then compared their successful completion rates for Transfer 1 composition with pass rates for the group of

Table 10.2 Beginning English Step by Cohort

Beginning composition level	Study population (%) n = 238,032	Generation 1.5 sample (%) n = 43,964
Beginning ESL	8.5	13.0
Advanced ESL	9.1	11.4
Pre-collegiate basic skills	23.2	41.3
Intermediate composition (AA)	31.9	18.4
College Transfer 1	22.2	13.1
College Transfer 2	5.1	2.8

Table 10.3 Highest Composition Course Passed in the Composition Sequence ($n = 231,522$)[i]

Starting point	n	Highest level passed					
		Beginning ESL (%)	Advanced ESL (%)	Pre-coll. basic (%)	AA-English (%)	Transfer 1 (%)	Transfer 2 (%)
Beginning ESL	18,752	38.8	23.4	2.4	5.4	2.0	0.6
Advanced ESL	19,918		40.2	5.9	13.2	10.9	4.8
Pre-coll. basic	53,319			28.6	18.2	14.8	6.9
AA-English	75,172				34.0	22.1	12.2
Transfer 1	52,312					49.4	25.3
Transfer 2	12,049						70.1

Note

i In Tables 10.3 and 10.4, attempted progressions (each higher level in the composition sequence, see Figure 10.1) are tracked upwards for all groups, starting with students who began their composition education with beginning ESL composition courses. Students who progressed from their starting course to a course outside of the composition sequence are excluded from this analysis, resulting in a slightly lower adjusted total n of 231,522. Pass rates in both tables reflect the highest course passed, though students who have passed a given level must have passed all pre-requisite courses. For example, in Table 10.3, 38.8% of the students who began in Beginning ESL passed that course and did not go on while 0.6% of the students who began in Beginning ESL passed the Transfer level 2 English course (and other courses that lead to that one). The complexities of the composition curriculum across our 14 institutions include inconsistent articulations between upper ESL and lower developmental English levels. At one college, for example, a student completing the highest ESL composition course may be directed towards College English I, while at a sister institution, a student completing a similar level of ESL composition will be directed to a course equivalent to "English Fundamentals." Therefore, we decided to present pre-collegiate composition course pass rates for ESL students even though the two levels are roughly equivalent in relationship to AA- and college-level English. On most participating campuses, there is in fact nothing to keep students in either discipline from enrolling in coursework in the other, and crossovers from ESL into developmental composition (or vice versa) are frequent. Some students drop out or fail and do not return, resulting in overall pass rates that do not add up to 100%.

students placed at that college level. Students were tracked only as far as they actually progressed in the sequence at any of the consortium community colleges.

Looking at the data in this way reveals distinct patterns of success and progress for different student groups. ESL students, who tend to pass their first course in higher numbers than developmental students, do not go on and progress through the college-composition curriculum at equivalent rates. This trend is particularly pronounced for beginning ESL students, with only 5.4% passing AA-English and less than 3% passing transfer-level English (2.0% passing Transfer 1 and less than 1% passing both Transfer 1 and Transfer 2). Pre-collegiate composition students who successfully complete their first English composition course fare better. That is, 40% of PC-basic students who attempt further progress up the English composition ladder succeed, with 22% successfully completing transfer-level work (14.8% completing Transfer 1 and 6.9% completing both Transfer 1 and Transfer 2). This compares favorably with the progress of even the more advanced ESL group; only 29% of those students eventually pass AA-English, and only 16% complete transfer-applicable composition.

Not surprisingly, students who begin their community college careers in college-level courses outperform all developmental groups. More than two-thirds of these students pass College English I, and a further 25% complete the subsequent transfer-applicable College English II; 70% of students starting with Transfer 2 pass that level. We suspect that a great many of the latter students are reverse-transfer students, that is, students who start their higher education at the university and only attend a community college to pick up a few required classes. It is worth recalling that students starting with college-level English were more than twice as likely to indicate transfer as their educational goal than students starting with developmental levels (see Table 10.1).

In addition to success and progression, we also examined failure rates and the likelihood of further coursework after a failed course in the comprehensive study. This separate analysis revealed that between 39% and 30% of ESL composition students fail their first course, as do 41% of developmental composition students. Substantial numbers of students began in one level and then ended up successfully completing a *lower* level. While these students represent only a small percentage of the whole population, they exist at all levels, raising questions regarding the student experience in composition or the fit with college curricula. Though we have evidence that about a quarter of those who fail try again and eventually pass and make progress, many more never get beyond a first failed course.

Our comprehensive study reveals that developmental progress is slow for many students. Beginning ESL students in particular appear to end their college studies where they began, in the ESL program—only 8% ever complete any college-applicable composition coursework, mostly AA-level English. Progress improves for the other two developmental groups, with 29% of Advanced ESL students and 40% of developmental English students completing at least AA-level English, but that is still fewer than half in either group. Table 10.4 presents a different picture of generation 1.5 students' movement through the composition sequence.

Generation 1.5 students perform differently from the larger cohort group shown in Table 10.3. Likely generation 1.5 students performed slightly better than the general population except for those entering in the Beginning ESL level. Of those starting in Advanced ESL, 37% progressed at least one level further and 28% completed college-applicable work, compared to 35% and 29% for the total population. Those starting in

Table 10.4 Highest Composition Course Passed in the Composition Sequence Generation 1.5 Cohort ($n = 43,964$)

Starting point	n	Highest level passed					
		Beginning ESL (%)	Advanced ESL (%)	Pre-coll. basic (%)	AA-English (%)	Transfer 1 (%)	Transfer 2 (%)
Beginning ESL	5,731	46.8	19.3	3.2	2.6	1.4	0.5
Advanced ESL	4,990		41.4	9.6	10.3	10.6	6.7
Pre-coll. basic	18,144			32.3	16.9	16.1	8.8
AA-English	8,108				32.4	26.2	18.3
Transfer 1	5,750					49.2	28.5
Transfer 2	1,241						77.0

pre-collegiate basic skills also were more successful: 42% completed college-applicable work and 25% completed transfer-applicable work, compared to 40% and 22% for the total population. For those deemed college-ready enough to begin their composition studies in AA-applicable English, success was even more noticeable: 45% eventually went on to complete transfer-applicable coursework, compared to 35% for the general population. In keeping with this trend, the Transfer 2 column also indicates slightly higher percentages of generation 1.5 students successfully completing that level despite lower beginning levels. Moreover, fewer generation 1.5 students failed their first composition course, with only between 21% and 26% failing and not succeeding at any other level. This compares favorably to the 30% to 41% of students failing their first composition course in the whole population.

As a final measure of success in the English composition sequence, we examine mean group grades in the AA-applicable and Transfer 1 composition courses. Each of these is important; the first for vocational students and the second for students aspiring to transfer. Each provides a means of comparison for the performance of students with different developmental histories. In principle, students who take college-preparatory coursework and complete it successfully should be equally well prepared for college-applicable coursework as those who start at that level. In reality, this might not be the case. Furthermore, frequent movements from ESL to pre-collegiate composition or the reverse path complicate our ability to say for certain what is happening for individual students without discussing individual case studies and losing the focus of this analysis.

Table 10.5 provides group GPAs for all students completing either AA-English or the first transfer composition course. In that same table, group GPAs achieved by the developmental groups in the comprehensive study are compared with those achieved by students who started at each respective level and with those achieved by likely generation 1.5 students.

Table 10.5 shows that likely generation 1.5 students achieve substantially lower English grades than students of the whole population in Transfer English. These data suggest that written academic communication presents a challenge for generation 1.5 students and at the same time, that generation 1.5 persist in their English classes, despite the likelihood of lower grades. Likely generation 1.5 students also received lower grades in AA-English than in Transfer 1 composition. They received even lower group GPAs than the total cohort pre-collegiate group in these two college-applicable courses, 2.31 for AA-English and 2.47 for Transfer 1. Total cohort students who started

Table 10.5 Group GPAs in AA- and Transfer 1 English

Level	Group	n	GPA
AA-English	Total population	95,749	2.39
	AA-starters	61,512	2.39
	Gen. 1.5 cohort	18,224	2.31
Transfer 1 English	Total sample	94,131	2.68
	Transfer 1-starters	44,373	2.76
	Gen. 1.5 cohort	16,362	2.47

their college career in pre-collegiate composition (the starting place for 41% of likely generation 1.5 students) received the second lowest group GPA of 2.37 for the AA-applicable composition course and the lowest group GPA of 2.50 in the Transfer 1 English course (Patthey-Chavez et al., 2005). In addition, all groups performed better in College English 1 than in the AA-applicable course, most likely a consequence of the greater academic diversity of the students served by AA-composition courses. Since AA-English courses serve more students with occupational goals, it is not surprising to find less academic achievement at that level. On the whole, results in Table 10.5 are consistent with the results of the comprehensive study. On the whole, the progress of likely generation 1.5 students through the composition sequence presents something of a mixed picture: they appear somewhat more likely to make some progress regardless of where they start, but earn lower grades in college-applicable courses. For both community college students as a whole and likely generation 1.5 students, an association between academic profile and outcome is emerging; the more academic a group of students, the better its English composition outcomes. However, does this association hold true across disciplinary boundaries? We examined college success in other coursework next.

Success in College: Patterns of Progress in Community College Coursework

While success in college-applicable composition is an important indicator of programmatic success (or failure) for developmental writing instruction, that course is rarely the goal of developmental students. Most include it in a more comprehensive course of studies, whether in a vocational or academic discipline. The extent to which they attempt and realize such a course of studies can be ascertained from their enrollment patterns and unit-completion rates. We now turn toward these more comprehensive measures of student achievement.

To conduct our unit-completion analysis, each student's course enrollments were totaled and a mean unit value was generated for the whole population, the whole population of students less than 22 years of age, and for the group of likely generation 1.5 students. Enrollments were further analyzed to ascertain the mean number of transferable general education (GE) units earned by each group. Table 10.6 presents our results, including a ratio of the transferable general education units (as accepted by universities and articulated in the Intersegmental General Education Transfer Curriculum, 2007) as a percent of total units earned.

Table 10.6 Patterns of Community College Course Unit Completion

Group	n	Mean units completed	Mean units transferable GE	Transferable units as % of total
All students	756,842	30.2	10.9	36
All students entering at age under 22	324,976	33.6	10.7	32
Generation 1.5 students	29,924	62.7	22.3	36

Table 10.6 reveals a surprising difference between likely generation 1.5 students and their peers: in comparison to both students of equivalent ages and all students in our database, they accumulate roughly twice as many units overall, and twice as many transferable units. It is worth noting that it typically takes about 24 units to earn a certificate, that most vocational degrees require between 45 and 60 units, and that a transfer-program requires 58 units. The total group mean accumulated by likely generation 1.5 students approaches the totals required for degree-candidacy, and they have accumulated a little over a third of required transferable GE units. According to our earlier analyses, most students who earned enough GE units to approach transfer- or degree-candidacy started their community college careers in the more advanced composition courses (Patthey-Chavez et al., 2005, pp. 271–272). In contrast, 66% of likely generation 1.5 students started in more basic composition courses through the English assessment process. These results prompted us to explore in greater detail the unit-accumulations achieved by likely generation 1.5 students. Since our database includes information about the students' primary language, we generated group means for each group of speakers and grouped those according to geographic proximity. Results of that more exploratory analysis are presented in Table 10.7.

Regardless of primary language, likely generation 1.5 students accumulated higher overall unit-totals and higher totals of transferable units than other students in the system. Speakers of Vietnamese distinguish themselves by accumulating the highest mean totals, and speakers of Filipino earn the highest proportion of transferable GE units. Most of the remaining groups performed comparably. Our results suggest that generation 1.5 students are using the community college system in precisely the way it was meant to be used, as an opportunity to complete college-preparatory coursework and then proceed with college-applicable coursework. If that is the case, transfer may be the next important goal for many of these students, and we examine their attempts to do so next.

Our final analysis focuses specifically on the transfer-rates between the community-college system and our two State University partners. The IPASS database includes all

Table 10.7 Patterns of Community College Course Unit Completion by Primary Language

Language	n	Mean units completed	Mean units transferable GE	Transferable units as % of total
Asian languages:				
Chinese	2,046	83.4	30.3	36
Japanese	229	62.1	22.6	36
Korean	1,668	72.4	27.0	37
Vietnamese	1,034	100.5	36.9	37
Filipino	1,806	70.8	29.7	42
Indo-European languages:				
Armenian	2,918	65.8	23.7	36
Farsi	1,370	83.7	30.3	36
Russian	1,302	62.8	22.6	36
Spanish	18,240	65.0	23.4	36

university course enrollments of our community-college students at our two partner institutions, and thus makes it possible to gauge intersegmental progress. Of the 43,964 likely generation 1.5 students, we found 18,257 had earned some units at one of our partner universities. That is equivalent to a 42% transfer rate, about five times higher than for the community college population as a whole. It also represents the majority of students who transferred. In other words, if a student transferred from one (or more) of the IPASS community college campuses to a partner university, chances are that it was a generation 1.5 student. While not all transfer students were tracked (since only two local universities participated in the data consortium), a greater percentage of generation 1.5 students eventually transferred compared to the total cohort.

College Composition as a Gauge for Academic Literacy

Enrollment and outcome patterns from the comprehensive study indicated some important trends. First, students that could be termed truly developmental, starting with very basic coursework, never quite caught up; though some progressed to college-applicable coursework, they performed noticeably less well once there. Second, university transfer students were the high achievers of their respective starting group, indicating a positive association between academic profiles and outcomes in English composition. Finally, advanced ESL students were the second-most successful post-transfer group in terms of university GPAs and group GPA in Transfer English. These findings were consistent with Bailey and Weininger's (2002) conclusion that "foreign-educated" students tended to outperform all other groups in their longitudinal study of City University of New York's community colleges. We speculated that unlike many remedial students, many upper-level ESL composition students come to the U.S. college with academic literacy in another language, a literacy they need to retool in the new one. That retooling may not be entirely easy, but it may be easier than starting from the beginning and learning college "ways with words" (Heath, 1983) later in life. In contrast, most developmental students fared more poorly, and were far less likely to complete any meaningful program of studies at the community college or to transfer to one of our partner universities. A subset of developmental students with success on all measures including transfer, however, indicated that at least some remedial students turn community colleges into a stepping stone to academic success. Our current study suggests strongly that these more successful developmental students were likely generation 1.5 students, whose patterns of success fall between those of developmental and college-ready students in the total population.

Our comprehensive study indicated that a student's initial placement in the college composition curriculum functions almost like a proxy for his or her academic literacy overall. The differences that emerged between students starting with pre-collegiate composition and those starting in upper ESL composition underscored the importance of that academic literacy in college success or failure. Students who are less prepared, students who arrive at the college with an English competency inadequate for the reading and writing demands of college coursework, have greater failure rates. Conversely, students coming into the institution with better academic literacy, even in another language, are more likely to acquire the written communication skills they need and succeed in college coursework. Yet we see a singular determination of generation 1.5 students to persist in their goals of college studies and transfer. Despite the fact of lower initial placements, and thus lower likely academic resources according to our proxy measure, these students go on to complete significant coursework at the community college, and a disproportionately large number of them transfer.

Summary and Recommendations

The most popular educational goal for generation 1.5 students entering the community colleges in our study is transfer for further education beyond the 2-year degree or certificate. This goal more closely matches the students who begin their community college career in college-level English, an unlikely starting point for most generation 1.5 students. Other students beginning in developmental English are more likely to choose a vocational goal than continuing in further education.

Generation 1.5 students were more likely to begin their community college English studies below college English. Only 16% began in college-level English compared to 27% of the total population studied. These different levels of college-readiness were not entirely due to ESL placement, since the generation 1.5 students began with 24% in ESL levels compared with 18% for the total population. By far the greatest disparity existed at the pre-collegiate basic skills and intermediate or associate's English levels, where we note that nearly twice as many generation 1.5 students begin their college sojourn as do students in the general population.

This ignominious beginning in college life for likely generation 1.5 students seems out of step with their eventual goals, especially since our research indicates the closer to college-level English students begin college, the more likely they are to transfer to a 4-year university. The odds seem stacked against such an achievement, yet likely generation 1.5 students persist. Despite a difficult beginning, generation 1.5 students are more likely to pass their initial English course (with the only exception being the lowest level of ESL). This higher rate of early success may be both an encouragement and a measure of the determination with which these students approach college studies. It seems unlikely that their success lies with superior resources or training in light of previous empirical evidence. In fact, once generation 1.5 students reach AA- and Transfer-level English, their low group GPAs in those classes indicate struggle with the material.

Successfully reaching a variety of educational goals, especially a transfer goal, includes a variety of other courses and steps to completion. Examining one of the most basic steps of completed course units, we find the likely generation 1.5 students outperforming their age counterparts. They successfully complete more transferable general education units than either students from their age peer-group or from the overall student population. Likely generation 1.5 students completed twice the number of total units than average community college students on the way to accumulating their transferable totals. Finally, against the general odds as established by the larger community college population, data indicate a significantly higher transfer rate for likely generation 1.5 students. The majority of transfer students in our studies were from the generation 1.5 cohort. Generation 1.5 students stand out as a separate cohort from other ESL students, basic skills students (who typically do not realize transfer goals), and from the overall student population. These students are more likely to begin in developmental levels, yet they are also more likely to persist through unit completion toward certificate and degree goals, as well as transfer to further education.

Several questions are raised by these findings for developmental programs. It appears that the fundamental objective of developmental programs, helping students overcome gaps in their academic preparation and acquire academic literacy, is only being met partially, but more so with likely generation 1.5 students than with their developmental peers. It appears that we may have something to learn from these students, who start their college studies with the odds stacked against them. Our earlier findings have highlighted the critical role of academic preparation in college success, a factor that has been shown to affect other, longer-term outcomes such as degree-completion (Adelman, 1999; Bailey & Weininger, 2002). How then do likely generation 1.5 students succeed where so many fail? What instructional and curriculum factors lead to their greater success? To answer these questions and assist in creating developmental programs that work for all students, future inquiries will have to examine instruction and learning through a different lens. More qualitative studies, particularly the longitudinal work carried out by Sternglass (1997), revealed both the value of developmental writing instruction and how students learned to use their academic literacy to make progress through degree programs and into employment. In addition, more interdisciplinary collaboration is clearly indicated, starting with research into the language and cultural factors that turn some generation 1.5 students into successful college students.

Research that only focuses on outcomes, such as ours, cannot inform such applied work, and yet, both developmental programs and writing programs as a whole aim not to function as gatekeepers, but to help "students emerge from our classrooms as more literate, more thoughtful, more accomplished human beings" (Applebee, 1999). We hope that by establishing realistic understandings of the effectiveness of developmental and writing programs through reasonable baselines and tempered expectations, our work helps such programs focus on their true mission of opening the doors to higher education and providing the kind of access to academic literacy apparently exploited by many generation 1.5 students.

References

Adelman, C. (1999). *Answers in the tool box: Academic intensity, attendance patterns, and bachelor's degree attainment.* Jessup, MD: U.S. Department of Education.

Applebee, A. (1999). Building a foundation for effective teaching and learning of English: A personal perspective on thirty years of research. *Research in the Teaching of English, 33*(4), 352–366.

August, D. & Hakuta, K. (Eds.) (1998). *Educating language-minority children.* Washington, DC: National Academy Press.

Bailey, T. & Weininger, E.B. (2002). Performance, graduation, and transfer of immigrants and natives in City University of New York community colleges. *Educational Evaluation and Policy Analysis, 24*(4), 359–377.

California Community Colleges Chancellor's Office. (2003). *Student right-to-know rate disclosure website: Student longitudinal outcomes tracking system (SLOTS—the first time freshman cohort study).* Retrieved March 9, 2003, from http://srtk.cccco.edu/index.asp.

California Department of Education. (2006, January 26). *Program overview: California high school exit examination (CAHSEE)*. Retrieved November 3, 2006, from www.cde.ca.gov/ta/tg/hs/overview.asp.

Clark, B.R. (1960). The "cooling-out" function in higher education. *American Journal of Sociology, 65*(6), 569–576.

Clark, B.R. (1980). The "cooling out" function revisited. In G.B. Vaughn (Ed.), *New directions for community colleges: Questioning the community college role* (pp. 15–31). San Francisco, CA: Jossey-Bass.

Council for Adult and Experiential Learning. (1999). *Serving adult learners in higher education: Findings from CAEL's benchmarking study*. Retrieved October 10, 2005, from www.cael.org/publications_research_whitepapers.htm.

Cummins, J. (1999). *BICS and CALP: Clarifying the distinction*. Retrieved August 31, 2007, from www.eric.ed.gov/ERICWebPortal/recordDetail?accno=ED438551.

Dillon, P.H. (2001, May). Parameters of multiple college attendance. Paper presented at the Accountability reporting performance: Have they made a difference? Research and Planning Group for California Community Colleges, Pasadena, CA.

Goen, S., Porter, P., Swanson, D., & VanDommelen, D. (2002). Working with generation 1.5 students and their teachers: ESL meets composition. *CATESOL Journal, 14*(1), 131–171.

Goossen, C.J.J. (2005, September 15). Is the high school exit exam unfair to English learners? *New America Media*.

Heath, S.B. (1983). *Ways with words: Language, life, and work in community and classroom*. New York: Cambridge University Press.

Intersegmental General Education Transfer Curriculum. (2007). *Intersegmental General Education Transfer Curriculum*. Retrieved August 31, 2007, from www.igetc.org.

Justice, E.M. & Dornan, T.M. (2001). Metacognitive differences between traditional-age and nontraditional-age college students. *Adult Education Quarterly, 51*(3), 236–249.

Lewiecki-Wilson, C. & Sommers, J. (1999). Professing at the fault lines: Composition at open admission institutions. *College Composition and Communication, 50*(3), 438–462.

Olsen, L. (2006). Ensuring academic success for English learners. *UC LMRI Newsletter, 15*(4), 1–7.

Patthey-Chavez, G.G., Dillon, P.H., & Thomas-Spiegel, J. (2005). How far do they get? Tracking students with different academic literacies through community college remediation. *Teaching English in the Two-Year College, 32*(3), 261–277.

Roueche, J.E. & Roueche, S.D. (1999). *High stakes, high performance: Making remedial education work*. Annapolis Junction, MD: American Association of Community Colleges.

Rumberger, R.W. & Gandara, P. (2004). Seeking equity in the education of California's English learners. *Teachers College Record, 106*(10), 2032–2056.

Sternglass, M.S. (1997). *Time to know them: A longitudinal study of writing and learning at the college level*. Mahwah, NJ: Lawrence Erlbaum.

Sternglass, M.S. (1999). Students deserve enough time to prove that they can succeed. *Journal of Basic Writing, 18*(1), 3–20.

Sullivan, P. (2003). What is "college-level" writing? *Teaching English in the Two-Year College, 30*(4), 374–390.

Part III

Curricular and Pedagogical Approaches

11 Situating Generation 1.5 in the Academy

Models for Building Academic Literacy and Acculturation

Robin Murie and Renata Fitzpatrick University of Minnesota

Marcos enters his first college course in the Commanding English Program at the University of Minnesota. His first homework assignment, typed in multicolored, size 14 font, offers a carefully constructed, relatively simple response to a set of questions. He is asked to read a chapter from Ronald Takaki's *A Different Mirror* (1993), a dense college-level multicultural history textbook. The first chapter assigned is on American Indian policies in the 1900s, something Marcos knows little about. He reads about Wounded Knee and John Collier's conflicts with Navajo sheep grazing. The teacher provides a scaffolding of questions; the class deconstructs some complex passages and discusses the main policies presented in the chapter. Marcos is then asked to reread the chapter and write a response to the questions: "What stands out in the chapter, what is confusing, and what connections can you make to your own experiences and knowledge?" This is a challenge for Marcos. The response, however, is not graded on organization, style, or mechanics. Students are encouraged to add quotes, to work closely with the text. The next chapter is on Mexican migration and conditions in U.S. "Barrios" in the 1930s. Again, students are given reading questions; they discuss the content, and are told to reread the chapter and write a response, working closely with the text to pull out quotes that they find interesting or confusing, and to discuss connections they can see. Marcos writes six pages this time, with an engaged response to the racism described in the chapter. He writes about his new insights into conditions facing Mexican families living in the Midwest today. Has he understood every vocabulary item in the reading? Hardly. Is his own writing fluent and error-free? Not yet. Is there a thesis? No, the assignments at this point only ask for engagement with the text, not focus. But he is building academic skills of reading extended texts, quoting and responding to passages, and filtering the content through the lens of his own experiences. By the fourth chapter assigned— the effects of World War II on various immigrant groups, in particular the history of Japanese-American internment camps—Marcos has developed a sense of the author's stance toward U.S. history; he has become more comfortable with writing an extended response, and he is building background knowledge that will serve him well in the immigration literature course the following semester. Marcos is grappling with entire chapters of text, learning to cite, interpret, and construct a response—in short, he is developing the kinds of literacy that are expected in college. In the process, his English fluency, vocabulary, and grammar are also improving, but these traditional ESL skills are not the focus of the course.

Students like Marcos are at risk for receiving a "deficit" model of instruction that limits reading of academic, expository text, and keeps the writing focus on error and careful control of shorter passages or paragraph writing. And yet, with appropriate scaffolding and course design, Marcos is capable of doing work that some might deem too difficult or beyond such students' comfort levels with the language. In fact, if Marcos is to develop the academic literacy needed in college, it is important that he be given opportunities for (1) extended reading, (2) challenging, compelling content, (3) writing tasks that develop competence and voice, and that focus on academic skills of recognizing main ideas, connecting information across chapters, citing, paraphrasing, and responding to text.

Designing assignments that foster academic acculturation needs to be done carefully and deliberately, however. To simply assign four chapters of the Takaki text would bring frustration to a reader who does not have the vocabulary to read college history with ease. To assign an essay, without unpacking the expectations and conventions of this style of writing, or without a drafting and revision process, and then to grade that essay by "college standards," could leave a novice writer silenced by red ink. And yet, to keep the curriculum simplistic and undemanding based on the assumption that students "can't do this yet" would be to delay access to critical literacy and to the education that students have come to college to receive. Immigrant students themselves are asking for coursework that is credit-bearing and will allow them to progress toward a degree (Abdimalik, 2006; Franko, Conner, Wambach, & Xie, 2006; Smalkoski, 2005). This chapter presents some ways of designing courses and writing assignments that honor these students' needs and abilities while cultivating the academic literacy that college work demands.

Through a Wider Lens

Increasing numbers of students find themselves at the intersection of ESL and basic writing as they transition from high school to college. While English placement scores identify language as a key issue, the pre-college experiences of our students complicate the picture and call for a wider perspective. The multilingual students we see in our program have typically experienced a disruption in their education due to the move to the U.S. and the switch to English as the language of instruction. For many of the current East African students, not unlike the Hmong students two decades ago, early schooling before arrival in the U.S. was also disrupted by war and years spent in refugee camps with limited access to formal education, so as a consequence, native-language education can be incomplete. These disruptions are compounded in the U.S. by tracking in urban high schools that can lead to limited preparation for college. Advanced placement coursework is typically reserved for the academically privileged students in high school. In Minnesota, for example, in 2004–2005, 86% of the students taking Advanced Placement exams were White, compared to 2% Black, 2% Hispanic, and 7% Asian (MMEP, 2006). Classes designed for mainstream students may not be a good fit, leaving administrators with the tracking dilemma that Harklau (1994) describes in her research: to place ELL students into rigorous courses, where the experience can be silencing, or to keep them on an academically lower track where there are often fewer opportunities to discuss, analyze, read extended text, or apply knowledge in ways that would prepare students for the academic literacy required in college (Fu, 1995; Harklau, 1994, 1999; Valdés, 2001). The implication of this is that many immigrant students come to college with less preparation than the monolingual college-bound who have had access to more rigorous high school coursework.

We know far more now than we did a decade ago about the needs and strengths of U.S.-educated students in our programs (Harklau, Losey, & Siegal, 1999; Roberge, 2002). Typical of any first generation college student, they have questions about how the "system" works: what the standards are, how one chooses a major, how one develops membership in the college community and an identity on campus. Career choices may be uninformed and inappropriate to the student's life plans and goals. If a student cannot find a major that works, it may delay or even inhibit graduation. Students who come to college "to become a doctor" face serious questions: what career information, internships, courses in medical technology, strategies, and science courses are needed to make it in this field? And the question we encourage students to add: what back-up plans and other related careers are available? We see low math placement scores and struggles in introductory science classes that, if left unaddressed, can create serious barriers to a student's ability to progress. For instructors and program directors, awareness of the issues beyond students' English language needs is valuable; by broadening our perspective, we are better positioned to respond to the questions and needs that students have as they enter college.

Other kinds of challenges faced by our students have been described elsewhere in this volume. In designing our program, we take into account not only the barriers with which students struggle, but also the uniqueness of the strengths they bring. The challenges they have faced often turn into sources of strong resilience, leading to a more focused sense of purpose in college, and a tenacity that is valuable. These college students are multilingual, not just "English deficient," and this multicultural expertise can serve them well in courses like anthropology, global studies, and immigration literature. This wider lens allows us to acknowledge the strengths and cultural capital students bring, and demands a broader approach to our work with generation 1.5 students, through a curriculum that resonates with students' own experiences and interests. It also demands courses where students can engage with academic content in ways that build academic literacy, a literacy that can only be acquired, over time, with practice and exposure (Adamson, 1993; Blanton 1998, 1999; Gee, 1998; Spack, 2004; Zamel, 1991).

A Model for Academic Literacy

For all of the reasons mentioned—the need to build stronger literacy at the college level, the importance of creating space for the development of identity and connectedness on campus, and the necessity to engage students in content that genuinely educates—generation 1.5 students benefit from coursework that is situated within the college curriculum. There are a number of ways to support students as they take college courses. Based on 26 years of experience with the Commanding English Program at the University of Minnesota, we discuss several components for connecting language and academic support with college coursework that could be applied in other institutions and programs. These elements include:

1. Supporting students' adjustment to the college environment and sense of belonging on campus through a learning community of linked courses.
2. Supporting academic work by offering reading adjuncts that are connected to introductory college courses in biology, sociology, etc., that fulfill college requirements.
3. Building intellectual content into writing and literature courses by developing projects that engage in reading, research, and making meaning about topics that are actively connected to students' experiences.

Common to all three of these features is an underlying search for ways to connect with other courses, services, advisors, and faculty in the college, so that the program responds to students in multiple ways, to address the "wider" perspective.

The Commanding English program is a first year program at the University of Minnesota for multilingual students who have been in U.S. schools for 8 or fewer years and whose test scores indicate a need for "ESL/academic" support at the University. In this two-semester program, linked courses provide content and offer ways to connect relevant language work, thus supporting students as they take biology, social science, and humanities courses. (See Appendix for a listing of courses in the program.) Students enroll in four or five academic classes each semester, often taking several courses together as a cohort. Reading adjuncts are linked to lecture classes; writing, editing, and speech courses are designed in ways that support college-level work, and an immigration literature course is intentionally constructed to make it accessible for multilingual students. With access to language and literacy support built into the college courses, students are doing sustained reading and writing in a variety of fields, acquiring academic literacy, and gaining the credit and education of their freshman year. (For a full discussion of the Commanding English program, see Christensen, Fitzpatrick, Murie & Zhang, 2005; Murie & Thomson, 2001.)

Table 11.1 illustrates the differences between a traditional Intensive ESL program and our academic program of content-based language support designed for generation 1.5 students.

Learning Community

One critical aspect of this model is building a community of students who share the experience of learning. Students know each other, because they are taking other courses together as a cohort. This creates a sense of belonging at the University—a sense of knowing others and of being known (Tinto, 1998). In the Commanding English program evaluations, this sense of community was often cited as one of the best features of the program. Students have noted: "vast diversity and interactions with each other," "meeting new students," "making new friends," "positive friendship with both students and instructors," "I felt like being in a family. Professors and students were friendly and kind. Small class size made me comfortable in a school environment" (Franko et al., 2006, pp. 44, 45). We should acknowledge that not all students appreciate the close-knit aspects of the program and would prefer more independence. However, given the impersonal nature of a large research university, beginning in a small, interconnected program has been beneficial to the majority of the participants. In some ways, it is the hidden strength of the program.

Table 11.1 Traditional ESL versus Model of Embedded Content-based Language Support

	Traditional ESL model	*Model for gen. 1.5 students*
1 Program goal	Acquiring language for college-level coursework.	Acquiring academic literacy and language for college-level work.
2 Level of instruction	Often at a pre-college level.	College level.
3 College credits	Often non-credit bearing.	Credit-bearing courses.
4 Pedagogical focus	Skills-based courses in: reading (shorter reading passages, reading skills, strategies); writing ("process approach," essay topics created by instructor); listening (strategies for comprehension of native speaker vernacular); grammar (mastery of grammar rules of English).	Content-based courses in: different content/discipline areas (e.g., biology, sociology, literature, writing, anthropology, arts); sustained reading in a discipline area; reading courses connected to college content courses; study strategies for reading two chapters per week; taking lecture notes; studying for college course tests (e.g., anatomy, biology, etc.); writing college-level academic/research papers in discipline areas such as anthropology and literature; acquiring grammar competence that is connected to developing editing strategies for writing.
5 Advising focus	Visa regulation, ESL support.	Course selection, choosing majors, financial aid, negotiating college.
6 Target population	International students: uninterrupted education in one language; literate, English learned formally as a linguistic system.	A complex mix of resident students who bring diverse language and literacy experiences to the first year of college; education disrupted by switch to another language of instruction; English may have been learned orally.

There are other advantages to a learning community. In a recent study of the outcomes of one multicultural learning community, James, Bruch and Jehangir (2006) comment that the "multifaceted environment of the linked courses offered culturally diverse first-generation students a means to use multiple ways to represent ideas, further enabling them to contribute to the intellectual life of the university" (p. 18). In the Commanding English program, there is shared content from the sociology, anthropology, and biology courses and their reading adjuncts, which can then be brought into the writing courses. This recursive layering gives students rich material to draw from; for example, readings from sociology in the fall are relevant in a research writing course in the spring. Instructors, who collaborate frequently on course plans and assignments, also share students and can observe student progress over time through multiple courses and multiple ways of evaluation. One recommended model, therefore, for supporting students in the coursework of college is to connect several courses together into a learning community. (See Mlynarczyk & Babbit, 2002, for a description of a learning community model at Kingsborough Community College.)

Reading Adjuncts

One specific way to link courses is through supplemental instruction. In Commanding English, this is offered through reading adjuncts that are connected to content classes students are taking in college. This model provides academic and language support that genuinely engages in the tasks required in college: how to read two chapters of sociology a week, navigate the complex wording of multiple choice exams in an anatomy course, critique an ethnocentric stance in cultural anthropology, take notes in a biology lecture, or read densely embedded articles about modern art.

Students who take sociology may, for example, read about the social construction of race or the problem of gender inequality in education. In doing so, they gain access to conventions of discourse and ways of thinking in the social sciences. They also make connections between the reading material and their views about how communities in the U.S. live. Without the support of a connected reading course, the dense reading load could easily become overwhelming, leading to the situation L. Kasper (2000) describes of the case of students who pass ESL courses but are unable to succeed in the general college curriculum (p. viii). However, with the supported adjunct course, students can gain confidence with the content of the readings, which then allows for fuller participation in the connected class. As one student wrote on the program evaluation survey:

> The sociology and cultural anthropology class(es) were the best experiences; it was a great mix of American born students and (Commanding English) students. I talked and made friends with American students who were open minded and friendly enough to correct me and helped me with my academic and social life transition ... to normal U of M classes and life.
>
> (Franko et al., 2006, p. 45)

Although not specifically mentioned by the student, behind this satisfaction in the two social science courses was the additional support that the reading courses provided. Our experience suggests that the supplementary instruction in the reading adjuncts facilitates students' ability to succeed in the content classes. In the reading courses, students work on note-taking, vocabulary, and other reading strategies, and write summaries of the content course readings, becoming more familiar with the academic concepts and theories of the core content. This allows for more confident participation in the mainstream classes, and leads to the kind of satisfaction expressed by the student cited above.

Designing a Literature Course for Generation 1.5 Writers

Another place in the curriculum where students build their academic literacy proficiency is in the course Literature of the American Immigrant Experience. The impetus for this 3 credit literature course grew out of discontent with non-credit skills-based reading courses in the curriculum and a desire to push a "fluency first" component

(MacGowan-Gilhooly, 1991). We worked in consultation with literature faculty to ensure that the course met standards of a credit-bearing college literature course, but we also drew on our expertise as ESL faculty, to ensure that the course was designed in ways that made it accessible to students who did not necessarily read fluently or write well-crafted essays, thus making it an accessible course that Marcos could take in his second semester. In the course, students read 50–80 pages before each class, write journal responses, and take focused reading notes to prepare for class discussion. Students do in-class essay writing, which in some cases provides the first draft for a richer, more polished paper. Typically there are four major graded papers that students must structure around an original thesis statement based on their interpretation of the literature. Instructors make the implicit explicit by modeling the kinds of essay writing expected, and there is a deliberate focus on grading essays for content, with a reasonable tolerance of language error.

Because students within the Commanding English program expressed a desire not to be separated from the general student body, and because students outside the Commanding English program expressed an interest in studying immigrant literature, we decided to open the course to all undergraduates, taking care that our students comprise a significant portion of the class. We are conscious of (and continually challenged by) the need to build discussion in ways that allow more hesitant students to formulate their thoughts in advance, and monitor group dynamics, making clear group assignments so that no one is "over-edited" or ignored in the group. Since the literature is focused on experiences that resonate with those of our students, they are often able to bring richer interpretations to the discussion than their native-born peers; the subject itself provides an opportunity to excel. Another way, then, of integrating college coursework is to design a college course in ways that accommodate and in many ways also advantage multilingual students.

Developing Academic Writing Competence

The importance of situating students in the academic work of college informs our writing curriculum as well. It is important that college writing courses for generation 1.5 students be rich in content and that they engage students in academic inquiry. We therefore take pains to provide source-based writing courses that incorporate substantial amounts of reading. Although there is much focus on content, it is also necessary to train students in some of the conventions of academic writing that will help them to succeed in the university at large. Like other developmental writers, our students need exposure to and practice with academic writing conventions such as:

- analyzing content, making meaning, developing a stance;
- writing from source material, knowing when and how to cite;
- developing a thesis and coherence, using the language of coherence;
- supporting main points with specific information and discussion;
- organizing ideas effectively;
- drafting, reviewing, and revising;
- using strategies for proofreading and editing;
- developing fluency in academic style.

Students are encouraged to read, think, and discuss critically, in order to articulate and capitalize on their own knowledge and experiences in the context of academic research. The assumption here is that "students marked as developmental are often made to feel ashamed of the language skills and knowledge they bring to school" (Bruch & Reynolds, 2005 p. 205). In an attempt to counteract this phenomenon, we are careful to give students multiple opportunities to articulate and express their ideas, free of the pressure of language expectations and grade anxiety: for example, in free writing that is explicitly not to be turned in, in pre-writing and drafts that receive feedback but not grades, and in small group discussions. All major papers are drafted at least twice. Student meaning is negotiated first, while attention to language and style are postponed until the final draft stage of writing the paper, in an effort to help students build confidence and voice as they grapple with complex ideas.

Support for students in this process comes from several sources. As mentioned in the discussion of learning community, students get to know each other well enough to generate mutual support. Class sizes are relatively small (15–18), so the instructors can work one-on-one with developing writers in a workshop setting, in a computerized classroom. An undergraduate writing consultant attends the classes, working with individual students, responding to their writing both in verbal consultations and written commentary. The consultants, who receive some extra training in responding to ESL writing, get to know the assignments and the students well. Students feel comfortable going to the writing center outside of class because they already have a connection with a consultant. When students are hesitant to approach an instructor for help, they have someone else to use as a resource. In a recent program evaluation, students reported very high rates of satisfaction with support received from the writing center (Franko et al., 2006).

Building an Education Narrative

The first writing course in the program is identified as basic writing and, like its parallel sections, it has typically centered around topics in literacy and education. Students read an autobiographical "literacy narrative"—current choices have included: James McBride's *Color of Water*, Gordon Parks' *A Choice of Weapons* or Loung Ung's *Lucky Child*—as well as a number of academic articles critiquing the education system. Students begin the course by reflecting on their own educational paths with the writing focus of finding a specific issue to analyze. The evidence gathered for this paper is drawn from the writer's own life experiences to support a focused discussion and a significant issue in the writer's educational history. The second project centers on the literacy narrative that students have been reading and discussing in class. Students are asked to formulate a thesis statement containing their interpretation of the book's overall message about a theme relating to the author's education. For some students, the task of quoting material from the narrative to support a thesis in their papers is a challenging transition from the earlier personal writing and we see considerable movement from the first draft to the second in terms of focus and organization. The third project pushes one step further, requiring that students read, summarize, and discuss various academic articles about U.S. high school education, finally building a thesis that synthesizes and discusses the theories in relation to their own experiences in U.S.

or home country high schools. Students work on such topics as the limitations of multicultural education in public school, the merits of bilingual programs, or the effects of tracking in high school. Most students are challenged by the academic tasks of summarizing several articles and writing an opinionated response using citation to support their thesis.

In the final project of this course, students expand the skills introduced in the third paper, and locate a number of related articles in order to construct an argument about U.S. education. An alternative assignment for this fourth project has been to research the life's work of one of the authors read earlier in the course (Ira Shor or Lisa Delpit, for example), to examine other publications by this person, and to develop a paper that analyzes this author's recurring interests and overall academic stance on education. Regardless of differences in final project specifics, by the end of the semester, students are introduced to research, both online and through class visits to a major campus library. In this first writing course, then, the sources of information progress from self, to another person's personal narrative, to a more academic discussion of an issue in education, to a process in which students independently select and connect several articles about a topic in education.

Extended Research Projects

Central to the pedagogy of writing courses in this model is the assumption that students will acquire academic literacy more readily by being steeped in a particular academic subject area for an entire semester, and that this academic subject should be meaningfully connected to students' interests and education. Extended reading and writing in a content area allows for opportunities to draw on material learned earlier in

Table 11.2 Typical Sequence of Writing Assignments Over Two Semesters

---

Writing I
Focused narrative on own education
  (3–5 pages, self as source)
Paper based on literacy narrative
  (4–5 pages, literacy text as source)
Summary and critique of academic articles
  (4–5 pages, 2–4 academic articles as sources)
Researched critique of educational system or of one author's work over time
  (5 pages, 3–5 sources, various)

Writing II: extended research
Defining terms, exploring topic
  (2–3 pages, 2–3 print sources)
Evaluating sources for authority/bias
  (2–3 pages, 2–3 website sources)
Position/argument paper
  (4–6 pages, 3–5 sources, various)
Extended research project including proposal and annotated bibliography
  (8–12 sources, various, self-selected, 10–20 pages)
Final reflection paper or short position paper or editorial

---

the semester, making connections between themes and across texts. In many cases, topics for the second semester writing class also relate to other academic work the students are doing. Current research topics developed by writing instructors in the program include: *International Human Rights, Life History of an Elder*, which builds on ethnographic studies discussed in the cultural anthropology course, *Biomedical Ethics* (which is often chosen by the students enrolled in the biology or anatomy courses), and *Race, Class, and Gender* (which links well with the sociology course). This linking is not mandatory, so that a student who took biology in the fall can opt for the life histories research course in the spring, but the informal connections are possible.

The use of these topics is intended to do a number of things: they allow students to internationalize their curriculum (life histories, international human rights), to create knowledge for others (life histories), and to explore issues pertinent to their lives (race, class, and gender) and to potential careers/majors (biomedical ethics). The controversial nature of many of these topics also encourages students to evaluate ideas and sources, to examine bias in arguments, and to develop their own critical stance in relation to something significant in society.

The research course, because it is designed for students who have had limited experience with academic writing, uses a sequence of smaller writing assignments that build to an extended research project. A typical sequencing might move from writing about terms and definitions (What is a definition of human rights? Or what is your culture's definition of an elder? Or how is race defined?) to writing a short exploration paper (What is interesting about this topic?). Students build on the skills acquired in the previous semester by reading and synthesizing main ideas from a selection of articles. Critical reading is a strong focus of the courses, both in terms of learning to identify author bias (especially in electronic sources) and for the purpose of learning to identify strengths and weaknesses of argumentation. After some preliminary computer-based research, students choose a focus and write a research proposal. Students are encouraged to use both the main library and specialized research centers such as the immigration history center and the law library. The next task might be to assemble an annotated bibliography and write a tentative thesis. Finally, the writer is ready to begin drafting and redrafting the final research project, which tends to vary in length from 10 to 20 pages.

Finding Relevance in the Curriculum

The International Human Rights course was developed to provide an opportunity to research social problems that are not necessarily limited to the United States. Since all of our students were born outside the U.S., and human rights issues are directly relevant to many of their life experiences, the subject offers a broad possibility for them to find a topic for independent research that is of genuine interest. Many of the former refugees research the issues that turned their families into displaced persons. One student, for example, did extensive research that compared published case studies of oppression against his ethnic group to the human rights instruments that his home country in East Africa had ratified. As a result, he became more fully involved in local activist groups and is now taking an upper-division course in human rights law. Another student examined the human rights controversy surrounding female circumcision, and then, through a series of interviews, analyzed the reasons why the practice persists in her own immigrant community. Like the life histories course described below, this human rights course has the potential for students to draw on their own backgrounds and communities; for example, interviewing elders is often a relevant part of the research. On the other hand, for students who do not wish to revisit painful or traumatic histories, the topic is broad enough that they can choose to research issues other than those pertaining to their own experiences. Some students focus on human rights theory, discussing, for example, the problem of international responsibility versus state sovereignty. In other words, the subject is rich in terms of relevance and variety. The relevance of many of the issues to current events also allows for field trips to lunchtime lectures and discussions at downtown lawyers' offices, and functions organized by groups such as Minnesota Advocates for Human Rights.

Another topic that offers students ways to find themselves in the curriculum by doing research on their own nations of origin and histories is the Life Histories of Elders project. This was developed with a grant from the University of Minnesota Center for Interdisciplinary Studies of Writing, utilizing the expertise of a professor in Family Social Science who had been conducting a life histories project with his graduate students in a course on aging (see Murie, Collins, & Detzner, 2004, for full discussion of this project). This course combines ethnography with library research, bringing together one person's life story with research on the political and social forces at play during that person's life.

Students begin the course discussing readings about aging (Detzner, 2004), defining an elder, and working on techniques for writing interview questions. Each writer in the course chooses an elder from his or her own community or, if the writer prefers, from another community, and prepares to do a series of three interviews about the elder's early, middle, and later years of life. At about the time of the second interview, students begin their library research using archives in the Immigration History Center on campus, and other general library and Internet sources. Students search for information that will illuminate some aspect of their subject's life, thus adding wider historical and cultural perspectives to the life history.

After the third interview, the task of assembling the project begins and writers find themselves having to choose which "pieces of the puzzle" to include. While this wealth of material from library research, interview data, and stories can be daunting, students often speak with pride about completing a writing project that is both creative and real: it becomes a document that is given to the elder as a gift, and the writing up of the life history is something most of the writers take quite seriously.

An important aspect of this project, to us, is that it positions students as bilingual experts rather than as "under-prepared, weak writers prone to making grammar errors." It takes tremendous cultural sensitivity and linguistic skill to interview an elder and transcribe and translate from the language of the interview into English. From a writing teacher's point of view, this type of project also provides a rich context for the library research. A typical problem with first-year research courses is that novice writers can become overwhelmed by decisions about what information to select and how to focus this topic. The elder's story creates a focus for the research, and, while students say it is difficult to find the information they are looking for, they are in a better position to discard information that is less relevant to their topics. As one student wrote in the final reflection paper, "I learned as a writer you have to be sincere when telling a story of a person, but at the same time you are the author and you decide what part of the story you want to tell and how will you use the research." Students who choose the life histories course rate it very highly.

While we have seen great success with the life histories course, it is important to us that students not be exclusively or restrictively positioned in the program as immigrants who can tell an immigrant story. Too often such students are immersed in immigration topics in an effort to create "relevant" content (and because immigration stories are of interest to us as teachers). The life histories course is always scheduled at the same time as one of the other research options, so that students choose the topic as an area of personal interest, and not because it meets at a particular time of day in the schedule.

An alternative research topic that is valued by many students is *Race, Class, and Gender*, a choice that was developed in response to the sociology course in the college. Students face complex issues on campus and in their lives. Generation 1.5 students, by definition, are situated "between cultures." They must juggle the simultaneous and sometimes contradictory demands and pressures of the multiple social worlds they inhabit, including family, community, workplace, and campus. For students of color, the move from their home country may mean being perceived for the first time as a "racialized minority" in the U.S. On our campus there have been occasions when campus busses have not stopped for veiled Somali women, assuming they were not students, and male students have reported perceptions of being profiled by campus police. In the sociology course People and Problems, students read about various social inequalities, do service learning at a local community center, and write about their experience, incorporating theory with observation. Picking up on this interest of students, one instructor has developed a research writing topic based on readings about race, class, and gender. Students read and summarize articles about the social construction of difference, social control, racism and sexism, and class inequalities, and in the process, many tell us that they feel they have a new way of articulating what they have been seeing in their own environment. In the words of one student:

> (The course) changed me. It changed the way that I look at the world, the way I look at things, because I would always say like "yeah, this person is racist" but I would never look at it as in the system. I would always blame the individuals who were racist. I would have a completely different point of view about racism than I do today.
>
> (Smidt, 2006, p. 36)

Another way to find oneself in the curriculum is to take courses that are relevant to one's intended field of study. For many of our current students, who hope to major in the health sciences, biology and chemistry are of prime importance. Having a research course in Biomedical Ethics allows students to gain experience reading in the scientific and medical fields about such topics as stem cell research, drug testing, and organ harvesting/donation. The richness of the topic allows students a broad range of choice as they search for an area of focus for research. The controversial nature of most of the issues also affords writing teachers ample opportunity to discuss point of view, ways of evaluating credibility of sources, and methods of structuring arguments so that the counter-arguments are also considered.

All of the topics for the extended research course are steeped in content. The reading material is difficult, often requiring class time to decipher passages and scaffold the arguments presented. Students falter when their understanding of academic articles is incomplete. There are moments of plagiarism, because the tasks are difficult and the temptation to lift passages from the web is present. It is not easy to create a thesis that is then supported by examples from academic research articles on biomedical ethics or human rights. However, by doing extended work within a single research area, students build a vocabulary and conceptual framework for examining the issues and are able to write papers that are substantial. Because major papers are drafted and revised multiple times, students gain competence, and grades reflect a student's tenacity in addition to current writing skill. We are concerned about some of the more anxious students in the program, who spend many hours in the writing center, seeking assistance from peer tutors. Nevertheless, most students looking back over what they have accomplished over a year of writing express great satisfaction at having written papers that were longer and better than they had believed themselves capable of, and evaluation of the writing component of the program is consistently very high.

Building Editing Skill

Working on editing for error and style can be complicated for students who have not learned English as a formal language system and who, consequently, may not have much grammar terminology to draw on. Grammar/editing concerns are typically addressed in the final draft for revision. In addition to teacher or peer-editing, first-semester students also enroll in a 2-credit editing course that is linked to the basic writing course. Here students study editing patterns, take grammar notes, do exercises, and, most important, bring their drafts from the writing class to the editing classroom for peer-work identifying patterns of error. The goal is not a perfectly edited paper, but a growth in confidence at finding errors. For example, a student who has difficulty with consistent use of past tense may need:

1. strategies for a slowed-down proofreading, to become a more deliberate and confident editor,
2. grammar knowledge about tense usage in English,
3. practice locating verbs, hearing soft –ed endings, and building a more intuitive awareness of the structure that is causing difficulty.

This is a three-pronged approach: strategies, knowledge, and practice, carried out within the context of the writer's own writing. However, what may benefit the student more than anything else is extended writing practice. Several students in the life histories course (described earlier in this chapter) commented in their reflection papers that control over verb tenses became more consistent because they were drafting and writing so much. The teacher lightly commented on past/present verb tense agreement, but it was the act of writing up the interviews and constructing a long project that seemed to give students a sense of mastery over tense.

Conclusion

It is not easy to write papers based on academic content. Some might argue that a heavy reading load may frustrate students who lack the vocabulary or background to fully understand academic articles and that reading detracts from time spent on writing instruction. However, by reading, students are acquiring a sense of what writing looks like, and, in fact, it is rare for students in our program to complain that the writing courses are a "waste of time" or stigmatizing. They recognize their gains in writing ability. The drafting and revising processes leave ample room for expression and feedback before grammatical accuracy and editing concerns are attended to. More importantly, these writing courses work with sustained academic content, in ways that allow students to connect with topics, build academic skills, and, we hope also, treat students as multilingual, competent thinkers, even when others in the academy might respond more negatively to surface features of the writing that are not "standard." The more we can connect coursework to the real work of college, the more we will be able to reduce the stigma of ESL, and to build the genuine academic literacy needed for success.

At the start of this piece, Marcos was beginning to learn to read ethnic history and relate the content of this reading to his own experiences: he was practicing with ways to quote passages, to paraphrase main ideas, and to build a journal response to specific content in the chapter. It is our goal that by the end of the academic year, Marcos will have written a major research project, read three textbooks for cultural anthropology, studied for five major biology exams, given numerous speeches and oral presentations in class, and written essays for four novels in immigration literature. He will have met with his advisor numerous times to figure out his next courses and his intended major. Will his writing be perfect? No. Will this have been an easy year? No. But will his English be as strong as if he had taken a year of developmental ESL coursework? We think stronger.

Appendix A Courses in the Commanding English Program

Fall Semester

Developing College Reading   2 credits
Comprehension and study strategies necessary for college textbook reading. This course uses the textbook from one of the content courses below. Previewing the textbook for content and organization, underlining and making marginal notes, outlining, anticipating test questions, and technical vocabulary.

Content courses—choose one[1]
People and Problems (sociology)   4 credits
General Art   3 credits
Principles of Biological Science   4 credits

Intro to College Writing: Workshop   2 credits
This is a grammar workshop that focuses on developing editing skills and accuracy in written English through practice with grammar trouble spots, editing strategies, and sentence combining.

Writing I   3 credits
This is the first of a two-semester writing sequence required at the University. The course focuses on the reading and writing of expository/analytical texts on topics of education and educational equity.

Oral Communication in the Public Sphere   3 credits
Through discussion, prepared speeches, and debates, students develop strategies for effective oral communication. Includes theories of communication, ethics, citizenship, persuasion, and language use. Fulfills college speech requirement.

Note

1. These all fill general education requirements at the University.

Spring Semester

Reading in Content Areas   2 credits
Taken in conjunction with an academic content course; additional practice with reading and study strategies specific to reading in a particular content area.

Content courses—choose one
Cultural Anthropology   4 credits
Biological Science: The Human Body   4 credits
General Art   3 credits

Writing II   3 credits
Academic, research-based writing. Readings and essay assignments explore a topic of contemporary interest. Summaries, analysis, and research writing. Fills U of M freshman writing requirement. Current topic choices: Biomedical Ethics, International Human Rights, Life History Ethnography, or Race, Class and Gender.

Literature of the American Immigrant Experience   3 credits
Exploration of American immigrant experiences, both historical and contemporary, through readings in fiction, expository prose, biography, and oral history. Course includes substantial reading, discussion, journal writing, essays, and a class project.

References

Abdimalik, A. (March, 2006). Best practices for recruitment and retention: a report on Somali colloquium in metro area. Meeting of the Metro Alliance Community Outreach Program, Minneapolis, MN. Unpublished proceedings.

Adamson, H.D. (1993). *Academic competence: Theory and classroom practice: Preparing ESL students for content courses.* White Plains, NY: Longman Publishing Group.

Blanton, L.L. (1998). Discourse, artifacts, and the Ozarks: Understanding academic literacy. In

V. Zamel & R. Spack (Eds.), *Negotiating academic literacies: Teaching and learning across languages and cultures* (pp. 219–236). Mahwah, NJ: Lawrence Erlbaum Associates.

Blanton, L.L. (1999). Classroom instruction and language minority students: On teaching to "smarter" readers and writers. In L. Harklau, K.M. Losey, & M. Siegal (Eds.), *Generation 1.5 meets college composition: Issues in the teaching of writing to U.S.-educated learners of ESL* (pp. 119–142). Mahwah, NJ: Lawrence Erlbaum Associates.

Bruch, P. & Reynolds, T. (2005). Multicultural writing instruction at the General College: A dialogical approach. In J.L. Higbee, D.B. Lundell, & D.R. Arendale (Eds.), *The General College vision: Integrating intellectual growth, multicultural perspectives, and student development* (pp. 201–218). Minneapolis, MN: General College and the Center for Research on Developmental Education and Urban Literacy.

Christensen, L., Fitzpatrick, R., Murie, R., & Zhang, X. (2005). Building voice and developing academic literacy for multilingual students: The Commanding English model. In J.L. Higbee, D.B. Lundell, & D.R. Arendale (Eds.), *The General College vision: Integrating intellectual growth, multicultural perspectives, and student development* (pp. 155–184). Minneapolis, MN: General College and the Center for Research on Developmental Education and Urban Literacy.

Detzner, D. (2004). *Eldervoices: Southeast Asian families in the United States.* Walnut Creek, CA: Altamira Press.

Franko, J., Conner, J., Wambach, C., & Xie, B. (2006). *Commanding English program evaluation.* Minneapolis, MN: University of Minnesota, General College Office of Research and Evaluation.

Fu, D. (1995). *"My trouble is my English": Asian students and the American dream.* Portsmouth, NH: Boynton/Cook.

Gee, J.P. (1998). What is literacy? In V. Zamel & R. Spack (Eds.), *Negotiating academic literacies: Teaching and learning across languages and culture* (pp. 51–59). Mahwah, NJ: Lawrence Erlbaum Associates.

Harklau, L. (1994). Tracking and linguistic minority students: Consequences of ability grouping for second language learners. *Linguistics and Education, 6*(3), 217–244.

Harklau, L. (1999). The ESL learning environment in secondary school. In C. Faltis & P. Wolfe (Eds.), *So much to say: Adolescents, bilingualism, and ESL in the secondary school* (pp. 42–60). Columbia University, NY: Columbia Teacher's College Press.

Harklau, L., Losey, K.M., & Siegal, M. (Eds.). (1999). *Generation 1.5 meets college composition: Issues in the teaching of writing to U.S.-educated learners of ESL.* Mahwah, NJ: Lawrence Erlbaum Associates.

James, P.A., Bruch, P.L., & Jehangir, R. (2006). Ideas in practice: Building bridges in a multicultural learning community. *Journal of Developmental Education, 29*(3), 10–18.

Kasper, L.F. (Ed.) (2000). *Content-based college ESL instruction.* Mahwah, NJ: Lawrence Erlbaum Associates.

McBride, J. (1996). *The color of water: A Black man's tribute to his white mother.* New York: Riverhead Books.

MacGowan-Gilhooly, A. (1991). Fluency before correctness: A whole language experiment in college ESL. *College ESL, 1*(1), 37–52.

Minnesota Minority Education Partnership, Inc. (2006). *The state of students of color.* Retrieved September 24, 2007, from www.mmep.org/ssoc.html.

Mlynarczyk, R.W. & Babbit, M. (2002). The power of academic learning communities. *Journal of Basic Writing, 21*(1), 71–89.

Murie, R., Collins, M., & Detzner, D. (2004). Building academic literacy from student strength: An interdisciplinary life history project. *Journal of Basic Writing, 23*(2), 70–92.

Murie, R. & Thomson, R. (2001). *When ESL is developmental: A model program for the freshman year.* In J.L. Higbee, D.B. Lundell, & D. Banerjee-Stevens (Eds.), *2001: A developmental odyssey* (pp. 15–28). Warrensburg, MO: National Association for Developmental Education.

Parks, G. (1986). *A choice of weapons.* St. Paul, MN: Minnesota Historical Society Press.

Roberge, M. (2002). California's generation 1.5 immigrants: What experiences, characteristics, and needs do they bring to our English classes? *CATESOL Journal, 14*(1), 107–130.

Smalkoski, K. (2005). Perceptions of academic progress and acculturation: A case study of two Somali women in college. Unpublished master's thesis, Hamline University, St. Paul, MN.

Smidt, E. (2006). Race, class, and gender: Immigrant identity in an English as a second language college writing class. In D.B. Lundell, J.L. Higbee, I.M. Duranczyk, & E. Goff (Eds.), *Student standpoints about access programs in higher education* (pp. 31–45). University of Minnesota: Center for Research on Developmental Education and Urban Literacy.

Spack, R. (2004). The acquisition of academic literacy in a second language: A longitudinal case study, updated. In V. Zamel & R. Spack (Eds.), *Crossing the curriculum: Multilingual learners in college classrooms* (pp. 19–45). Mahwah NJ: Lawrence Erlbaum Associates.

Takaki, R. (1993). *A different mirror: A history of multicultural America.* New York: Little, Brown, and Co.

Tinto, V. (1998). Research on student persistence. *Review of Higher Education, 21*(2), 167–177.

Ung, L. (2005). *Lucky child: A daughter of Cambodia reunites with the sister she left behind.* New York: HarperCollins Publishers Inc.

Valdés, G. (2001). *Learning and not learning English: Latino students in American schools.* Columbia University, NY: Columbia Teacher's College Press.

Zamel, V. (1991). Acquiring language, literacy, and academic discourse: Entering ever new conversations. *College ESL, 1*(1), 10–18.

12 Creating an Inter-Departmental Course for Generation 1.5 ESL Writers
Challenges Faced and Lessons Learned

Christine Holten University of California, Los Angeles

In the opening chapter of their volume, *Generation 1.5 meets college composition*, Harklau, Siegal, and Losey (1999) point to some of the "political and ethical dilemmas" that accompany college writing requirements for multilingual and bilingual students. These issues include: (1) how to appropriately and fairly assess generation 1.5 ESL students for placement; (2) which courses to place them in: ESL writing courses, developmental writing courses or freshman composition courses; (3) what instructional paradigms to use; (4) how to acknowledge students' prior academic successes while letting students know that they have weaknesses in academic writing; and (5) whether this group of students should be held to exactly the same writing and language standards as their monolingual English-speaking counterparts.

ESL professionals at community colleges and universities across the country have been working on ways to address the above issues for some time. The university ESL program that is the focus of this article is no different. Like many programs, our ESL program for matriculated students at the University of California, Los Angeles, has been serving U.S.-educated immigrant students for well over a decade. Most of these students have been in the U.S. less than 7 years, i.e. under the 8-year limit for acquisition of academic literacy set forth in Collier (1987). But over the past 5 years, we have experienced a tripling of entering first year students who have been in the U.S. longer than 7 years—in other words, students who would clearly fit into the "generation 1.5 ESL" group described by Harklau et al. (1999). In fact, many of these new students have been educated in U.S. schools since the primary grades.

In the early stages of this demographic shift, the ESL program attempted to serve the needs of generation 1.5 ESL students using existing placement mechanisms and course structures. On our campus, first year students whose writing proficiency exams exhibited language and vocabulary issues similar to those of typical ESL students were placed either in a developmental writing course or in an equivalent ESL course. The final placement decision depended on the type and severity of grammar problems in their writing and the length of time they had spent in U.S. schools. If students' writing samples contained many ESL-type errors in vocabulary and grammar, and if their SAT verbal scores were below the average set by the university, they were usually placed in the ESL course regardless of how long they had lived in the U.S. and regardless of whether they identified themselves as native speakers of English. In other words, the language control exhibited in their writing exams trumped their prior educational and language use background. Many of the generation 1.5 students who were placed in the

ESL courses had not been in courses labeled "ESL" since elementary school and some had never taken an "ESL course" before. It is therefore understandable that some of them were very unhappy with their ESL placement. And their ESL instructors were often equally unhappy.

The generation 1.5 ESL students and their teachers had further cause for dissatisfaction because the curriculum for the ESL course was not designed for proficient bilinguals who were highly fluent in English yet lacked preparation in academic reading and writing. It had been formulated primarily with traditional ESL students in mind, i.e., international undergraduates in the U.S. on F1 visas and more recently arrived English language learners who had done most of their formal schooling in non-English medium schools. Solving the problem of how best to serve this growing group of students involved collaboration between ESL and college composition faculty. The intent of this chapter is to describe how we worked together to solve the problem, how we overcame obstacles, and what we learned along the way.

The Challenges of Course Placement for Generation 1.5 Writers

The heart of the problem faced by our institution was to determine where to place freshman generation 1.5 writers who were not yet ready for the reading and writing demands of "freshman composition." We were presented with an either/or choice: we could place the students in either an ESL course or a native-speaker-oriented developmental writing course. The grammar and mechanical errors in their writing suggested the need for ESL instruction, which focuses on both academic writing and grammar issues such as verb form and tense, articles, and relative clauses. Their bilingualism and their cultural and educational backgrounds argued for placement in college composition courses, which tend to limit grammar instruction to stylistic issues and a small set of grammatical errors such as comma splices and fragments. For reasons outlined below neither choice was satisfactory.

Drawbacks of Placing Generation 1.5 Students in ESL Courses

Placing generation 1.5 students into an ESL course had several drawbacks. First, as noted already, generation 1.5 ESL students at our university tended to resent this placement. In fact, it is an understatement to say that many of them were astonished (perhaps "appalled" would be a more apt word) to find themselves labeled as ESL students and required to take an ESL course to satisfy their developmental writing requirement. Because of their resentment, they often ended up "resisting" the course, the curriculum, and the teacher. This, in and of itself, was enough to reduce the efficacy of the ESL course.

A second problem had to do with the differences in language learning experience between the generation 1.5 ESL students and the other students enrolled in the ESL course. At our university, students enrolled in the ESL courses were a heterogeneous group. In a given quarter, approximately one-third of the students in a typical ESL course were international undergraduates on F1 visas and one-third were recently arrived immigrants. These two groups of students typically had learned English grammar in a formal way either in EFL or ESL classes. The remaining one-third of the students, the generation 1.5 ESL students, generally had learned English "naturalistically," by living and going to school in an English-speaking environment from a young age. Thus, the student groups brought very different sets of knowledge and language learning practice to the class, and very different expectations about the kind of composition instruction they should receive.

It was difficult to address these differing student needs, backgrounds, abilities, and expectations in one course with one curriculum. From student evaluations and teacher reports, it was apparent that the curriculum, which had been designed with traditional ESL writers and their problems in mind, could not fit the needs, work paces, and self-perceptions of these very different groups. While all three groups benefited from the college-level reading texts and writing tasks, the way they needed to approach these tasks and texts and the help they needed with grammar and vocabulary were often quite different. Whereas the more traditional ESL students often preferred a metalinguistic approach to grammar instruction and could label, recognize, and talk about many grammar structures in their writing, the generation 1.5 ESL students often expressed frustration at this type of language analysis and they tended to have difficulty matching the most basic grammar terms with structures in their own texts. While the traditional ESL students approached issues of editing and correctness via rules, many generation 1.5 ESL students relied almost exclusively on their "ear" or language intuition ("It sounds right," cf. Reid, 1998). And the grammar problems found in the writing of each group were quite distinct. For example, international students sometimes produced constructions that were highly unidiomatic. Generation 1.5 students, on the other hand, would more often produce constructions that *sounded* quite close to academic English expressions, but were just slightly inaccurate, for example in the choice of preposition.

Drawbacks of Placement in College Composition Courses

Clearly, the generation 1.5 ESL students on our campus would have felt more at home in a developmental writing course because their fellow students in such a course would have been their classmates in high school English courses. In addition, placement in a composition course would have avoided the stigma attached to placement in a course labeled "ESL".

This "path of least resistance" solution, however, would not have appropriately served these student writers and their language and editing issues. The instructors of the college composition courses themselves admitted feeling ill-equipped to deal with what they considered to be the pressing language and vocabulary needs of generation 1.5 ESL students. In fact, instructors of developmental writing courses routinely advised writers with the most marked and persistent language problems to drop the course and enroll in an equivalent ESL course.

Crossing Departmental Lines: Collaborative Course Design

The ESL composition instructors and the college composition instructors decided to join forces to tackle the dilemmas associated with our "either/or" placement dilemma. As a faculty, we met and discussed the unique profile of our population of generation 1.5 ESL students who did not qualify for direct entrance into freshman composition. In particular, we looked at their lower-than-required SAT verbal scores (below 520 verbal SAT), their length of residence (more than 8 years in U.S. schools), their bilingual status (most report speaking a language other than English at home), the language and vocabulary errors present in their writing—a combination of what might be considered "typical" native-speaker basic writing errors (fragments, run-on sentences, oral spellings, misuse of academic vocabulary) and "typical" ESL errors (verb form and tense, subject–verb agreement, singular and plural nouns, prepositions, sentence structure, vocabulary, and idioms). We also considered generation 1.5 students' reported dissatisfaction at being forced to satisfy their developmental writing requirement by taking an ESL course. We then explored alternatives to teach them in a way that would be more satisfying for the students and for their instructors. Options we entertained included: (1) adopting an adjunct model whereby students would simultaneously take a college composition course and a special two-unit workshop course taught by an ESL professional;[1] (2) requiring these students to get extra tutoring; (3) creating a special course just for the entering generation 1.5 ESL students. In the end, we opted to design a special course that would be taught by an ESL composition expert but offered by UCLA Writing Programs, carrying its name and numbering (English Composition 2— Approaches to University Discourse). Instead of meeting 4 hours a week as the ESL and college composition courses do, the class would be an intensive 6-hour a week section.

In opting to create a special course, we were making some firm statements in response to ethical and political questions surrounding college composition requirements for generation 1.5 ESL students. We were acknowledging the hard work that had earned them a place at one of the state's most prestigious universities and we wanted to reduce the stigma that students would have felt if they were placed in an "ESL" course. However, we were also emphasizing that these students would be held to the same writing requirements as their monolingual counterparts, with the appropriate instructional support. Finally, the decision to increase the number of contact hours recognized that the students have two areas of academic literacy that need equal attention—language and academic writing/reading skills—and that the university needs to give them time, focused instruction, and expert faculty to work on these two areas simultaneously. Our approach was different from that of many universities: we did not label these students "remedial writers." We did not "off-load" their instruction, i.e., send them to the community college system to complete "remedial work" before allowing them to return to do "regular" English coursework. And we did not expect these students to take pre-university writing courses leading to a "gatekeeping" writing exam required for admittance to freshman composition.

Rethinking Assessment of Generation 1.5 ESL Students

Creating the course that has come to be known as English Comp. 2i raised questions about the assessment procedures we used to place students in writing courses. At first, we decided to keep the two-part assessment process that had been in place for many years. In this two-part process, students first took the university's entry-level writing exam. Any student who failed that exam because of the ESL language features in their writing would then be instructed to take the university's ESL placement exam before their ultimate course placement could be decided. This procedure had several advantages. Essentially it allowed a student to submit two writing samples produced several months apart, the first in the spring prior to their freshman year and the second in the fall just prior to the start of classes. An added advantage to this system was that the two writing tasks were quite different. The university's writing exam is a reading-based writing task whereas the ESL writing exam is an analytical or argumentative task about a topic of general interest. The procedure ensured the careful review and consideration of each student's case, at least as much as possible based on the information we had access to: a student's SAT scores and the information about language and residency provided on the "intent to register" questionnaire she or he returned to the campus.

Although our long-standing placement process gave us a comprehensive view of students' abilities, it created some logistical problems for students and for both the ESL and the composition programs. Entering first year students at our university participate in a week-long orientation program in the summer prior to their freshman year. During this week, they enroll in their fall quarter courses and plan their course schedule for the rest of the academic year. The students who were directed to take the ESL exam in the fall were not able to enroll in any fall composition courses during summer orientation. This was, of course, inconvenient for them because it impacted their ability to enroll in courses required for their degrees or majors. For our two academic programs, this delay impeded course planning as we never knew how many sections of the ESL or the generation 1.5 courses to offer in a given year until right before the start of the academic year.

To overcome these problems of timing, we eventually simplified the process. Instead of having the students sit for two exams, the students only sit for the university's entry-level writing exam in the spring before they enter the university. A group comprised of both ESL and college composition faculty reread the exams that have been marked as containing ESL-type errors. Each exam is read twice, once by an ESL instructor and once by a college composition instructor. Based on these two readings, students are placed in one of three courses that prepare students for "freshman composition": a developmental writing course, an ESL writing course, or the course for generation 1.5 ESL writers. Although the readers suggest placement in one of the three courses, this is not finalized until the demographic data on file for each student is checked. For example, a reader may recommend that a student be placed in the ESL composition course because of the number and type of grammar and vocabulary errors in the writer's text. If, however, upon examining the demographic data, it is discovered that the student has attended U.S. schools since third grade and identifies English as their native language, readers will carefully reconsider their decision to place that student in an ESL course. Instead, the student may be placed in the composition course for generation 1.5 ESL writers.

The new assessment process has the advantage of being timed better to the academic and administrative schedule while ensuring appropriate placement. Moreover, the process encourages ESL and composition faculty to work together on placement decisions, a collaboration that can be beneficial not only for validity of placement decisions, but for curriculum and teaching in both programs.

Involving Generation 1.5 ESL Students in Placement Decisions

While it is important that we make accurate placement decisions based on students' language and literacy needs, it is equally important that we take into consideration their affective needs, personal histories, and desire to participate actively in choices about their education. It is especially important to acknowledge students' prior educational successes: they have graduated from American high schools as honors students and they have been accepted to a prestigious public university. Many have even successfully completed college-level AP courses while in high school. To promote buy-in from students, we involve them in the placement process by encouraging them to meet with faculty to discuss their placement before the start of classes. These private meetings are designed to help students understand their placement (what it is and how it was determined) and to describe the developmental writing course they will take. The meeting also allows them to tell us about themselves— their language background, their experience in U.S. schools, and the profile of language use in their homes. The meeting also allows us to determine if the background information we used to place the students was comprehensive and accurate. In some cases, talking to the students makes it clear whether the original placement is appropriate.

These placement conversations have given us a window into how the students identify themselves, which has, in turn, informed both our placement process and classroom practice. As many researchers discuss, what students call themselves (Rodby, 1999) and what they claim as their native language (Harklau et al., 1999) are crucial parts of the equation when working with generation 1.5 ESL writers. The students who are ultimately placed in the generation 1.5 course have often been in the U.S. since first or second grade and readily acknowledge speaking another home language. But, when asked what their first language is, most say that they know English better than the other language or languages that are spoken in their environments.

Finally, being able to discuss their placement seems to have an important impact on their attitude going into the course. Rather than feeling "punished" or "stigmatized," most students seem glad to have been given information about fulfilling their composition requirement. In the final analysis, the most important outcome of involving students in the placement decision is a marked improvement in the class atmosphere and the students' participation in the course over what they were when students were automatically placed in an ESL course.

Course Design and Instructional Choices

Like its ESL and college composition counterparts, the generation 1.5 course familiarizes students with university-level reading texts and writing tasks. In its design, it is essentially a blend of its "parent" courses and, thus, maintains the parts of each course that are most suited to and work the best with generation 1.5 ESL writers. See Table 12.1 for a complete comparison of the three courses.

Table 12.1 Comparison of the Three Courses

Developmental writing course	Generation 1.5 course	ESL course
	Contact hours/week	
4 hours	6 hours	4 hours
Writing assignments 3–4 graded papers: approx. 20 revised pages expository writing that synthesizes course readings teacher-assigned tasks (often the type of writing is somewhat open and is decided by the student)	*Writing assignments* 3–4 graded papers: approx. 20 revised pages writing that synthesizes course readings teacher-assigned tasks that correspond to central academic text types	2 graded papers: approx. 15 revised pages writing that synthesizes course readings teacher-assigned tasks that correspond to central academic text types
Reading 15–20 pieces, some of which are over 20–25 pages in length (over 100 pages of text)	15 pieces, none of which is longer than 10 pages (50–60 total pages)	15 pieces, none of which is longer than 10 pages (50–60 total pages)
Reading-related assignments and class activities Class discussion Discussion board postings on the class website related to self-selected questions about the readings	Class discussion Discussion board postings on the class website related to teacher-formulated questions about the readings	Class discussion Reading guides (handouts with comprehension and discussion questions)
Writing-related assignments In-class quick writes on topics related to readings or writing assignments Journal and website posting activities	Pre-writing tasks (not mandatory) In-class quick writes on topics related to readings or writing assignments Style imitation exercises (focused on conclusion strategies)	Guided pre-writing and outlining activities (must be completed)
Grammar and proofreading activities Teacher error marking or correction Teacher discussion of common problems Referral to handbook and/or tutoring	Teacher error marking Learning and identifying parts of speech and sentence structures Strategies for self-editing of specific grammar points	Teacher error marking Grammar activities focused on recurring problems Rule-based grammar activities focused on a specific grammar point Strategies for self-editing of specific grammar points
Conferences 3–4 times per quarter, on a voluntary basis	7–8 times per quarter, mandatory, becoming voluntary later in the quarter	3–4 times per quarter, mandatory

Focusing on Academic Reading and Writing

When designing the curriculum, it seemed important to align the course goals with those of the developmental writing course offered by the university's writing program. Thus, the generation 1.5 course requires the students to submit approximately 20 revised pages or three to four final draft essays, the same number of drafted pages as the developmental writing course. This is more than the two drafted essays turned in by writers in the ESL course. Also, students read a set of theme-based, university-level reading texts. These are the focal point for all student writing, including journals, discussion board postings, and drafted essays.

In contrast to the developmental writing course, however, students read fewer texts. Instead of reading entire books or long essays, students read texts of no longer than ten pages. We made the decision to assign shorter readings because, in their course final evaluations, the generation 1.5 ESL students in our program reported that some of the longer academic texts were too difficult or, in their own words, "boring." This, in turn, dampened their enthusiasm for writing on the assigned topics. For their part, instructors reported that students didn't understand the reading or, in the case of longer readings, weren't able to finish them. Teachers then had to spend valuable class time catching students up on unread material. Therefore, we determined that "less is more" and opted to choose a few readings that students would enjoy and do more with them. Reducing the reading load also allows time to have students read about writing and the writing process, and it frees class time for language work, time that would otherwise be spent discussing assigned reading.

In addition, the generation 1.5 course places more emphasis on and scaffolds the writing process, as is typically done in ESL courses (cf. Hyon, 1996). This is a more systematic approach to teaching the structure of essays than is typically adopted in developmental writing courses for native speakers of English. Commonly, developmental writing courses focus on the "what" of the writing process, emphasizing idea generation and extended discussions of the assigned readings. The link between these activities and "how" students are to go about writing the subsequent essay assignment may not be explicitly made. In the generation 1.5 course, the writing process is specific to each writing task and is broken down into steps the students follow to complete the assignment. They include not only idea-generation activities, but also tasks that will help students in organizing and revising ideas in their essays.

While this scaffolding is useful for all developing writers, whether they are monolingual English writers or multilingual writers, it has particular benefits for the generation 1.5 ESL writers. First, it allows these novice academic writers to glean and rehearse vocabulary and phrases that they will use in their essays. The strength of generation 1.5 ESL students is their oral English. They have the linguistic resources to talk and write comfortably about their own experiences but may find themselves a bit at a loss when summarizing or writing about ideas from published texts. With each pre-writing exercise they do, they can add and experiment with academic vocabulary and the grammar needed to express their ideas about the topic. In the long run, this has to make generating an essay easier. Second, it helps them develop an effective process for approaching any writing task. Developing a structured writing process makes writing more efficient for all freshmen writers, but it is quite important for generation 1.5 ESL students who need to spend more time on generating and editing their texts because of language and vocabulary constraints.

Developing an Approach to Language and Vocabulary Instruction

In addition to the adjustments made to the reading and writing components of the course, the other aspect of the generation 1.5 course that makes it distinct from both its ESL and college composition equivalents is the amount of time devoted to teaching grammar, vocabulary, and editing as well as the instructional approaches used to tackle these issues. As noted earlier, the course meets 2 more hours than the college and ESL composition courses. The 2 hours devoted to grammar and vocabulary are used flexibly. Sometimes they are used for in-class language and editing activities. Sometimes the teacher will use them to extend conference time so that work can be done on students' individual editing, grammar, and vocabulary problems.

But it isn't enough simply to add hours. Those hours have to be usefully spent. And this has not been easy. In fact, discovering an approach to language and vocabulary that works well has undoubtedly been the greatest course design challenge because the typical approaches to language in writing—either from the first language composition world or from the ESL composition world—seem to need adjusting for generation 1.5 ESL students.

Problems with Existing Approaches to Correctness

As mentioned earlier, the generation 1.5 ESL students may be bored or confused, or may feel demeaned by traditional ESL approaches to teaching grammar and mechanics. This is especially true of the approach that focuses on reviewing or learning grammar rules for a certain grammatical structure. Such activities require knowledge of formal grammar terminology and an ability to identify these structures in one's own and others' writing. Generation 1.5 ESL writers have essentially approached and been taught to approach issues of correctness in writing as native speakers of English would, and thus, they not only vary as a group in their knowledge of formal English grammar, but their approach to accuracy is anchored in and governed not by formal grammar rules, but by strong intuitions about how written English works based on their years speaking and reading English in school.

A second approach that is employed with both ESL and developmental writers involves the teacher marking errors in students' essays followed by an in-class discussion of language issues common to all students. The teacher may then either have students do error correction activities in class or refer students to relevant pages in a writing handbook. Students are expected to use the marks on their texts in combination with information from the handbook to proofread their texts. We have found that this approach has several drawbacks when implemented with the generation 1.5 ESL writers in our program. For example, handbooks treat a handful of errors (e.g., comma splice, fragments, pronoun reference, etc.) based on those usually found in the texts of developmental writers. However, the errors found in the texts of the generation 1.5 ESL writers in our program do not always fall into such neat and recurring patterns. Instead, their grammar and vocabulary errors are often varied and inconsistent—even within a generation 1.5 ESL writer's text, a structure may be correct in one sentence and incorrect in subsequent sentences. This makes error marking a much more labor intensive proposition, and the errors that are marked may defy easy categorization, in turn making it difficult to refer students to pages in a writing handbook. In addition, we found that many of our generation 1.5 ESL students who have gone to large public high schools are not used to getting such consistent and focused feedback on the errors in their texts.[2] Thus, they may not attend to or know how to use the error correction to improve their own proofreading abilities. Finally, if they are referred to handbook pages, they may not find them that useful, given that they lack familiarity with the terminology that is used in even the most accessible writing handbooks. In addition, they may also be unfamiliar with how to use such a handbook to help them improve their proofreading skills.

More discourse-based approaches such as having students analyze published texts to discover how a given language feature functions in a written text seem more suited to the intuitions that generation 1.5 ESL writers have for English. While such activities help student writers pay attention to stylistic and linguistic choices in writing and show them the range of structures and vocabulary open to writers, it is unclear how much this influences the language in their own written texts, and particularly, the accuracy of that language.

Developing our Approaches to Correctness

In the 7 years of work with the generation 1.5 course, we have found that each group of students is different both in the language they need to work on and in the approaches to language work that suit their needs and learning styles. Thus, instructors devote the first 3 weeks of each course to three activities: (1) assessing students' knowledge of formal grammar terminology and rules; (2) examining the error patterns in the writing of the group and individual students; and (3) trying and evaluating various task types for working on language, proofreading, and vocabulary to see which the students find most interesting and useful. The choice of any task is driven by several guiding principles. The language activities must first address language problems evident in the students' writing—both the essay drafts they submit and their discussion board postings, which are more informal than the essays. The tasks have to be discourse-based; that is, they have to involve students in examining grammatical structures and vocabulary in paragraph-level text and help the students discover what they already know about how written English works. Further, any task has to transfer into helping them produce more accurate academic English in their essay drafts.

In the course of this 7-year trial and error process, we have found several consistently useful and well-received language focused tasks. Students have been interested in tasks that entail learning terminology for parts of speech, verb types (e.g., transitive and intransitive), and sentence parts, and learning to pick out and label these sentence constituents in their own writing and in the writing of the published texts they read. They have also found it useful to practice concrete strategies for editing their own writing for verb tense shift and subject–verb agreement with complex subjects. The process moves from one that is teacher-guided to one in which the students are more responsible for editing their own texts. In self-editing for subject–verb agreement, for example, students first learn to identify and mark the subjects and verbs in their paragraphs, editing any errors they discover. They are subsequently asked to complete the process as homework. The results are looked over by the instructor, who marks any errors that students haven't been able to find. Finally, they are expected to find all subject–verb agreement errors in their texts by independent self-editing before handing in an essay draft. On these drafts, the teacher will make a general comment "subject–verb agreement errors" in the margin of paragraphs in drafts that still contain errors, and students will try again. This instructional cycle is very much in keeping with suggestions made by Ferris (1995, 2002). Students work through the same process when learning to edit for verb tense shift, highlighting the verbs in their written paragraphs in different colored markers to see if they can detect shifts in tense that are inappropriate or that need to be more clearly signaled to readers.

Another area of language work that we have found important for generation 1.5 ESL writers is vocabulary use. As stated earlier, the vocabulary use errors in our students' writing are idiosyncratic. This makes it difficult to teach, and thus, much instruction on vocabulary is done via text marking with follow-up in individual writing conferences. However, there is one area of lexicon that lends itself to whole class instruction: logical connectors—subordinators, coordinators, and conjunctive adverbs. Many of our generation 1.5 students have trouble with logical connectors—the number they know and use is often limited, they misuse them, or omit them where they could have been used to signal the logic of their argument. To help students employ these phrases and structures more effectively in their academic writing, we review the different words, phrases, and structures used to signal logical relationships, including any grammar or usage constraints and punctuation conventions. They then rewrite incorrectly signaled paragraphs taken randomly from student drafts, using structures and vocabulary they have learned. After these guided class exercises, problems with logical connectors are marked in their own drafts, and they then edit these.

The final prong of language work is consistent and focused marking of errors on their paper drafts. This process has been tweaked somewhat to account for the generation 1.5 ESL writers. Text marking is confined to three types of problems per draft: lexical problems (word choice, idiomatic phrasing problems, and unclear phrases), the language aspects for which they have learned editing strategies in class (subject–verb agreement, verb tense shift, etc.), and one or two errors that occur consistently throughout a given student's texts. Problematic choices of lexicon are usually marked with a symbol (word choice or word grammar) or, in the case of incorrect idioms, directly revised. Grammatical or syntactic problems are marked with the same symbols that most ESL writing instructors use (Ferris, 2002; Lane & Lange, 1999) and these are explained in class and discussed in conference. They are discussed in conference as well as in class to determine which mistakes students could edit for if they took the time and which aspects of the language they aren't sure about. Students have reported that these discussions are helpful and quite different from what they experienced in high school. According to some students, the feedback on language errors they had received in high school consisted of having teachers mark errors without correcting or explaining the problem or having teachers write general comments such as "interesting ideas, but watch your grammar."

No Magic Formula

All this is not to say that the course for generation 1.5 ESL writers is a magic formula for students' control of written academic English. The 10 weeks do not allow enough time for all of our students to make improvements in their language. At the end of any given quarter, some students are not really ready to go on to freshman composition, a course that requires them to write more independently and to produce more error-free texts. Even with 60 hours of instruction, it is difficult to balance work on language, style, and vocabulary with reading discussions, peer response, and lessons on important aspects of academic writing.

In addition, many of our students are not successful in independently and consistently applying the self-editing strategies they have learned. As stated earlier, students practice text-marking strategies to edit their writing for errors such as subject–verb agreement with complex subjects. The hope is that they will adopt these strategies when proofreading their own papers. Often, however, the drafts these writers produce—even after 10 weeks—still contain the same errors as they did at the outset. When asked why self-editing is still problematic for them, our students tend to provide two answers. Some report that the self-editing strategies are too time-consuming and require too much attention to detail. Their opinion on this matter is understandable, given that in other areas of English usage, many of our students have probably approached language as monolingual English speakers do—via intuition and often with little effort. Some have even said that they are unsure whether the investment of time will "pay off," given the amount of time and effort necessary to find just a few errors. Others report that they are unable to "see" the problematic grammatical structures in their own texts. When a student is editing for verb tense shift in a paragraph, it is not unusual for her to see and mark only one verb in a sentence, usually the verb in the main clause, and ignore one or two other verbs in relative clauses, dependent clauses, or auxiliary verbs. The failure to see problems in the stream of their own written discourse is a problem they share with most developing writers (Shaughnessy, 1977).

Lessons Learned

When colleagues in the college writing and ESL programs began conceiving this course for generation 1.5 ESL writers, we were working in unknown territory. After 5 years, we have learned several important lessons.

First, we have worked out a clearer profile of generation 1.5 ESL writers (as opposed to ESL students and native speaker writers) on our campus and of the students that benefit from the generation 1.5 course. In our first attempt at identifying this special group of multilingual writers, we arbitrarily decided that students who had attended school in the U.S. for more than 9 years would be placed in the newly created course. All other criteria (SAT verbal scores below 520 and a non-passing score on the university's writing proficiency exam and the ESL 35 placement exam) remained the same. This left two questions open: How suitable is this placement for U.S.-born bilingual students? Should students who have attended U.S. high school for less than 9 years also have the option of taking the generation 1.5 course? Time, experience, and research have answered these questions. There seem to be several variables that are useful in considering whether students are generation 1.5 ESL students and will be well served in the specialized composition course: (1) length of time in U.S. schools, (2) the language and culture of the students' home, and (3) their parents' educational background. It appears that the students for whom the generation 1.5 course works best are those who have done most of their high school and junior high school education in U.S. schools. This can be explained by the identities that today's college-bound high school students form. Before they arrive at university, generation 1.5 ESL students have been first and foremost college-bound (U.S. college-bound). They have taken AP courses in a variety of subjects, taken SAT preparation courses, engaged in extra-curricular activities necessary to be accepted to prestigious schools, and worked hard to keep their GPAs high. These experiences have deeply influenced their views of themselves. Although they have influences from other cultures at home and their writing exhibits ESL markers, they are hyper-accomplished, highly successful products of the American high school system. For this reason, we now use 4 or more years in U.S. schools as the benchmark for placing students in the generation 1.5 course.

However, students who were born in the U.S. and who have never lived or studied anywhere other than U.S. schools frequently resent being placed in the special composition course for generation 1.5 ESL writers. Here are some typical complaints: "English is my native language. Why am I in a course with foreign students?" (These same "foreign students" might have been their high school classmates.) Or "I want to take a regular English class, not an ESL class." From the very first day of instruction, we try to figure out who these students are and look carefully at their first day writing exercise to verify the placement in the course. If their writing does contain ESL markers, we look together at the language issues in their writing and discuss the benefits of the course in addressing these. But, ultimately, we let them decide if they wish to continue in the course or switch to a section of the developmental writing course. Fighting a student's negative attitude toward the course is usually a losing proposition for both parties involved.

A further constellation of key variables for defining generation 1.5 ESL writers has also come into greater relief—the students' home language and culture, the students' relationship to it, and their parents' education level. In a case study of six of the students in the first year's generation 1.5 course, Janssen (2005) found that some of the students spoke (and sometimes read and wrote) the language(s) spoken by their parents and grandparents. In effect, these students lived in two very separate cultures—their family's culture and their high school culture. In addition, the parents of the students that Janssen studied often had less than a high school education. Students with this type of cultural, linguistic, and educational background seem to find the generation 1.5 course helpful in many ways. As first generation college students, they value the extra help and explicit instruction the course provides. As multilingual and multicultural young adults, they appreciate being in a class where they can openly acknowledge and discuss the roles culture and language play in their lives.

We have also learned important lessons about the curriculum. In particular, student course evaluations have provided important insights about what territory this specialized composition course should take in. According to the students, the most valuable aspect of the course is the individual attention they and their writing receive in the course. One student wrote the following comment in a course final evaluation: "I really appreciate that you actually read the entire essay and give feedback. Conference is very helpful in giving me more ideas to write which makes me enjoy what I write." Students also consistently comment that they find the explicit and guided writing instruction in the course helpful in clarifying the mysteries of academic writing. When they leave the class, they are proud to know how to structure paragraphs, how to organize certain types of essays, and how to tackle recurring grammar problems in their drafts. Finally, they seem to welcome the course's heavy writing workload because they know that the only way to become better writers is to write.

They also appreciate that grammar is an explicit and constant thread that runs through the course. Some even express pride in the fact that they probably know more about grammar in writing than their peers in subsequent writing courses. Yet, we have also learned important lessons about how to improve this tricky part of the course. One student said, "Do we always have to look at our grammar problems?" This verbal "two-by-four" is sufficient warning against an approach to language instruction that focuses primarily on student errors. Another student asked that grammar be more consistently taught from the very beginning of the class. This student observed that "grammar worksheets from the beginning would make us more aware" of editing and language issues in writing.

Conclusion

As experts in language and as human beings, we believe that naming a thing helps us better understand the thing we name. This is true and not true in the case of generation 1.5 ESL students in college composition courses. On the one hand, when the term *generation 1.5 learners* began to appear in the second language writing literature, it replaced less satisfying terms such as the general terms "second language writer" or "ESL writer" and pejorative terms such as "language minority student." The term also accurately captures the cultural, educational, and linguistic reality of these students who have been educated in U.S. schools and who tend to use English as the primary language of academic literacy.[3]

On the other hand, the coining of the term has not removed the fundamental challenges these students present to our colleges and universities; these challenges include issues of appropriate placement, of designing courses that address their needs, and of taking appropriate account of these students' personal, cultural, and linguistic backgrounds. In the same way, creating this special course for generation 1.5 ESL students does not remove or diminish the challenge they present to the college composition and ESL programs on our campus. It has, however, helped the ESL and college composition faculty more clearly define the students who comprise our university's generation 1.5 ESL population. And this, in turn, has made their needs more visible. And seeing them and their needs more clearly has helped our two programs begin to work together to transform our approaches to assessing, placing, and teaching them.

Notes

1. This is a model that has been tried at several universities including the University of California at Santa Barbara. In this model, students who fail the university writing proficiency exam because of the ESL markers in their writing are either required or strongly recommended to take the workshop.
2. Many students in the generation 1.5 course have reported receiving little or no feedback on the errors in their writing, and when they have, it usually came from peers in peer editing sessions. This is not surprising given the workload of most high school teachers.
3. Many of our generation 1.5 students are not only bilingual or multilingual, but also bi- or multiliterate thanks to instruction in other languages at home, Saturday schools, after school programs, or language immersion programs. Nonetheless, for most of them, English is the primary language of academic literacy, owing to their years in the U.S. school system.

References

Collier, V. (1987). Age and rate of acquisition of second language for academic purposes. *TESOL Quarterly, 21*(4), 617–641.

Ferris, D.R. (1995). Teaching ESL composition students to become independent self-editors. *TESOL Journal, 4*(4), 18–22.

Ferris, D.R. (2002). *Treatment of error in second language student writing.* Ann Arbor: University of Michigan Press.

Harklau, L., Siegal, M., & Losey, K. (1999). Linguistically diverse students and college writing: What is equitable and appropriate? In L. Harklau, K. Losey, & M. Siegal (Eds.), *Generation 1.5 meets college composition: Issues in the teaching of writing to U.S.-educated learners of ESL* (pp. 1–16). Mahwah, NJ: Lawrence Erlbaum Associates.

Hyon, S. (1996). Genre in three traditions: Implications for ESL. *TESOL Quarterly, 30*(4), 693–722.

Janssen, G. (2005). The changes in the academic writing of generation 1.5 students. Unpublished master's thesis, University of California, Los Angeles.

Lane, J. & Lange, E. (1999). *Writing clearly: An editing guide.* Boston, MA: Heinle & Heinle.

Reid, J. (1998). "Eye" learners and "ear" learners: Identifying the language needs of international student and U.S. resident writers. In P. Byrd & J. Reid (Eds.), *Grammar in the composition classroom: Essays on teaching ESL for college-bound students* (pp. 3–17). Boston, MA: Heinle & Heinle.

Rodby, J. (1999). Contingent literacy: The social construction of writing for nonnative English-speaking college freshmen. In L. Harklau, K. Losey, & M. Siegal (Eds.), *Generation 1.5 meets college composition: Issues in the teaching of writing to U.S.-educated learners of ESL* (pp. 45–60). Mahwah, NJ: Lawrence Erlbaum Associates.

Shaughnessy, M. (1977). *Errors and expectations.* New York: Oxford University Press.

13 Individualizing Pedagogy

Responding to Diverse Needs in Freshman Composition for Non-Native Speakers

Dudley W. Reynolds Carnegie Mellon University – Qatar
Kyung-Hee Bae University of Houston
Jennifer Shade Wilson Ontario Institute for Studies in
Education/University of Toronto

This chapter describes the process of needs analysis and pedagogical planning in a two-semester core composition sequence for "non-native speakers" at the University of Houston (UH), a large, urban, public institution that describes itself as "the most ethnically diverse research university in the [United States]" (University of Houston, 2006). Traditionally positioned as an option for students educated outside of the U.S., the non-native sequence has increasingly attracted U.S. high school graduates as the number of international students dropped after 9/11 and immigrant students who previously were dispersed throughout sections of the general composition sequence discovered it as an option. These changing demographics—and our growing awareness of them—have posed a challenge: how to meet the needs of diverse students with a single set of courses.

The chapter begins with a description of the authors' initial attempts to teach the courses and conduct needs analysis—experiences that led us to realize a basic need within the courses to "individualize pedagogy." What follows is a discussion of our revisions to the course and the ongoing challenges faced in trying to institutionalize adaptability.

Background

In the fall of 1999, Reynolds took over supervision of the non-native composition courses at the same time that he was teaching a graduate course on second language writing using the just-published book *Generation 1.5 Meets College Composition* (Harklau, Losey, & Siegal, 1999). The institutional understanding at the time was that the course should be equivalent to the first-semester general composition course, which focused on reading and writing expository texts, but should also include language-focused activities useful for non-native speakers. Using a composition textbook with multicultural readings, a second textbook specifically targeted for ESL writers, and a writing handbook, the students worked through four major assignments in a computer classroom. The syllabus cycled through four iterations of reading a text, discussing it, working on a text analysis or grammar activity supplied by the class website, producing a draft, receiving peer or instructor feedback, and revising the draft for final submission.

Unfortunately, the foregrounding of the readings as the start of every assignment, combined with the disparate nature of the reading topics and the fact that they were excerpted from popular published texts rather than academic papers, made it very difficult to give the class coherence or a sense of purpose. Furthermore, the range of grammatical competencies in the class created issues in designing language activities useful for everyone. The one redeeming feature of the course seemed to be the days spent on writing conferences and working on activities presented via the class website when Reynolds was able to move through the class and talk with students one-on-one.

At the same time that we were realizing the limitations of our traditional curriculum, we were also trying to find out more about our students. Following Ferris and Hedgcock, we felt that "we need[ed] a systematic way of inquiring into the diverse background features, skills, schemata, and expectations of ESL writers so that we [could] take this information into account when planning instruction" (2005, p. 73). We were also driven by an underlying question: how many of the students who found their way into the composition sequence for non-native speakers matched the profiles of generation 1.5 students discussed in Harklau et al. (1999)?[1]

We gathered data about our students through a series of university-wide surveys, student information sheets submitted to course instructors, and action research projects conducted by graduate students in UH's MA in Applied English Linguistics program. Across these instruments we asked students whether they graduated from a U.S. high school, the age they began learning English, languages in which they felt comfortable speaking and writing, whether they held jobs in addition to their studies, and their intended majors. An action research project conducted by Wilson and Poltavtchenko (2004) further focused on students' motivation to write and participate in both the general and non-native composition sequences.

The picture that emerged from the data is one of diversity and change. Prior to 9/11, fewer than 20% of students in the first-semester non-native course were U.S. high school graduates. In the years following 9/11, when the number of international visa students at the university dropped significantly, this number rose dramatically to 74%, but by the fall of 2005 it appeared to have leveled off at 45%. With respect to the length of time learning English, at least half reported beginning English studies in their middle school years (i.e., age 12) or later, which meant that approximately 30–40% of the students had some exposure to English since they were in elementary school. Nearly half of the students reported using English as an additional language at home and almost 90% when among friends. When asked what language they felt most comfortable writing in, over a quarter responded English, and almost half listed multiple languages. Their intended majors were typically fairly evenly distributed between majors in the liberal arts or social sciences, business, natural or physical sciences, and over half reported that they wanted to complete a master's or doctoral degree.

Wilson and Poltavtchenko's survey of attitudes thought to relate to motivation further indicated that while students fairly consistently believed that working hard in class would pay off, writing would be important for their futures, and their past English classes had been a positive experience, there was much more variation with respect to whether they perceived themselves as an English speaker, their self-confidence in their writing ability, and their expectations about how easy the writing class would be.

As evidenced by this quick summary, our efforts at needs analysis were focused on trying to build a picture of the students as a group, as a population that was somehow distinct from students in the general composition sequence. The picture that emerged led us to conclude, however, that it would be naive to formulate a curriculum in terms of uniform linguistic or content needs. The presumed usefulness of needs analysis in the literature seems to be as a basis for choosing and sequencing activities and assignments, but our experience taught us that we simply could not make generalizations about our students. We believe that for the many universities located in what the urban sociologist Saskia Sassen (2005) refers to as "global cities," the direct linkage between needs analysis and curricular activities is no longer possible—if it ever was—because it is based on a myth of homogeneous, isolatable communities. It assumes that students in a given class share an identifiable set of characteristics—derived either from their past experiences learning languages, their future academic orientations, or labels placed upon them by society such as "non-native speaker"—that can be used to define and sequence "teaching points" (cf., Allwright, 2005). The challenge presented by twenty-first century urban settings then is to find conceptualizations of content and models for structuring interaction that permit and encourage autonomous, life-long learning—hence, our impetus for individualizing pedagogy.[2]

Conceptualizations of Content

The catalog description for the first-semester course states that it "provides practice in reading and writing expository texts" while the second course "provides practice in reading and writing argumentative texts." These are bare-boned phrasings, intentionally worded not to restrict how the courses are actually taught. Nevertheless, they specify a means of learning (practice) as well as focus modes (reading and writing) and rhetorical purposes (expository/argumentative) that provide a summary of the way in which content was originally conceived for the course: students would learn through activities to read and write specific types of text.

The problem with such a conceptualization is that it objectifies the content solely in terms of text types while ignoring the development of the students and their interactions with social contexts. As Johns argues, students also must "acquire a literacy strategy repertoire and develop the confidence that enables them to approach and negotiate a variety of literacy tasks in many environments" (1999, p. 159). Not surprisingly, the process of writing this chapter has forced us to articulate our re-conceptualizations, and we offer the following as a set of goals for a composition sequence that supports individualized learning practices and academic purposes:

- students will develop personalized strategies for researching writing tasks, reader expectations, and source content;
- students will develop confidence in their abilities to achieve their expository and argumentative aims in a variety of intertextual and expressive discourses;
- students will develop their meta-awareness of the craft of writing and their abilities to assess and respond critically to the writing of others.

These goals do not necessarily play out in specific activities but rather represent parameters for the individual "learning opportunities" (cf., Allwright, 2005) that arise in the course. As a result we have begun to think of the courses not in terms of how content is sequenced but rather how opportunities for interaction are structured in order to support these course goals on a student-by-student basis.

Structuring Interaction

In this part of the chapter we provide a more nuts-and-bolts description of the two courses as a way of illustrating the structures where students interact with each other, with instructors, and with texts and the ways in which individualized pedagogy can be combined with a traditional class structure. We pay specific attention to four areas: use of contact time, major and supplemental assignments, technology, and assessment.

Contact Time

In an early acknowledgment of the issues presented by diversity in the composition classroom, Harris and Silva write:

> We should recognize that along with different linguistic backgrounds, *ESL students have a diversity of concerns that can only be dealt with in the one-to-one setting where the focus of attention is on that particular student* and his or her questions, concerns, cultural presuppositions, writing processes, language learning experiences, and conceptions of what writing in English is all about.
>
> (1993, p. 525, emphasis added)

Kroll likewise argues that "[English language learners] in a writing class need to have individual conferences with their teacher even more than native speaker students do" (2001, p. 228). We agree. The problem with individual conferences, however, is the amount of contact time required of the instructor. Our solution has been to adapt the approach used in the developmental writing course at UH, where students work through four writing assignments with a consultant in the Writing Center who meets with them individually and in small groups.[3]

In our first-semester course, student contact hours are divided between six whole class meetings led by the instructor and weekly small group and individual meetings led by writing consultants to whom the students are assigned for the semester. Table 13.1 shows the frequency and duration of the different formats and illustrates how the same topic might be treated in each. The whole class meetings are held during the first and last weeks of the semester and on the 3 days that a new assignment is introduced, with the small groups meeting during the same time slot in the other weeks. While this arrangement limits the amount of "teacher-fronted" class time, we have been willing to make that sacrifice to provide students with the opportunity to work individually on their writing with the consultants.

The extensive use of the writing consultants in the first-semester course maximizes students' opportunities initially for individualized interaction with someone who has already demonstrated their ability to write successfully in the university academic

Table 13.1 Comparison of Meeting Formats in First-Semester Course

Type	Whole class meetings	Small group meetings	Individual conferences
Number of students	30–35	3–8	1
Frequency	6, 50-minute sessions per semester	Weekly 50-minute sessions	Weekly 30–60 minute sessions
Treatment of a thesis sentence	Discuss concept	Identify thesis sentences in sample texts; discuss good and bad examples	Ask the student to identify the thesis sentence in his/her own essay; give advice strengthening it if necessary
Treatment of particular genre	Explain concept of an academic genre (e.g., a comparative essay)	Analyze a sample text, identifying particular sections or linguistic patterns	Analyze student's text in terms of genre framework
Treatment of plagiarism	Discuss concept of plagiarism and source documentation	Practice documentation conventions	Help the student to figure out how to document his/her sources accurately and correctly
Treatment of grammar	Introduction to a concept such as the use of modal verbs to qualify a claim	Grammar lessons on issues shared by these particular students	Grammar lessons on issues specific to the student, using his/her own writing as an authentic teaching text

context—to ask them questions, to hear their take on what assignments really mean, and to experience first hand the often implicit values that people may use to evaluate a piece of writing.[4] In the second semester, the balance shifts with weekly whole class meetings led by the instructor and then a second either small group or individual meeting with the writing consultant. This provides students with more direct interactions with the instructor who can speak both as someone who designs and grades academic assignments and who has the authority and experience expected by students accustomed to teacher-fronted classes, while at the same time maintaining the individualized input from the consultant. Thus the consultant's role changes slightly in the second semester from being the student's primary resource to being one among several resources. This change in structure allows students to transition from depending solely on their consultants and moves them toward utilizing their peers (classmates in other classes or friends) once they leave the class and no longer have the benefit of regular contact with writing consultants.

Obviously much of the success of the program depends on the writing consultants.[5] Consultants are hired based on a writing sample and a personal interview with the executive and assistant directors of the writing center. During the interview, applicants' areas of interest and previous tutoring experiences are assessed for use in assigning them to appropriate programs (developmental writing, writing in the disciplines, and ESL writing). Initially all consultants working with the composition sequence had previously taught in the center's developmental program; however, with the expansion of the center, some newly hired consultants have been incorporated. Because the consultants work for the writing center and not just the composition sequence, if a consultant's skills and interests are not a good match with the ESL program, it is possible to transfer him or her to other projects.

Consultant training consists of a general orientation to tutoring at the writing center; three to six in-service training sessions each semester on topics such as "Prioritizing in a Consultation," "Working with ESL Writers," "Building a Resource Bank," and "Motivating Student Writers"; and weekly meetings led by the course instructors. We have found the weekly meetings to be the most productive form of training. In these meetings, the instructors allow time for discussion of topics specific to the courses (e.g., issues students are having with the current assignment, procedural questions), as well as general topics such as global vs. local errors (Harris & Silva, 1993), cultural awareness (Reid, 1993), views of tutor authority (Thonus, 2004), etc. Because many consultants expect to work with international students and have attendant stereotypes, considerable time is also devoted to discussing student demographics and attitudes, differences between "ear-learners" and "eye-learners" (Reid, 1997) and language learner identity construction (Chiang & Schmida, 1999; Leung, Harris, & Rampton, 1997). In a sense these meetings model our notions about individualized pedagogy for the consultants. They build rapport between the consultants and the instructors and among the consultants themselves, with veteran consultants generally falling into the role of mentoring new consultants. The interactions at the meetings also model how content can be addressed through discussion and interaction as opposed to purely presentation.

To ensure that consultants are working effectively with their students, we employ anonymous mid- and end-of-semester student evaluations of the consultants that ask targeted questions like "What could be improved about your individual conferences?" and "Can your writing consultant do anything different to help you understand the assignments and improve your writing?" Although negative feedback is rare, these forms, especially at mid-semester, have helped us identify any individual consultants who might benefit from additional training or who are not following course guidelines (e.g., not spending enough time with their students, frequently cancelling appointments). Additionally, the instructors observe the consultants in at least one small group meeting and during one individual consultation each semester as recommended by Weigle and Nelson (2004).

Assignments

Major Assignments

During each semester of the program, students complete four major, scaffolded writing assignments. One by-product of our individualized approach is that students need time to meet with their consultants both in the small groups and individually before submitting each assignment. Thus, while four assignments may seem a limited number, it is the maximum that we can fit into a 14-week semester. In the first semester, the assignments (loosely connected to the theme of the American university) progress from more public and supported writing to more personal and original writing. Complete descriptions of each assignment can be found in Appendix A, but broadly speaking the first assignment asks students to write a response essay to a single provided text, the second to compare two provided texts, the third to find outside sources in support of a proposal, and the final to call on their own powers of observation and reflection to describe a place or scene. This sequence stands in contrast to curricula grounded in expressivist theories where personal narratives and descriptive essays segue to more public writing following the rationale that invention will be easier when students can call on first-hand experiences. We agree that students need initial support for invention, which is why we provide source texts for the first two assignments. As noted by Ramanathan and Atkinson (1999), however, cultures differ on the acceptability of sharing personal information and perspectives, hence our decision to delay personal writing to the final assignment. Additionally, this move from text-based to more abstract and personal reasoning is intended to scaffold the development of critical thinking skills frequently mentioned as characteristic of university-level writing (Reid, 1993; Spack, 2001). Language learning activities to support these assignments are generally chosen by the writing consultants in accordance with the specific demands of the assignment and their perceptions of their students' individual needs (cf., Hyland, 2003).

In contrast to the more generalized exposure to U.S. academic writing provided by the first-semester course, the second-semester course emphasizes the development of "students as researchers" (Johns, 1997, p. 93). Students begin with a summary of a provided article on a controversial scientific topic, then progress to a position paper on the topic using multiple provided sources, and then step-up to an academic, research-based argumentative paper. For the final assignment, students switch to researching material for a group-produced website.[6] (More complete descriptions of each are provided in Appendix B) Across the four assignments, instructors emphasize in accord with Johns' socio-literate approach that what students are learning is a process that will serve them in the future as independent academic writers. They are learning to see each academic assignment, not as a prescribed form, but as something that they must individually research. In-class activities require students to find and analyze sample texts on the Internet, research writing guides, discuss the apparent conventions, and even formulate evaluation guidelines. In the course of these activities, they learn to identify text purposes, research audiences and their expectations, create plans to achieve a purpose, and devise ongoing strategies to determine if the goals are being achieved. This approach, which places the burden for articulating patterns and conclusions on the student, is especially well suited for students who have not had formal, metalinguistic training (Holten, 2002) and further allows each student to "customize" their learning to meet their individual needs at an individual pace.

Supplemental Assignments

Leki (1995 as cited in Johns, 1997) argues that while an ESL composition class should help its students ease their anxiety about writing, it should not just be a "safe refuge" and should give students sufficient writing experiences through which they can develop different strategies necessary to accommodate the diversity of writing tasks they may encounter in their future. Because limiting students to composing only four texts over the course of a semester paints an unrealistic picture of the multiplicity of texts that most students work on at any given time, we have incorporated weekly supplemental writing assignments into both courses. With their varied purposes and forms, these supplemental assignments also provide a much greater opportunity for individual writing issues to surface.

To encourage critical analytical reading early on and respond to the frequently heard call for connections between extensive reading and writing (e.g., Grabe, 2001; Leki, 2001), students keep a reading response journal in the first-semester course. These journals expose students to a larger variety of texts than would be possible with such a limited number of whole class meetings. Texts for each week are provided by the instructor and range from newspaper or magazine articles to an argumentative piece taken from a textbook. An attempt is made to select readings based on their relevance for the students and their academic lives. Writing consultants also are encouraged to choose readings for their group as long as the selections are discussed with the instructor in advance, thus allowing this activity to be personalized to the interests of the students in each small group. Students receive only a completion grade for the assignments and are told that they may respond to the reading in whatever format they wish, but that they should be prepared to discuss what they have written with their consultant.

In the second-semester course, students produce a series of short texts—frequently no longer than a paragraph—in response to prompts that target a wide range of academic, professional, and even popular purposes and audiences. Assignments include writing instructions for a word processor's reviewing features, a restaurant review, an annotated bibliography, and a professionally oriented series incorporating a job ad, an application letter, a résumé, and a thank-you note for an interview. Following the student-as-researcher emphasis in this course, for some assignments students are provided links to different sample texts or writing guides that they can use to research the text-type, while for others they are encouraged to search the Internet and find their own examples. For each activity, students receive personalized feedback from a peer reviewer and their writing consultant.

Across both courses the rationale behind the selection of major and supplemental assignments has more to do with exposing students to writing for a variety of purposes and audiences—both academic and professional—than ensuring that they have been taught a canon of academic modes or genres. In the postmodern world of English as a global language (cf., Graddol, 2000, 2006), doing otherwise would be a disservice to our students. Therefore, one of the key goals for individualizing pedagogy and developing autonomous learners is getting students to see assignments not as something they need to know how to do but as stepping stones to the processes of a mature writer. We believe that the frequent consultations and peer interactions during which students engage in metacognitive talk about their writing propels their composing experiences to enter "their repertoire of ways of constructing and representing meaning, resources upon which they can draw in other activities" (Chapman, 1999, p. 482).

Technology Use

In keeping with this emphasis on individual capacity building is our approach to technology use. No composition course today can escape the changes in literacy practices that have accompanied the evolution of production tools like word processors and html editors, the increasing opportunities for online communication, and the Internet as a source of multimedia print and image. These developments have also altered the construction of instructional spaces across academia. Hirvela writes:

> Though students may still utilize traditional print-based source texts, composing processes, and strategies in their writing and thus operate in conventional print culture to some extent, they must be conversant in the ways of screen culture as well. Enabling them to do so, and understanding what this entails, is one of the major tasks now facing L2 writing specialists.
>
> (2005, p. 340)

As gateway courses to the broader university curriculum, composition courses need to introduce students to these varied uses for technology.

Incorporating technology and technology instruction into the composition courses leads to the same dilemma that we face with choosing appropriate content, however—the diversity of student experiences. We generally will have at least a few students who have never used a spell checker and who do not know that the library has a website; at the same time, we will have some students whose expertise in web design far exceeds our own. Our response has been to set a common expectation that technology will be used extensively at the same time that we rely on the courses' variable interaction structures to accommodate the range of student experiences.

Both courses use a web content management system for e-mail, presentation of resources and in-class activities, and assignment management. The only exchanges of paper occur in the first-semester course, where students generate hard copies of their assignments for consultations and to submit for grading. In the second-semester course, where there is a strong emphasis on peer interaction, students use a word processor's reviewing tool to give and receive peer feedback on the supplemental assignments and complete a group website-design project as the final major assignment. For both courses, students must also submit their major assignments to a web-based service that highlights portions of the paper where the wording appears similar to wording found on Internet sites and in previously submitted papers (Turnitin.com). This extensive use of technology is not a problem for many students, but it is for some. Instructors limit their technology instruction for the whole class to presentations about using the web content management software, the library databases, and designing and posting a website. Students also may seek individual help on an as needed basis from their consultant, from other students during a group task, or by reading online help guides provided on the course website.

As with the writing assignments, the goal for incorporating technology is more to introduce students to the possibilities than to demand competence. Especially in the second course where there are more whole class meetings, in-class activities frequently direct students to example texts from the Internet or online writing guides authored by university writing centers. Students individually or as a small group then answer questions aimed at raising awareness of genre characteristics. When students begin working on their research papers, activities focus on using search engines and library databases to locate materials for their individual topics. Such activities allow students to use the Internet as an individualized resource not only for finding source material but also for researching writing genres and identifying their stylistic conventions.

Technology is introduced also as a vehicle for addressing language-related issues. As noted earlier, whole class grammar activities are not successful with this population because of the diversity of students' language learning backgrounds and the range of their formal metalinguistic knowledge (cf., Roberge, 2002). Instead, students in both courses are provided with links to Internet-based language learning activities that they can complete at their own pace. Because of the wealth of materials already available, we have not felt the need to create our own materials. In line with the course goals, we also believe that it is important for students to find resources that they can access after they complete the class. Links include corpus-based vocabulary development sites, traditional grammar-focused, pattern practice exercises, and sites with listening comprehension activities. Since most of these sites offer activities at different levels, students can work on activities most appropriate for their personal level of language command.

Assessment

Clearly one of the best tools that a composition instructor has for individualizing pedagogy is assessment in the form of feedback on writing assignments. Discussions of assessment practices in second language composition classes and writing centers (e.g., Ferris & Hedgcock, 2005; Liu & Sadler, 2003; Thonus, 2004; Williams, 2004; Zhu, 2001) typically focus on issues of method: written feedback versus oral conferencing, ways to improve grammatical accuracy, techniques for effective peer review, rubric development, and portfolio use. The central issue for many of these discussions is how to maximize feedback to the individual while minimizing the burden on the instructor who has many "individuals" in a class. To address this issue, it has been helpful for us to draw a clear distinction between formative and summative assessment within the courses (cf., Black and Wiliam, 1998). Students engage in formative assessment of their writing with their peers and writing consultants, while summative assessments are reserved for the course instructor.

Formative assessment in the first semester is highly individualized; students participate in structured peer review activities in their consultant groups and during the one-on-one meetings with the consultants. In the second-semester course, feedback on the major assignments is generated during the individual consultant meetings, while students engage in peer review of the supplemental assignments using a word processor reviewing tool. In this way, students receive spontaneous as well as guided input on specific writing assignments from more than one reader (peer, consultant) using both face-to-face and electronic means. In both courses, the people providing the feedback are working with a small number of papers so they can hopefully engage in more in-depth interaction than an instructor who has to provide feedback to a whole class. Finally, the provision of feedback in all cases is geared toward revising a piece of writing before it is submitted to the course instructor for summative grading.

All major assignments are graded by the course instructors using rubrics that evaluate targeted traits. Reflecting the broader, more introductory aims of the first-semester course, the same rubric is used for all assignments. The rubric, which is based on one cited by Hamp-Lyons (1991), targets ideas and content, organization, and language control. It provides five level descriptors (corresponding to letter grades A–F) for each trait and determines an overall grade by averaging the three traits (see Appendix C). The analytic nature of the rubric allows the instructor to target individual issues for each student to work on as well as track areas in which individual students are showing progress across assignments. Additionally, we have found this rubric to be easy for the writing consultants to use when explaining grades or instructor comments to their students. (Because there is room at the end of the rubric form for the instructor to provide any narrative comments, the instructor generally provides few written comments on the paper itself.) For the second-semester course, different rubrics are used for each assignment, reflecting the more specialized nature of the writing tasks in that course. These rubrics do not include level descriptors but rather require narrative evaluations for each trait and assign an overall grade based on the instructor's appraisal of the paper. An example from the second assignment appears in Appendix D.

One of the issues raised by individualizing pedagogy is the degree to which assessment also should be individualized. This is similar to the dilemma of whether to grade on individual progress or achievement of group goals. Our response has been to use consultants and peers for providing more individualized feedback while reserving decisions about performance vis-à-vis group standards to course instructors. We believe that this separation avoids some of the confusion that can emerge when instructors switch from providing suggestive to evaluative feedback. It also allows us to stress that, at least within academia, writing is typically assessed as both a process of thinking and sorting through ideas and as a product that demonstrates targeted learning. Finally, by acknowledging the importance of peer feedback, we hope to foster students' meta-awareness of writing as a craft and confidence in their own ability to serve as readers.

Ongoing Challenges

In writing this chapter we have attempted to provide both details and rationale for a composition sequence designed to encompass the needs of generation 1.5, international, and a wide range of other students whose experiences, characteristics, and educational needs cannot easily be classified. We believe that there is one thing these students have in common: their desire to succeed in their future academic/professional endeavor—to become legitimate, contributing members of their chosen discourse communities. To that end, we have advocated a curricular focus on learning strategies, meta-awareness, and contextualization. As a way of concluding we would like to discuss the ongoing challenges that we face with the sequence.

The first challenge we face is the course title, "Freshman Composition for Non-native Speakers." Both students and university colleagues frequently assume based on the course title that the focus will be more grammar than composition. They may therefore perceive it as somehow remedial or at least easier than the regular composition sequence.

(Although on several occasions we have had complaints from enrolled students that they are having to work harder than their friends in the regular sequence.) We have also had requests from former students who are trying to transfer to another institution for letters explaining that the courses in fact satisfy the core composition requirement. The title is also problematic for generation 1.5 students, who may not perceive themselves or who do not wish to be stigmatized as "non-native speakers." We want people to see the sequence as a place where students can work through language-related issues, but that at the same time the focus is writing.

A second challenge we face is incorporating new instructors. Having designed the template of assignments, procedures, and policies regarding writing consultants, evaluation rubrics, and course websites, we feel a sense of ownership. There is a strong temptation simply to hand the materials to new instructors and say "Teach the course." We recognize, however, that it is important for any new instructor also to feel a sense of ownership and investment in the course. If we are operating in what Kumaravadivelu refers to as the "post method condition," then individual instructors should be able to "generate location-specific, classroom-oriented, innovative strategies" (2003, p. 33). New teachers need room to tinker and experiment, to try different assignments and activities, or to implement new policies.

A related issue is how to maintain the spirit of innovation that has created our own investment in the course. The description we have provided of the sequence is fairly static and implies a fairly top-down regimented template for the courses. It is very easy for what we initially perceived as goals and parameters to become fixed as requirements and rules. One of the greatest lessons generated by the belated recognition of generation 1.5 students' presence in composition classes has been that student populations are never static. What works today may not tomorrow. The very goal of individualizing pedagogy relies on the ability to maintain flexibility.

The final challenge is one faced by every course—how do we know if it is working? We have described goals and practices and have made hermeneutic arguments for their worthiness; we have not provided positivistic proof, however. We believe strongly that courses that make claims about innovation and re-conceptualizations should be sites of ongoing action research as exemplified by a project Bae is initiating on how the use of technology affects second language writers' learning. We are developing beginning- and end-of-course surveys that we hope will provide indirect measures of how the courses change students' attitudes and beliefs about writing. We also admit that we are still searching for ways to measure more directly the specific goals listed above. Thus, we offer these descriptions and rationales not as proven practices, but as assumptions that should be questioned by localized contexts in order to truly individualize pedagogy.

Appendix A   First-Semester Assignments

Assignment	Format	Rationale
Response paper	Students read an assigned, online article from either a major U.S. newspaper or an academic periodical about a current, often controversial, topic related to the U.S. educational system and write a response. Emphasis is placed on crafting a response that is more than just disagreeing or agreeing with the claim.	Students can respond through multiple modes, including analysis of the source text, relating personal experiences that support a counter-claim, or hypothetical scenarios. As a common type of academic assignment, it prepares them for longer research papers as well as critiquing journal articles. Finally, the topic encourages students to explore issues and/or popular conceptions of the educational system they are entering.
Comparison paper	Students are provided links to three paired sets of newspaper articles; each pair addresses the same topic, and each contains an article from a university paper and one from a daily mass circulation newspaper. They compare the authors' treatment of the topic, analyzing such factors as audience, purpose, and style and using the sources to support their claim.	This task underscores the use of outside source material to support an argument. Students move from considering the content of a single text to thinking analytically about multiple texts and must identify strategies for incorporating multiple references into their own writing.
Proposal	Students propose a written, original solution to a problem they feel exists either on the UH campus or in the U.S. higher education system. They define the problem, then explain and defend their solution. They are required to use a minimum of two sources to reinforce the idea that the proposal should be professional and fact based (not a personal diatribe).	This assignment extends students' experiences from analyzing preselected sources to finding the sources they need to bolster their claims. Also, the proposal is a genre used in many disciplines our students plan to pursue.
Interpretation of a scene	Students write a description of an existing physical location, showing either why this place is important or what this location reveals about a particular culture or society.	Students practice their description skills and extend their vocabulary. This task concludes the sequence from public, supported writing to personal and original writing.

Appendix B Second-Semester Assignments

Assignment	Format	Rationale
Summary	Students write a detailed summary of a controversial, scientific article from a peer-reviewed scholarly journal.	Because the ability to read precisely and identify main ideas is requisite to writing that involves outside sources, this assignment prepares them for any number of inter-textual writing assignments.
Recommendation paper	Students are given the scenario that they work for a congresswoman who needs a two-page position paper related to the topic of the article used for the first assignment. They are given an additional three sources to use in preparing the paper.	This assignment scaffolds off the proposal written in the first semester, showing how academic genres may also exist in real-world contexts. By providing the sources for the paper, instructors also have a greater awareness of the texts students are drawing on in their writing.
Job prospects research paper	The third assignment, a job prospects research paper, asks students to identify career opportunities within a particular field of interest which are most likely to show increased employment opportunities within the next 5 years and to argue why they have come to such a conclusion.	Asking students to write a research paper that may truly be useful for them enhances their motivation. This paper functions as a capstone assignment, requiring them to identify and synthesize source material in an extended text.
Cultural group profile (website)	Students work in groups of five to six to create a website that profiles one of Houston's ethnic communities. Students plan the site's content, delegate research responsibilities, agree on a strategy for presenting the information, and assign writing tasks. Websites are reviewed and graded based on the following criteria: group effectiveness, site informativeness, and site creativity.	The last assignment is designed to promote the act of writing as a collaborative process and the development of web authoring skills. It also encourages students to explore identity issues related to intercultural communities.

Appendix C Grading Rubic for First-Semester Assignments

Ideas and content

A   This essay has a clear purpose. It treats the subject as complex and makes it interesting for an identifiable audience. It presents substantial arguments or well-developed ideas, as appropriate for its purpose.

B   This essay has a clear purpose. It presents developed arguments or ideas as appropriate for its purpose but some may provide better support than others. The intended audience may be less clear.

C   This essay may substitute an organizational statement for a controlling purpose or present a purpose that lacks a clear focus. Not all of the arguments or supporting ideas bear a clear relationship to the purpose and some are left undeveloped.

D   It is not clear what this essay is about. There may be individual segments that present coherent arguments or interesting details but there is little coherence to the ideas of the essay as a whole.

F   This essay is a collection of undeveloped and often unmotivated ideas.

Organization

A   This essay has a clear structure both at the level of the essay as a whole and within individual paragraphs. The writer uses appropriate rhetorical devices to signal the structure and prevent the reader from being confused.

B   This essay shows evidence of planning by the writer. There may be some rough transitions or occasional redundancies. There may be some claims that need further support.

C   The organizational structure of this essay breaks down in places. There may be paragraphs that stray from their stated purpose or ideas presented at inappropriate moments. Transitional expressions may be inappropriate or absent. The reader may be forced to infer the writer's plan.

D   The overall organizational structure of this essay is not clear. There may be paragraphs that exhibit some organization, but the structure as a whole makes it difficult to determine the writer's plan.

F   This essay makes numerous abrupt and/or illogical transitions. The writer's plan cannot be inferred.

Language control

A   This essay evidences the intentional use of language to create an effect on the reader. The language chosen represents an appropriate level of formality for the intended purpose and audience. Although there may be occasional language errors, the reader is not constantly aware of them.

B   The language in this essay may be more basic or conversational in tone, although not overly so. Language errors may be slightly more common but the reader is still not constantly aware of them.

C   This essay has more frequent and distracting language errors, some of which make it difficult to determine the writer's intentions. The language chosen may also be inappropriate at times for the complexity of topic.

D   This essay has frequent language errors that make it difficult to determine the writer's intentions. The language is often simplistic and inappropriate for the topic.

F   Language errors in this paper make it impossible to determine the writer's intentions.

Appendix D Rubric for Second Assignments, Second Semester

Criteria	Evaluation
The clarity of your position about the risks of nanotechnology.	
The clarity of your explanation of what nanotechnology is.	
Whether you make it clear what are the potential benefits and what are the potential risks.	
The proper use of citations.	
Whether the language you use sounds appropriate for a paper directed to a member of the U.S. Congress.	
How carefully you have edited your work—did you check for spelling mistakes, complete sentences, proper use of definite and indefinite articles?	
Other	
Letter grade:	

Notes

1. As with the general composition sequence, students may qualify to take the non-native sequence by passing the writing portion of a state-mandated academic-readiness exam, by virtue of their high school GPA or SAT score, or by completing the developmental writing course. Students who wish to take the non-native sequence may also use a TOEFL writing score of 4.5 or a passing score on a locally administered, holistically scored placement essay. Between the fall 2003 and fall 2005 semesters, 40% of the students entered via the developmental writing course, 25% used a TOEFL score, 20% passed the local test, and 16% used one of the criteria for the general composition sequence.
2. Use of the word "autonomous" is not meant to imply that learning is anything other than a social act. What we want to emphasize is that individuals must be prepared to adapt constantly to new social contexts.
3. When assigning students to groups, we try to achieve a mix of first languages, based on the personal information form that students complete on the first day of class. Beyond this, however, we manipulate the composition of the groups very little (such as grouping them according to their language abilities). Not only is it quite difficult to assess accurately their language performance, we also believe it is unnecessary to divide students in such a way because of the individual attention each student receives.
4. At the beginning of each assignment, consultants are given benchmark papers (sample papers from previous semesters with the instructor's comments) and specific expectations are discussed. Occasionally, however, there may be consultants whose formative feedback to students is at odds with the instructor's final evaluation. These situations generally are brought to the instructor's attention either by individual students or through a pattern in a group's papers. Though we believe that it is beneficial for students to realize that different readers react to pieces of writing in disparate ways, when these situations arise, the instructor does meet with the consultant to address the misunderstanding.

5. The expense of hiring writing consultants in addition to a lead instructor is partially covered by raising the quota for the first-semester course from 20 to 35. Since the majority of meetings occur in small groups or individually, we feel that raising the quota does not compromise the quality of instruction, nor does it place an undue burden on the instructor whose primary responsibilities are course management and grading. Even with the higher quotas, however, the course is still subsidized by the writing center and reflects a commitment to educating all students that we feel should be applauded.

6. Although this is the only assignment in either semester that requires group work, students have become used to working in groups by this point because of the small group meetings they have had every week. Moreover, students are required to submit an essay reflecting their team work and evaluating their group members' contribution. The consultants serve as moderators should issues arise between team members during this assignment.

References

Allwright, D. (2005). From teaching points to learning opportunities and beyond. *TESOL Quarterly, 39*(1), 9–31.

Black, P. & Wiliam, D. (1998). Assessment and classroom learning. *Assessment in Education: Principles, Policy & Practice, 5*(1), 7–75.

Chapman, M. (1999). Situated, social, active: Rewriting genre in the elementary classroom. *Written Communication, 16*(4), 469–490.

Chiang, Y.-S.D. & Schmida, M. (1999). Language identity and language ownership: Linguistic conflicts of first-year university writing students. In L. Harklau, K.M. Losey, & M. Siegal (Eds.), *Generation 1.5 meets college composition: Issues in the teaching of writing to U.S.-educated learners of ESL* (pp. 81–96). Mahwah, NJ: Lawrence Erlbaum Associates.

Ferris, D. & Hedgcock, J. (2005). *Teaching ESL composition: Purpose, process, and practice* (2nd ed.). Mahwah, NJ: Lawrence Erlbaum Associates.

Grabe, W. (2001). Reading–writing relations: Theoretical perspectives and instructional practices. In D. Belcher & A. Hirvela (Eds.), *Linking literacies: Perspectives on L2 reading–writing connections.* Ann Arbor: University of Michigan Press.

Graddol, D. (2000). The future of English? A guide to forecasting the popularity of the English language in the 21st century. London: The British Council.

Graddol, D. (2006). English next. London: The British Council.

Hamp-Lyons, L. (1991). Scoring procedures for ESL contexts. In L. Hamp-Lyons (Ed.), *Assessing second language writing in academic contexts* (pp. 241–276). Norwood, NJ: Ablex.

Harklau, L., Losey, K.M., & Siegal, M. (Eds.) (1999). *Generation 1.5 meets college composition: Issues in the teaching of writing to U.S.-educated learners of ESL.* Mahwah, NJ: Lawrence Erlbaum Associates.

Harris, M. & Silva, T. (1993). Tutoring ESL students: Issues and options. *College Composition and Communication, 44*(4), 525–537.

Hirvela, A. (2005). Computer-based reading and writing across the curriculum: Two case studies of 12 writers. *Computers and Composition, 22*(3), 337–356.

Holten, C. (2002). Charting new territory: Creating an interdepartmental course for generation 1.5 writers. *CATESOL Journal, 14*(1), 173–189.

Hyland, K. (2003). *Second language writing.* Cambridge, UK: Cambridge University Press.

Johns, A.M. (1997). *Text, role, and context: Developing academic literacies.* New York: Cambridge University Press.

Johns, A.M. (1999). Opening our doors: Applying socioliterate approaches (SA) to language minority classrooms. In L. Harklau, K.M. Losey, & M. Siegal (Eds.), *Generation 1.5 meets college composition: Issues in the teaching of writing to U.S.-educated learners of ESL* (pp. 159–171). Mahwah, NJ: Lawrence Erlbaum Associates.

Kroll, B. (2001). Considerations for teaching an ESL/EFL writing course. In M. Celce-Murcia (Ed.), *Teaching English as a second or foreign language* (3rd ed., pp. 219–232). Boston, MA: Heinle & Heinle.

Kumaravadivelu, B. (2003). *Beyond methods: Macrostrategies for language teaching.* New Haven: Yale University Press.

Leki, I. (1995). Coping strategies of ESL students in writing tasks across the curriculum. *TESOL Quarterly, 29*(2), 235–260.

Leki, I. (2001). Reciprocal themes: In ESL reading and writing. In T. Silva & P.K. Matsuda (Eds.), *Landmark essays on ESL writing.* Mahwah, NJ: Lawrence Erlbaum.

Leung, C., Harris, R., & Rampton, B. (1997). The idealised native speaker, reified ethnicities, and classroom realities. *TESOL Quarterly, 31*(3), 543–560.

Liu, J. & Sadler, R.W. (2003). The effect and affect of peer review in electronic versus traditional modes on L2 writing. *Journal of English for Academic Purposes, 2*(3), 193–227.

Ramanathan, V. & Atkinson, D. (1999). Individualism, academic writing, and ESL writers. *Journal of Second Language Writing, 8*(1), 45–75.

Reid, J.M. (1993). *Teaching ESL writing.* Englewood Cliffs, NJ: Prentice Hall Regents.

Reid, J.M. (1997). Which non-native speaker? Differences between international students and U.S. resident (language minority) students. In D.L. Sigsbee, B.W. Speck, & B. Maylath (Eds.), *Approaches to teaching non-native English speakers across the curriculum* (pp. 17–27). San Francisco: Jossey-Bass.

Roberge, M. (2002). California's generation 1.5 immigrants: What experiences, characteristics, and needs do they bring to our English classes? *CATESOL Journal, 14*(1), 107–129.

Sassen, S. (2005). The global city: Introducing a concept. *Brown Journal of World Affairs, 11*(2), 27–43.

Spack, R. (2001). Initiating ESL students into the academic discourse community: How far should we go? In T. Silva & P.K. Matsuda (Eds.), *Landmark essays on ESL writing* (pp. 91–108). Mahwah, NJ: Lawrence Erlbaum.

Thonus, T. (2004). What are the differences? Tutor interactions with first- and second-language writers. *Journal of Second Language Writing, 13*(3), 227–242.

University of Houston. (2006). *UH at a glance.* Retrieved July 1, 2006, from www.uh.edu/uh_glance/index.php?page=info.

Weigle, S.C. & Nelson, G.L. (2004). Novice tutors and their ESL tutees: Three case studies of tutor roles and perceptions of tutorial success. *Journal of Second Language Writing, 13*(3), 203–225.

Williams, J. (2004). Tutoring and revision: Second language writers in the writing center. *Journal of Second Language Writing, 13*(3), 173–201.

Wilson, J.S. & Poltavtchenko, E. (2004, March). Motivation differences between international and immigrant writers. Poster presented at the TESOL 2004 conference, Long Beach, CA.

Zhu, W. (2001). Interaction and feedback in mixed peer response groups. *Journal of Second Language Writing, 10*(4), 251–276.

14 Situated Invention and Genres

Assisting Generation 1.5 Students in Developing Rhetorical Flexibility

Ann M. Johns *San Diego State University*

Increasingly, secondary schools and colleges are enrolling students spoken of as "generation 1.5," a group discussed at length in this volume. From immigrant backgrounds but raised principally in the United States, often fluent in spoken English and familiar with American school cultures, these students still tend to be placed in college ESL or "remedial" classes with international or new immigrant students whose needs and backgrounds are quite different from their own (Harklau, 2003). The "drill and practice" and grammar-dependent approaches in many of these literacy classes are demotivating for generation 1.5 students and can lead to discouragement and drop-out. In this chapter, I will argue that through drawing from these students' prior knowledge of academic and everyday genres in American cultures and through encouraging them to use context-sensitive invention strategies, we can motivate them to ask the right questions about—and produce—appropriate texts for academic contexts, thus contributing to their success.

Drawing from Prior Knowledge

It has long been argued that students' prior knowledge of content should be a major intertextual resource for their writing. This claim was central in the eras of Expressionism and "The Process Movement" (see Silva, 1990), during which classrooms were self-consciously student-centered. In these types of classrooms, which are still common, students are given open-ended prompts for writing and encouraged to brainstorm about familiar topics before they compose their texts. As a result, they tend to write essays about their families and friends or on issues that they have confronted while growing up. Particularly with generation 1.5 students, for whom academic and professional cultures, languages, tasks, and genres can be foreign and intimidating (Harklau, 2003; MacBeth, 2006), drawing from everyday content knowledge can provide an important bridge to academic writing.

In addition to drawing from students' prior knowledge of content, teachers of generation 1.5 students—who are often considered "remedial" because of their surface-level grammatical errors—draw from and exploit students' prior knowledge of text structures. Because of their remedial placement, generation 1.5 students have often been asked to produce the same types of texts over and over again in their classrooms, perhaps because teachers believe that they are incapable of producing a variety of text types or that they shouldn't be taught new genres until they control with complete confidence the grammar of standard English. For many years, I have been asking my so-called remedial and ESL college freshmen, many of whom could be classified as generation 1.5, to identify the academic genres they have been taught; and, once these have been identified, to tell me how to organize texts in these genres. The genre most frequently identified, year after year, is *the five paragraph essay*, and inevitably, at least half of my students can recite exactly how this essay should be organized at the macro-structure level (Johns, 2002). In fact, students who have studied under the Jane Schafer method[1] can recite the putative functions of each sentence in this essay form. Because our generation 1.5 students are often thought to be "incapable of doing more creative work" (a quote from a colleague who teaches writing), they tend to be particularly familiar with this genre. Harklau, Losey, & Siegal (1999) summarize these points when they note that many generation 1.5 students have had "low track" instruction that may have included substitution drills, dictation, short answer questions, or writing from models.

Personalizing of the curriculum by drawing from everyday content and textual knowledge definitely has its merits. Generation 1.5 students, who are orally fluent, are more motivated to discuss a familiar topic in a classroom, and they may be more comfortable writing in a structure that they have practiced, over and over again. If these students are to succeed in colleges and universities, however, instructors need to be concerned with much more than student motivation and oral fluency. As considerable writing-across-the-curriculum research indicates (e.g., Carter, 2007; Melzer, 2003), to be successful in postsecondary contexts, students need to move from their comfort zones into analyzing and critiquing unfamiliar topics, language, arguments, and contexts for a variety of texts. In order to succeed, students must be motivated to develop the *rhetorical flexibility* that enables them to move from the familiar, assess an academic situation, and write successfully in the genre that each situation requires.

The Role of Genre

There is much more to successful academic writing than what occurs at an isolated sentence level or in the personal essay, something I have discovered when completing my own research and reading the extensive published literature on literacies in academic disciplines. In fact, an understanding of discipline-valued genres, approaches to argument, integration of sources, and a deep understanding of academic language appear to be much more central to students' academic success, particularly in some of their majors, than sentence-level correctness. Perhaps by discussing the results of two of my own studies in disciplines, these points will be further explained. In 1991, I published a case study of a Vietnamese-American student ("Luc") whose high school education had been completed in the United States and whose spoken English was at the near-native level. When I interviewed him, he was an upper-division student, maintaining an A–/B+ average in classes in his major, biology, and was planning to enter dental school when he completed his undergraduate education. Nonetheless, he was a student in my "remedial" writing class and had failed the university's writing competency examination twice. How could there be such a disparity between his grades in his major and his examination scores? It is because the biology department valued primarily his knowledge of the specific content, concepts, and genres of the discipline that he displayed in his written work. Luc had also mastered the principles of argumentation in biology, ways in which to make claims and use evidence. Herrington, in her ground-breaking 1985 article on writing in the disciplines, says that it is crucial that writers know "the types of knowledge claims [they] can make and what counts as a good reason to support those claims" (p. 355) in their disciplines. Despite these abilities, Luc's written work indicated that he made a number of sentence-level errors which, among other things, led to his repeated failure on examinations set by writing teachers.[2]

Another study I conducted, this time when I was teaching undergraduate engineering majors, resulted in similar findings (Johns, 1993). In this case, I interviewed the two most effective grant writers in the engineering college on my campus, both of whom had been born and raised abroad, to determine what was valued in that discipline's discourse. According to these experts, argumentation, particularly as displayed in non-linear texts (charts, graphs, formulae), was the most important element in successful grant writing. To make their case, the engineers showed me their successful proposals and explained why they have succeeded. To my surprise, all of the proposals were replete with the sentence-level errors with which we are familiar, e.g., the absence of the definite article or the third person singular "–s" in the present tense. The engineers explained that grant reviewers are not interested in grammatical errors but in appropriate argumentation.

After completing these studies, I am loath to conclude that the types of sentence-level errors our generation 1.5 students continue to make are not important. They are important in many contexts, of course; however, how these errors are identified, studied, and corrected needs to be influenced by other factors: the students' own backgrounds and needs, certainly (Ferris, 1999), but disciplinary values related to argumentation and textual conventions as well.

Given this complexity, how can we assist students to grasp what is important to academic texts within the disciplines? How can we take them beyond traditional approaches to sentence-level error and the model-based five paragraph essay? Genre, the most social constructivist of literacy concepts, is a term that provides an intellectual and practical lens through which students can look as they become more rhetorically flexible and through which instructors can work to take students from their known texts to the situated language and texts of academic contexts.

Before discussing how this might be done, it is important to give a brief overview of the genre theory, which provides the basis for this discussion.[3] In her ground-breaking article, Miller (1984) spoke of genres as "actions we want to accomplish" (p. 151). Building upon that definition, Paltridge (2006) refers to genres as "ways in which people get things done through their use of *language in particular contexts*" (p. 236, italics mine). These two quotes suggest that genres are purposeful, social, and situated—and that the language of texts is directly related to genre and writers' purposes. Miller also tells us that genres are *repeated*, for what Coe (2006) calls "genre-provoking situations" (p. 247). Thus, for example, many writers employ the genre of the résumé every time they apply for a job. As they write a number of résumés for different jobs, they become increasingly skilled in producing this genre. Therefore, as I have noted elsewhere:

[Writers] are able to separate texts into genre categories in order to assist themselves, and other readers and writers, in identifying, processing, and remembering textual experiences. Thus, as individuals have repeated, situated experiences with texts from a genre category, their schematic memories of those texts and relevant contexts become increasingly reliable. They are able to identify texts by a community-designated name, and read, comprehend, and perhaps write similar texts with increasing ease and effectiveness. Genre knowledge provides a shortcut for the initiated to the processing and production of familiar texts.

(Johns, 1997, p. 21)

It is important to note, however, that in each situation a writer confronts where a genre is "provoked," a successful text may be different from a previous text from the same genre; and, as a result, the writer's genre schema must be revised. A good résumé in one situation may not be appropriate for another situation, for example. Therefore, we need to consider not only what is repeated or conventional about a genre ("the central tendencies") but the situational features that make a text from a genre different from that in the previous, analogous situation. Theorists speak of the centripetal forces that contribute to the prototypicality of a genre ("central tendencies") and centrifugal forces from the immediate situation that influence the writing of a successful text (Berkenkotter & Huckin, 1995).

This brief commentary on genre theory originates from the New Rhetoric, a theoretical camp that draws from Perelman and Olbrechts-Tyteca (1969), among others, and focuses on what makes texts, and the arguments within them, both repeated and variable. The concern fronted in this theory is for the values of the readers and writers and their communities that infuse rhetorical contexts—rather than for absolutes such as the rigid text structure of the traditional five paragraph essay. Perelman and Olbrechts-Tyteca note that "since argumentation aims at securing the adherence of those to whom it is addressed, it is, in its entirety, *relative* to the audience to be influenced" (1969, p. 19).

For the undergraduate, *the academic essay* is a genre that is infinitely open to variation, one of the problems that "Luc" faced in my study of his efforts to pass the writing competency examinations (Johns, 1991). On high-stakes examinations, students are presented with what assessors call "essay prompts," which have a few conventions or "central tendencies" (a title, no headings, paragraphing, often, an argument) but vary in a number of ways. Here are three examples:

Timed writing 1: Read the text provided. Then, in an essay, answer the following questions: a. What argument is the author making? b. What are the strengths and weaknesses of the argument? c. What strategies does the writer use to persuade the audience?

(From the Upper-Division Writing Examination, San Diego State University. Students who fail must enroll in "remedial" classes)

Timed writing 2: In recent years, there have been many negative criticisms of large corporations such as Wal-Mart and McDonalds. What do you think about these criticisms? Using the sources you have been studying, write an essay in which you explain, describe, and evaluate some of the major arguments against large corporations.

> (From an end-of-class writing examination at San Diego State, determining whether "remedial" students will advance to "regular" writing classes)

Timed writing 3: We pass the word around; we ponder how the case is put by different people, we read the poetry; we meditate over the literature; we play the music in our minds; we reach an understanding. Society evolves this way, not by shouting each other down, but by the unique capacity of unique individuals to comprehend each other.

Read the passage above from *The Medusa and the Snail* (1979) by biologist Lewis Thomas, carefully. Then, drawing from your own reading and experience, write an essay that defends, challenges, or qualifies Thomas's claims.

> (From an AP Language and Composition Essay Examination, retrieved February 6, 2008, from www.collegeboard.com/apstudents)

Though in each example given above, the genre identified is an *essay*, the texts that would impress the grader audience in each situation are considerably different from each other and from the familiar five paragraph essay still common in the writing classes in which our generation 1.5 students tend to be enrolled. One common element is the focus upon argumentation: understanding an argument in a text or developing one's own. Another element that is central to these prompts is intertextuality, i.e., the integration of information outside of the writer into the text. In the examples presented above, the immediate intertextual influence is the prompt; however, the secondary influences, the written sources, are also important to successful academic texts. Timed writing 1 requires a rhetorical reading of single, short text; it asks students to analyze the strategies that the writer uses to make an argument. Timed writing 2 requires a reading of several sources to "describe, explain, and evaluate" their claims. Timed writing 3, from an AP examination, requires students to read a short text and "defend, challenge, or qualify" the author's claims. In each writing situation, the important issue is not the number of paragraphs or paragraph structure. Instead, the students are asked to process and integrate the sources in different ways: to analyze a writer's argument, to explain, evaluate, challenge, or qualify arguments in one or more sources. As can be seen, the *academic essay* used to assess secondary or undergraduate students is a genre that becomes the catch-all name for a variety of texts requiring rhetorical stances and different approaches to argumentation and sources.

This discussion of "the essay" points to a student characteristic required for success in academic and professional reading and writing: *rhetorical flexibility*, that is, *the ability to analyze ("research") a situation in which writing is required and to produce a text from a genre appropriate for the audience in that situation.* In addition to noting the name of the text ("essay") and drawing from their genre schemata "central tendencies" or conventions of that amorphous genre, the students must assess the immediate situation (e.g., How am I to read the prompt? How are sources used? Who's grading the exam? How will it be graded? What language must be used? How carefully should it be edited? What should it be edited (or revised) for? How much time do I have to respond to the prompts?) and respond accordingly. The term "genre" then becomes a jumping off place—a way for writers to draw from their prior knowledge of "central tendencies" but then to assess the immediate writing situation, revise their genre schema, and produce an appropriate text for the context.

The "essay" genre is particularly troubling in academic situations because so many different types of texts are called essays by assessors and college and university faculty; and, as can be seen in the research that I conducted (Johns, 1991, 1993), criteria for evaluating written work may vary considerably.

Invention

So what are our responsibilities for preparing generation 1.5 students to become rhetorically flexible, to draw from prior genre knowledge, and assess a writing situation? How can we assist this particular group of students to become confident and proficient academic readers and writers? Keeping in mind the social nature of genres, we can focus in our classrooms on another New Rhetoric concept, taken from Aristotle: invention. Useful modern work on invention has been completed by Anis Bawarshi, whose volume, *Genre and the invention of the writer* (2003) and other writings (2006) can illuminate our pedagogies. Bawarshi (2006) speaks of invention as:

> stages in the writing process in which writers situate themselves within the genre they are writing ... orienting themselves within the social, rhetorical, and linguistic contexts they will need to inhabit before they can participate effectively and critically within these contexts.
>
> (p. 246)

This author contrasts his description of invention with the types of classroom prewriting for the personal essay described at the beginning of this chapter. In the "process" classrooms, "writers explore, discover, and *generate what they want to write* and how they want to go about writing it" (Bawarshi, 2006, p. 247). This practice is "pre-social," for it does not consider the contextual ("social") forces in play. Bawarshi argues that contextually situated approaches to invention should be central to classrooms throughout the writing process as students become increasingly familiar with an immediate writing context and the "best possible means of persuasion" for that situation. This means, among other things, that students develop a sensitivity to a variety of authentic writing situations and the demands of these situations upon the writer, something that Reid (1992) has advocated for this population for a number of years. What it also means, as I am implying throughout this text, is that generation 1.5 students, often overwhelmed by the multiple demands of academic literacies, need to determine what factors are central to a task and genre and devote their efforts to working on these.

Pedagogy

As I have noted here and we know from other chapters in this volume, generation 1.5 students are often placed in de-motivating and inappropriate classes where the emphasis is upon "skill and drill" grammar instruction (Harklau, 2003) and the structured, five paragraph essay. I am suggesting a completely different approach, one that has been motivating and empowering for my students, assisting them to understand what makes texts from genres successful in specific academic contexts. In what follows, I will suggest basic pedagogical approaches that assist generation 1.5 students to leave their comfort zones and take on the roles of literacy researchers in academic contexts while at the same time enriching their invention strategies. In this discussion, I am drawing principally from New Rhetoric theory and research as well as my own experiences with teaching "remedial" college freshmen (Johns, 1997) and working with secondary teachers who are preparing students for university through the AVID program.[4] Here are my suggested approaches.

Approach 1: Exploring Invention Through Familiar Genres

What is required to read or produce texts in the "social worlds" that our students will inhabit? Considerable research into faculty assigned writing (and reading) tasks across the disciplines have convinced me that we cannot predict the specific writing tasks and situations that students will face in every classroom—simply because there are too many variables. Instead, we need to prepare students to be researchers in each writing situation (Johns, 1997) and to empower them with invention and discovery strategies to be successful in these contexts and with the tasks and genres that are present.

At various points in the semester, I separate students into groups to complete genre analyses of texts from their own communities that they bring to class, e.g., flyers, church programs, and invitations to "raves," and advertisements. Drawing on their prior knowledge of the texts and situations in which they have been successful gives students feelings of control, comfort, and awareness that are motivating and enjoyable. They are the teachers of texts and I am the learner. Using Table 14.1, an "Invention Grid," they answer the questions in the first two sections, "Genre name" and "Community or context," about the familiar texts they have brought. We discuss what they already know about the writing situation and the texts that have resulted, and we consider the writing processes that may have taken place as the texts were produced.

Early in the semester, they use this technique with known academic texts: how they have been taught and processed texts in the past, particularly in their literacy classrooms. I ask them to examine all parts of Table 14.1, and then they reflect, in writing, on the following:

> Compare how you have "invented" texts before with what the "Invention Chart" suggests. How did you plan for writing or revision in your English/Language Arts classrooms and elsewhere? What does this "Invention Grid" add for your consideration? Does the chart leave anything out that the writer must consider?

Students share their reflections and we discuss what it means to write successfully in one of the genres they have been analyzing or in the five paragraph essay. We also draw from their prior knowledge of secondary school tasks and ask: What was most important to these tasks? How did your teachers grade? How did you prepare?

Table 14.1 Invention grid

Feature	Questions	Comments
Genre name	What is this type of text called?	
Community or context	Where does a text like this appear, according to the prompt?	
Audience(s)	For whom is this text written? Does the instructor specify an audience?	
Audience evaluation	How will the audience evaluate how well the text is written? [Scoring criteria or other indicators.]	
Writer's purposes	Why would you, or someone else, write a text in this genre?	
Conventional features	What characteristics of a text from this genre help you to identify it? What is repeated in texts from this genre? [Text structure, font type, use of headings...?]	
Situated features	What particular features does this text have? What does the prompt tell you about text organization, content or other elements?	
Other features	What else does the prompt tell you about the text that would help you to write it? How long should it be? What types of language should you use?	

Approach 2: Augmenting Invention Practices Through Timed Writing

At other times, we turn to assessment tasks, such as the timed writings that appear in the first part of this chapter. Timed Writing 3 is a good example. After some discussion about whether the use of quotes from famous people is common practice in the examinations they have taken, the students move into their groups, and using Table 14.1, come up with the "givens" in the Timed Writing 3 prompt. We discuss what is *not* stated in the prompt and how students might find out ("research") these situational requirements[5] before they write. We also discuss how, even in a timed examination, they might be able to obtain more information from the instructor or assessor about expectations. Finally, we talk about *when and how* it is important to correct errors. For example, in some of their examinations in the content areas, it might be much more important to respond appropriately to the prompt, create a well-organized answer and make use of appropriate language and argumentation than it is to correct every error.

Since much of the writing that students complete during their first years at university is in the form of in-class, timed responses to a prompt (see Melzer, 2003), the students are given the opportunity to respond to this prompt under timed conditions. Before writing, the students, with my assistance, devise an analytical scoring scheme based upon what we have discovered, through Table 14.1, about the prompt. For this particular prompt, the scheme could be the following, based upon 25 points:

Element	Score
Use of the quote	3 pts
Selection and development of one function: defend, challenge, *or* qualify	7 pts
Effective text structure	5 pts
Use of detail and other forms of support	7 pts
Sentence-level features (since it's timed)	3 pts

Because the students are becoming literacy researchers, I advise them to ask their instructors to give them scoring criteria for the writing tasks that they have been assigned or are tested on in other classes. Because, through experience, I know that many faculty across the curriculum do not create scoring criteria, I provide opportunities for students to role-play successful ways to elicit the criteria from the instructor. They might ask, "What are the most important elements of a good response?" or "When you grade these papers, what do you look for?" After the students have studied prompts at some length, they are given opportunity to plan and write responses under timed conditions.

What I am arguing then, is that because generation 1.5 students, often inexperienced with complex academic prompts and discourses, may not be able to give equal attention to grammar, content, prompt type and structure, audience, and other factors, they need to analyze what may be most important in a given writing situation and focus their invention strategies upon what may be most important—or, to be more specific—what factors may most influence their grades.

Approach 3: Analyzing a Variety of Authentic Classroom Tasks

Fortunately, my years as director of the campus Writing-across-the-curriculum and Center for Teaching and Learning Programs, and 15 years of co-teaching with instructors from other disciplines in a learning communities program (Johns, 1997, 2001), augmented by an excellent master's thesis by one of my students (Oberem, 2004), have provided me with many examples of authentic writing tasks from a number of disciplines.[6]

Again stressing rhetorical flexibility and situated invention, I assign each group of students to an out-of-class writing prompt from a list provided, an example of which is found in Appendix A. Using Table 14.1, the "Invention Grid," the student groups analyze the prompt they have been assigned. This is a good time for oral and/or visual presentations of the assigned prompts or for one group of students to exchange their prompts and analyses with another group to determine if their answers are the same. When they have completed this work, students are asked to develop questions for the faculty prompt writer that are not answered in the prompt itself. If time permits, I ask a faculty member who wrote one of the prompts to come to my class so that the answers to student questions can be provided.

After considerable discussion, students develop scoring criteria for the authentic prompts they have been assigned and discuss the difficulties they might have in preparing a paper based upon them. This experience often leads to student collection of writing prompts from their other classes and presentation of these prompts to the class.

The possibilities for this approach are endless, and the discussions are rich—because students are making discoveries about genres and academic cultures that may be new to them.

Approach 4: Relating Prompts to "Macro-Genres"

Recently, I have discovered a useful four-part "macro-genre" taxonomy (see Appendix B) for writing in the disciplines (Carter, 2007). Using this taxonomy, students are asked to hypothesize about what types of writing their chosen majors might value and the genres that result. I then ask students to examine the authentic prompts they have been assigned or that they have collected in their classes to discover how the tasks in the prompts compare with the macro-genre taxonomy. This discussion may lead to confusion since the tasks do not parallel, in a precise way, the macro-genres. However, I ask students to look beyond specifics to some of the questions that the "macro-genres" raise:

1. What types of data or sources are valued by various disciplines?
2. How and when are claims presented?
3. What is the basic organization of the papers that result from the different macro-genres?
4. Why do you think that texts are organized in these ways?
5. Which types of "macro-genres" are you most familiar with? What, for example, does your typical English class research paper look like?

Approach 5: Varying Writing Assignments

The types of analyses discussed here continue throughout the class, and they are accompanied, if possible, by analyses of successful (model) papers that respond to academic prompts. What and how, then, should students write? They write under a variety of conditions (timed/process) and in response to a variety of prompt types, eliciting a variety of texts, as Reid (1992) has advocated for the generation 1.5 student. Each time a prompt for writing is assigned, students complete Table 14.1, the Invention Grid. In addition, they are either given the criteria for scoring their papers or they ask questions in order to create criteria that appear to be appropriate. The criteria and their answers to invention questions in Table 14.1 then become the bases for peer review and eventual scoring of the texts that result.

The ideal final assessment for this type of class is a portfolio in which students can place a variety of their best work in a number of genres, reflections upon their invention and writing processes, and comments on what they learned from the prompt and text analyses (Johns, 1997).

Approach 6: Linking Language and Writing

At this point, the teacher/reader may be asking "So what do you do about language? My generation 1.5 students are still making those pesky grammatical errors." The students begin to understand as they develop their rhetorical flexibility that grammar is *one* factor upon which they will be assessed. For some instructors, such as those teaching and testing composition, editing carefully may be very important (cf., Johns, 1991). However, in other classes, particularly on timed, in-class examinations, other factors may be much more important to their success. In some of their writing assignments, written under "process" conditions, students are advised that correctness is very important and given practice in identifying their own, and each other's errors, through teacher modeling of error correction using their papers and other approaches suggested by Ferris (2003). As Ferris (1999) suggests, for generation 1.5 students, the teaching of formal grammar may be in order so that they can use a handbook and develop a grammar metalanguage.

But we need to go considerably beyond the classic editing and revision strategies if we are to be true to theory. If we want to teach language as genre-based and situated, then we need to analyze what language *does* in the text. Ann Snow and I co-edited a 2006 special issue of *Journal of English for Academic Purposes* (Vol. 5, Issue 4), dedicated to academic English in secondary schools, which contains several articles discussing the functions of language within genres and disciplines. In one of these, Schleppergrell and de Oliveira argue that in order for students to understand what academic English *does*, they must work with the constructs of a discipline and its valued genres to see how language assists writers to perpetuate knowledge in content areas. Using these authors' suggestions for classroom activities, the students and I examine model prompt responses and authentic prompts from the disciplines, generally from the majors that students in the class have selected.

To augment this work, we use Dutro and Moran's (2003) classification of academic words into "brick" and "mortar" categories, giving further salience to our classroom discussions. Brick words are those that take on special meanings in a discipline or reading and include central concepts, among other elements. Thus, for example, "adaptation," "assimilation," and "kinship" are brick words that serve special purposes in the discipline of anthropology. Mortar words are the "general-utility vocabulary required for constructing sentences—the words that determine the relationship between and among words, [sentences and paragraphs]" (Dutro & Moran, 2003, p. 239). These include conjunctions and other metadiscourse words and phrases ("So far, I have discussed"), citation verbs ("argue," "note," "suggest"), cohesive devices, such as pronouns, and "stance and evaluation" terms that authors use to express their attitudes toward a topic (Hyland, 2005).

Thus, we devote a considerable amount of time to the languages of the disciplines and, especially, to the categories of words that provide the mortar for writing in many disciplines. As students work with invention strategies and their analyses of prompts, we discuss language they can use and what it can do. As they draft and revise their texts, we pay special attention to the language they have chosen, suggesting words from a "mortar" collection that we post. As we post these words, we can practice their use in the familiar grids such as Table 14.2 to augment their understanding of parts of speech (Ferris, 1999).

Table 14.2 Word Grid

Key mortar word	Synonym	Noun	Adverb	Adjective
argue (verb)	claim	argument	arguably	argued (?)

Conclusion

In this chapter, I have attempted to show how instructors can create a different kind of class for generation 1.5 students, taking them from their known genres and contexts into situated invention and genre analysis. I have argued that these students can learn to be academic researchers through a "social" invention process that includes analysis of the task, the text, the context, the textual language, and the writer. I have also argued that the relationships between language, text, and situation must be transparent and discussed, thereby enabling students to develop their higher order thinking skills. If our goals are student motivation and context analysis, as well as transfer of skills, then we must make major changes in the ways in which we approach the teaching of academic writing (and reading), particularly to generation 1.5 students. We must understand better what they have experienced, what they need, and how the study of academic language and texts can benefit them.

In my freshman classes, I have been working on "social" invention and encouraging students to be researchers for a number of years (e.g., Johns, 1997). As teachers, our purposes are to ensure success and high student motivation, and my former students report that when they are more rhetorically flexible and open, they are much more confident and successful in their academic classrooms.

Appendix A Authentic Academic Writing Prompts[7]

These writing prompts are taken from classrooms in a number of disciplines. Complete the "Invention Grid," Table 14.1, using one of these prompts. Decide what the prompts do not tell you—and you will have to find out from the instructor before you begin work on the paper.

---

1. From Philosophy 329 (Ethics: General Education)

Consider the following questions: What purpose should the Supreme Court serve? Should it simply strike down laws that violate specific constitutional provisions? Or is its purpose to strike down laws that are based on a notion of morality found objectionable to the majority? Should the focus of the Court be simply procedural, or does the Court have a role in narrowing the gap between the nation's constitutional ideals and the truths of everyday existence?

- Your essay should draw on the Gobitis and Barnette law cases.
- Your essay should draw a distinction between procedural and substantive justice and explain the importance of that distinction.

2. From Geography 101 (General Education)

Illegal international migration between Mexico and the United States has commanded a great deal of attention from policy makers in both countries. A sound policy needs to be grounded in an understanding of the magnitude of the flows as well as the forces that generate this form of migration. In your memo, you are to assume the role of a policy analyst who is responsible for providing this information and a discussion of the impacts of this migration on both countries. Additionally you are to suggest a plan of action for the United States' government to shape its immigration policy towards Mexico as well as justification for the policy that you suggest. In addition to lectures and the textbook, draw upon at least two web-based sources for your text. [Use sources that will convince your audience!]

3. From Human Sexuality 102

Role: A friend has written to you about her up-and-coming wedding. She knows that you have taken a human sexuality course and has asked you for any advice you might give for her and her husband to have a good sex life in marriage.

Audience: Imagine someone that is a friend and is similar to you in many ways. You might even imagine a real friend. Assume the friend is like you in terms of educational background, religion, ethnicity—and make these assumptions clear to the reader (e.g., Now, Mary, I know that since both you and Fred are Catholics...). The tone of the letter should be casual; however, you can still include academic, technical material.

Genre: A letter, obviously, but you may have sections with headings for easier reading. The assignment can be completed in three to four pages. Organize the material any way you wish but try to have an organizational scheme that is obvious and logical to the reader.

Theme: You may select any topics from the course, from the book, lectures, or classroom discussion. Please include at least two outside sources (a magazine, academic journal, book, or sources from the web). Be sure to reference sources properly at the end of the assignment, using APA.

Criteria:	*Points*:
Organization	4
Use of outside references	8
Selection of relevant material	8
Accurate information	6
Spelling, grammar, and punctuation	4
Writing process (drafts, peer review)	10

4. From Exercise and Nutritional Sciences 441C: Field Games

(Group assignment): Using the *Sport Education* text and other sources, type a plan to be implemented in class for a 2-day, end-of-season culminating competition. Describe all of the games and mini-games that will be played, any special rules, playing field considerations (equipment, dimensions, and organization), player numbers, duration of each contest, and outcome and process points/ rewards. Each group will also implement this plan by presenting and organizing the selected sport's culminating tournament's activities.

(Individual assignment): Observe an entire soccer or softball game at the youth, interscholastic, collegiate, or professional level. Take complete notes during your observation so that you can prepare a typed report in which you *fully* describe five primary features of the sport context that are diagramed in Figure 1.1 of the textbook. Using material from Chapter One and your observation notes, describe how three of your observations/features of sport could be implemented in a secondary physical education setting.

5. From a History 110 (American History)

The paper assignment for this course involves researching a particular historical event or episode in the twentieth century through contemporary newspaper and/or popular magazines. First, choose a topic from the list below [60 were listed, e.g., the 1948 Truman election, Jackie Robinson's first game] and find at least six to eight articles or editorials on your topic in newspapers or magazines from the period you are researching. From these, you are to analyze and discuss the attitudes, beliefs, or responses of Americans during that period to the event. Depending upon your topic, you should try to explore it for several days after the initial episode. Be sure to use ideas or quotes from the articles to support your claims about writer perspectives. Rather than simply describing the response or attitudes you find, try to construct some form of argument, which will help your paper take a coherent direction.

Your paper is to be at least five pp. in length, double spaced with normal font and margins and is due April 23rd. You must also provide proper footnotes to document your evidence. You must allot the bulk of your paper to examining and analyzing sources, allowing no more than one page for the background and introduction.

Possible sources found in the SDSU library include: *San Diego Union, L.A. times, Life Magazine, Saturday Evening Post,* and *Newsweek.* In the UCSD Library, you can find.... [If you have any difficulties, consult the reference librarian. The Internet, however, is not an acceptable resource for this assignment.]

6. From Religious Studies 305: New Testament

An Exegetical Paper

Text: Select from one of the following: 1 and 2 Thessalonians; 1 and 2 Corinthians

Format: While you can write in almost any format you like (as long as it's narrative, and not poetry!), your paper should include the following elements, and not be longer than two pages. [Sources: at least one Biblical commentary and two different translations.]

1.   Introductory paragraph which sets the stage.
2.   The historical context, perhaps including:

   • the "occasion" on which Paul wrote a letter;
   • the setting in which the gospel was written;
   • the audience for whom the letter or gospel was written;
   • any historical details that will put the passage in the proper historical context.

3.   Literary context: Put the passage in the context of the bigger picture. This means:

   • Where does it occur in the book you are studying?
   • How does it advance the plot or argument of the writer?
   • How and where does it fit in the narrative?
   • How do the versions (translations) differ?

4.   The textual context:

   • Are any words problematic? Why?
   • Are there translation difficulties?
   • Do your Bible and commentary indicate any issues or questions?

5.   Your analysis of what the passage means, given the context mentioned above. I want your analysis, not the biblical commentators'!

The paper should give credit to any sources you quote or use. It should be written in proper English style and grammar. Use Spell-Check and then *read* your paper out loud. You will catch grammar errors when you read your paper.

Appendix B Disciplinary Macro-genres (Carter, 2007)

In his study, Carter found that there are four categories of genre responses within the disciplines. In this appendix, the four types are outlined. The genres and disciplines in which they tend to appear are also included.

1. A Problem-Solving/System-Generating Response
    Disciplines: Business, Social Work, Engineering, Nursing
    a. Identify, define, and analyze the problem;
    b. determine what information and disciplinary concepts are appropriate for solving the problem;
    c. collect data;
    d. offer viable solutions; and
    e. evaluate the solutions using specific discipline-driven criteria.
    Genres: case studies, project reports and proposals, business plans.

2. A Response Calling for Empirical Inquiry (An IMRD Paper)
    Disciplines: Sciences, Nursing, and the Social Sciences
    a. Ask questions/formulate hypotheses;
    b. test hypotheses (or answer questions) using empirical methods;
    c. organize and analyze data for verbal and visual summaries;
    d. conclude by explaining the results.
    Genres: lab reports, posters, a research report, or article.

3. A Response Calling for Research from Written Sources
    Disciplines: Humanities, English and other literatures, Classics, History
    a. Critically evaluate the sources "in terms of credibility, authenticity, interpretive stance, audience, potential biases, and value for answering research questions;" and
    b. marshall evidence to support an argument that answers the research question.
    Genre: "*The quintessential academic genre: the research paper*" (MLA style).

4. A Response Calling for Performance
    Disciplines: Art, Music, Composition (writing)
    a. Learn about the principles, concepts, media, or formats appropriate for the discipline;
    b. attempt to master the techniques and approaches;
    c. develop a working knowledge and process; and
    d. perform and/or critique a performance.

Notes

1. For an example, see http://ecs.ovhs.info/dsp.subpage.cfm?uid=38&id=627 (retrieved April 12, 2007).
2. I am happy to say that this story has a happy ending. Luc passed the writing competency examination on his third attempt; and after completing dental school at the University of Southern California, he began a promising practice in San Diego.

3. Hyon (1996) speaks of three theoretical genre camps: English for Specific Purposes (ESP), the New Rhetoric, and "The Sydney School" (Systemic Functional). Though I am an ESP product, I find that the New Rhetoric has more to offer our generation 1.5 students, considering their backgrounds. See Johns (2008) for a more complete discussion of the three theories and their applications to academic writing.

4. AVID is a long-established, secondary in-school program dedicated to encouraging diverse students (often generation 1.5) to attend universities. See www.avidonline.org/info/? tabid=1&ID=548. (retrieved May 10, 2007).

5. It is important to note here, and throughout a writing class, that many college and university faculty do *not* give students sufficient information about their writing tasks for them to successfully complete them. What is necessary, then, is role play, a classroom activity that fluent generation 1.5 students enjoy. I give students certain problems and roles ("You are a student who needs to find out more information about a writing task from your professor." and "You are the professor who has assigned the task."). Students then act out what they might say in this situation. Needless to say, the job of teacher and the rest of the class is to critique their approaches, some of which will probably be unsuccessful, e.g., student asks: "What do you want?" "How long should this be?" We then discuss some possibilities for improved approaches to task research through interviewing the instructor.

6. For those instructors lacking the access I have had, the Internet provides many opportunities for task retrieval. I suggest that instructors begin with the Melzer (2003) article, which is online—and then move to websites of faculty on their own campuses. The Political Science Department at San Diego State, for example, includes postings of syllabi and reading/writing tasks for every faculty member.

7 The "Human Sexuality" prompt is taken from Walvoord, Barbara E. & Lucille P. McCarthy (1990). *Thinking and Writing in College: A Naturalistic Study of Students in Four Disciplines.* Urbana, IL: National Council of Teachers of English. All other prompts are taken, with permission, from interviews with faculty at San Diego State University.

References

Bawarshi, A. (2003). *Genre and the invention of the writer: Reconsidering the place of invention in composition.* Logan, Utah: Utah State University Press.

Bawarshi, A. (2006). Crossing the boundaries of genre studies. [Co-written with A.M. Johns, R.M. Coe, K. Hyland, B. Paltridge, M.J. Reiff, & C.M. Tardy] *Journal of Second Language Writing, 15*(3), 234–249.

Berkenkotter, C. & Huckin, T. (1995). *Genre knowledge in disciplinary communities.* Hillsdale, NJ: Lawrence Erlbaum.

Carter, M. (2007). Ways of knowing, doing, and writing in the disciplines. *College Composition and Communication, 58*(3), 385–418.

Coe, R.M. (2006). Crossing the boundaries of genre studies. [Co-written with A.M. Johns, A. Bawarshi, K. Hyland, B. Paltridge, M.J. Reiff, & C.M. Tardy] *Journal of Second Language Writing, 15*(3), 234–249.

Dutro, S. & Moran, C. (2003). Rethinking English language instruction: An architectural approach. In G.G. Garcia (Ed.), *English learners: Reaching the highest level of English proficiency* (pp. 227–258). Newark, DE: International Reading Association.

Ferris, D. (1999). One size does not fit all: Response and revision issues for immigrant student writers. In L. Harklau, K.M. Losey, & M. Siegal (Eds.), *Generation 1.5 meets college composition: Issues in the teaching of writing to U.S.-educated learners of ESL.* Mahwah, NJ: Lawrence Erlbaum Associates.

Ferris, D. (2003). *Response to student writing: Implications for second language students.* Mahwah, NJ: Lawrence Erlbaum.

Harklau, L. (2003). *Generation 1.5 students and college writing*. Center for Applied Linguistics website: Retrieved September 24, 2007 from www.cal.org/resources/Digest/0305harklau.html.

Harklau, L., Losey, K.M., & Siegal, M. (Eds.) (1999). *Generation 1.5 meets college composition: Issues in the teaching of writing to U.S.-educated learners of ESL*. Mahwah, NJ: Lawrence Erlbaum Associates.

Herrington, A. (1985). Writing in academic settings: A study of the contexts for writing in two college chemical engineering courses. *Research in the Teaching of English, 19*(3), 331–359.

Hyland, K. (2005). Stance and engagement: A model of interaction in academic discourse. *Discourse Studies, 2*(1), 173–192.

Hyon, S. (1996). Genres in three traditions: Implications for ESL. *TESOL Quarterly, 30*(3), 693–722.

Johns, A.M. (1991). Interpreting an English competency examination: The frustrations of an ESL science student. *Written Communication, 8*(4), 379–401.

Johns, A.M. (1993). Written argumentation for real audiences: Suggestions for teacher research and classroom practice. *TESOL Quarterly, 27*(1), 75–90.

Johns, A.M. (1997). *Text, role, and context: Developing academic literacies*. New York: Cambridge University Press.

Johns, A.M. (2001). An interdisciplinary, interinstitutional, learning communities program: Student involvement and student success. In I. Leki (Ed.), *Academic writing programs* (pp. 61–72). Alexandria, VA: TESOL.

Johns, A.M. (2002). Destabilizing and enriching students' genre theories. In A.M. Johns (Ed.), *Genre in the classroom: Multiple perspectives* (pp. 237–248). Mahwah, NJ: Lawrence Erlbaum.

Johns, A.M. (2008). Genre awareness for the novice academic student: An on-going quest. *Language Teaching, 41*(2), 237–252.

Johns, A.M., Bawarshi, A., Coe, R.M., Hyland, K., Paltridge, B., Reiff, M.J., et al. (2006). Crossing the boundaries of genre studies: Commentaries by experts. *Journal of Second Language Writing, 15*(3), 234–249.

MacBeth, K.P. (2006). Diverse, unforeseen, and quaint difficulties: The sensible responses of novices to learning to follow directions in academic writing. *Research in the Teaching of English, 27*(2), 222–251.

Melzer, D. (2003). Assignments across the curriculum: A survey of college writing [Electronic version]. *Across the Disciplines, 6*(1), 86–110.

Miller, C. (1984). Genre as social action. *Quarterly Journal of Speech, 70*(2), 151–167.

Oberem, T.L. (2004). Academic literacy demands: Case studies of faculty perceptions. Unpublished master's thesis, San Diego State University, CA.

Paltridge, B. (2006). Crossing the boundaries of genre studies [co-written with A.M. Johns, A. Bawarshi, R.M. Coe, K. Hyland, M.J. Reiff, & C.M. Tardy] *Journal of Second Language Writing, 15*(3), 234–249.

Perelman, C. & Olbrechts-Tyteca, L. (1969). *The new rhetoric: A treatise on argumentation* (J. Wilkinson & P. Weaver, Trans.). Notre Dame, France: Notre Dame University Press.

Reid, J. (1992). Helping students write for an academic audience. In P. Richard-Amato & M.A. Snow (Eds.), *The multicultural classroom* (pp. 210–221). Reading, MA: Addison-Wesley.

Schleppergrell, M. & Oliveira, L.C. (2006). An integrated language and content approach for history teachers. *Journal of English for Academic Purposes, 5*(4), 254–269.

Silva, T. (1990). Second language composition instruction: Developments, issues, and direction in ESL. In B. Kroll (Ed.), *Second language writing: Research insights for the classroom* (pp. 11–23). New York: Cambridge University Press.

15 Grammar for Generation 1.5

A Focus on Meaning

Mary J. Schleppegrell *University of Michigan*

This chapter offers ways of talking about grammar through a functional linguistics approach that enables instructors and students to analyze a text and consider alternative language choices a writer could make to further develop and strengthen it. It presents a grammatical framework that supports talk about language at the level of the clause, sentence, and text in ways that stimulate discussion about meaning and help students recognize the resources available to them in the systems of English grammar for strengthening their academic writing.

Generation 1.5 and Functional Grammar

In the classroom with generation 1.5 writers, grammar is always in the background, and often in the foreground, as students continue to make language errors as they write ever more complex texts and often make language choices that are unclear, awkward, or informal. Some instructors teach grammar regularly, others provide explanations and mark errors inconsistently, and others reject any explicit grammar teaching. Some students know rules, others can label parts of speech, and others know nothing about grammar. Grammar is talked about in research and pedagogy in ways that are ambiguous: sometimes as something a student "has," other times as something to be "learned." Sometimes grammar refers to the students' unconscious knowledge of language and sometimes to the set of prescriptive rules that we call Standard English: rules for subject–verb agreement and other formalities whose use plagues both native and non-native writers.

This chapter takes a different perspective on grammar, drawing on systemic functional linguistics (SFL) (Halliday & Mattheissen, 2004; for accessible introductions see Eggins, 2004; Lock, 1996; Schleppegrell, 2004; Thompson, 2004). Rather than treating language as a set of rules about what cannot be done with language, SFL approaches language as a set of systems that offer options that can be taken up in different ways according to the context and purposes of the writer. SFL provides a framework for recognizing meanings of three kinds that are always simultaneously presented in every use of language: meanings related to the content (experiential meaning), relationship with the reader (interpersonal meaning), and mode through which the message is communicated (textual meaning). With a focus on meaning, SFL approaches grammar through mood, modality, transitivity, conjunction, and information structuring (Martin & Rose, 2007). This enables us to look beyond clause and sentence structure at how meaning is presented in a text as a whole. Rather than focus on the forms of word classes (nouns, verbs, etc.) and errors in sentence structure, SFL offers a way of talking about alternatives for meaning that systematically correspond to a writer's goals and audience.

For example, conjunction is a system of English grammar that offers resources for making logical connections. The grammatical resources available in the system of conjunction cut across grammatical word classes; the "same" logical relationship can be expressed in conjunctions, verbs, prepositions, or nouns:

> Some children do poorly in school *because* they watch too much TV.
> Watching too much TV can *lead to* poor school performance.
> Some poor performance at school is *because of* too much TV watching.
> One *reason* for students' poor school performance is too much TV.

The consequential relationships construed in these sentences are realized in the conjunction *because*, the verb phrase *lead to*, the prepositional phrase *because of*, and the noun *reason*. None of these options is the "correct" way to express this idea. Each of them might be most appropriate in a particular situational context or at a particular point in a developing text. But having all of these options as possibilities enriches a writer's "palette" of expression. Flexibility in choosing among options comes from a richer understanding of English grammar and its systems of meaning-making.

Many generation 1.5 students live in communities where they hear and use different varieties of non-standard English. They come to the composition classroom with different voices in their minds that suggest different ways of formulating the meanings they want to present. They have knowledge about English and ways of expression that have served them well in other contexts, but many have not had an opportunity to expand their range of English grammatical resources for the tasks they face as college writers. They may be fluent in a variety of registers that reflect their experiences, but less fluent in the academic registers that construe the educational contexts in which they are now participating. Instructors can help them expand their range of grammatical options and ability to make choices that lead to more effective writing by helping them analyze their writing and by explicitly modeling different options. SFL offers constructs and analytical approaches that can help instructors systematically and explicitly present grammatical options that expand students' range of expression, building their repertoires and adding options for meaning-making to develop their potential.

Structuring Information: Organization, Logic, and Voice

One system of English grammar that a functional approach illuminates is the system of information structuring. Students who are able to explain something informally in oral language, backtracking and inserting background material as the explanation evolves, often still need to develop new ways of structuring language in order to present a highly valued expository text. One grammatical construct that SFL offers for making these options a focus of attention is theme/rheme structure, and this chapter suggests an approach instructors can take in leading students through a theme/rheme analysis of the texts they write. Focusing students' attention on theme/rheme structure provides a way of showing that every text, sentence, and clause has a point of departure from which it moves into new territory and helps writers recognize how they have organized their texts and explore other options. It can help students explore how different language choices enable them to stay focused on developing a point and to elaborate and expand their ideas, develop the logical reasoning in their texts, and consider the ways that different realizations of those possibilities in language enable them to present a more authoritative voice.

The theme is the point of departure for the clause that establishes in some sense what it is about. The rheme of the clause introduces what is new, the point of the clause. The movement from theme to rheme is called thematic progression. Because many students from generation 1.5 may not be familiar with grammatical terminology nor have experience identifying and thinking about clause structure, thematic progression is a useful construct to introduce attention to language form. Themes can be identified through their position at the beginning of a clause, and identifying themes can help students begin to recognize constituent structure in sentences and focus on different types of clauses and the meaning relationships they introduce. In addition, analysis of themes highlights another grammatical system, the system of conjunction, which contributes to the logical reasoning that the text constructs. Further, some issues of stance and voice can also be discussed through the analysis of themes. For these reasons, theme/rheme structure is a useful starting point for developing a meaning-based approach to grammar.

In this chapter, essays by two first year college writers illustrate how analysis of theme/rheme structuring can illuminate how clearly focused and developed the writers' points are, how effectively logical connections are established, and how assertive a voice the writer projects. The essays were written as examinations in first year university writing classes; one student wrote about superstition in response to class readings, and the other wrote about friends, drawing on personal experience. As examination texts, the essays were written under time pressure and not edited or revised by their authors. Such texts provide useful examples of the kind of writing an instructor might see as first drafts and so offer rich contexts for demonstrating how development of students' language resources can be proactively addressed as they revise and expand a text with feedback and instruction. Engaging in such analysis as a classroom activity, students can think about how they have developed the points they want to present and how they have constructed their logic and stance, identifying issues that can stimulate discussion and help expand their repertoires of grammatical options.

Organization and Development of Ideas

In analyzing the organization of a text we identify how writers move from clause to clause as they build toward a point. The Superstition text does not synthesize and discuss the examples the writer provides and so exemplifies the challenges a writer faces in moving into analysis. The Friends text does attempt synthesis and discussion and in doing so illustrates the challenges that writers face in controlling the complex language needed for analysis. Analysis of the theme/rheme structuring of these essays illuminates these issues.

To analyze theme, we identify the first noun phrase, verb phrase, or prepositional phrase in each clause, along with any other grammatical constituents such as adverbs or conjunctions that precede it. The rheme is then the remainder of the clause. Because identifying clauses may initially be challenging for students, as a first step they can identify the theme/rheme structure of their sentences. Below is the first paragraph of the Superstition text with the sentence themes in bold.

Paragraph One of Superstition Text
People believe in superstitions because it brings them a great deal of security. **Superstitions** to many people have magical power which give them good luck along with good health. **In** *Superstitious Minds*, Letty Cottin Pogrebin told us her mother of Hungarian descent will never allow the full moon to shine on the sleeping children. **Her mother** would use window shades or cloths to protect her children from the spirits. **The reasons** was because the full moon only shines on cemeteries. **Furthermore, in** *New Superstitions for Old*, Margaret Mead said how, "one must leave by the back door when you are going on a journey or wear a green dress when you are taking an examination." **Once again, these** are superstitions that makes people feel safer in a living environment. **At home,** I would give three bow to my deceased grandparents whenever I walk past their black and white portrait. I see that this religious practice is a form of respect, but I understand that it is also asking for protection from my ancestors.

While this text has some typical infelicities of a writer from generation 1.5, rather than focus on errors, the functional linguistics approach looks more broadly at the meanings the student presents and the systems of language that are at stake for making those meanings. Generation 1.5 writers need to be able to grapple with increasingly complex writing tasks without being discouraged by the errors that are inevitable as they attempt genres that require moving beyond narrative exemplification into argument and persuasive writing. Using a functional perspective on grammar, composition instructors can help students work on revising their drafts without having to mark or respond to every infelicity, leaving sentence-level editing for the final stages when the meaning and structure of the text are well established. By looking at this text in terms of its thematic structure and progression, the student can recognize the choices she has made in the way the information flows and can consider ways to enhance and focus what she has written, taking responsibility for revision and improvement by reflecting on and developing the meaning, rather than by correcting language forms.

Two typical strategies for thematic progression are to hold the theme constant while information is built up in a series of rhemes, or, alternatively, to introduce information in a rheme that is then taken up in a subsequent theme. The first is a constant theme strategy and the second a rheme-to-theme strategy, in which information from a rheme is recast in a new way so that the points it presents can be further developed. Both strategies are important for presenting and developing points and synthesizing and analyzing what has been presented, but the rheme-to-theme strategy is especially important for building an explanation or argument.

Variation in theme is a resource for introducing the sentence variety that is typically valued in academic writing. In this paragraph, five of the nine sentences have the subject as theme (*People, Superstitions, Her mother, The reasons, I*). Two of the themes are prepositional phrases that orient the clause and introduce a new focus to the text. *In Superstitious Minds* introduces the text the writer is responding to and *At home* shifts the focus to the writer's own context of superstition. Two themes, *Furthermore, in New Superstitions for Old,* and *Once again, these* [*superstitions*] indicate that the writer is building a case, adding to the information or underscoring a point. It is important to identify all the elements of the theme in order to consider the complexity of the theme and what it contributes to the evolution of information in the text.

The analysis of thematic progression reveals how ideas that are introduced are developed and elaborated. Students can analyze the choices they have made as they began each sentence and consider what is presented in the rhemes to evaluate how they build their main points. Recognizing how they move from theme to rheme and then back to theme can help writers chart the overall structure and flow of organization in their texts. In this case, the writer uses the generic *people* as the initiating theme of the paragraph, with the rheme introducing the notion that superstitions offer security.[1] *Superstition* and the text the writer is responding to on that topic then become thematic, and after the sentences that introduce Pogrebin's mother in the rheme, *her mother* is taken up as theme. *The reasons* introduces the point of the example about the mother. *Furthermore, in New Superstitions for Old* introduces additional examples of superstitions from Margaret Mead and *Once again, these* [*superstitions*] introduces evaluation of the examples supporting the main point of the paragraph. This is followed by another example. *At home* shifts the focus to the writer, who thematizes herself (*I*) in the concluding sentence that relates her own practice to a quest for security (*protection*).

Analysis of the information built up in the rhemes highlights the points developed in the paragraph. Security is introduced in the rheme of the first sentence and is returned to in the rhemes that elaborate the notion of security in the phrases *good luck along with good health, to protect her children from the spirits, feel safer in a living environment,* and *protection from my ancestors.* In this way the theme/rheme structure builds the point of the paragraph as a whole, with superstitions and those who enact them as themes and the notion of security built up in the rhemes.

Analyzing thematic structure reveals when a text does not clearly build toward a point. This can be illustrated by comparing paragraph one with paragraph two of the same essay. Here is paragraph two with the sentence themes again in bold.

Paragraph Two of the Superstition Text
Superstitions give a huge amount of hope to people. **At many times,** people believing in superstitions hope to avoid bad luck and bring them good luck. **According to Pogrebin,** her mother and her would tried to distract the "Evil Eye" attention in keeping their good fortune. "Evil Eye" is a jealous spirit that kept track of those who had "too much" happiness and zapped them with sickness and misery to even the score. **In doing so,** her mother practiced rituals of interference to tried to get rid of the "Evil Eye" from their home. **In addition, Margaret Mead** mentioned that no matter it's new-belief or old-belief it reflects one's wish to having something come true or to prevent something bad from happening. **Nevertheless, Superstitions** serve as a hope to block misfortune to earn luck (bring in luck).

In this paragraph, *superstitions* is the initiating theme and the notion of *giving people hope* is introduced in the first rheme. The second theme, *At many times*, is an infelicitous expression of usuality (*often* people...). The rheme again focuses on *hope*, introducing a contrast between *bad luck* and *good luck* that appears throughout the paragraph. The writer again cites Pogebrin and Mead, but does not analyze how the Pogebrin example relates to good fortune or hope. Analysis of the theme–rheme progression indicates that the example of the *Evil Eye* is not well integrated into the paragraph, as the movement from what Pogrebin and her mother did to distract the *Evil Eye* to the theme *In doing so* two sentences later is interrupted by a definition of *Evil Eye*, making the connection less cohesive. The writer makes no thematic connection to *hope* from this example in the way the previous paragraph used *The reasons* to come back to the point she was building. The last sentence, introduced with *Nevertheless*, draws a conclusion but does not connect to the examples she has used as she asserts again the point she had made in the first sentence of the paragraph.

The differences in the two paragraphs are illustrated in Tables 15.1 and 15.2, in which the clauses, and not just the sentences, are presented in their theme/rheme structure, with the subordinate clauses indented. The language that presents notions

Table 15.1 Analysis of Paragraph One

Theme	Rheme
People	believe in superstitions
because it	brings them **a great deal of security.**
Superstitions	to many people have magical power which give them **good luck along with good health.**
In *Superstitious Minds,*	Letty Cottin Pogrebin told us
her mother of Hungarian descent	will never allow the full moon to shine on the sleeping children.
Her mother	would use window shades or cloths **to protect her children from the spirits.**
The reasons	was because the full moon only shines on cemeteries.
Furthermore, in *New Superstitions for Old,*	Margaret Mead said
how, "one	must leave by the back door when you are going on a journey or wear a green dress when you are taking an examination."[i]
Once again, these	are superstitions that makes people **feel safer in a living environment.**
At home, I	would give three bow to my deceased grandparents
whenever I	walk past their black and white portrait.
I	see
that this religious practice	as a form of respect,
but I	understand
that it	is also asking for **protection from my ancestors.**

Note

i The clauses in the quote from Mead are not analyzed for their theme/rheme structuring, as these do not represent the student writer's language choices.

Table 15.2 Analysis of Paragraph Two

Theme	Rheme
Superstitions	give a huge amount of **hope** to people.
At many times, people	believing in superstitions **hope to avoid bad luck and bring them good luck.**
According to Pogrebin,	her mother and her would tried to distract the "Evil Eye" attention in **keeping their good fortune.**
"Evil Eye"	is a jealous spirit that kept track of those who had "too much" happiness and zapped them with sickness and misery to even the score.
In doing so, her mother	practiced rituals of interference to tried to get rid of the "Evil Eye" from their home.
In addition, Margaret Mead	mentioned that no matter it's new-belief or old-belief it reflects **one's wish to having something come true or to prevent something bad from happening.**
Nevertheless, Superstitions	serve as a **hope to block misfortune to earn luck (bring in luck).**

about security and hope in the clause rhemes is in bold. Students can create charts like this to analyze their choice of theme and assess how they are building their points. As Table 15.1 shows, the first paragraph returns consistently to the notion of security, but uses no themes that suggest analysis of the examples. The second paragraph does not relate the Pogrebin example to the notion of hope, leaving that example unanalyzed.

By analyzing theme/rheme structure, writers can explore how they have developed and elaborated a point by looking at what is presented in the rhemes and how they have moved from theme to rheme and back again to theme. They can also see which points are elaborated and which are not, as themes remain constant or change and as information presented in the rhemes is picked up in a subsequent theme. Where writers keep a constant theme and develop information about it, they are accumulating information toward a point, and they can assess whether they have provided sufficient development. Where information in the rheme is taken up in the following theme, writers can look at the point they are developing and whether it is clearly focused. In these two paragraphs, such analysis can help the writer recognize that the notions of security and hope are never taken up in themes. This indicates that she has not discussed or evaluated these notions or their relationships to superstition. The lack of security or hope in the themes indicates that the writer has not drawn a concluding point that evaluates the importance or significance of the two constructs that she is associating with superstition.

Drawing a larger point often means constructing a theme that distills or condenses the point the writer has been building toward in an abstract noun or complex nominal group. The themes in the Superstition paragraphs are mainly simple nominal constituents, with little expansion, modification, or complexity. Only two themes, *The reasons* and *this religious practice* (in paragraph one) make cohesive links that build on what has been said and recast it in a more abstract form. This is an area for potential intervention and development of language resources. Nominal group complexity is a distinguishing feature of academic language, as students need to be able to construct themes that are more than simple nouns or pronouns in order to move from narrative to expository modes of writing (Schleppegrell, 2004). Analysis of theme can be a springboard for talking with students about nominal group structure, complexity, abstraction, and movement toward more academic language choices.

We can see some development of more complex themes in the essay on friends. Below is the first paragraph with sentence themes of the Friends text in bold.

Paragraph One of the Friends Text

I have all types of friends. **Some of them** are very honest that they usually tell the truth. **They** tell the truth probably is because they want to keep friendship forever. **These kinds of friends** feel that why lie to me, later on I still will know the truth. **They** scare that if they lie to me, our relationship will end. **On the other hand, some of my friends** do lie to me all the time. **They** feel that if they tell the truth, they might hurt my feelings. **However, I** believe that lies and truth can be harmful and helpful. I receive many benefits of these two types of friendship. **Well, sometimes it** is good for me not to know the truth so I won't feel bad. **But hearing the truth** can give me knowing what to do to escape from happening. **Thus, I** prefer to have friends who tell me the truth than friends who tell lies to me.

The student compares two kinds of friends: those who are always truthful, even if the truth hurts, and those who lie in order not to offend or lose the friendship. The writer evaluates each of these types of friends and concludes that she prefers the truthful ones. The organizational structure takes the writer (*I*) as point of departure, focuses in turn on one kind of friend and then on the other, and then gives the writer's judgment about the two types of friends. The *friends* that are introduced in the rheme of the first clause are picked up again in the theme of the second clause as *some of them*, with the rhemes of these clauses describing the attributes of the honest friends, who, in various forms (*they, these kinds of friend*) remain the theme until the connector *On the other hand* changes the focus to *friends who lie*, with information then built up about them.

The theme *However, I* introduces the writer's analysis as she evaluates the two kinds of friends and the value she places on honesty, and the theme *Thus, I* introduces an explicit conclusion. These are key moves in which the writer is analyzing and drawing out larger points from her discussion of the two types of friends, so they are worth looking at in greater detail. Table 15.3 is an analysis of the theme/rheme structure of the clauses in the final sentences of the Friends text.

Analysis and evaluation are difficult moves that put stress on the grammatical resources of the developing writer. In order to draw conclusions, the writer needs to construct the abstract notions that she is going to evaluate. We can recognize the writer's attempt here and the challenges it presents. She uses two thematic nominal constituents that are abstractions: *lies and truth*, and *hearing the truth*. These complex noun phrases enable her to go beyond just reporting what she and her friends do, feel, and want, in order to generalize and make the judgments that are necessary in exposi-

Table 15.3 Themes and Rhemes in the Final Sentences of the Friends Text

Theme	Rheme
However, I	believe
that lies and truth	can be harmful and helpful.
I	receive many benefits of these two types of friendship.
Well, sometimes it	is good for me not to know the truth
so I	won't feel bad.
But hearing the truth	can give me knowing what to do to escape from happening.
Thus, I	prefer to have friends who tell me the truth than friends who tell lies to me.

tory writing. She is focused on drawing conclusions from and evaluating the behaviors she has described, and so needs more abstract language than the *friends* and herself (*I*), and needs to construct complex sentences that present her analysis. Building from an example by constructing an abstraction in a nominal constituent that captures the point of the example is a means of doing this. The theme *hearing the truth* draws a contrast with *is good for me not to know the truth* in the previous sentence, and casting this in a nominal form allows the writer to evaluate the benefit of knowing the truth. At the same time, she is challenged in drawing on grammatical resources that will enable her to effectively accomplish this important move. She uses the abstract themes but has difficulty constructing the rest of the clause in each case (*lies and truth can be harmful and helpful; hearing the truth can give me knowing what to do to escape from happening*). The analysis of theme/rheme structuring highlights these infelicitous constructions in the rhemes and suggests where modeling of grammatical options would be valuable.

Logical Reasoning

The theme/rheme analysis also helps students analyze their reasoning and the logic they have employed. Conjunctions and connectors often appear in clause themes and are an important resource for clause combining, helping a writer make logical links from one clause or one part of the text to another. Conjunctive meanings can be categorized as additive, temporal, comparative, and consequential, and analyzed according to whether they construct an external logic (related to events outside the text) or internal logic (constructing the logic of the text itself) (Martin & Rose, 2007). As in the Superstition and Friends essays, connectors in academic writing often construct the logic of the unfolding text through internal conjunction that helps readers recognize how the writer is building the explanation or argument.

In the Superstition text, for example, the logic of both paragraphs is an internal logic of addition, the accumulation of examples to support the idea that superstitions bring feelings of security and hope. This logic is signaled in the internal conjunction constructed with *Furthermore, Once again,* and *In addition. Furthermore* and *In addition* introduce examples and *Once again,* although temporal in its surface meaning, introduces a reiteration of the writer's point about superstitions making people feel secure and helps construct the internal logic of the text from the writer's point of view. These connectors signal in yet another way that the writer is just adding examples, not engaging in analysis and synthesis to build to a larger point about superstition. Only the phrase *The reason was because* constructs any causal thinking, and this draws the intermediate point about the particular example, rather than reasoning about security. No connectors in either paragraph (except *Nevertheless*) indicate that any logical connection other than just addition of information is being developed.

The connector *Nevertheless* at the end of the second paragraph would seem to suggest that the writer has presented some evidence that might be construed as contradicting her main point about superstition, and that she wants to underscore that in spite of that evidence, her main thesis holds. However, this concessive meaning is not established in the text. In fact, the example from Mead does not contradict the overall point she is building, and so *Nevertheless* is an inappropriate connector to introduce the concluding sentence.

The writer of the Friends text has used a number of conjunctions to scaffold its logic, including *because, if, On the other hand, However, Well, so, But,* and *Thus.* From this list, it is clear that the logic of the text is a logic of comparison and consequence, stating conditions, comparing, contrasting, and drawing conclusions, and not just a logic of adding information. The theme *On the other hand, some of my friends* signals a pivot point, introducing the other set of friends that will serve as the point of comparison. *However* signals yet another turning point in the paragraph, where the writer moves into analysis of the two types of friendships. But again in this essay, the contrast/concessive meaning expected when *however* is chosen is not established. Following the statement that some of her friends believe they will hurt her feelings by telling the truth, the *however* leads the reader to expect something that counters that belief, rather than the statement that both lies and truth have their advantages and disadvantages.

Analysis of what is being connected through conjunctions can help students recognize the logic they are constructing. Formal and informal registers use connectors and conjunctions in very different ways to structure a text and present logical relationships. Second language writers have been shown to overuse connectors and to use them in ways more typical of informal spoken registers than registers of academic writing (Schleppegrell, 1996). The focus on themes can help students analyze whether the choice of connector matches the meaning they intend. They can look at the overall logic of the text and how it is supported and presented. Where a change of focus is intended, writers can think about the choice of marker and whether it effectively guides the reader in recognizing the shift. They can ask themselves whether the logic they are constructing fits with the points they are developing and identify places where further work may be needed to develop the logical meaning.

The same meanings construed by connectors can also be incorporated into a clause through choice of verbs or nouns (Achugar & Schleppegrell, 2005). For example, in the Friends text, instead of *They tell the truth probably is because,* the writer might use the nominal *Their motivation for telling the truth is.* Building up a wider repertoire of vocabulary that constructs logical relationships is an important part of academic language development. When a topic is assigned that elicits particular semantic motifs, such as the motif of comparison in the Friends text, the language needed for this kind of meaning can become a focus of instruction to help writers develop the grammatical resources that enable presentation of a point like *lies and truth can be harmful and helpful* in a more effective way. Comparison is complex, calling on resources that involve more than just conjunctions and connectors. Determiners (*some* lies can be harmful; *other* lies can be helpful), adverbs (lying is *more* harmful; *so* harmful), and conjunctions (lies can be harmful, *but so* can the truth; lies are harmful, *whereas* the truth is helpful; the truth is helpful, *similarly*, lies can sometimes also be helpful, etc.) as well as adjectives and nouns help construct similarity and difference. The clausal structure of comparison involves complex embedding (lies are *more harmful than the truth*). Students can explore ways of construing the "same" meaning in different wording and will need many opportunities to engage with comparative meaning to develop these language resources for academic writing.

Stance and Voice

The thematic analysis can also reveal something about the voice the writer has adopted. In the Friends text, for example, the sentence *Well, sometimes it is good for me not to know the truth so I won't feel bad* is an attempt at concession, but including *Well* in the theme introduces an oral-like tone of informality and interaction. The discourse marker *well* is not typically used for this concessive meaning in academic text. Such informal expressions often occur at the beginning of a sentence and are highlighted by analysis of themes. The oral tone of the essay can be addressed by working with alternative ways of construing the intended meanings.

Another aspect of voice that the thematic analysis can illuminate is how the writer uses her own feeling and thinking and the words, thoughts, and feelings of others, as clauses that project saying, thinking, and feeling emerge from the analysis. The writer of the Superstition text, for example, projects the views of *people, Pogrebin, Mead,* and herself (*I*), and the writer of the Friends text projects the views of the *two kinds of friends* and herself. Table 15.4 gives the themes of both the projecting clauses and the projected clauses at four points in the Friends paragraph where the writer constructs clauses that report the thinking or feeling of her friends or herself through the verbs *feel, scare,* and *believe.*

Analyzing the clauses that project the thinking, feeling, and saying of others can help writers consider whose voices they have included and analyze how they have presented their own positions and judgments. Analysis of the projected clauses can help the writer explore alternative strategies for incorporating these points into their texts. For example, the representation of speech in *Why lie to me* might become a focus of attention. The theme/rheme structure of the clauses that are projected through verbs of thinking, feeling, and saying can also be analyzed in terms of their contributions to textual organization and logical reasoning. Here the themes of the projected clauses indicate that they introduce the conditions and consequences of telling the truth or lying (*why, if they*). Many infelicities occur in the construal of the conditions, making this another opportunity for exploration of the grammar of conditionality and alternative ways of presenting conditions.

Table 15.4 Friends Text

Theme	Rheme
These kinds of friends	feel
that why	lie to me,
later on I	still will know the truth.
They	scare
that if they	lie to me,
our relationship	will end.
On the other hand, some of my friends	do lie to me all the time.
They	feel
that if they	tell the truth,
they	might hurt my feelings.
However, I	believe
that lies and truth	can be harmful and helpful.

Many academic writing tasks ask students to use and synthesize information from other sources, whether from class readings, as in the Superstition text, or from their own experience, as in the Friends text. There are many ways to introduce such information, but developing writers often rely heavily on verbs of saying, thinking, and feeling to project the views of others. When these projections mainly offer evidence and examples, and instructors could work with the writers to explore alternative ways such evidence might be presented.

Composition instructors often advise writers to avoid projecting their own views through a verb of thinking such as believe. We can see the validity of such advice when we look at the theme of the projected clause in the sentence *I believe that lies and truth can be harmful and helpful.* Here the writer is summarizing her main point, and as discussed above, has constructed a noun phrase (*lies and truth*) that incorporates the points of comparison. Making this nominal construction the point of departure for the main clause, rather than a projection of the writer's beliefs in a subordinate clause could be encouraged, as it would enable the writer to state the position more assertively. Projecting clauses such as *I believe* and *I think* often construe a modality of possibility in the same way *maybe* or *probably* would, and so attenuate the force of the conclusion that is being drawn (Schleppegrell, 2002). This is why such projections are typically discouraged by instructors.

The key to being authoritative in writing is to construct a stance that is appropriate for a particular task. Much more could be said about the construal of stance and voice, as other grammatical systems such as mood and modality are also involved in important ways. The focus here has been on how analysis of themes can help writers assess the use of some informal expressions and enable analysis of the way the writer's own and other voices are incorporated into the text.

Summary

Dividing clauses into themes and rhemes reveals the point of departure for each new clause and helps the writer assess how well information flows from clause to clause, identify the logical connections being made, and assess some aspects of the stance and voice the text presents. This chapter has shown how an analysis of thematic progression and the elements of theme and rheme can help a writer focus on organization, elaboration of ideas, logical reasoning, and presentation of an authoritative stance. To organize and develop their points, writers can analyze the information they are developing in clause rhemes. They can ask whether they have recast information in a nominalization or complex noun phrase as they draw their points or make judgments. They can practice naming the notions they are exemplifying to raise the level of abstraction and analysis in their texts. They can analyze the logical connections they have introduced and assess the overall reasoning they construct. They can evaluate whether they have established appropriate related meanings in the clauses connected by conjunctions, especially concessive and other complex meanings. They can identify the language choices that construe an informal stance and decide whether that is the stance they want to present. They can assess the level of formality of their themes and analyze the clauses that introduce thinking, feeling, and saying in order to examine the role these projections play in the explanations and arguments they have developed. Each of these ways into the text enables them to consider the meanings they have constructed and use concrete tools for engaging in deeper analysis and development of their ideas and perspectives.

Conclusions

This chapter has suggested an approach to discussion about language choices that can help students see how their organization of ideas, elaboration of key points into analysis and synthesis, logical reasoning, and an authoritative stance are all dependent on the language resources they choose. The point of a functional analysis is to help students see how meaning changes with changes in wording, and how those changes in meaning may be related to stance, logic, or organization as well as content. The goal is to foster discussion about language choices and their effects, giving students a more nuanced perspective on the meanings they are construing. Writers in the generation 1.5 classroom bring language resources that can be expanded as they incorporate new constellations of features that enable them to participate in new contexts. SFL provides a theoretically grounded basis for presenting students with different possibilities from the language systems that are available to them and for helping writers see the power of different grammatical options. The students can then make their own choices about the language they want to take up in relation to their purposes and needs. Language is a powerful resource for construing meanings of different kinds, and an enhanced linguistic repertoire can enable students to make meaning in new ways.

Acknowledgment

I would like to thank Anne Curzan, Anne Gere, Megan Sweeney, and the editors of this volume for helpful comments on an earlier draft of this chapter, without holding them in any way responsible for the final product.

Note

1. This is done in two clauses, each with a theme/rheme structure, as seen in Table 15.1, in which themes are listed by clause rather than by sentence. The theme of the second clause includes *because* and the *it* that refers back to *belief in superstitions*; the rheme introduces the notion of *security*.

References

Achugar, M. & Schleppegrell, M.J. (2005). Beyond connectors: The construction of *cause* in history textbooks. *Linguistics and Education, 16*(3), 298–318.

Eggins, S. (2004). *An introduction to systemic functional linguistics* (2nd ed.). London: Pinter.

Halliday, M.A.K. & Matthiessen, C.M.I.M. (2004). *An introduction to functional grammar* (3rd ed.). London: Arnold.

Lock, G. (1996). *Functional English grammar: An introduction for second language teachers.* Cambridge, UK: Cambridge University Press.

Martin, J.R. & Rose, D. (2007). *Working with discourse: Meaning beyond the clause* (2nd ed.). London: Continuum.

Schleppegrell, M.J. (1996). Conjunction in spoken English and ESL writing. *Applied Linguistics, 17*(3), 271–285.

Schleppegrell, M.J. (2002). Challenges of the science register for ESL students: Errors and meaning making. In M.J. Schleppegrell & M.C. Colombi (Eds.), *Developing advanced literacy in first and second languages: Meaning with power* (pp. 119–142). Mahwah, NJ: Lawrence Erlbaum.

Schleppegrell, M.J. (2004). *The language of schooling: A functional linguistics perspective.* Mahwah, NJ: Lawrence Erlbaum.

Thompson, G. (2004). *Introducing functional grammar* (2nd ed.). London: Arnold.

16 Working with Generation 1.5

Pedagogical Principles and Practices

Sugie Goen-Salter, Patricia Porter, and Deborah vanDommelen San Francisco State University

Our work with generation 1.5 students and their teachers began over a decade ago when we jointly served on San Francisco State University's (SFSU) Committee on Written English Proficiency. As part of our committee work, we embarked on an examination of the progress of students placed in SFSU's ESL and basic writing programs toward meeting the University's written English requirements. In our examination, we identified many students who were different from international students in that they brought to the classroom a comfortable fluency, an ease with the English language and American popular culture alongside a rich and varied background from growing up in multilingual and multicultural environments. But they were also different from native speaker basic writers, for they had characteristics that marked them as second language writers, characteristics that all too often are inappropriately subsumed in composition research and literature under the label of academic "under preparation." We initially referred to this group as long-term bilinguals, but along with a growing number of researchers adopted the term "generation 1.5."

As a follow-up to our committee report, we conducted a two-year research study focusing on generation 1.5 students and their teachers (Goen, Porter, Swanson & van-Dommelen, 2002). We conducted the study with two goals in mind, and with the overall aim to help us better address the obstacles these students face in becoming proficient speakers, readers, and writers of English. The first goal of our study was to acknowledge these students' presence on our campus by profiling in greater detail the linguistic and educational experiences they bring to their college studies. We collected and analyzed language profile and educational history data from a sample of 85 first-year students enrolled in basic writing and ESL courses. We also conducted a number of follow-up interviews with students, a component of which asked them to respond in writing to prompts about their perceptions of themselves as language users.

Our analysis of the survey of students' language use and their responses to the writing prompts identified a group of students for whom we adopted the term generation 1.5. Comprising 79% of the total number of students we surveyed, they are students who have varied ways and contexts in which they use language. They move in and out of different languages depending on the situation and their relationships to the people with whom they are communicating. For a majority, English may play a minor role in their language use outside school, or what they identify as a "home language" may be the language they use primarily at home, but not the language they use with peers or at school. The versions of English that they and their teenage friends use is filled with what one student referred to as "short cuts" in terms of vocabulary and form, hybrid forms of English that reflect the urban American youth culture that they identify with. Our survey showed that these students may be using language differently from recently arrived ESL students who are still in the process of acquiring oral fluency. Even so, the fact that 42% of these generation 1.5 students consider their "home language" their best language suggests that they are using English in a more limited way than we might imagine. Our survey also indicated that these are students who, by and large, are comfortable communicating in the oral mode (whether in their home language and/or English), but who lack confidence and skill in reading and writing in any of their languages. Sixty-nine percent of the generation 1.5 students reported oral fluency in English and 95% reported oral fluency in their home language. By contrast, two-thirds of these students ranked their literacy proficiency as weak in both English and their home language. Despite this reported lack of confidence in reading and writing in English, 67% of these students indicated that they are most comfortable reading and writing in English compared to their home language.

The second goal of our study was to bring together faculty from both ESL and basic writing in an effort to start bridging the disciplinary gap between these two programs. In a one-day workshop, 48 instructors from both our ESL and native speaker composition programs examined the tendencies, preconceptions, and assumptions that inform the ways we respond to the writing of second language students (for more information about this workshop, see Goen et al., 2002). The results of the workshop revealed what may be the biggest challenges for us at SFSU. In working with generation 1.5 learners, we need to get outside the confines of our own institutional categories, which lead us to label writing as "ESL" or "basic writing" based on the quantity and/or type of error. And, as we make placement decisions and curricular choices, we need to move beyond what we see on the page to include thoughtful consideration of the person behind the words. Too often, by assuming that as educators we know what is "best" for their literacy development, we can undermine students' self-confidence and even thwart their progress by not paying attention to what they say about themselves as language users and what support they need to attain greater proficiency in English.

This increased awareness of the long-term bilingual students on our campus, coupled with opening up this dialogue between programs, has led both directly and indirectly to a number of changes on the San Francisco State campus. In the past, once entering students were placed via established institutional criteria (e.g., English placement test scores, number of years in the U.S., etc.) into one of two parallel pathways to meeting the university's writing requirement—either composition/basic writing or ESL—they remained throughout their college career in whichever program they began. It was a rare occurrence for a student who was initially placed in basic writing to transfer to an ESL class, or vice versa. And it was even more unusual for the student's own perceptions and experiences as a language user to be taken into account in placement decisions. We have since instituted mechanisms for increasing communication between the two programs, making the barriers between the two programs more permeable, changing assessment and placement policies so students meet with an advisor individually and have substantial input into their own placement, and providing support to faculty working with second language writers in their classrooms. San Francisco State has also made changes to our ESL and basic writing programs, not the least of which is a change to the ESL program name. To help dismantle some of the punitive and negative associations with the institutional label of "ESL," the program is now called Composition for Multilingual Students (CMS). To help students focus on grammar-for-writing conventions within the context of their upper level course work, the CMS program has developed adjunct workshop classes for three reading/composition courses. In addition, the basic writing program, consisting of a vast majority of multilingual students, has fully integrated what used to be separate reading and writing classes into a single curriculum that offers baccalaureate credit. The integrated program encourages the formation of peer communities, allowing students to learn from each other in an enriched literacy environment. This integrated program benefits both native speakers of English and generation 1.5 learners by offering them extended opportunities to interact with each other using all four channels of communication. They get to hear, speak, read, and write English in a community of trusted peers that develops over time. As the CMS and integrated programs have evolved, so has the Learning Assistance Center (LAC) Writing Workshop Program, which offers a comfortable small group setting in which groups of four to five students meet twice weekly with graduate students from MATESOL and/or Composition. These workshops were originally conceptualized as grammar workshops designed primarily for ESL students. They have since evolved into more general writing workshops that strive to bridge "the disciplinary gap," mentioned earlier, by providing a learning environment that supports the goals of both the CMS and integrated reading and writing programs.

The institutional changes we've made so far provide a vital infrastructure for working with generation 1.5 students inside classrooms and/or learning assistance centers. The rest of this chapter looks more closely at this work, specifically on principles and practices for classroom teachers.

Principle I: Use Knowledge of Students' Backgrounds to Inform Teaching and Classroom Practice

We have found that students often come to language classes with the previously conceived idea that they are entering an arena where their language histories and practices are commonly seen as deficits rather than as strengths. From working with generation 1.5 students in our classes and in the tutoring center, we have found that not only is it critical for effective teaching to find out about students' educational backgrounds and diverse language histories and practices, but also it is important to provide an opportunity for students to comfortably describe how they identify themselves. Through the information we learn from students, we have come to recognize the rich diversity of this heterogeneous group and have become better equipped to listen well, to avoid making assumptions, and to respond to learners as individuals. Described below are activities that allow students to become more proficient in academic English by building directly upon their competence and experiences as multi-language users. These activities are based on the following teaching practices:

- developing surveys to get to know students and inform classroom practice;
- developing writing topics for students to explore their language use and identities.

Activity 1. Using a Survey to Get Background Information

We have found student surveys to be helpful as a quick reference for planning in-class activities, for framing questions on content and grammar, for developing reading and writing assignments, and for preparing for student–teacher conferences. The survey shown in the handout for Activity 1 invites students to share information about their educational and language backgrounds as well as about their experiences with reading and writing and in other English classes. In response to our request to write about personal factors that might determine how well they do in class, students' comments such as "I need help scheduling study time because I have to work in the evenings," or "I have to take my little brother to school on Monday and Wednesday mornings," provide valuable information and help us be more tolerant and appreciative of the complexities of students' lives. Their responses may also lead us to plan in-class time-management activities coupled with reading and writing assignments, for example, a daily journal that helps students explore and comment on their patterns and successes in managing their time responsibly.

Handout for Activity 1, Student survey

Your Student Info

Family Name: First Name: Nickname you want to be called in class:
Student ID: e-mail: Phone Number:
Class level: Freshman   Sophomore   Junior   Senior   Grad   Other:
Major (or major you're considering, if you're not sure yet):
How many units are you taking this semester?
Are you a California resident, out of state student, short-term exchange student, or an international student pursuing a degree?

Your College Reading and Writing Experiences
What English classes have you taken at this school?
What English classes have you taken at other schools over the past few years?
Name of last college attended and last course you took:
Have you worked with a tutor before?   Yes   No   If so, where?
Do you think you'd like to work with a tutor this semester?   Yes   No   Not sure
How can I help you do well in this class?
Are you working this semester?   Yes   No   If so, how many hours/week?
On the back of the paper, please write about one or two things that would be good for me to know about: your work schedule, family responsibilities, other commitments, or information about your learning style.

Your Language Background: If you speak a language in addition to English:
What language(s) do you speak in addition to English?
Do you read and write another language? If so, which one(s)?
What language(s) would you consider your "home" language(s)?
What's your strongest language for listening and speaking?
   English___ My other language(s) ___ Both (all) are strong ___

What's your strongest language for reading and writing?
  English___ My other language(s) ___ Both (all) are strong

If you were born in another country, please write a bit below about where you were born, when you arrived, and when you started school in this country. This background will help in planning different types of activities we do in class.

Activities 2 and 3. Writing About Your Languages and Your Language Identity

In working to set a tone of openness and to reinforce the positive aspects of students' multilingualism that we begin to acknowledge with the student survey, we often get students writing early in the semester with informal topics such as the ones described in the handouts for Activities 2 and 3, which ask students to write about the languages they use and about their language identities. These writing tasks are always preceded by some pre-writing warm-up activity such as brainstorming, clustering, and/or discussing or interviewing in pairs. The results of activities such as these warm-ups and informal writing tasks are that students get to know each other, discover parallels in their backgrounds, and feel that their linguistic practices are appreciated. Teachers receive the benefit of gaining a deeper understanding of the complexities of students' language histories, an understanding that directly influences the multiplicity and diversity of instructional options that teachers can make available to students.

Handout for Activity 2, Writing about your languages

Directions:
Write about the languages you use on a daily basis at home, at work, at school, and/or with friends. Discuss the situations when you use a particular language and how you feel when you use it. Include the following in your paper:

- what the languages are
- which language
  - you feel is your *best* language and why
  - you are *most comfortable speaking* and why
  - you are *most comfortable reading* and why
  - you are *most comfortable writing* and why.

Handout for Activity 3, Writing about your language identity

Background:
In our group discussion, we brainstormed ideas about identity and the words we choose to identify ourselves. We also talked about how other people identify us and how we feel about the names they use.

Directions:
Please respond to the statements below in the space provided. Then, in writing, on a separate piece of paper, explain the reasons why you answered the way you

did. Use details and examples from your own experience as support for your ideas. (1 to 2 pages)

1. I am a native speaker of English.   Yes   No
2. I am a non-native speaker of English. Yes   No
3. I speak English as a second language. Yes   No
4. I am an ESL student.   Yes   No
5. I am bilingual or multilingual.   Yes   No
6. I am none of the above. I am _____.
   (the word(s) that best describe(s) your language background)

The complex linguistic background of generation 1.5 students and the role English plays in their lives are illustrated by the written response to the topic in Activity 2 by a student named Wan, who is multilingual, names English as her "best" language, and refers to Chinese as "my own language."

> There are different ways language can be use in communication. The language I use in school, family, and friends are all different. In school, I use English to talk to my instructors and fellow classmates. At home, I speak three different languages. I speak English to my brothers and sister, while speaking Mandarin to my parents and speaking Laotian with my brother-in-law. With all these different languages I use in my daily life, I find I am most comfortable with the language I use with my friends.
>
> When I speak to my friends, I always use English. Even if some of my friends are Chinese and can speak the same language as I can, I have never spoke Chinese with any of my friends. I find myself to communicate better in English than my own language. When I speak to my friends, I don't pay attention to my grammars. We often talk to each other using slangs, that others might find it weird. But to us, it's fun because instead of saying one complete word, we tend to say a short cut of the word. Although I find myself speaking English, my best language, to my friends, it has somewhat affected me in my grammars.

The snapshot profiles provided to us by students have been invaluable in helping us shape in-class activities and out-of-class assignments. Knowing which students are more comfortable speaking English helps us form small groups for oral-based activities such as interviews or discussions. With this information, we are able to create groups with a balance of confident and less secure learners. Written assignments can be more effective when we plan out steps carefully for learners who struggle with the academic conventions of research, analysis, and explication. In these assignments, we offer ample time for breaking down the task and recycling academic skills, such as quoting, citing sources, and interpreting text. Knowing more about our students also helps us develop more varied and appropriate options for assessing their learning, such as letting "products" be in the form of oral and visual presentations in addition to written work, utilizing such informal writing venues as blogs or iLearn forums (SFSU's course management environment) and not just formal papers or other high-stakes assessments.

Principle II: Help Students Raise Awareness—Connections Between Learning Preferences, Spoken Language, and Written Discourse

Prior to the committee work and study previously described, we began to notice a shift in the population in our ESL classrooms: many resident "long-term bilingual" students, while not proficient in traditional academic skills, began emerging as orally proficient in English, communicating verbally with ease and facility. This was in contrast to their international counterparts, who often lacked this level of comfort with spoken English but nevertheless excelled in their ability to identify and produce rule-based grammatical forms. Since the residents had acquired English in ways similar to native speakers, learning and applying the rules of grammar seemed foreign to them.

Acknowledging the struggles generation 1.5 learners face in learning the conventions of academic English, we, as ESL and Composition faculty, began to evaluate our traditional approaches to teaching. As a result of assessing our practices, we have worked to develop a different pedagogical model that better serves students by acknowledging and drawing upon their strengths as oral communicators and by helping them make connections between how they speak and how they write. In approaching this second principle, we have followed these practices:

- developing activities that help students discover learning preferences: oral, aural, and written modes;
- using activities and assignments that help students make connections between how they speak and how they write.

In both the classroom and the tutoring center, we use Activities 4, 5, and 6, which ask students to participate in both oral and written modes, thus starting the process of raising awareness about the differences. We find these activities useful for both students and teachers to get to know one another, for students possibly to discover learning style preferences, and as techniques for drawing on students' backgrounds to promote language learning.

Activity 4. Warm-Up: Comparing Language Backgrounds and Ways of Learning

On one of the first days of class, we use a warm-up discussion activity in which students report on their language learning experience with English and their other languages. We set up three columns on the board with the following headings: (1) Name (2) What language did you learn first? (3) How/when did you learn English? Students go up to the board and fill in information underneath each column. When they are done writing, the whole class examines the similarities and differences.

In our experience, this simple activity evokes much discussion and often discovery. Students have responded to the question about their first language with traditional names of languages, but also with such names as "Ebonics" or "Spanglish." When responding to the third question, students also respond in varied ways: "at home," "in preschool by reading/writing," "by mimicking teachers," or "from the dictionary." The responses from this activity create a grounded context for Activity 5.

Activity 5. Writing About Learning in the Aural Mode Compared With Learning in the Written Mode

In this activity, students engage in varying levels of self-discovery as they learn about themselves and find common ground with peers. This activity asks students to come up with and discuss definitions of "eye learner" and "ear learner," interview a partner about their learning, and report on the interview (as indicated in the handout for Activity 5). To follow up, we put the summaries generated in step four of the activity on the board, or on the overhead projector, to discuss the content and/or grammar patterns. (See Principle III for approaches to using student writing for teaching.)

Handout for Activity 5, Writing about learning in the aural mode compared with learning in the written mode

Directions:
1. With a partner, use the information from the introductory activity about how you learned English to come up with two definitions: one for "eye learner" and the other for "ear learner." Write your definitions on the board.
2. As a large group, discuss the different ideas on the board to decide on two definitions that work for the class.
3. With your partner, interview each other using the following question: Are you an "eye learner" or "ear learner" of English? Ask your partner to explain why. Take notes.
4. For homework (on paper or overhead transparencies), write a summary of your interview.

Below are samples of student summaries in response to Activity 5:

Fernando learns better by eye learning. He said that with ear learning only he easily gets bored, but with eye learning he learns more. He noticed he was a better learner by certain types of eye learning when he was 14 yrs old, when he read a book and understood nothing, but when he watched a movie and listened to the characters, he understood it all.

Loan is an eye and ear learner that uses both of her learning experiences to learn more. She uses both most of the time, but she can adopt any of the learning techniques depending on the situation. She said that for chemistry she uses both and for grammar only uses eye learning. She realize that she uses both last night when she answer the homework question.

The student responses are revealing for them and for us with the contradictions in the students' written analyses becoming rich sources for class discussion of learning styles and individual patterns. In addition, we have found that these activities provide useful context for more structured activities such as 6 and 7, and they also lay the groundwork for learners to begin to discover their strengths as oral communicators in relationship to the challenges they face with written academic tasks.

Activity 6. Dictocomp: Listening, Reconstructing Text, Negotiating Meaning and Form

We have found the following two activities to be useful vehicles for capitalizing on generation 1.5 learners' oral fluency, helping them pay attention to language in order to express ideas and learn conventions of written academic discourse.

In a dictocomp activity, students listen to a text read two or more times by the teacher, take notes on key words as they listen, then working in pairs or small groups, negotiate meaning and form to reconstruct their own text based on the notes they have taken (Wajnryb, 1990). The text can be a piece of adapted student writing, an excerpt from a reading, or a brief paragraph constructed by the teacher. The text that the students produce conveys the meaning of the original but is not necessarily identical to it, as is expected when learners respond to a dictation.

Steps for the dictocomp:

1. The teacher reads the whole text through at a normal pace, pausing slightly between sentences. Students don't write.
2. The teacher rereads the text at a normal pace, pausing briefly between clauses. Students take notes.
3. Students, in pairs, triads, or small groups, compare notes to reconstruct the text. Groups can write on the board, on overhead transparencies, or at their desks.
4. After constructing their texts, students apply their active editing strategies, negotiate form and meaning with one another, and revise and correct their work.
5. As a class, students, with the teacher guiding, compare different versions, examining the relationship between form and meaning, between spoken word and written text. Students look for evidence of oral forms or patterns in their written work: dropped endings, missing subjects, missing time expressions, or joining words.

Telling students to take notes on "key" information only (not complete sentences) when introducing a dictocomp activity helps learners develop active listening skills. Teachers can also help students pay attention to both content and form by asking them in a pre-listening activity to identify the language forms or features they have been focusing on in the course and discussing how to identify them during the reading by the teacher. For example, teachers might ask students to notice the time expressions that occur during the preliminary reading of the text and think about what tenses are used to show appropriate time–tense relationships. During the text reconstruction, students will negotiate both content and grammar, thus having to pay attention to both features simultaneously, and thus raising awareness of links between form and meaning. (For additional examples and information about dictocomp activities, see Porter and vanDommelen (2005).) Below is a sample dictocomp text adapted from student writing that could be used to help students focus on verb endings and/or understanding appropriate shifts between present and past tenses.

I interviewed Don yesterday about what it means to be either an ear learner or an eye learner. He has some interesting ideas about this topic, mostly because he speaks two different languages that he learned in two different ways. For his first language, he speaks Cambodian, and he has been learning this language at home since he was a baby. From learning a language as a child, he understands that you listen, imitate, and repeat what others say. Learning Cambodian made him an ear learner. Yet, he also learned English when he was in grade school. He learned the language of English differently from the way he learned Cambodian. He learned by reading, which requires seeing then writing, and by memorizing, which requires studying worksheets and reading notes. Learning English made him an eye learner as well as an ear learner.

Activity 7. Oral/Written Project: Analyzing Spoken and Written Language

Another activity that we have used to raise students' awareness of differences between spoken and written English is an oral/written project (modified from Kutz, Groden & Zamel, 1993), which builds explicitly on students' competence as oral language users in order to develop their confidence with written academic English. The project engages students in a study of spoken and written communication and is specifically intended to help students discover for themselves how what they already know and do as speakers provides a basis for understanding what is required of them as writers communicating to an academic audience.

Steps for the oral/written project:

1. Students tell a story into a tape recorder and prepare transcriptions.
2. Students write the same story.
3. Students prepare a four- to six-page written report of their comparative analysis of the written and oral story.
4. Students write a self-reflection about what they have learned from the comparative experience of telling a story, writing a story, and writing a report for an academic audience.

Throughout the project, students record their observations about speaking and writing and ask questions about what they are noticing: What do they do differently when they speak compared to when they write? What advantages does speaking offer that writing does not? What advantages does writing offer? As they transcribe the tapes, they become aware of such written conventions as punctuation, capitalization, and sentence boundaries and begin to ask questions about these conventions. They become aware of audience, the differing roles and needs of a listener compared to a reader, and what understanding the differences between these two types of audience requires of them as communicators. They also become aware that writers and speakers have reasons for the choices they make, that rules and conventions are not arbitrary, and that meaning is conveyed not just in language, but also in how language is presented and in how well it achieves its purpose. These discoveries then become the basis for discussions about speaking and writing in different contexts (in class discussions, among friends, in text messaging, over e-mail, in formal essays, and written reports). The following is an excerpt from students' written self-reflections:

Many times idea just seem to come out, when telling or writing a story, but it is hard to prepare them to form sentences. In my oral, I was so lost, I did not know where to begin and had so many things going on in my head at once. I laughed and giggled a lot and used to interact with my audience. I tried to make eye contact to see if they were paying attention or if they were rolling their eyes at me or having a strange look. It was a lot harder to interact with my reader, but I had time to plan out what I was going to say and I was not scared because I could stop and go back to it when I remembered what was going; which was I could not do in my oral.

By analyzing the similarities and differences between speaking and writing, these students show an awareness of what they know about audience and how to anticipate what their audience needs from them both in terms of word choice and in terms of how text is organized on the page. These reflections also reveal what students know about the unplanned and spontaneous nature of spoken language, and how repairs and revisions get made on the spot, often unconsciously, in response to visual and verbal cues from their listener.

By contrast, writing requires sustained planning and revision as students learn to anticipate in advance of communication what their reader needs from them. In stark contrast to what many generation 1.5 learners may have experienced in their educational histories—that their spoken English is a potential minefield of error to be steadfastly avoided during writing—the oral/written project allows students to critically compare their oral competence in English with their emerging understandings of what is required of them as academic readers and writers.

Principle III: Make Grammar Information Accessible

Developing appropriate grammar approaches for generation 1.5 students at our institution was a complex process. We needed to look beyond the various pedagogical models from our individual disciplines (ESL and basic writing) to find new ways to help learners access and use relevant grammar information they need to improve the accuracy of their academic writing. We realized that the primary reason for teaching grammar would be to enable students to *read, revise, and edit* their work with a critical eye. Thus the questions we faced were: What kinds of information and skills do students need to do this? And how do we assist students in acquiring that information and those skills?

When working with any students who are in the process of developing their academic writing skills, a crucial first step is assessing the students' skills and needs—beginning with analysis of writing samples—in order to prioritize the grammar features we need to focus on. What we have found with multilingual generation 1.5 learners in particular, however, is a diversity of skills and needs that reflects an exposure to formal analysis and "rules" of grammar that is similar to that of monolingual native English speakers. Realizing the impossibility of developing a class syllabus to address this complexity of grammar and lexical issues, we have relied on various practices for making grammar accessible, including:

- limiting the grammar focus to key, "teachable" features such as verb tense, sentence structure, use of subordinators and coordinators, and structures for attribution and stance;
- assessing students' knowledge of grammar, metalanguage, and strategies for editing;
- using accessible texts, including student writing;
- addressing individual differences, with students setting priorities and developing their own reference materials.

Activity 8. Analyzing Writing to Identify Parts of Speech

One activity that helps us assess students' understanding of grammar terminology and structures is a task in which students examine a piece of writing and identify examples of grammatical structures, as illustrated in the handout for Activity 8. The goal is not only to see what students know, but also to get them to begin to talk about grammar in context using the appropriate metalanguage.

Handout for Activity 8, Identifying parts of speech

Directions:
Read the paragraph below, and write each italic word next to the corresponding part of speech in the list. Then try to find other examples of the part of speech.

Proper noun	Article
Count noun	Adjective
Noncount noun	Adverb
Verb: infinitive	Preposition
Verb: state of being	Pronoun
Verb: action	Possessive determiner
Verb + ing	

One thing that I'm addicted to is making crafts. *I* love *to make* things *with* my hands, and I *am* most *happy* when I'm working on a crafts *project*. It makes me feel very special that I can *do* things by myself. I feel great when I learn to make something new, and I *frequently* hang out at *Crafts' World* to find new things to make. Whenever I have *a* new project, I spend so much time on it that *my* life gets out of control. I like to work on the project until I get things right, and I often keep *working* on it all night. The worst part is that sometimes I also drink *coffee* while I work. Because I don't sleep, I can't concentrate on my studies.

Activity 9. Editing Student Writing for Basic Grammar

To determine students' ability to edit text, we ask them to examine a text that contains selected types of errors, analyze and mark it using their preferred procedures, indicate locations of errors, and correct those errors if they can. The handout for Activity 9 shows an example of this type of task, this one focusing on three grammar areas: articles and nouns, verb tense, and word form. Students would have reviewed this terminology in class and done some work with rules on these three features. In general, we encourage students to use their own strategies for marking and analyzing that are helpful to them.

Handout for Activity 9, Editing for basic grammar

Directions:
- Read the paragraph.
- Use strategies for marking and analyzing that are helpful to you.
- Highlight/circle errors related to articles and nouns (five errors), verb tense (eight errors), and word form (six errors).
- Write corrections in the space above each error.

I once experienced my own problem with communication. I still remember that embarrassed situation at the American restaurant, Peppermill. After I had lived in United States for a year, a group of friends ask me out for dinner at the Peppermill. I had never been to any American restaurant before. Since this is the first time, I wanted to observe and understand how American enjoy their dinner. Therefore, I accept my friend's invitation. When I arrived at the restaurant, I went to the counter and gave my friends' names. The host looked down the list and polite led me to the table. After I joined the group, we started to order meal. I looked over menu, but I don't know what to order. Most of my friends order steak, so I did the same. When the food came, I started to cut the steak. I was shock because blood came out of the meat. Since it was not completely cooked, I called the waitress over and asked her what was wrong with the meat. Then she look at her order list and said that I ordered the steak to be cook "very rare." I told her that was corrected. She looked very confusing. I tried to explain that it wasn't completely cooked. Then she realized that I didn't understand the word "rare." After her explanation, I felt very embarrassed in front of my friends. The people near our table looked at me as if I were from outer space. At that moment, I really want to find a place to hide.

Throughout the semester, when we are assessing students' knowledge or their writing, teaching grammar inductively, preparing and implementing practice activities, and promoting self-editing, we regularly use student texts, such as those in Activity 8 and Activity 9, because their comprehensibility in terms of vocabulary and syntax makes the grammar more transparent and accessible. We can also monitor the students' comprehension of grammar information by their performance on various practice activities such as dictocomps, structural identification and analysis, sentence and text-level writing, editing of teacher-prepared texts based on student writing, editing of their own texts, and editing of peers' texts in response to questions posed by the writers.

Activity 10. Developing Grammar Reference Cards

We have found that traditional grammar reference materials, which have unfamiliar metalanguage and detailed explanations, are usually not accessible to our students: the information from these sources is often confusing and irrelevant. To resolve this problem, we encourage students to make and use their own reference materials. One kind of reference material we regularly use is grammar reference cards, which are learner-prepared index cards with examples, rules, and information about correct form (see sample, Figure 16.1). These cards can be developed for various features of grammar. As described in the following steps, the activity of preparing grammar reference cards for tense and time relationships, for example, not only requires analyzing text and looking at the relationship between tense and time expressions, but also looking at tense shifts, namely present vs. past, in academic writing. We find that this analysis moves students from thinking in the narrative mode, which they are usually most comfortable with, to the expository mode, a genre that is not as familiar to them.

The steps for developing grammar reference cards are:

1. We work from a template for a card, always starting with examples taken from student writing that demonstrate the grammar feature or problem, and then working toward the definition or rule that gives the grammar explanation. Using example sentences, students use a system they have learned for analyzing and developing active editing strategies: in this case, drawing wiggly lines, underlining, circling.
2. We work inductively, asking questions to help students understand how the verbs of the sentences carry the meaning of general truth statements: for example, when presenting sentence #1, "Many people spend too much time shopping," the teacher asks, "What is the time here, present or past? Now? What about tomorrow? Was it also true yesterday?" Answering these questions leads students to an understanding of how to appropriately use tense to formulate generalizations, a key concept in academic writing.
3. Students move through each example, questioning as they go, labeling the statements either fact or opinion until they get to the past-tense examples that actually support the statements in the first three sentences.
4. When students complete the analysis of the series of examples, they are able to articulate the rule in their own words. For example students might write, "Use present tense for fact, opinion, general truth statements; use past tense for examples of events from the past that support statements of opinion."

Creating and using grammar reference cards offers students a personalized, learner-based reference tool that provides them with a portable and succinct resource designed for their particular needs. An additional feature of this activity is that preparing and referring to the cards, which may be hole-punched and secured with a metal ring, appeals to kinesthetic and tactile learners.

Figure 16.1 Grammar reference card.

Activity 11. Developing Personal Item Reference Cards or Lists

In line with our practice of addressing individual differences by getting students to work on their particular grammar concerns, we have found that students can also benefit from using their own reference materials for "item" grammar, i.e., word forms, prepositions, idioms, and lexical/collocational patterns. Before students write about a particular topic, we ask them to think about relevant grammar, vocabulary, and ideas in relation to the topic. We generally follow these steps:

1. Students brainstorm ideas on the topic of the particular paper: in groups, students write down some phrases or expressions they might need to use when writing about the topic.
2. Students put these on the board or overheads. For example, for the topic of addictions, with our help, students might come up with these examples:

   I am/He is/They are addicted to movies/sudoku puzzles/playing computer games/TV.

   I *spend time* watching TV/playing computer games/surfing the web/shopping/text-messaging my friends/talking on the phone.

3. As a class, we focus on the "be" and "to" with "addicted" and also note the "ing" verb form that follows "spend time" and "be addicted to."
4. Students keep track of these lexical items and collocations by writing them on lists or on index cards that they use when they are writing and editing their papers.

We then use the following procedure after students have submitted a paper:

1. When evaluating the paper, we highlight two or three lexical/idiomatic/word form problems that have come up and give the correction. (We select only a few such

Table 16.1 Example of Teacher Feedback

Numbered sentence in essay	Our correction (at bottom of page)
Most people addicted on watching tv.	Most people *are* addicted *to* watching tv.
This can help me not to be so stressful.	This can help me not to be so *stressed.* (adjective: describes how a person feels) My life is *stressful.* (adjective: describes where the stress comes from)

items in each paper because we have found that more than a few becomes burdensome.) An example appears in Table 16.1; we highlight and number these selected problem sentences in the essay and provide the corrections at the bottom of the relevant pages.

2. Students add these items to their grammar reference lists or cards so they can refer to them when editing in the future.

Principle IV: Help Students Take an Active Role in Working on Grammar and Editing

In our conversations with generation 1.5 students in class, in office hours, and in the tutoring center, we repeatedly would hear that students had strong desires to be diligent and check their work. But we also learned that many of these students lacked concrete strategies for actually taking ownership of the drafting, revising, editing, and proofreading process. In recalling their high school writing experiences and their experiences writing for other college courses, students typically spoke of 1-draft papers—papers that were quite different from the complex, multi-draft, highly polished analytical papers that we were asking them to produce. We therefore needed to broaden students' repertoires of strategies and instill in them the confidence that they could be in charge of their writing processes and their learning processes. Among the practices we have followed to meet this goal are the following:

* developing systems for editing and encouraging students to use them;
* using various feedback forms to facilitate student–teacher communication;
* assigning follow-up tasks on compositions to extend students' learning.

Activity 12. Setting Up a System for Active Editing

In working to support students to become more confident editors, we have found it is useful to set up a system to actively edit work (see Porter & vanDommelen, 2005). Our goal is to help students develop focused strategies for editing beyond simply trying to check their work: we want them to think about their readers and what their readers need in order to understand the meaning the students want to convey. One activity that sets up such a system involves asking students to read a text, mark it in various ways related to a particular grammatical feature, and analyze and respond to grammatical as well as content concerns (see handout for Activity 12). To prepare materials for such activities, we select a student text that will be meaningful to the students and that helps teach a particular language feature and adapt it by editing out any distracting errors that would sidetrack the students from the focus for teaching. The students begin by reading the text in its entirety, to encourage them to think about how language works at the discourse level and to avoid becoming derailed by individual sentences. They then work with the text following instructions related to the grammar features.

Handout for Activity 12, Setting up a system for active editing

Directions:
First, read the student writing below all the way through once. Then, follow the steps. If you can't do any of the steps because you don't understand the words in the directions, put a star next to the word(s) you have questions about.

1. Identify grammar structures.
    - Draw a wiggly line under any *time expressions* you find.
    - Underline the *verbs* that show tense in the sentences below.
    - Circle all the *subjects* of the verbs.
    - Put a box around *modals* in these sentences.
2. Identify grammar errors.
    - Write "s–v" in the margin in front of any line where you think there is a *subject–verb agreement* error.
    - Put an *x* in the margin in front of any line where you think there is a *tense* error.
3. Make corrections.

I think being addicted to something can be a serious problem and can also be harmful, too. I am also addicted to a few things. although I knew it is not wisest for me. One of the things that I'm addicted to most is shopping for clothes and spending too much time on crafts. It seemed like it is part of me and I will do it forever. It is something that I really like to do to make myself feel happy.

Ever since I've got a job last year in the summer, I started to shop more than I usually do. I was afraid to lose my job and didn't worry much about school. All I cared for is what I wanted. As soon as the program ended, I felt terrible. I didn't have the money to go shopping anymore. My attitude start to change dramatically and I got very lazy. I feel like I would never be happy if I do not get what I want. I am always in my room and I never want to go out. Sometimes I'm afraid to see my friends and if they have something nice on, I would feel very uncomfortable that I don't have it.

For this activity to be successful, we have learned that consistency and extended practice are especially important, and students continue to use this technique of drawing wiggly lines, underlining, and circling throughout the semester in order to reinforce this system for focusing on subject–verb agreement and tense. Although perhaps not an easy task for some learners, this basic activity of identifying sentence parts allows students to focus on the relationship between tense and expressions that mark shifts in time. As students work through the first paragraph of the excerpt following the steps, they will discover two shifts from present to past tense in lines two and four but no time expression to indicate these changes of tense. When we ask the question, "If you are the reader of this writing, is the meaning clear to you?" students quickly figure out that without the inclusion of markers to clearly designate time references, readers become confused. The focus here is not just on "finding errors," but rather, on figuring out what forms and markers the reader needs to have in order to understand what the writer wants to convey.

Activity 13. Developing Self-Editing Sheets

One resource that helps students develop independent editing skills is the self-editing sheet, as illustrated in the handout for Activity 13. A self-editing sheet includes two basic elements: (1) ways to mark up texts for various grammatical features, and (2) questions that students need to ask themselves to analyze their grammar and meaning and that can then lead them to make corrections as needed. Students use these self-editing sheets as they work with drafts of their papers: as a reference guide at home, during peer review, and during in-class essay writing. The steps we use to develop self-editing sheets are as follows:

1. We work at the board and elicit (a) the steps that students need to check for accuracy for a particular grammar feature and (b) the questions that learners need to ask themselves in order to successfully edit their work for that point.
2. Students copy the information in their notebooks for future use and/or we type up the procedure to hand back to learners.

Handout for Activity 13, Self-editing sheets

Directions:
Follow all the steps below on your essay. When you correct or edit, use a brightly colored pen. Use your grammar reference cards to help you.

Tenses Checklist
For each sentence:
1. Underline main verbs, circle subjects, wiggly line time expressions, box modals.
2. Think about *your meaning* in relationship to other sentences in the paragraph.
3. Ask yourself the following questions:
    • Do I want to show *past time, present time*, OR
    • Do I want to use *present tense* for fact, opinion, or general truth?
    • Have I shifted tenses?
    • Do I have a clear *reason* for shifting?
    • Are my time expressions clear?
4. Correct and edit: correct verbs for tense and agreement.

Encouraging learners to develop and use self-editing steps and questions in conjunction with grammar reference cards, described earlier, helps them follow up on language analysis activities from earlier class sessions. With self-editing sheets, students are presented the same information as in previous activities but in a different format, in this case, a series of inductive questions to ask themselves as they analyze their writing. Accordingly, as students determine the answers to the questions, they benefit from the recycling of previous material and apply what they have learned to their own writing.

In addition to developing these editing strategies and resources, we have found it essential to practice their use. We give students short texts, including their own writing, for editing practice, and we often review this editing as a whole class. We also regularly ask students to turn in a marked-up editing draft along with the final clean draft.

Activity 14. Completing a Final Draft Cover Sheet

In conjunction with focused self-editing, we have developed various feedback procedures to encourage students to reflect on their work and communicate with us. One of these is a brief cover sheet for students to complete and submit along with the final draft. The cover sheet can include questions such as these:

* What do you like best about your paper?
* What do you think you did well on this paper (content and grammar)?
* What did you have difficulty with? How did you try to overcome it?
* What part of the paper would you like most to improve?
* What questions or difficulties did you have related to the readings for this paper?

With this activity, we are essentially asking students to evaluate their papers before we do. Some teachers in our composition program assign a more extensive cover memo such as the one described in the handout for Activity 14.

Handout for Activity 14, Cover memo for final draft

Directions:
When you turn in your essay, make sure that you include a cover memo in which you discuss:

1. what you liked/disliked about this unit, the readings, and the essay assignment;
2. what you found easy/difficult about this unit, the readings, and the essay assignment;
3. a brief description of how your paper changed and developed as you revised it;
4. a summary of advice that your peer reviewers gave you during peer response and a brief discussion about how you used that advice;

5.   a brief discussion of the current strengths of your paper;
6.   a brief discussion of things you would work on more, if you had more time;
7.   a list of grammar points that you focused on during proofreading and a description of the proofreading techniques that you used to work on them;
8.   any other questions that you have for me about this assignment or anything else in the course.

Note: The cover memo is 10% of the final paper grade.

We have found that this task fosters a sense of ownership and responsibility and allows students to recognize and enjoy their accomplishments. Additionally, it gives us a richer context in which to evaluate their writing and often provides us with additional focus points for feedback.

Activity 15. Getting Clear Feedback Through a Rubric

In our experience, generation 1.5 students can be overwhelmed by excessive teacher feedback on papers. In light of this, when giving feedback on papers, we try to promote good teacher–student communication by making minimal marks on the paper, writing an end note that highlights strengths and perhaps one salient point to attend to, and using a grading rubric for guidance and clarity. Our grading rubrics generally include the categories of content, grammar and editing, and mechanics. (For an example, see the handout for Activity 15.) We mark each point with a +, √, or –. We use rubric points that are specific to the content required by the actual writing assignment, and include a section on the grammar features that were to be focused on as well as a section on the extent to which the student was using editing strategies. The rubric provides space for a final summative comment about the paper, including what was done well and what needs more work.

Handout for Activity 15, Grading rubric

Essay #2   Name: _____
Grading Criteria
Content/Fulfilling the assignment
____ You have clearly focused on a topic and stated a point from the reading about this topic.
____ You have provided an explanation, with details and information, about how the reading supports your point.
____ You have illustrated this point by a description of a personal experience (your own or someone else's).
____ Your description of this experience is well written with clear details.
____ You explain ideas and information thoroughly.
____ You have made clear connections between the point related to the reading and your personal example.
____ You successfully tie your ideas together in the introduction and conclusion.

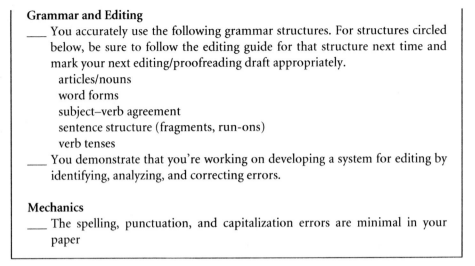

Grammar and Editing

____ You accurately use the following grammar structures. For structures circled below, be sure to follow the editing guide for that structure next time and mark your next editing/proofreading draft appropriately.

articles/nouns
word forms
subject–verb agreement
sentence structure (fragments, run-ons)
verb tenses

____ You demonstrate that you're working on developing a system for editing by identifying, analyzing, and correcting errors.

Mechanics

____ The spelling, punctuation, and capitalization errors are minimal in your paper

---

Activity 16. Responding to Teacher Feedback on Papers Using the Editing Log Assignment

An additional way to encourage students' attention to forms they need to work on is an assignment to insure further work on their papers, such as an editing log (see the handout for Activity 16). Consistent with this principle of helping students take an active role in working on their grammar and editing, the editing log asks students to do some follow-up activities after papers are returned, such as (1) setting goals for their next paper based on successes and problems in their papers, (2) logging particular highlighted errors and writing out corrections of them for us to check, and (3) adding our notations of lexical, collocational, or word form corrections of errors to their personal reference lists or cards. These activities require students once more to respond to their work and use it to enhance learning.

Handout for Activity 16, Editing log assignment

Background:

For every essay I return, you will need to complete an Editing Log on a separate piece of paper, and to turn it in within 1 week from the day your portfolio is returned. An Editing Log is a way for you to:

• consider comments on your portfolio, and make sure you understand them;
• address some of the grammatical issues you may be struggling with.

Directions:

1. Consider Comments. Go through comments on your portfolio, from the margins and on the response sheet, and write a brief summary of (a) the strengths and (b) the concerns. Then, (c) try to come up with specific concrete strategies for addressing those concerns.

2. Find the Errors. Go through the final draft and look for errors that have been marked, such as run-together sentences (R.T.S.), subject–verb agreement problems (S–V), sentence fragments (frag.), verb tense problems (V.T.), spelling errors (Sp.), and missing articles (the/a). If the error seems to be a pattern, you will see that the first few errors have been marked. The rest are indicated by check marks in the right margin to show that somewhere in that line you'll find another error of the same type.
3. Fix the Errors. Indicate what the error is that you are fixing (a fragment, a verb tense problem, etc.), and rewrite the sentence correctly, underlining the correction you made.
4. Make new entries to your personal grammar reference cards.

Principle V: Give Students a Voice in Directing Teaching and Learning: Goal Setting and Self-Assessment

One of the themes underlying the principles and practices we have described so far is our belief that learners need to take an active role in their learning, both inside and outside the classroom, and that we can help them do this by giving them a voice in the direction the class takes. One of the reasons we feel so strongly about this is the well-known fact that teaching does not necessarily lead to learning. We have found that if learners can set up their own goals for learning, making their needs clear to themselves and to us, and can evaluate their progress along the way, they have greater success in improving their writing. But we have also found that students are not necessarily familiar (or completely comfortable) with this self-directed manner of learning. And as a result, we need to explicitly discuss with them how self-assessment and goal setting, like completing compositions and other projects, are in fact formative procedures, not just hurdles to be jumped but activities that can help them learn. Described below are several activities we have used to implement this practice of giving learners a voice through self-assessment and goal setting.

Activity 17. Assessing Strengths and Weaknesses; Setting Goals for the Semester

One activity that asks students to identify needed skills, strengths and weaknesses, and learning goals is done as a class activity at the beginning of the course, following these steps:

1. The group brainstorms grammar and writing skills they know that they want to work on.
2. Individual students write down particular areas they feel are strengths and also skills they need to improve.
3. Then, working together, the group brainstorms ways to improve their skills and check their progress.

As facilitators, we help learners make links between writing skills and grammar skills (e.g., using correct verb tenses when writing about readings; using subordinators to make clear statements of ideas) and also assist students in coming up with concrete strategies for improving (e.g., practice, take risks with language, check work with partners) and techniques for evaluating progress (e.g., pay attention to feedback from teachers, compare final essays with rough drafts). We have found that this activity has benefits for both teachers and students. The student-generated lists, rather than instructor-mandated criteria, help us as teachers understand what students need and how we can best frame in-class activities and out-of-class assignments. By making skills and goals explicit, this activity encourages students to take responsibility for their own learning and gives them a voice in the process. It also helps them get used to using unfamiliar terminology, articulate the skills appropriate to their tasks, and begin to understand the transferable nature of the skills they are acquiring—from their reading and writing classes to courses across disciplines. As the semester progresses, students come back to initial goals to review them, check their progress in achieving them, and reformulate their plans as appropriate.

Activity 18. Evaluating Progress With an End-of-Semester Self-Assessment

At the end of the course, we refer learners back to:

1. the initial goal-setting activity,
2. other goals they may have set throughout the course (e.g., using reference materials, giving good peer feedback, citing sources),
3. grammar-for-writing skills that they may have worked on that were not part of their initial goal setting (e.g., using pronouns for reference, correctly punctuating joining words, quoting correctly).

As they engage in this process, we find that students are able to see the complexity and developmental nature of learning and to better understand their role in the process. We use an end-of-course self-assessment worksheet (Handout for Activity 18), which has a format that can be adapted for different purposes and can be used at midterm or at the end of a specific unit.

Handout for Activity 18, End-of-course self-assessment

Directions:
Refer back to your goals that you set at the beginning of the course (or important goals that you set during the course). Choose two grammar-for-writing skills that you have worked on and would like to assess, and write them below on the lines.

Using the 0–100 scale below, do the following three things. Keep in mind that "0" means you know absolutely nothing and "100" means you have mastered this skill.

1. *Draw a mark* on the scale and *write a number* for your long-term goal for that grammar-for-writing skill. This is where you want to be by the time you complete your writing courses. Write "long-term goal" above that mark.

2. *Draw a mark* on the scale and *write a number* for where you feel you were before you began this course. Write "before" above that mark.
3. *Draw a mark* on the scale and *write a number* for where you feel you are now. Write "now" above that mark.

Skill #1 _____

0   25   50   75   100

Skill #2 _____

0   25   50   75   100

Using the back of this sheet, describe why you rated yourself the way you did.

Activity 19. Writing About Developing Your "Voice" in the Writing Workshop

By eliciting student input into the initial student self-assessment activity described in Activity 17 and setting goals for the semester based on learner-generated criteria, we include students in the process of directing course content. Allowing students to have a voice and encouraging their participation not only helps them develop skills but also helps create a positive learning environment. Additionally, at the end of the semester, we want them to write about their learning; we have used topics such as the one shown in the handout for Activity 19.

Handout for Activity 19, Writing about your voice

Background:
In our group discussion, we brainstormed associations with the word "voice." We also talked about different ideas for what the phrase "to have a voice" might mean.

Directions:
Think about the writing workshop: activities, discussion, and topics we worked on this semester. What connections can you make between what we did in the workshop and the process of developing your voice as a college writer?

In writing, please respond to the following questions: Has the workshop helped you develop your voice as a writer? How?

Some excerpts from student responses show how this approach benefits students' skill development and self-confidence:

I like the fact that we get to decide what we need help on.

Having a voice in English class helped me because I speak up in class now and ask a lot of questions about what I didn't understand. Before I was quiet and didn't want to get involved and be active in class.

I have learned to work with groups and to care [about] my opinion and when I need help or I'm seeking information I am now willing to raise my hand and ask. I've learned that confusion is a common thing and if you don't know something, don't be discouraged, just keep trying.

The writing workshop helped me express myself more when being around people who had different points of view than me.

Conclusion

We began our work with generation 1.5 learners all too aware of how easily we can undermine students' confidence when we pay insufficient attention to what they say about themselves as language users, especially in their new role as academic readers and writers, and what support they need from us to attain greater proficiency in English. In the development of these five principles, we have challenged ourselves to look beyond the words on the page to see the person behind those words and to create an approach that brings this person into a central and dynamic relationship with the learning environment. Tom Fox (1999) has noted that perhaps 90% of what we need to do as educators is to create environments where students faced with linguistic and/or socio-economic hurdles (hurdles that traditionally render these students "at risk" for dropping out or failure) are inclined to "hang out" with us long enough to see what is in it for them, to discover on their own terms the benefits of higher education. Once students become self-affirming in their pursuit of higher education, their potential to reach their academic goals is greatly enhanced. Our experience suggests that the approach we have outlined in this chapter creates just such a space for students to become self-affirming, to feel confident and comfortable, and to see themselves as participants in the academic community.

Acknowledgments

The authors wish to acknowledge the contributions of LAC teachers Jennifer Peters and Sheila Botein for their assistance in developing and piloting the writing topics in principles I, II, and IV and Deborah Swanson for her earlier work on this project.

The end-of-course self-assessment worksheet for Activity 18 is adapted from procedures developed by Mario Rivas and Peter Ingmire for the Learning Assistance Center, San Francisco State University, San Francisco, CA.

References

Fox, T. (1999). *Defending access: A critique of standards in higher education.* Portsmouth, NH: Boynton Cook.

Goen, S., Porter, P., Swanson, D., & vanDommelen, D. (2002). Working with generation 1.5 students and their teachers: ESL meets composition. *CATESOL Journal, 14*(1), 131–171.

Kutz, E., Groden, S.Q., & Zamel, V. (1993). *The discovery of competence: Teaching and learning with diverse student writers.* Portsmouth, NH: Boynton Cook.

Porter, P. & vanDommelen, D. (2005). *Read, write, edit: Grammar for college writers.* Boston, MA: Heinle Cengage Learning.

Wajnryb, R. (1990). *Grammar dictation.* Oxford, UK: Oxford University Press.

Contributors

Harriett Allison is a doctoral student at the University of Georgia. Her most recent position was Assistant Professor of ESL/English and Director of the ESL Program and Steps-to-College, a for-credit summer program for area high school language minority students, at Gainesville College, Gainesville, Georgia. Her interests include college reading pedagogy for generation 1.5 students, language minority students' access to higher education, and generation 1.5 students' literacy and discourse transition from high school to college. She is editor of Georgia TESOL's *TESOL in Action* and has given numerous presentations on generation 1.5 students and related social and pedagogical concerns.

Kyung-Hee Bae is Assistant Director of the University of Houston Writing Center, where she has also worked as the ESL program manager, developing curriculum for ESL students across campus. Holding an MA in Applied English Linguistics from the University of Houston, she has taught various writing courses including the non-native speaker equivalent of freshman composition. She has served on TESOL's Awards Standing Committee and is interested in second language writing pedagogy in relation to academic literacy development at the college level.

Sarah Benesch is Professor of English, College of Staten Island, City University of New York. Her research interests include English for academic purposes, critical pedagogies, critical media analysis, and identity constructions of English language learners. Her book, *Critical English for Academic Purposes: Theory, Politics, and Practice* (Erlbaum, 2001) proposes a relationship between EAP and critical pedagogies. She edited a special issue on critical EAP for the *Journal of English for Academic Purposes* (2008).

Cathryn Crosby is Assistant Professor of TESOL, in the Department of Second and Foreign Languages at West Chester University in Pennsylvania. Her dissertation focused on academic reading and writing difficulties and strategies of generation 1.5 learners. In addition, she taught in the ESL Composition and Spoken English Programs at Ohio State University, and presented and published on second language writing, technology and generation 1.5 learners. She is current co-editor of *Second Language Writing News*.

Paul Dillon is an applied anthropologist in Peru and works as an intersegmental researcher for the "Intersegmental Project to Achieve Student Success" at Los

Angeles City College. He also has designed and taught on-line courses for composition and critical thinking.

Renata Fitzpatrick is a Senior Teaching Specialist at the Department of Postsecondary Teaching and Learning at the University of Minnesota. She teaches various courses to immigrant and refugee freshmen in the Commanding English program, including writing, grammar/editing workshop, literature of the American immigrant experience, and reading for general arts.

Jan Frodesen is Director of ESL in the Department of Linguistics at the University of California, Santa Barbara, where she teaches ESL and Teaching English as a Second Language (TESL) Methods. Her areas of interest include second language writing, pedagogical grammar, content-based instruction, and pronunciation. She has co-authored several ESL textbooks and has contributed to edited volumes concerned with second language writing.

Sugie Goen-Salter is Professor of English at San Francisco State University. She teaches basic writing courses as well as graduate courses in theory and pedagogy, research methods, and reading/writing integration. In addition to her work with generation 1.5 student writers, she also co-directs San Francisco State's integrated reading/writing program. Goen-Salter has published articles on topics related to generation 1.5 learners and on reading/writing integration and currently she sits on the Executive Board of the Conference on Basic Writing.

Linda Harklau is Professor in the Teaching Additional Languages program and the Linguistics program at the University of Georgia. Her research has explored the high school experiences of college-bound students and the high school to college transition of language minority youth in California, New York, and Georgia. Harklau's work has appeared in *Anthropology and Education Quarterly*, *Educational Policy*, *Journal of Literacy Research*, *Linguistics and Education*, *TESOL Quarterly*, *The Handbook on Research in Second Language Learning and Teaching*, and the forthcoming *International Handbook of English Language Education*. Harklau co-edited *Generation 1.5 Meets College Composition: Issues in the Teaching of Writing to U.S.-Educated Learners of ESL* (Erlbaum, 1999). She is currently concluding a 5-year case study of college-bound immigrants in the southeastern U.S.

Christine Holten is a lecturer in the Department of Applied Linguistics and TESL at the University of California, Los Angeles, where she teaches ESL writing courses for graduate and undergraduate students and also TESL courses for graduate students. She has presented and published on writing conferences, grammar and language in writing instruction, composition tutoring, and curriculum options for generation 1.5 writers.

Ann M. Johns is Professor (Emerita) of Linguistics and Writing Studies at San Diego State University. She has published more than 50 articles and book chapters and five books, including *Text, Role Context: Developing Academic Literacies* (Cambridge University Press, 1997) and *Genre in the Classroom: Multiple Perspectives* (Erlbaum, 2002). Her most recent interest is in the gap between secondary school pedagogies and assessments and faculty expectations in postsecondary classes. In attempting to fill that gap, she works with secondary teachers to develop curricula for critical reading, writing, and research across the disciplines.

Vivian Louie, Associate Professor in the Graduate School of Education at Harvard University, is a sociologist who studies how the children of immigrants and adult migrants acquire the necessary educational credentials and skills for upward mobility in a globalized world and experience cultural shifts through the process of migration. Louie draws on a K-16 comparative approach and interview data to examine how the incorporation of immigrants in the United States influences their children's access to, preparation for, and choice of college, with a focus on the key high school to college transition, and further, how these experiences both intersect with and are distinct from those of native Blacks, Latinos, and Whites, particularly in urban schools. In addition to her first book, *Compelled to Excel: Immigration, Education, and Opportunity among Chinese Americans* (Stanford University Press, 2004), she has a second book manuscript in preparation, focusing on Dominicans and Colombians, and several articles comparing immigrant and native groups around the transition to college, the identities that the children of immigrants develop inside and outside of schools, and the extent to which these differ from their immigrant parents.

Aya Matsuda is Assistant Professor of Language and Literacy at Arizona State University. Her research interests include the use of English as an international language, the linguistic and pedagogical implications of the global spread of English, and issues related to non-native English-speaking teachers in the TESOL profession. Her work focusing on these issues has appeared in various books and journals including *English Today*, *CATESOL Journal*, *JALT Journal*, *TESOL Quarterly*, and *World Englishes*.

Paul Kei Matsuda is Associate Professor of English at Arizona State University. Founding chair of the Symposium on Second Language Writing and of the CCCC Committee on Second Language Writing, he has edited several books, including *On Second Language Writing* (Erlbaum, 2001), *Landmark Essays on ESL Writing* (Erlbaum, 2001), *Second Language Writing Research* (Erlbaum, 2005), *Second-Language Writing in the Composition Classroom* (NCTE and Bedford/St. Martin's, 2006) and *Politics of Second Language Writing* (Parlor Press, 2006). His articles on second language writing appear in various books and journals in both applied linguistics and composition studies.

Jennifer A. Mott-Smith is Assistant Professor and ESOL Coordinator at Towson University in Maryland. Her teaching and research interests include language ideologies, writing theory and assessment, racial/ethnic identities of ESL students, minority access to higher education and academic standards, White teachers' understandings of race and whiteness, and the achievement gap. She has given numerous conference presentations in Boston and in Japan, where she previously taught English as a Foreign Language.

Robin Murie directs the Commanding English program at the University of Minnesota, working with first year college students as well as postsecondary outreach programs in several area high schools. Murie's interests include second-language writing, editing, immigrant education, and building college access initiatives for first generation students. She has been co-editor of the *MinneTESOL/WITESOL Journal*, and has written and presented extensively on the importance of building language and literacy support into college coursework so that students can earn the credit of the freshman year.

Genevieve Patthey is an applied linguist who directs the Intersegmental Project to Assure Student Success at Los Angeles City College, where she also teaches English and ESL. Her research focuses on language minority students and she has published in the *Elementary School Journal, Research in the Teaching of English, Written Communication, Discourse Processes, Issues in Applied Linguistics, Annual Review of Applied Linguistics, Anthropology and Education Quarterly*, and *Journal of Basic Writing*.

Patricia Porter is Professor Emerita of English at San Francisco State University, where she served as the Coordinator of the ESL Program for non-native speakers for 18 years and taught composition, grammar-for-writing, and oral communication in that program. Her work in the MA/TESOL Program at SFSU included teaching graduate courses in pedagogical grammar, methodology for listening and speaking, curriculum and assessment, and supervision of student teachers. She has published ESL textbooks on oral communication and on grammar. Her most recent publication, co-authored with Deborah vanDommelen, is entitled *Read, Write, Edit: Grammar for College Writers* (Houghton Mifflin, 2004).

Dudley W. Reynolds is Associate Teaching Professor and Director of Research in English Language Learning at Carnegie Mellon University in Qatar where he teaches freshman composition. Formerly the supervisor of the non-native composition program at the University of Houston and an associate professor in its MA in Applied English Linguistics program, he has published in the areas of second language writing development, writing assessment, and quantitative approaches to researching second language writers. He currently serves on TESOL's Standing Committee for Research.

Mark Roberge is Associate Professor of English in the Composition program at San Francisco State University. His research focuses on immigrant education, postsecondary ESL instruction, program administration, and teacher training. He has given numerous presentations and faculty development workshops on teaching academic writing in linguistically and culturally diverse English classes at the secondary and postsecondary level. For the past 7 years he has served as editor of the *CATESOL Journal* (the Journal of the California TESOL Association).

Mary J. Schleppegrell is Professor of Education at the University of Michigan, Ann Arbor. Her research focuses on the academic literacy development of English language learners, with interests in second language writing and teacher education. She is the author of *The Language of Schooling: A functional linguistics perspective* (Erlbaum, 2004) and co-editor, with M. Cecilia Colombi, of *Developing Advanced Literacy in First and Second Languages: Meaning with Power* (Erlbaum, 2002). She has worked with teachers from the California History Project for the last several years to help them improve English language learners' academic literacy in history.

Meryl Siegal, an applied linguist specializing in interactional pragmatics, second language learning and teaching, and issues in language, ideology, and education, teaches English at Laney College in Oakland, California. As a teacher trainer and researcher, Siegal has worked both in Japan and West Africa. Her research has focused on the socio-cultural and historical context of face-to-face learner interactions in Japan. Siegal's work has appeared in *Applied Linguistics, Japanese Language and Literature, Anthropology and Education,* and *TESOL Methods.* She co-edited *Generation 1.5 Meets College Composition: Issues in the Teaching of Writing to U.S.-Educated Learners of ESL* (Erlbaum, 1999).

Joan Thomas-Spiegel teaches psychology at Los Angeles Harbor College. With over 30 years of experience in mental health and educational research, her primary interest involves increasing student success through active learning andragogy. Her doctoral studies focused on adult learning at community colleges and academic self-efficacy. Previous publications have included tracking English and English as a Second Language learners in community colleges with numerous presentations on student progression in math and English through her involvement in the IPASS and Cal-PASS consortiums.

Deborah vanDommelen is Director of the San Francisco State University Learning Assistance Center (LAC), where she mentors graduate students who teach Grammar-for-Writing Workshops, an academic support program designed for generation 1.5 learners from ESL and composition classes. For over 20 years, through the LAC and the SFSU ESL Program, she has taught reading, composition, literature, and grammar-for-writing. She has published in the *CATESOL Journal,* is co-author of the literature and composition text *Inside Out/Outside In: Exploring American Literature* (Houghton Mifflin, 2000), and with Patricia Porter, has developed an approach for working with multilingual students in *Read, Write, Edit: Grammar for College Writers* (Houghton Mifflin, 2004).

Jennifer Shade Wilson is completing a doctoral program in second language education at Ontario Institute for Studies in Education (University of Toronto) after earning an MA in Applied English Linguistics at the University of Houston. At the University of Houston she taught freshman composition for non-native speakers of English and later served as the assistant director of the writing center. Her research interests include motivational profiles of second language writers and the development of immigrant students' academic literacy.

Index

eBooks – at www.eBookstore.tandf.co.uk

A library at your fingertips!

eBooks are electronic versions of printed books. You can store them on your PC/laptop or browse them online.

They have advantages for anyone needing rapid access to a wide variety of published, copyright information.

eBooks can help your research by enabling you to bookmark chapters, annotate text and use instant searches to find specific words or phrases. Several eBook files would fit on even a small laptop or PDA.

NEW: Save money by eSubscribing: cheap, online access to any eBook for as long as you need it.

Annual subscription packages

We now offer special low-cost bulk subscriptions to packages of eBooks in certain subject areas. These are available to libraries or to individuals.

For more information please contact webmaster.ebooks@tandf.co.uk

We're continually developing the eBook concept, so keep up to date by visiting the website.

www.eBookstore.tandf.co.uk